Stars of '90s Dance Pop

ALSO BY JAMES ARENA
AND FROM MCFARLAND

Legends of Disco: Forty Stars Discuss Their Careers (2016)

First Ladies of Disco: 32 Stars Discuss the Era
and Their Singing Careers (2013)

Fright Night on Channel 9: Saturday Night Horror Films
on New York's WOR-TV, 1973–1987 (2012)

Stars of '90s Dance Pop

29 Hitmakers Discuss Their Careers

JAMES ARENA

Foreword by Larry Flick
Afterword by Susan Morabito

McFarland & Company, Inc., Publishers
Jefferson, North Carolina

LIBRARY OF CONGRESS CATALOGUING-IN-PUBLICATION DATA

Names: Arena, James, 1960– interviewer.
Title: Stars of '90s dance pop : 29 hitmakers discuss their careers / [interviews by] James Arena ; foreword by Larry Flick ; afterword by Susan Morabito.
Description: Jefferson, North Carolina : McFarland & Company, 2017 | Includes index.
Identifiers: LCCN 2016051896 | ISBN 9781476667560 (softcover : acid free paper) ∞
Subjects: LCSH: Singers—Interviews. | Sound recording executives and producers—Interviews. | Popular music—1991–2000—History and criticism.
Classification: LCC ML3470 .S754 2017 | DDC 781.64809/049—dc23
LC record available at https://lccn.loc.gov/2016051896

BRITISH LIBRARY CATALOGUING DATA ARE AVAILABLE

ISBN (print) 978-1-4766-6756-0
ISBN (ebook) 978-1-4766-2661-1

© 2017 James Arena. All rights reserved

No part of this book may be reproduced or transmitted in any form or by any means, electronic or mechanical, including photocopying or recording, or by any information storage and retrieval system, without permission in writing from the publisher.

Cover photograph by James Washington and James Arena

Printed in the United States of America

*McFarland & Company, Inc., Publishers
Box 611, Jefferson, North Carolina 28640
www.mcfarlandpub.com*

To my wonderful parents
and to the artists featured here,
whose uplifting works hold a
special place in my heart.

Table of Contents

Acknowledgments ix
Foreword by Larry Flick 1
Special Commentary by the Berman Brothers 5
Preface 9

The Stars

Thea Austin, formerly of Snap!—"Rhythm Is a Dancer" (1992)	13
Angie Brown, formerly of Bizarre Inc—"I'm Gonna Get You" (1992)	21
Sannie Carlson, also known as Whigfield—"Saturday Night" (1994)	30
Marty Cintron, formerly of No Mercy—"Where Do You Go" (1996)	39
Nance Coolen, formerly of Twenty 4 Seven—"Slave to the Music" (1993)	47
Fred and Richard Fairbrass of Right Said Fred—"I'm Too Sexy" (1991)	55
Nicki French—"Total Eclipse of the Heart" (1995)	68
Nestor Haddaway, also known as Haddaway—"What Is Love" (1992)	77
Sten Hallström, also known as StoneBridge, DJ, Producer, Remixer—"Show Me Love" (Robin S, 1992)	86
Nosie Katzman, Composer, Lyricist—"Mr. Vain" (Culture Beat, 1993)	97
Sybil Lynch, also known as Sybil—"The Love I Lost" (West End featuring Sybil, 1993)	107
Robin Jackson Maynard, also known as Robin S—"Show Me Love" (1993)	116
Lane McCray of La Bouche—"Be My Lover" (1995)	123

Rozalla Miller, also known as Rozalla—"Everybody's Free (To Feel Good)" (1992)   133

Tony Moran, DJ, Producer, Remixer—"HIStory" (Michael Jackson, 1997)   144

Ultra Naté—"Free" (1997)   153

Alban Nwapa, also known as Dr. Alban—"It's My Life" (1992)   164

CeCe Peniston—"Finally" (1991)   171

Frank Peterson, formerly of Enigma, Producer—"Sadeness Part I" (Enigma, 1990)   178

Alfredo "Larry" Pignagnoli, Producer, Label Owner—"Saturday Night" (Whigfield, 1994)   191

Paul Spencer, also known as Dario G—"Sunchyme" (1997)   195

Rafael "Dose" Vargas, formerly of 2 in a Room—"Wiggle It" (1990)   204

Martha Wash, former guest vocalist with C + C Music Factory, Black Box—"Gonna Make You Sweat (Everybody Dance Now)" (1990)   210

Kristine Weitz, also known as Kristine W—"One More Try" (1996)   218

Afterword by Susan Morabito   227
The CD Rack: Recommended Listening   231
Index   239

Acknowledgments

I wish to thank all the artists featured in this book, who kindly and generously granted me the extraordinary privilege of sharing their stories and memories.

This chronicle of '90s dance music history was only possible because a small village helped me complete it. I'd like to express my gratitude to the many people who stood by me, gave me support and offered truly invaluable assistance.

I am extremely grateful to Nick Bunning, who spent many hours helping me edit this project. He is a great friend, and his contribution to this book has been immeasurable.

Though it was but one part of his ever-expanding career in media, Larry Flick represents the '90s as distinctly as any singer, songwriter or producer in this book. I thank him for his wonderful, insightful opening commentary.

My great thanks to Frank and Christian Berman for the groundbreaking sounds they produced in the '90s and for their warm, memory-rich introductory commentary. Though busily moving forward with exciting new music projects, they still managed to find time to share their thoughts with me about this important genre and music era.

I am very grateful to acclaimed DJ Susan Morabito, whose name is synonymous with the energy of '90s nightlife in New York City and who kindly consented to compose a thoughtful closing commentary piece for this book.

I'd like to acknowledge the following individuals for their invaluable assistance: Jeff Dorta, Dr. Hans Reinisch, Michele L. Ruiz, Ruben D. Martinez, Barbara Pennington, Howard Lee Gatch, Maggie Kent, Troy Bronstein, Eileen Pekelharing, Letzia Pignagnoli and Barbara Sobel.

Special thanks to James Washington for his guidance, friendship and belief in me. "Are we still talking about this?"

Special thanks to Miss Martha Wash.

A special thank you to Frank Peterson for his kindness and belief in my work.

I am very grateful to Taco Ockerse, Harriette Weels, Norma Jean Wright, Carol Williams, Amil Stewart, Linda Clifford, Evelyn "Champagne" King, Robert and Maureen Arena and Elvis Bramble for your support.

I'd also like to thank Bruce Imber and Phillie Purpero for hiring me at Record World, which introduced me to much of the music discussed in this book. Later, Bruce brought me on board as an executive at Bertelsmann Direct North America, for which I am also extremely grateful. I'd like to give a special shout out to my friends from the 42nd floor (where the BMG International music department resided), especially Laura Psaroudis Lavery, who let me borrow all the latest European dance CDs stockpiled in their super cool storage room. It was like Christmas every time I entered it, and she kindly loaned me the key.

I'd like to make note that Discogs (discogs.com), Joel Whitburn's *Billboard's Hot Dance/Disco 1974–2003* (2004, Record Research Inc.) and my collection of Music & Media charts were most helpful as data verification resources.

There were many others who took an interest in this project and offered their encouragement and assistance. If I have neglected to mention you, please forgive the oversight and know that I am deeply grateful for your contribution.

Foreword by Larry Flick

You might know Larry Flick from his cameo appearance (playing himself and representing the emerging power of gay media) in Chris Rock's 2014 hit film, Top Five. *But throughout the better part of the '90s, Larry Flick was synonymous with dance music (and an artist in his own right) whose canvas was the pages of the U.S. music business bible* Billboard *magazine. For much of the decade, Flick's column supporting the dance genre was the page every fan and dance music industry professional had to flip to first.*

The publication is one of the world's oldest trade magazines and has played host to some of the most important American music charts for decades, including the Billboard Hot 100. *Beginning some 25 years ago, Larry's dance column ran in conjunction with what is known today as the* Dance Club Songs *chart (formerly called* Disco Action, Hot Dance Club Songs *and* Club Play Singles, *among other titles). His commentary provided vital insights into the genre, its artists, DJs and culture. Despite the explosion of clubland during the era and the prevalence of dance music on the radio and on the charts, there were few media outlets critiquing the genre—so all eyes were on Larry. Though some failed to appreciate Flick as a weekly harbinger of good taste, most members of the dance industry of the '90s will agree he set the bar high for the quality measure of its music. His observations about the culture of club music were a barometer of the prevailing conditions that existed at the time.*

During the latter part of his 14-year tenure at Billboard, *Larry served as the weekly journal's primary singles reviewer and Senior Talent Editor. Moving on from the publication, he began producing and hosting two popular shows at SiriusXM Satellite Radio in 2003,* The Morning Jolt *and* Feel the Spin, *programs which were frequented by such notable guests as Kylie Minogue, Adele, Florence + the Machine and many other stars. Larry continues to remain a popular talk and music show host on SiriusXM, currently connected with their Studio 54 channel.*

Larry was invited to share his perspective on '90s dance music.

I was the first actual journalist *Billboard* hired to write the dance column late in 1989/ early 1990. It was around the same time "Groove Is in the Heart" by Deee-Lite came out; that's how I remember when it happened. They had previously hired DJs to handle this editorial function, such as the great Tom Moulton. While each previous contributor had his own style, all of which were very popular, my arrival marked the first time they had someone who didn't just want to say, "Here are the new records out this week." I went into the field and asked questions. I wanted to do the column because I loved dance music, the culture, the whole scene. I wanted to be part of it. I wanted to become a tastemaker.

I succeeded Bill Coleman in the role, who was also a DJ and who mentored me to take over the column. He knew I was going to handle it differently, and he encouraged it. Bill was managing Deee-Lite at the time, and he left the position because of the release of their hit record. In the beginning, the dance music community didn't like the way I handled the column. I had a very tough first year. I'd go so far as to say that it was brutal. A typical Bill Coleman column offered his unique view of music and trends, but it also offered a long list of the records released that week. When I came on board, I would say, "Yeah, we're gonna talk about just these four records." And I'd interview an artist. So many people in the industry (artists, managers, label reps) started saying, "What the fuck? How come I'm not in the column?" I didn't list records; I wrote about them, and many people didn't go for that. I didn't know how to do a column their way; I had to do it my way. I almost gave up at one point and thought about quitting, but I had a great editor and managing editor who held my hand through it all. I made enemies, and I made many mistakes. I also made several new friends and even managed to have a few really good moments that first year. I came out as a gay man in my column and won a GLAD award for that.

My dance column for *Billboard* became something you had to fight to get into. It became a big deal to make it into the column, thank goodness. I was very lucky. I think what people eventually realized was that I wasn't being a bitch about it; I was writing commentary on the music I cared about. I wasn't being a jerk; I just really needed to like the track I wrote about. In the process, the column became a little bit more exclusive. Let's face it; it was *Billboard*, the big gun. There was no place else to go. It wasn't like there were 20 magazines, 50 websites and 30 blogs you could utilize. There was *Billboard* and *DMA* (*Dance Music Authority*) magazine. That was it. So they learned to play ball with me. I also stopped caring what people thought. I focused not on other people's opinions, but on what I was doing—cultivating and fostering great music and great artists. (Believe me, there was a lot of bad dance music during the era.) I kept my head clear. I didn't go out every night to the clubs—your head would just get filled with too much stuff. I focused on my column as my art—it wasn't traditional art, but it was my contribution to pop culture. If you let people know that, eventually they would come to respect it. And if they didn't—well, life goes on.

Everyone wondered if disco would ever come back, and for a while in the '90s it did. It was a period when there seemed to be an organized effort among a lot of different people, communities and in a lot of clubs around the world to foster a sound that would be as big as disco. And what a mix it was—house music, Hi-nrg, freestyle, Euro-dance, dance-pop, techno. The list goes on and on. The great thing about disco was how multi-cultural it was and how reflective it was of the fringe parts of society, despite eventually becoming so mainstream. Gays, blacks, Latinos—disco was originally a melting pot of ideas, cultures, people and sounds. These same elements came together in the '90s, only this time you saw the music industry take it all seriously. Dance music departments returned to major labels with a fresh focus on marketing and promoting artists and songs. Artists whose popularity had begun to wane were finding a new energy and life in dance music. A great example is Gloria Estefan (who had enjoyed massive pop success years before). With her dance hits of the period, she found youth and energy again in the club world. The '90s are what turned Madonna from a potential flash-in-the-pan to a serious artist, in a way her music hadn't in the '80s. She established herself as a songwriter and a sales force, while maintaining her primary aim—to conquer the clubs.

You had dance music that was very above ground, very pop, very major label–friendly, and you had the music from indie labels becoming massively profitable and influential (think Strictly Rhythm Records, Micmac and Eightball Records). If you prefer a sports analogy, an artist usually honed his or her skills on these indie labels, the so-called amateur leagues, and it could very well lead to something huge—the big leagues. Or it could work the other way. Take Ultra Naté, for example. She had her major label moment, but it didn't quite work out beyond the clubs, where she had a series of dance-floor hits. Off she went to Strictly Rhythm, and she released "Free," a worldwide mainstream pop phenomenon. Look at Boy George; he had a rebirth during the '90s. He'd bottomed out as a pop artist, so he became a club DJ and started a label—More Protein Records. That label was extremely important during the '90s, and was one of the most influential house labels to come out of the UK.

The '90s was a time when everybody wanted to dance again, and people were feeling inspired. The glue that connected the people with the music were such elements as those massive gospel choruses and big vocals. It became the era of the diva, but in a different way than in the '70s or '80s. We had gone beyond Donna Summer. We had a new breed of divas like Martha Wash (a '70s and '80s artist who managed to keep reinventing herself), Amber, Kristine W and Robin S. Unlike the disco era, which was often viewed as an American phenomenon (with European hits largely staying in their corners of the world), the '90s opened everything up. The sounds became bigger because the world got smaller. Music made in Germany and the UK was as at home in the U.S. as it was in their native lands. In Europe and in the U.S., club and house music became pop music—"Finally" by CeCe Peniston, "Everybody's Free" by Rozalla, Snap!'s "Rhythm Is a Dancer," "Another Night" by Real McCoy—everywhere in the world these songs, and many others that were nurtured in the clubs, became gigantic pop records.

We also saw the rise of the DJ, people like Junior Vasquez, Frankie Knuckles, Deep Dish, Steve "Silk" Hurley, Farley "Jackmaster" Funk, E-Smoove, David Morales, Tony Moran, Todd Terry and many more. It became big business for these DJs to play American clubs and the big venues overseas. The DJ world was a very communal experience, with these artists being followed by extremely loyal and devoted fans. It was a competitive environment to be sure—everyone wanted to be the best DJ on the club scene. You had to have the best grooves; you had to be the one that Madonna came to for her latest remix. The '90s also gave DJs their first opportunities not to just extend a song, like Jellybean had in the '80s, but completely rewrite, reconfigure and re-imagine the song.

I think about those legendary moments, like when Masters at Work (Louie Vega and Kenny "Dope" Gonzalez) took a song like "Losin' Myself" by Debbie Gibson and just created an entirely new song out of it. It was a game-changing reinvention. They had a major hit with it, and Debbie earned house music credibility that she never had before. After a while, the labels would go hunting for remixers like Masters at Work and Junior Vasquez to turn "okay" songs into something special. There was a point where it was more interesting to know that a label hired one of these DJs to mix a new Michael Jackson record than to know about the record itself. We were less interested in Michael's song than what they were gonna do with it. This scene eventually caved in and cannibalized itself, but for many years in the '90s, it was a very exciting experience to watch it unfold. These DJs were brilliant people working with great artists and saving many of their records from mediocrity.

The EDM (electronic dance music) star DJs of today, like David Guetta, are following the blueprints set forth by the legendary DJs of the '90s. Unfortunately, nobody back then could quite figure out how to break these club mixes to Top 40 radio. I wrote countless columns trying to figure it out—nobody ever could. By contrast, today's DJs seem to have learned how to successfully monetize their work.

The aspect of '90s dance music culture that moved me most was the clubs—you could go to a club and see a lot of people having a great time, just as in the '70s. But what I found more exciting about the '90s was that these venues and nightlife experiences were far more creative than their counterparts in previous decades. The themes, decor, atmosphere and the power of the events were remarkable. Club culture of the '90s was so artistic—it was unlike anything I'd seen before or have seen since.

The heyday of '90s dance music ended as the decade drew to a close. Music tends to change every ten years or so, so this shift was right on schedule. I noticed many artists changing their attitude about dance music, the genre that had brought them success. There's this old joke about the actor who starts saying, "What I really want to do is direct." In dance music, you'd talk to a big club star, DJ or singer, and they would say, "What I really want to do is R&B." Or pop. Or rock. Or alternative rock. Everybody got too big for the clubs, for dance music. The heroes were falling out of love with their own genre, and they started releasing material in these other styles. Very often, they weren't good records, and, obviously, they were unsuccessful endeavors. (These same artists usually ended up going back to the clubs, because the pop and rock genres were like diving into the ocean—and you can drown there.) At the same time, a lot of young people who started the rave movement, a sort of punk expression of dance music, were gaining momentum. Suddenly, the music was moving in a direction I didn't care for. Soon the clubs would start to change as well. Honestly, it became a lot less fun, a lot less passionate and a lot more mechanical. I grew restless, and it all coincided with other opportunities for me at *Billboard*.

When people want to express their most primal emotions—they move; they dance. Disco grew out of a community of people that wanted to go someplace safe, to feel freedom and to express their emotions. They went to these crummy buildings with colorful lights where they could hear music that would take them away from the hardships of their world. Disco was born in these dens, where a circle of queens would be turning in one corner, blacks, Latinos and gays were all getting along together, and straight people might very well be doing their mating dances beside all of them. People used dance music to exorcize the demons of the world. It's no coincidence that many people referred to hitting the clubs as "going to church." The music was tribal. At its peak, the '90s was an equally amazing experience and an extraordinary time in dance music history. The '90s brought back the best aspects of disco, such as its ability to supply hope and an uplifting soundtrack (that, in this case, defied the daunting gloom and massive challenges of the AIDS crisis). And by its power, for a time, it restored a communal sense to the world. That's not meant to sound dramatic—it *was* dramatic.

I feel very much a part of the great dance music that represents the '90s, and, having fostered the sounds and the artists from this time at *Billboard*, I feel a very deep, emotional attachment to the era. We built something that will live forever. The dance music of the '90s doesn't have a catchy name like disco, but we were the second wave of that music explosion and nightlife phenomenon, and we took our sounds around the world. I think the decade speaks for itself, and we can be very proud of that.

Special Commentary by the Berman Brothers

Breaking into the business as young musicians in Germany, brothers Frank and Christian Berman rose from relative anonymity to superstardom in the world of '90s dance-pop music. As songwriters, producers and remixers of several of the era's most popular hits, the Berman Brothers worked with many of the decade's hottest acts. Their infectious production of Real McCoy's 1993 floor-filler "Another Night" took the song all the way to the number one position on Billboard's dance chart, a Top 10 ranking on the pop chart and paved the way for the gentlemen's prolific association with Arista Records and other major U.S. labels.

In addition to their hits with Real McCoy, the brothers enjoyed great success fashioning irresistibly upbeat sounds for Amber, No Mercy, She Moves, Hanson and other stars of the period. Frank and Christian's production of "If You Could Read My Mind" by the female trio known as Stars on 54 (from the 1998 film 54) became a widely lauded dance anthem and yet another Billboard Hot 100 hit for the brothers. The Bermans earned a Grammy for Best Dance Recording in 2001 for their production work on the Baha Men's smash dance single "Who Let the Dogs Out" and have reportedly amassed over 80 gold and platinum records worldwide. In addition, they've contributed to the soundtracks of such hugely popular films and TV series as The Hangover, Sex and the City *and* The Sopranos.

Frank and Christian co-produced all the tracks on the hit 2006 album Rhythms del Mundo—Cuba *(which featured artists such as Coldplay, Sting, Maroon 5 and Ibrahim Ferrer & Omara Portuondo from Buena Vista Social Club), well ahead of the country's recent shift into 21st century pop culture. The album is said to have sold over 1.5 million copies, a highly significant accomplishment in the music industry. In 2014, the brothers produced the* Studio Rio Presents—The Brazil Connection *compilation for Sony/Legacy, which utilized the original vocals of such legends as Billie Holliday, Marvin Gaye, Nina Simone and Bill Withers. They continue to comb the world on a quest to find the perfect rhythm—one they describe as being "authentic and crafted by the best local musicians, while also having a mainstream appeal." Following recording sessions for a new project conducted in Cuba, the brothers composed their vivid recollections of the '90s and the role they played in fueling the era's dance beat explosion.*

The '90s was an amazing decade where people wanted to simply have a good time and dance again. It was all about enjoying one's self with the sounds of upbeat, positive music. For us, it marked our incredible beginning in the professional music industry.

We were in our early 20s back then and originally came from a background in live music (funk, soul, acid jazz and world). But the excitement building for dance music in the U.S. would lead us to move all the way from our home in Germany to New York City, which is still our favorite place in world.

When we produced "Another Night" by Real McCoy in a recording studio in Hamburg, Germany, at first it was only a minor hit in Europe, barely making it into the Top 100 of several countries. Thanks to BMG Canada and (former international A&R VP at RCA) Vince Degiorgio, the song suddenly hit number one in that country and stayed there for several weeks. That got Arista and Clive Davis on board, who championed the record in the U.S. Clive Davis became the executive producer of the Real McCoy debut album, and then our amazing run really began in earnest.

We will never forget the day we received a call from Clive Davis' office, inviting us to come to New York to begin work on more productions. We had never been to America before, but when we landed at JFK airport, we just knew we were in the right place. The week we landed, "Another Night" was number one on the *Billboard* airplay charts. And we quickly learned just how powerful that top spot can be.

In a taxi on the way from the airport to our hotel, we heard the song played twice on the radio. We also heard a commercial for the album. On top of that, when we passed through Times Square, we saw a huge billboard advertising our album. For us, it was like being in a movie. Shortly after, the album debuted in the Top Five of the *Billboard* album charts and the single stayed in the Top 10 on the pop chart for 23 weeks. Both the album and single went on to achieve platinum status. "Run Away," the second single we produced for Real McCoy, reached the Top Three and went gold.

We remember our first meeting with Clive Davis (at his amazing office) very well—what a visionary, powerful, music-loving person he was. He helped us in so many ways and hired us on the spot to handle several other productions and remixes for Arista. He was also very involved in the new songs we produced for Real McCoy's follow-up album, which was made in New York. When we were sitting in his office, he received a call from a woman named "Annie," and he asked if he could put her on speaker phone, allowing us to listen to the conversation. It took us a while to figure out that this lovely, distinguished English voice was, indeed, Annie Lennox, who had just penned a song for Whitney Houston. All this happened in just our first meeting in America.

When we left Germany, we brought with us the rough demo of a dance-pop song called "This Is Your Night." We produced and co-wrote it just before we left. Our second big meeting in New York was with Tom Silverman, founder of Tommy Boy Records, and Victor Lee, an important executive there. Tommy Boy was coming off an amazing run with Coolio, Naughty by Nature, House of Pain and other top artists. They fell in love with "This Is Your Night" and wanted to sign a full album right away. The performer of the song was a great singer from the Netherlands named Marie-Claire Cremers. The project name was Amber. "Sexual," "One More Night" and "Love One Another" were follow-up singles we produced as well. All became big club and mainstream records.

We will never forget that first meeting with Tom Silverman. When we decided to sign with Tommy Boy, he offered us the key to his beautiful private city apartment on the Upper East Side, so we could really experience and enjoy the city. We had been staying in a hotel. Those were incredible days in New York, with the amazing views from his apartment and the generosity he showed us by letting us stay in his private place for such a long time (and for free). Tommy Boy's A&R head at the time, Victor Lee, introduced us to so many wonderful DJs, remixers and artists from the New York dance scene. We were very glad we signed with Tommy Boy. They really made us feel at home.

Shortly after, *Billboard* magazine announced the Top 20 most successful producers of the year, and we were listed among icons such as R. Kelly, Mutt Lange and Babyface. We teamed up with Jerry Ade, who was representing the extremely popular remixer Hex Hector (who added his touch to some of our projects). The pace just wouldn't ease up, and we next signed a multi-album production deal with Tommy Mottola, Don Ienner (the head honchos over at Columbia/Sony) and Will Botwin, a major talent executive. The marketing meetings we attended at Sony with famous executives such as Jerry Blair and (future Epic label president) Charlie Walk were just amazing. Wow, these certainly were the crazy '90s. (Interestingly enough, we produced another project for Sony Music U.S. last year. When we entered their office building, all the memories from the '90s came flooding back.)

During the '90s, *DJ Times* magazine featured us on their cover, calling us "Crossover Kings." We believe that growing up in Germany and listening to pop radio, where they played ABBA, along with Tears for Fears, New Order, Rolling Stones and the like, perhaps helped us to create records that were able to reach the top spot on the dance charts—but also had the kind of appeal that made them radio/mainstream successes.

Back in Germany, the type of music we were creating was seen more as a kind of "cheesy" pop, but in America, there was a totally different attitude. Commercial music wasn't something bad. It was actually the opposite. When we received a BMI award for "This Is Your Night" for ranking as one of the most performed songs on the radio in America, we were sitting at the same table as Sheryl Crow, actress Charlize Theron, Matchbox Twenty's Rob Thomas and many more. And we weren't sure how they would react to us when we were called on stage to receive our award. But when the song was played, every one of them sang along with the song and applauded. This was a wonderful moment for us.

Our favorite production during the '90s was the song "If You Could Read My Mind" by the group Stars on 54. It was the title track for the movie *54*, starring Mike Myers, Salma Hayek and Ryan Phillippe. It featured Ultra Naté (to date, our favorite female singer), as well as Amber and Jocelyn Enriquez. Except for the short (but intense) "discussion" between the three performers about who would get the first verse, it was an amazing session. In the end, the film company Miramax re-shot the conclusion of the movie and had the group perform the track. That's how much they loved the song.

Not all of the experiences we had were necessarily smooth sailing. One such incident comes to mind—working with Mariah Carey and her team when they signed one of our artists to her new label Crave, connected with Sony. Collaborating with Mariah's team, we cast an additional rapper/singer for our band. The plan was to first launch the album in Japan. So, Ms. Carey got the Sony Japan bosses to come to New York and shoot some promo material with the band (including the new rapper), which they started airing in Japan. We were all surprised and extremely excited about the unusual fact that this new rapper fluently spoke Japanese. Two weeks before the band was supposed to fly to Japan, the rapper called us, saying there was a little problem. Long story short, he confessed that he had been in Japan before (with the Marines) and was caught in some kind of drug smuggling scheme and had been in jail there for a long time. Guess that's a great way to really learn the Japanese language. We will never forget the frantic days that followed, with the Sony corporate lawyers and other international "crime" experts on the phone, all trying to solve this situation. Needless to say, the rapper never made it to Japan.

There are so many stories from this time, we could go on for the length of this book. By and large, when we look back, it really was an amazing and incredibly fun time for us. It is very gratifying to have received several awards for our work and to have been told by many fans that our music brought them such great pleasure. (To this day, we still meet people in the States who tell us their children were conceived while our songs were playing!) We are very honored to have been a part of the '90s dance-pop music movement. It was our start in the music industry and opened so many important doors for us.

We are pleased to be a part of this project and to share in the joy of commemorating the era and our fellow artists.

Preface

After coming of age during the heyday of disco in the late '70s and exploring the intense pleasures of synth-fueled '80s dance music, I spent the '90s immersed in and actually earning a living from the American music industry. I served as the editor of the Record World retail music chain magazine *The Street* during the first years of the decade and went on to a long and successful career working in New York City as an executive with the U.S. division of the (Germany-based) Bertelsmann entertainment organization. At the time, Bertelsmann was the corporate parent of record labels such as Hansa, Ariola, RCA and Arista, as well as other business ventures, such as the publishing giant Doubleday. They also owned the entertainment marketing firm BMG Direct North America (my stomping ground), housed in a massive office building located right in the heart of New York's Times Square on Broadway.

My career path with Record World and Bertelsmann gave me a tremendous education into the workings of the music industry and my first up-close encounters with a wide range of international music stars, everyone from Donny Osmond and TLC to La Bouche and Italian superstar Eros Ramazzotti. I truly had the time of my young adult life in the '90s, and though there was plenty of work to get done, I can't imagine a better or more enjoyable nine to five experience. Connections with many of those I worked with continue to this day, I'm happy to say.

The '90s was a time of great prosperity in the U.S. music industry. For a good portion of the decade, CD sales were growing exponentially, year after year. Record labels were rolling in cash. It was a period of tremendous variety in music, with artists from nearly all genres sharing the pop charts. The tendency to marginalize different forms of music seemed to dissipate as *Billboard's* pop singles survey reflected a wider range of sounds than in the past. Hip-hop (Jay-Z, Wu-Tang Clan, 2Pac, Snoop Doggy Dog) was on the rise, and indie, grunge and alternative rock (Green Day, Nirvana, Counting Crows) were gaining mainstream popularity. Country was unstoppable (Garth Brooks, Shania Twain, Alan Jackson) and R&B/soul (Whitney Houston, Janet Jackson, Boyz II Men, En Vogue—and Mariah Carey, *Billboard's* Artist of the Decade) was on fire. Pure pop was everywhere. The delicious harmonies of NSYNC, the Spice Girls, Hanson and the Backstreet Boys exemplified that niche. Whatever one was into, it was out there in abundance. If music lovers didn't mind coughing up some coin ($12–$18 for a CD album, $7–$10 for a CD single, on average in the U.S.), your crib could be all that with some phat tunes. (*I can assure you, I never actually spoke like that.*)

It was also one of the most popular periods (arguably *ever*) for dance music. Electronic styles from this era (not to be confused with present day EDM, though similarities exist) generally ratcheted up the tempo, and new and powerful sub-genres emerged, such as techno, trance, Euro-dance, house and hip-house. Germany, Italy, Sweden and the UK became major

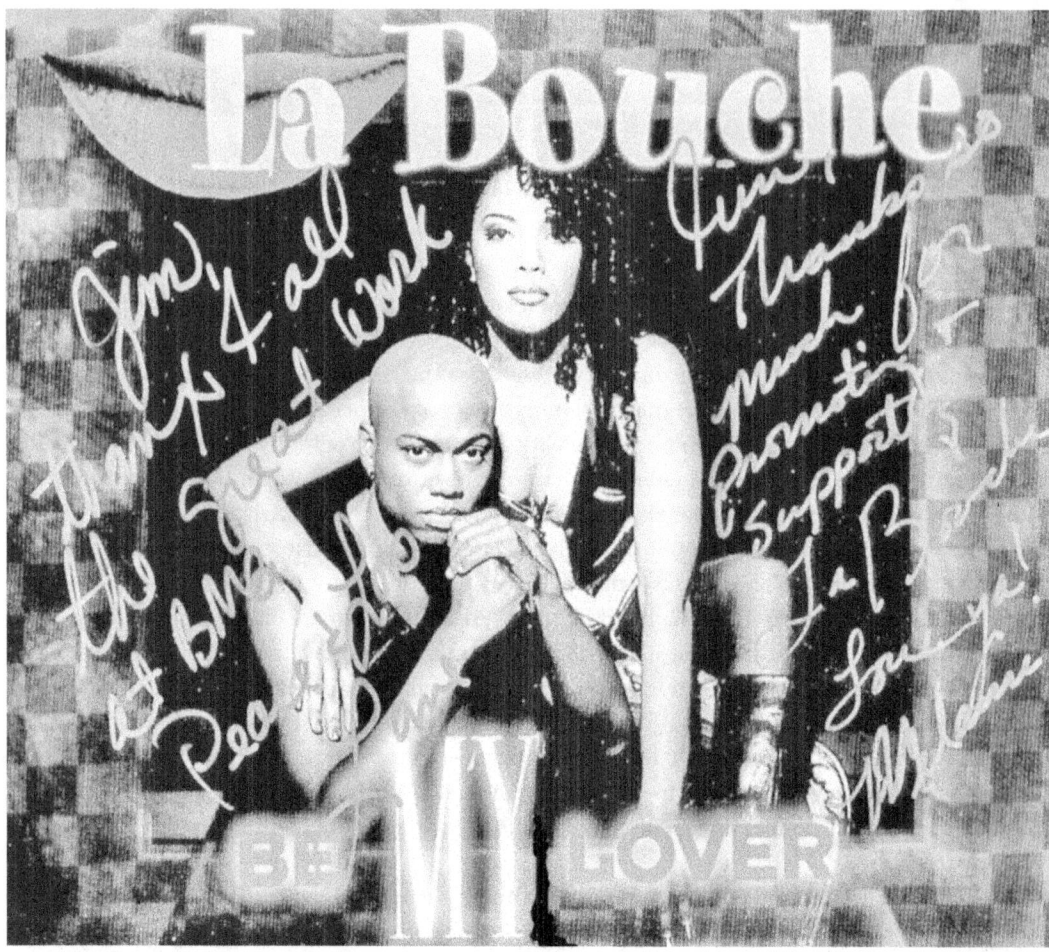

This European CD single jacket for the hit "Be My Lover" was autographed for the author by La Bouche stars Lane McCray and Melanie Thornton, who visited the offices of BMG International in New York City in 1995.

exporters of floor-filling beats. U.S. radio, clubs and consumers welcomed international artists like Haddaway, Right Said Fred, 2 Unlimited, Snap!, Ace of Base, M People, Enigma and Real McCoy with open arms. American artists equally shared the spotlight, with stars such as CeCe Peniston, Robin S, C + C Music Factory, Deee-Lite, Cher and Madonna reaching top positions on all the major charts.

It was a hugely explosive era for the clubs, which for decades had been the launching pad for dance music hits. Enormous, state-of-the-art venues sprang up whose focus was to create an unparalleled, otherworldly dance floor experience. The quaint neon of the discothèques and new wave nightspots became a distant memory. In both gay and straight cultures, big club and rave happenings became the hippest and most sought after of weekly adventures by 20- and 30-somethings. The White Party and Black Party became legendary in the LBGT community during this period. Leading the beat-fused charge were star DJs and remixers, who could whip a song into a massive club anthem and give a beat hungry crowd a fix they wouldn't soon forget. Among the most celebrated spin masters of the period were house legend Frankie

Knuckles, Danny Tenaglia, Little Louie Vega, David Morales, Junior Vasquez, Tony Moran, Todd Terry, Armand Van Helden, Hex Hector, Peter Rauhofer, Susan Morabito, Roger Sanchez, Steve "Silk" Hurley and Deep Dish, in addition to many other celebrated names.

The '90s saw dance music and club culture at its most heightened level of popularity since the disco frenzy of the '70s. There were good reasons to feel up—some legitimate, others not so much. The music was making people feel alive, that's for sure, and popular, mood-altering drugs like "X" and "Special K" were numbingly abundant in the club environments, often helping quite a bit to create a surreal "I love everyone" atmosphere of chaotic bliss among the flashing lights.

For the gay community (still cited as dance music's biggest supporters by many of this era's artists), the main event of the '90s was the end of automatically rubber-stamping a skull and crossbones on the heads of those who contracted HIV and AIDS. The difference between a manageable condition and the panic of a terrifying deadly epidemic became increasingly palpable, and the sense of growing relief and optimism was vividly on display in the clubs and at pride celebrations.

Life seemed good in the '90s, and music was, once again, providing a fabulous soundtrack for all of it.

By the summer of 1999, the music industry, driving full speed down a golden highway (with a pile of cash in the trunk), was sideswiped. At first, the industry didn't seem to fully know it had been dealt such a critical blow. However, the arrival of Napster and the ensuing debacle with the very modern day issue of peer-to-peer file sharing ended up nearly wrecking the commercial music business model that had existed for decades. The dawn of the 21st century saw the industry face its most daunting challenges ever. Unlike the disco backlash of 1979 (that targeted dance music artists exclusively), this time every artist, musician and record company executive would feel the blow to some degree. As if that weren't challenging enough, a worsening trend towards corporate control of radio station (and later Internet outlet) music programming that reflected big business interests rather than the regional tastes of audiences would prove decidedly unhealthy for artists worldwide.

But I digress.

Let's get back to the ten years which preceded this dramatic reversal of fortune, a period that was, indeed, a bull market for dance-pop music. I feel quite blessed that I was able to experience this extraordinary and eruptive time, both as a music fan and as a professional within the industry. The exhilarating tracks that so distinctly defined this era are vividly engrained in my memory, and the artists who brought them to life made a powerful, uplifting impression upon me. One listen to the songs discussed in these pages and you'll instantly feel a fresh surge of the amazing, infectious energy that permeated those years. You'll know exactly what I'm talking about. If you missed the '90s experience, I feel sure the history captured in this volume will make you wish you hadn't. In any event, I suggest keeping your mp3 player, iTunes, Amazon, Vevo, Vimeo, YouTube or the cloud where your musical memories are stored close by when reading these chapters. You'll surely want to see and hear these songs performed again.

Forgive me if I now borrow a few explanatory points from my previous books (*First Ladies of Disco, Legends of Disco* and *Stars of 80s Dance Pop*), as they are certainly relevant to this tome. To the distinguished assemblage of professionals contained herein, I posed questions about their lives and careers. These are their answers, given from the perspective of maturity they all have in common. These are the thoughts they want to share with you. Their struggles and triumphs are both relevant to the present and reflective of the past. The lessons in positivity and determination their steadfastness teaches us are sure to inspire, and I hope you will learn a great deal about what makes each of these artists tick. (I think you'll also find their answers to *The Lightning Round* questions found in several artist chapters both revealing and a lot of fun as well.) While relishing their past musical accomplishments, I encourage you to explore and enjoy all that they offer us today and all that they will in the future. By the way, I have chosen to share these interviews with you in Q&A style, a departure from the formats of my previous books. I believe doing so reflects the trend toward speed and short-burst dissemination of information that characterized the '90s.

I deeply thank the world stars who shared their stories with me in this examination of the nitro-fused '90s. You have done something truly marvelous, making this planet a more enjoyable place to be with your talents and music. As our world currently struggles against violence, intolerance and defensiveness, the positivity and inclusive spirit of '90s dance music (and all the great dance sounds of the 20th century) become increasingly prized.

As time goes by, I feel certain we will need more, more, more.

Peace out.

The Stars

Thea Austin, formerly of Snap!
"Rhythm Is a Dancer" (1992)

"The music is so unique in that there was and is no other song that sounds like 'Rhythm Is a Dancer.' To me, it was a perfect marriage of music and voice."—Thea Austin

From its distinctively electrifying opening chords to its powerful rolling beat, unusually poetic lyrical depth and robust vocals, "Rhythm Is a Dancer," by a studio concept known as Snap!, is one of the most recognizable success stories of the '90s. Thea Austin co-wrote and sang the track, and, along with rapper Maurice Butler (aka Turbo B.), she contributed to the group's visual identity. The song turned out to be Snap!'s biggest hit ever, reaching the number one position on the charts of Germany, Italy, France, the Netherlands, Ireland and the UK. "Rhythm Is a Dancer" was also a mammoth hit in the U.S., where it reached the Top Five of Billboard's pop singles chart in January of 1993, surrounded by the likes of Whitney Houston, Boyz II Men, Madonna and Mary J. Blige.

Snap!'s origins go a bit further back in time to an idea developed by producers and co-writers Michael Münzing and Luca Anzilotti—working under the aliases Benito Benites and John "Virgo" Garrett III—who had previously enjoyed huge success in Germany in the late '80s with an act known as 16 Bit ("Where Are You?"). Shifting their focus to Snap!, they scored a worldwide hit with the fist-pumping, anthemic dance smash "The Power" sung by Penny Ford (featuring rhymes by Turbo B.) in 1990.

In the aftermath of "Rhythm Is a Dancer," Austin's tenure with Snap! was relatively short, the result of frequent personnel changes within the group. However, the artist was able to continue lending her vocal and songwriting skills to a number of releases during the era, including a version of the Soulsearcher's bass-heavy house hit "Can't Get Enough," which reached the UK Top 10 and the Top 20 of the Billboard dance chart late in the decade. The artist enjoyed more hits with "I'm Addicted (You're the Worst Thing for Me)" by Pusaka on Tommy Boy Records in 2000 and "Just About Had Enough" with Beat Hustlerz in 2003.

Thea is upbeat as she speaks about her '90s success from her home in California, revealing a strong sense of spirituality that she believes has always kept her moving forward.

I'd like to know a little about your early years growing up in Pennsylvania, Thea.

Life for me actually began in McKeesport Hospital. My mother and father raised my sisters and brother in the small steel mill town of Clairton, Pennsylvania. My sister, Vontelle, was my mentor, and she is still a singer. She's amazing and was very inspiring to me, and it was her voice that I heard the most growing up. She put me on to Aretha, Chaka, Phyllis Hyman, Minnie Riperton, the Jackson 5, and the list goes on and on. My mother and father were dedicated parents who worked hard to develop a better lifestyle for our family. They bought property in Jefferson Hills, PA, and built our family home (not contractors) with a little help from a few family members and close friends. They were and are my heroes because they showed us, with focus and dedication, that things can get done. Whatever it took to purchase that property and get their home built, they did it. They had a strong work ethic and believed every goal is attainable.

I always knew I would be a singer (and my career as a paid singer actually began when I was just eight years old). After graduating from the University of Pittsburgh, my friend (Donna Miller) asked me to move to California with her. So, we hitched up a U-Haul trailer on the back of my car and drove across country. My personal life was in a bit of turmoil in those days. After a job as a writer for the *R&B Report* came to a halt due to bankruptcy of the publication, I moved to Japan to work as a singer. Although my experience in Japan was awesome in many ways, I was almost murdered there—it was only by grace and sheer physical manipulation and the help of some good people (like Leon Wesley, Osafune, Kobaiashi and Maggie) that I was able to handle those challenges. When I returned home to the U.S., a friend named Jonas introduced me to Penny Ford, a super talented vocalist and songwriter.

"My music was right up there with the best of them—it elevated 'Rhythm Is a Dancer' beyond being just another dance song," says singer/songwriter Thea Austin (photograph by David Burgoyne, courtesy Thea Austin).

Penny had been the lead vocalist for Snap!'s mega-hit "The Power." How did you come to be part of the Snap! project?

It was a divine blessing that my path crossed with Penny Ford. She introduced me to Luca Anzilotti and Michael Münzing, Snap!'s producers. Penny was interested in recording a song I'd written (which she wanted for her solo album), and she knew they were looking for a new singer for Snap! So we helped each other out. She had been singing with them and was now pursuing her own solo career. She was more of an R&B/jazz singer than electronic dance music. So I went with Penny to Germany, and Logic Records flew us over, ambassador class, on Lufthansa. We stayed in a very nice hotel. We worked diligently on a couple of songs with the guys, and then Penny left.

They played me the music for "Rhythm Is a Dancer" (which did not have a name at the time) and gave me some ideas that didn't work that well. So, I sat in a corner of the studio, by myself, and prayed to God to please give me something that people could feel. I got quiet and then the inspiration came. I could hear the lyrics and melody, and eventually the verse just spilled out of me. "Rhythm Is a Dancer" was birthed. The producers loved what I brought to the table. That was it.

It wasn't just me coming up with the song; it was a team effort. But once I was in the booth alone and kind of surrendered myself, it took about 45 minutes or an hour [to get it written]. Sometimes with the creative process, if you have too many people in your face trying to brainstorm and pull ideas out of you, you can come up with ideas—but [you might not get] that key verse. When you're alone, you have the time to think things out without the outside influences. I remember I came out of the vocal booth and said, "Hey, I think I've got it."

During this creative process, was there a positive atmosphere in the studio?

We got along well, Luca, Michael and I. They were very formal and business-like in the beginning, but with a touch of warmth, especially from Mr. Anzilotti. Michael was cordial and very much the business backbone. Luca was a freer spirit and more of the creative musical person behind it. They were fun in the studio, and they had many other worker bees with them. There was a guy there named DJ Rico that I heard contributed to "Rhythm Is a Dancer." I heard a rumor that he was the one that came up with the lick that you hear at the beginning of the song. There were other talented DJs/musicians in the studio that shared their gifts and helped create some of the sounds in the Snap! recordings. The producers seemed happy with our creative process. It was a nice and easy going experience for me. The studio was clean, professional and legit.

What do you think the producers were looking for as far as your talents were concerned in regard to "Rhythm Is a Dancer"?

I think the producers were looking for me to pour my R&B soul into their songs. They wanted to capture the feelings, the sound and the power that African American soul singers are known for possessing. The producers were successful at marrying soulful vocals with the powerful rap vocals of Turbo B., along with their dynamic Euro-dance music style. This was a working formula for them, and the world embraced it. It was a certain vibe and texture of all the sounds that worked so well together.

Did you sense any pressure among the group to keep the momentum going that had begun with the hit "The Power"?

I'm sure there existed some pressure [to match the success of "The Power"]. However, the producers never put pressure on me by saying anything like, "You gotta write something as incredible as 'The Power.'" Of course, a bit of anxiety and certainly the excitement was there in the studio. They were very, very happy with "Rhythm Is a Dancer."

"Rhythm Is a Dancer" held the top spot in the UK for several weeks and was a mammoth success worldwide. Reaching the Top Five in the U.S. (via Arista Records) took the song to

another level. It has truly become one of those classic songs that define the sound of the '90s. It's been remixed numerous times and seems to strike the right chord with many generations, regardless of whatever styles may be in current favor. Why has this song resonated so powerfully with the public and stood the test of time so well?

I believe "Rhythm Is a Dancer" resonates so powerfully because it is spiritually and creatively blessed. The producers and I had amazing energy and great intent in our creative processes. The melodies are hypnotic and make people feel good, like a great nursery rhyme that people gravitate towards. The music is so unique in that there was and is no other song that sounds like "Rhythm Is a Dancer." To me, it was a perfect marriage of music and voice. Spiritually, I believe the song has a divine God energy in it because I surrendered myself to God in prayer and was blessed to receive the melody and lyrics. I believe the song touches the spirit of people—music is spiritual, after all.

People wanted a song like that back then—something to kickstart their day, free them up. It was a time in life that people were being liberated, like in South Africa or for the LGBT community in the States, and the song represents that liberation for many people.

I went to South Africa for the first time a few years ago—I've got goosebumps telling you this story—and the guys that were meeting us, road managers and personal drivers, they were sharing with us their experience with the song. It was an old school tour with MC Hammer, Vanilla Ice, Turbo B. and myself. They were telling us that "Rhythm Is a Dancer" was so huge there because it was one of the first songs that they were able to freely hear from the outside world. They had been pretty limited to hearing only music from their country. The song really hit their souls, and in turn, their support gave the song more life and energy and made it even more loved.

It's funny. The song clearly received a joyful response, as you say, but I always felt "Rhythm Is a Dancer" had a kind of ominous quality about it, a darker sound.

That's a cool way to describe it, too. I can feel that as well. When I listen to the music separate from my vocals, I hear myself sounding very melancholy, with a lot of pleasure and pain. That may be what you're picking up. I had gone through a lot by that time. When I hear my voice and listen to the songs I wrote at that time, I can identify that combination of happiness and the tug on my soul that I was going through.

How did you react to your success with Snap! and the fame that came with your hit?

I was enormously surprised by the success of the song. As you said, it reached the Top Five on the U.S. *Billboard* Hot 100 and number one in the UK, where it was the second biggest selling single of 1992, surpassed only by Whitney Houston's version of "I Will Always Love You." These facts are important and cherished by me as an artist and songwriter. They show what I am capable of doing, and I am very proud of that. To have "Rhythm Is a Dancer" mentioned in the same sentence with one of the loves of my life, Whitney Houston (and her classic song), is as impactful to me as the phenomenal chart level the song reached. My music was right up there with the best of them—it elevated "Rhythm Is a Dancer" beyond being just another dance song.

My life was—and forever will be—changed by it. It's my favorite song on the planet, and not just because I wrote it and sang it. I know where it came from, and it was the biggest blessing of my life. That's why I will never get tired of singing it or hearing it. There are times where it still seems to divinely pop out of nowhere. I can be in a fitness class at the gym, and it comes on, and the people go crazy. And they don't know that it's me. That's the beauty of it. I can stay listening to it with a humble spirit and a grateful attitude. I was in the right place at the right time—and it wasn't just me. It was everybody involved with that song that poured their hopes into it and loved it as I did.

It took months—a very long time—before any money came in from it. It took a while before we made the video, too. And it took a while for a tour to come about—and it didn't come from Luca or Michael. We did not get support from them. To his credit, Turbo B. and his manager, Johnny Wright (who managed Janet Jackson, Justin Timberlake, Britney Spears and so many great artists) created the tours. I remember they flew me down to Florida for a few weeks of rehearsal.

The funny thing was Turbo wasn't that crazy about "Rhythm Is a Dancer." We learned [the routine for the song] kind of at the last minute. Turbo liked the song; he just didn't love it in the beginning. He learned to *love* it.

Being on tour with Snap! was really an elevated level—arenas and clubs. Snap! already had a worldwide reputation, so people anticipated something good—and it was happening. I didn't realize how big it was at the time. I was just doing what I was supposed to do. But then I saw the results—the interviews increasing, the TV shows, like *Top of the Pops*. I think it was CNN that first said the song was one of the Top 20 of the year—that's when it became real for me. I had been a bit blind to the success. I was just glad to be singing and performing and doing the day-to-day grind. I wasn't even that curious.

Do you recall a standout event performing the track for an audience?
We opened for Michael Jackson's HBO concert in Bucharest, Romania. It was incredibly exciting to see Michael perform—it's like an out-of-body experience. I was like, "I'm going to run across the same stage *he's* gonna run across?" You know? Amazing! To hit that same stage, sing our song, and have that same audience singing "Rhythm Is a Dancer," word-for-word, and their first language wasn't English, well—thank God it was an easy verse. [*Thea laughs.*] Their applause and excitement sounded like a mix of thunder, lightning and joy.

Turbo B. left the group to pursue a solo career, and there was a new female vocalist representing Snap! by the release of the third album, Welcome to Tomorrow, in 1994. What disconnected you from the group?
When the producers tried to contact me [about starting the next album]—back then we didn't have the communication options we have now—they weren't able to reach me, as I was touring. By the time I got back to the States and tried to contact them, they had already moved on to find singer Niki Harris, who I believe was a background singer for Madonna. Once they had done a few records with her, they moved on to the next singer, Summer ["The First the Last Eternity"]. That's how it was.

The story gets a bit worse, however. About seven or eight years ago, there was an opportunity for me to do a television show in Germany. [The show's producers] wanted me to sing "The Power," but I told them I wasn't the original singer of that track. Penny did the show, and that kind of catapulted her back into Snap! Penny, along with an unknown rapper, became the choice to tour as Snap! by the producers, who own the rights to the name. This was extremely challenging to deal with for Turbo B. (since he had been the main voice) and me, as we had been the artists touring and representing Snap! songs for so many years.

Despite this setback, I will always respect that Penny was the first Snap! vocalist, and I will always love her for introducing me to the producers.

You did, however, enjoy some significant success beyond Snap! with Marc Pomeroy's Soulsearcher project in 1999.

Yes, I had a hit with Soulsearcher called "Can't Get Enough," which took me back to *Top of the Pops*. I arrived at the hotel before performing on the show and turned on MTV, and—boom—my video came on. I was back in it again; it was a wonderful feeling.

As a result of this hit, I was also invited to perform at a Prince Charles and Princess Diana event called *Party in the Park*. It was an annual event with about 120,000 people gathering in Hyde Park. There was a sea of people there, and I wanted to be their ear and eye candy. I wanted them to feel good. It was a phenomenal concert, and I sang "Can't Get Enough"—and threw in a little bit of "Rhythm Is a Dancer." That was one of my best moments. It marked success for me without Snap!, and at that time in my life, I was, indeed, a soulsearcher. Again, it was a challenging point in my life—my mother was dying and not much had been happening in my career. I felt I was bottoming out again. And then this song came along and saved me again—from depression, money problems, doubting myself, and the sadness of my mother's eventual passing.

It just made me feel, spiritually—as I still do today—that I am supposed to sing all of my life and never stop. When you step into that kind of success with the right song and the right feeling, it is really spiritual bliss.

The dance music landscape is much different today from the way it was in the '90s. Opportunities for heritage stars are fewer, and the DJ, in many cases, has become the focal point. What are your thoughts about these changes?

I would agree. Thank God for the DJs and the people who really *do* love the music. If it weren't for them, so many singers' careers would tank. Many associated with dance are treated as more disposable that artists of other genres. They are easily replaced. I feel that so many DJs built their careers on our songs. I just want to ask them to please reach back and help pull us forward. Give us an opportunity to write a song with you and perform it. They sometime act is if we're too old or washed up, but we are still able—and they know that.

I was at a party and talking with a professional dancer in the business, and we got onto the subject of dance music. We talked about Madonna. He surprised me by saying, "Nobody wants to see an old bitch like that," blah, blah, blah. I said, "Excuse me? I beg your pardon, but she's a colleague. I love her, and I'm in the same age range. So what are you saying? *I'm an old bitch too?*" He said, "Oh, no, no, no. *Not you!*" He said he was referring to some of the personal things she's done. But we weren't talking about her personal life. We were talking about her songs and innovative approach as a performer. Are people ready to just forget about her? There was a 20-year-old kid there, and he actually said, "Who is Madonna?" I was like, "You must be kidding." You could see in his eyes he had no idea who she was.

It's sad to think even someone like Madonna could be disposable. It's crazy. I think a lot of people hate on her because she still has energy, she still looks good, and she doesn't play down sexy. Some people can only see her as a middle aged woman now and want her to stop being sexy and assertive. Well, that's like saying, "Stop being Madonna." So let her be herself, and stop being so damn jealous and envious. If you don't like her, stop flapping your lips about her, and mind your own business. She has enough money to put on her own tours, and the people who *do* love her *will* be there.

I recently did a gig at an event called *Out & Equal Workplace Summit*, and Lee Daniels (*Empire, Precious, The Butler*), the producer and writer, was a guest speaker. Part of his speech focused on the fact that even though he's received a lot of accolades for his work, he still walks into big meetings in Hollywood, and they look at him with doubt in their eyes. They still look at him with uncertainty—like the gay black dude, not the acclaimed producer. This is the battle he faces, and Madonna has hers. So I guess we're all going to have to battle some kind of discrimination—race, age, sexual orientation, you name it. It seems like that no matter what level you are at, at some point we all drink that bitter water.

Where would you like to take your career in the years ahead?

I'd like to stay healthy so that I can successfully continue touring around the world, writing and singing more hit songs. Also, I'd like to further develop as CEO of my record label, RIAD Music, helping people achieve their dreams as successful songwriters and recording artists. I'm a guitarist now, and would like to become a stronger player of the instrument and produce great music.

Beyond my personal health and career goals, I'd love to continue mentoring children, working with various non-profit organizations, such as Journey Sistahs, APLA (as an advocate for HIV/AIDS awareness), aiding in the needs of the homeless and being a caregiver to those in need. I believe there is lasting joy in giving.

In regard to the music business itself, it's a little sad how the business of selling recordings has been diminished. There's a huge plus on the one side because technology and innovations have allowed us to be able to make our own music and release it without a label contract. But it's also dumbed down the business. The ability for musicians, singers and songwriters to make a living from music has been severely compromised. Times are continuing to change.

You helped create one of dance music's biggest hits and have seen its power on the dance floor first hand. Does dance music serve a valuable purpose in society?

I've always thought all forms of dance music have great value. Its value is in its good energy, and that's something we all need. The energy of dance music gives people a certain feeling that inspires them. It's really that simple. Its value is in its good energy. Dance music is an amazing emotional pick-up!

Lightning Round with Thea

Diana Ross or Donna Summer?

[*Thea bursts into laughter.*] How can I possibly choose? Ok, I'll say Diana Ross because of her legendary breakthrough with Motown.

Extended versions or radio edits?

Radio edits. It takes a skill to make a three-minute song that works.

Applause or record sales?

Wow! Interesting. I don't sing for applause, and record sales are the reward of a job well done as a singer and songwriter. So I'll pick record sales.

Perfect hair or perfect teeth?
　Perfect teeth. All day long.

Meet your ancestors or meet your descendants?
　Another tough one. I'll say ancestors because of the value of their struggles, triumphs and wisdom.

'70s or '80s?
　[*There's a long pause.*] There's no lightning happening for me in these questions. [*She laughs.*] I love the '70s, and that's what I kind of came up with when I was young. But then the wealth of music styles grew for me tremendously in the '80s. I'm so sorry—I'll have to pass on deciding this one!

Angie Brown, formerly of Bizarre Inc
"I'm Gonna Get You" (1992)

"All of us, the performers and producers making this '90s music, didn't analyze it. We were just in the moment. I never had a clue that house music would ever stay in the hearts of people that lived through that era."—Angie Brown

Some dance songs of the '90s had the charm of veritable Pied Pipers, luring dancers onto club floors in droves with their hypnotically infectious hooks, arousing beats and scintillating vocals. As 1992 drew to a close, "I'm Gonna Get You," conceived by a British techno-house-dance-pop outfit known as Bizarre Inc, proved to be one of the most irresistible of these anthems. Among the song's most distinctive qualities was the roof-raising voice of singer Angie Brown, which sparked tremendous excitement on radio and in the clubs on both sides of the Atlantic.

In some ways, Angie was a reluctant participant in the house and rave scene of the day. However, she readily admits her association with Bizarre Inc and "I'm Gonna Get You" has served her well and continues to create demand for her live performances (including a spot on the UK version of TV's The Voice *in 2014) nearly 25 years later. She has continued to stay busy in the studio working as a featured vocalist, with releases such as the 2015 single "Deep" by the artist Istabile garnering much attention.*

From her home in Britain, she bubbles with enthusiasm and eagerly shares details of her experience as the diva behind one the era's most exuberant, foot-stomping jams.

If you would, Angie, tell me a little about growing up in Britain and how you discovered your voice.

My parents are both from Kingston, Jamaica, and they moved to the UK in the 1950s. After they settled, following a few years taking various jobs, my father, Alfred, finally got a good position as a carpenter. My mother, Almatine, became a nurse. They started a family in 1959. My brother Leon arrived first, and in 1963, they had me. My mother had a difficult birth, and couldn't hold me properly for a few days. Since she was not well enough to do it herself, I would be taken away to be fed and looked after by the nurses. When my mother was back on her feet, she would gingerly walk to where lots of babies were being cared for, and, she swears, she never ever had to look in any of the cribs to find me. She said she could always tell my voice amidst all those babies. In her words, "It rang like a bell."

My mother had a strong and beautiful voice. When she was a girl, she sang in church and told me that many people used to come to hear her sing, recite poetry or read from the bible. That's where I think I got my voice from. Even though my father could play a little bit of the harmonica, I really think my musicality came from my mother's side.

I grew up in Brixton, South London, a place where a lot of people who move to the UK settled. It was, and still is, a place where different people, cultures, religions and attitudes all come together and successfully live side-by-side. I think that mixture of cultures went on to spill over into the music we grew up listening to. When I was growing up, there was one radio station which everyone listened to. It was called Radio One. We didn't have a huge choice of radio stations with each playing one genre of music, like we do nowadays. Radio One always played a huge variety of music. You would hear the Jackson 5, David Bowie, the Four Tops and Elton John, all in the same show.

While growing up in the '60s and '70s, I had a wealth of great American music to listen to that was frequently on the British charts—like the Supremes, Stevie Wonder, and Tina Turner. Of course, I adored the great Brits, too, singers like Dusty and Lulu, and I think that my sound was definitely influenced by them. I also listened to a lot of reggae music, which was called ska. My mum used to have parties, and I would regularly hear and enjoy hits from popular reggae artists of the day, like Jimmy Cliff ("Many Rivers to Cross"), Millie [Small], who sang "My Boy Lollipop," and, of course, Desmond Dekker's "Israelites." I loved all that music, too. I'm sure they have all influenced me in one way or another.

When I was about 14, I joined theatre groups, sang in the choir at school and appeared in some amateur productions. I was told I had a very good voice, and that's where my confidence as a singer grew. Around the age of 17, I went on holiday with my family. My patents also fostered children by then, and a family holiday with lots to do was just perfect for us. During the holiday, I entered a singing competition and won. My mum quickly realized that I could sing but suggested that I needed some singing lessons so I wouldn't strain or hurt my voice in any way. Mum knew it was important to use my voice in the right way. So, I eventually found a singing teacher in Clapham (near Brixton), and I still see her today. Her name is Annette ("Nettie") Batam. A wonderful woman, who taught me well—a woman who had the privilege to work with Maria Callas and who, as a young girl, was trained as a dancer in New York.

Nettie went on to me teach a lot of things that have shaped my professional and social life. She taught me how to sing in French and to appreciate art, poetry, jazz, classical music and all things cultural. She said I had a good, solid, soulful voice, but I could be an even better singer if I had a good technique. She said that we British people tend to speak and sing from our throats, while American people tend to place their voices in their heads and smile throughout their performance, which makes it easier for them to produce a gospel sound. I went to Nettie's classes twice a week, where I would concentrate on my scales and basically broaden my vocal range. She treated me like a daughter, and I loved it! I was basically a Brixton kid, experiencing a very middle-class arty life.

After many years of working intensely with Nettie, I finally understood how to get a bright sound out of the top end of my voice. She helped to produce that "belter" sound, while maintaining beautiful control. That's how good American singers do it! Their voices naturally resonate.

So, while trying to create some singing work for myself, I needed an income, and I became a waitress. I also did catering and cleaning jobs. I didn't want a day job or a "proper job" that I couldn't get out of should I strike gold with singing. I worked for various employment agencies, and I called the shots. I told them whether I was working on that day or not, so I could always go off to my session work in the studios without explaining anything to anybody. No questions asked; I'm singing today! Plus, I'd also attend auditions as well. I tried my hand at a bit of everything to find my destiny.

In the mid-to-late '80s, I finally started getting more and more session work. I turned up at the studios, put my headphones on and quickly learned the choruses. Bam—I was on a pop song. But I didn't find choral or group singing interesting; it didn't push me enough. I really wanted people to hear me above everybody else. I tried everything to get into the top London vocal agencies. I didn't read music, so that really didn't help me to get professional session work. Back then, I'd knock on a few agency doors or send off my cassette tapes and curriculum vitae to try and generate some work. But a lot of agents had their favorite or regular singers. And those singers were excellent and very professional at their jobs. They were used on adverts, major artists' albums and tours. Sadly, those doors were closed for me, but I knew that I had to get noticed. So I gave it everything I had every time I had a chance to perform live.

Then, in the late '80s, the "open mic nights" were popping up all over the London club and pub scene, and I started going to them at least three days a week. And those clubs were perfect! It was the ideal learning ground for crafting my art, and perfecting my delivery of a song. Working with an enthusiastic audience on a weekly basis, I gained lots of experience of how to work the stage. I always sang something uptempo when it was my turn on those nights. I loved singing Aretha Franklin's "Respect." I could hit the high notes and people would go crazy. I also loved singing "What's Going On" and "We Are Family," songs that I still enjoy singing today.

This provided a means of breaking into the rapidly growing UK house music scene?
Yes. I started to get work as a professional vocalist in my own right. That's when I also got asked to be a featured artist. It was the '90s now, and there were a lot of singers with strong, high gospel voices featured on house music. These vocals were mostly found on bootlegs vinyl records that got sampled time and time again, and then got played (and treasured) by the new and adventurous up and coming DJs. American house music was blowing up on the club scene, and British DJs and producers were also looking to get in on the action. So they started looking for singers in the UK that could replicate the same styles as the American singers. It would be easier for them because they wouldn't have to fly anyone in from the States. Plus, Brit girls, in all honesty, were going to be a lot cheaper to hire.

Luckily for me, there weren't a lot of British girls who could actually produce that earth-shattering full bodied chest voice that was required on house music. The voice psychologically feels like it's coming from your toes and powers right through you. I knew if I could get what they wanted in the bag (and save the producers and their record company a fortune), I could be well on my way to the kind of success I had been waiting for.

This brings us to your connection with the group Bizarre Inc, who were already a very successful trio of DJs on the British house music scene and pop chart.
Exactly. Bizarre Inc were very successful, and I was introduced to them through an agent. The agency called me out of the blue and asked if I was interested in doing some session

work. I said that would be fantastic and asked who it would be for. She went on to explain all about Bizarre Inc. She said that they had already had a Top 10 hit in the UK with a track called "Playing with Knives" in 1991. The agent asked me if I could sing like Jocelyn Brown, and, of course, I immediately said, "Yes!" It really didn't matter if I could or I couldn't. I knew that I needed a break, and these DJs seem to have the world at their feet. If I could use my minimal drama school training and sing anywhere near the original bootleg they played for me, I knew I would get the gig! But you have to visualize it. That's how you pull people in. If you believe it, they believe it. If your audience believes you as a performer, then your job is done. So, I went into that session believing I could sing like Jocelyn Brown.

In the studio, I met three young, enthusiastic guys named Dean Meredith, Andrew Meecham and Carl Turner—they were Bizarre Inc. They played me a sample of Jocelyn singing her heart out. The bootleg sample had other big-voiced singers on it, like Loleatta Holloway and Martha Wash. Finally, they played me "I'm Gonna Get You." They really and truly wanted to use that original sample, but it was going to cost them a lot of money (otherwise they couldn't use it legally). So, [it was my job to] re-sing it. They only wanted two or three parts of the track, but it sounded way out of my range. I knew that if I was going to replicate that sound in any way, I was going to have to dig really, *really* deep. "Let's get this thing done," I thought to myself. If I could mimic Jocelyn and basically use the singing technique that Nettie taught me, I could have this recorded in no time. It felt like every muscle in my backside and lower abdomen were used to get the strength and the power I needed to get those notes out. I had never sung like that in my life—and I was impressed with myself because I thought it sounded just like the sample.

I really nailed it in about 20 minutes. The three DJs were jumping like crazy, punching the air and shouting "yeah—yeah—yeah!" They were so happy with it, they could hardly contain themselves. Then they asked for some additional ad-libs that they explained would "fly in" on certain parts of the track.

When it all wrapped up that day, how did you feel about the project?

Well, I was really happy because they were paying me well, and even offering me points if and when the track was released. But in my heart, I wasn't thinking that the track could do very well at all. I thought I would just take the money and run. Why? I just really thought the track was far too repetitive. Remember, I was classically trained, so I was in a different mindset about how a song should be. I was thinking on a completely different level.

I really didn't understand house music and how people liked the fact that a song went over and over the same hook. House music was pretty new to me at that time. I had no idea about raves, parties, or the whole acid house scene. This was all new territory for me. I was in a different mindset about what and how I sang, and house music was way too predictable for my taste.

Though you may have had misgivings about it, "I'm Gonna Get You" was a monster on both sides of the Atlantic and across Europe. In addition to being a chart smash in the UK, it reached number one on Billboard's dance chart, further fueled by Todd Terry's extremely popular remixes, and it was a Top 50 pop hit in the U.S. The track is regarded as a signature house classic of the era, with an uncanny ability to pack dance floors. Tell me about the explosion of attention that enveloped you with the release of this song.

Three months after I recorded the track, it was in all the High Street shops, up and down the streets of the UK, like Woolworths, Tower Records and Virgin Records—just everywhere! It was such an honor, and everyone who knew me felt exceptionally proud. "Bizarre Inc featuring Angie Brown" was emblazoned, loud and proud, in big bold print on the front of every record.

It began when I received a phone call from the record company, who told me that the record had gotten over 44,000 pre-sales. Good pre-sales meant pretty much you were shaping up to have a massive hit, or at least some kind of chart entry, and that it was doing exceptionally well in the clubs. It was clear that people were really liking the song and asking for it. Once the track was finally released, it entered the British charts straight in at number 17! Wow, what an achievement!

The people around me, people who personally knew me—everybody was so happy for me. By everybody, I mean *everybody*—from the lady who did my dry cleaning to the man who fixed my shoes. They knew how hard I had worked and how great a moment this was in my career. It felt as if I no longer had to explain myself. It felt like everything in the universe just came together and fell right into place.

Sometimes you get a window in life, and you just have to get through it. You have to get through the opening before you're too old or the moment passes you by. Well, this was my moment to soak up all the glory! "I'm Gonna Get You" was doing really well in the UK, but I remember filling up with even more pride one night while watching a clip of Casey Kasem (in the U.S.) doing his enthusiastic countdown of the American dance charts. "Oh my God," I thought. There we were on the chart with Prince and Whitney Houston and Boys II Men. I thought I'd died and gone to heaven. I was overjoyed!

The record company in the UK got in touch with me and gave me the fantastic news that we were going to be on *Top of the Pops*. This was an amazing feeling. Everything I'd worked for—it all finally seemed worth it. The show was the equivalent of being on *American Bandstand* over there in America, and if you were on the show you'd made it!

I'm so happy that my father was alive when the song became this massive hit. He'd watch me on TV, but because he was from another generation, he just couldn't get over the fact that I could be on the tube as well as beside him watching it. He was in total disbelief, and I had to keep explaining to him (through my laughter) that they had recorded it the day before. It really reminded me of when, as a child, I used to look behind the television to see if there were people in it. Well, my dad was kind of acting the same way. He was absolutely dumbstruck and said, "How-how-how de 'ell dem do dat?" in a thick Jamaican accent. My dad had a stutter, and it took him a little while to get that sentence out. He was so proud of me.

"I'm Gonna Get You" proceeded to climb the charts to the number two spot in the UK. Tasmin Archer's "Sleeping Satellite" kept us out of the top spot. We just sat there at number two while the telephone rang off the hook. My whole family—cousins, aunts, everyone—were buzzing about "Hangie on de telly"—a typical sentence I would hear during my mother's telephone conversations.

Anyway, the record stayed in the Top 10 here for eight weeks, and it was really an exciting time. I'd be walking down the street, and you'd hear it on people's car radios, coming from a store and in the nightclubs. Sometimes I'd be in a club with some friends after I'd been on the road for a while. The DJ would spot me, and I would get an immediate shout-out. Straightaway, you would hear the intro to the song, the "da dup dup be do do dah dup," coming from the speakers. That DJ would be straight on it! It was so exhilarating!

I hear the raves in those days were pretty crazy. What was it like performing at them?

Oh wow. We did these *crazy* raves that were so completely foreign to me. I thought we'd always be in lovely, sophisticated clubs and venues, but we did so many of these events that were like quickly erected circuses, full of people, extremely loud and with plenty of drugs mixed up in all of it. The music at these events sounded so repetitive—I was often like, "Give me my money, and let me get out of here!" I liked that people liked my voice and were dancing so crazily to this sort of contemporary, sped-up disco, but I just found that the sound was designed to simply race up your heartbeat, right to the edge.

I never did any of the drugs that were everywhere—I am the daughter of a nurse, and my mum said, "If you get into the music business, you have to be careful. People die from doing drugs." I'd been in bands and saw many people doing the stuff. I always figured I'd be the unlucky one who would try it and my system would reject it, and I'd be the one to keel over. Then my mum would be really, *really* pissed off at me.

Most of the raves were hastily built on wasteland, farms, and just huge abandoned areas. Back then, it was a mobile phone the size of a brick that would keep everybody in contact with each other. The police would come and sometimes be chasing us. They would try to stop these illegal raves, but the show had to go on, as they say. Promoters, DJs, dancers, fire-eaters—everyone had their part to play. Plus, there was a lot of money to be made out of everyone's insatiable appetite to be a part of the madness that came with the "house" movement.

It's only in hindsight that I realize just how exciting that time really was. But back then, it went against everything I had been taught. I really thought when I made it, I would be singing in a sophisticated venue or even the theatre with live musicians. Instead, it was the complete opposite. Four-to-the-floor at 128 beats-per-minute would bass its way through your chest, along with glow sticks, bright clothes and wild dance moves. MCs would control the microphones as DJs became the new rock gods. The era was electric, and people totally embraced it. That's why I think people who were around that whole scene in the '90s will never forget it. Just like people who were young in the '60s. You were young, you were making a statement, you were changing the way people saw the world, you were wearing the most outrageous clothes, and music was doing its thing. Parts of it were shady, to be sure, and sometimes it felt really grubby. It felt like everyone was in a Mad Max movie. It was impromptu, and we were just all thrown together, making an unforgettable impact!

All of us, the performers and producers making this '90s music, didn't analyze it. We were just in the moment. I never had a clue that house music would ever stay in the hearts of people that lived through that era. House music has carried on, over and over, into younger generations. That's why I think '90s house music still gets played on the radio; it still sounds really good today! I learned so much back then, and I'm really grateful for the whole experience now. When I was younger, I must admit I didn't like it much, but now I know that I experienced a really great time.

The Energique **album followed, along with the second single, "Took My Love." The track reached the top of the U.S. dance chart, but it seemed like Bizarre Inc had lost some steam by the time the follow-up came out. What happened?**

That's the downside of the story. Mind you, I did like the Bizarre Inc boys because we spent a lot of time together, including touring all over the States. I even went to Fresno, California with them, of all places. We played the Limelight and many big clubs in the U.S. After that success, everyone wanted to work with me because of the record—except for Bizarre Inc. Now, it wasn't entirely the boys' decision; it was probably pressure from the record company. I don't know; maybe their record company didn't want to develop me as an artist, and I know that sex and sexy marketing really sells. I'm not that kind of girl. I'm an understated girl-next-door type. In truth, it felt as if Bizarre Inc's bubble had burst by the second single. This track (another Jocelyn Brown sample that I sang) was supposed to ground us and show the serious side of us. Bizarre Inc wanted to be taken seriously, as a collective band and as serious musicians.

So, "Took My Love" had a more of a soulful vibe to it (and it also had verses). It wasn't as lighthearted and definitely wasn't as catchy as "I'm Gonna Get You." And just about everywhere I went or socialized, people said they didn't like it as much as the first one. But those decisions, like what tracks are released, weren't up to me. That was in the hands of the record company. I had aspirations, albeit all in my head, for all of us to be like M People. I wanted us to be a real band and for me to sing all the Bizarre Inc songs; I didn't want to feel like a featured singer any more.

On the actual video shoot for "Took My Love," there was a model miming to my vocals. I felt so rejected and so sad. I felt that I was disposable! I reckon record companies are always going to think about music as a commodity. And between major labels and the smaller dance labels, artist development eventually became less and less important. In my opinion, artists like George Michael and bands like Queen and U2, who had careers for well over 30 years, were a thing of the past.

I think the girl in the video was prettier than me. And it was definitely an artistic decision to use her. But that didn't help me feeling any better. I felt completely underrated by their decision, and I actually got very ill around that time. I was still singing live most nights as the demand for "I'm Gonna Get You" was still high, but with the forthcoming release of "Took My Love," I just felt really shitty! But, you know what? I concluded, "Well fine, but you can't keep a good woman down."

The boys went off and did their radio interviews for the new song; I soldiered on. I'm sure the record company wanted me out of the picture, but in every single interview, the radio station DJs would always ask about me. In my opinion, the boys were not very effervescent, shall we say, in their interviews. So, I became a personality in my own right, and I appeared on breakfast television and did a lot of radio interviews of my own. And that helped make up for the fact that I was quite depressed when "Took My Love" got released. The song got to number 12 in the British charts, but, as I mentioned before, the record buying public just didn't embrace it as much as the previous hit. I finally got over those bad feelings regarding the video shoot and the whole marketing process.

I was okay about all of it in the end because I still went out, week after week, performing both songs and "Playing with Knives" to cheering fans in nightclubs around the world. And I'm *still* doing it today.

I was wondering about the other major UK hit you had in 1994, "Rockin' for Myself," with the electronic artist Motiv8 and your other accomplishments during the decade.

"Rockin' for Myself" was a paid session—not very much money—and I didn't get on that well with [Steve Rodway, a songwriter, remixer and producer who used the moniker Motiv8]. He went on to cause a bit of a stir in the music business. He caused some problems for people; let's put it that way. I was happy to once again take an old sample and reproduce the sound, note-for-note, but I didn't have much to do with him after that. I went on to do some work with the Hed Kandi compilation albums, voiceovers, and sampling work (which still shows up on records today). I also sang backing vocals on Mark Morrison's massive 1996 hit, "Return of the Mack," and went on the road with Heaven 17, Neneh Cherry, Lisa Stansfield and other stars of the day. I never really went away; I just didn't get another massive hit like those two singles.

So much has changed in dance music since the '90s, including the overshadowing of vocalists by DJs. In some ways, today's trends are not unlike the conditions under which you recorded "I'm Gonna Get You."

Yes, that's true. I spent many a night discussing with my fellow vocalists why dance music has gone in this direction. I don't think we've come up with the answer. I'd rather see the glass half full than half empty, though. If you look at it half empty, then you get rotten and bitter. You have to just face it and work with it. The man playing the records has the record deal today. Music isn't like pork bellies, gold or silver commodities, where you can predict what will do well. The creative direction of music can't be predicted. If a DJ/producer/remixer comes up with a sound on a song that becomes a hit, they start pushing the DJ as the artist. Maybe it is easier for labels to deal with a DJ than hissy fit divas or vocalists who were hard work.

But the positive thing about it? I've had three record deals—with EastWest, Elektra and Mercury. I was in my 20s when I had these deals, and then the window was closed almost as quickly as it opened. They promised to put money behind you, and they treated you like gold for about a year. Then they put one single out, it doesn't do well enough, and bang—you're dropped. I am quite sure that U2 would have been dropped by their label had *The Joshua Tree* set not taken off (after their other albums hadn't).

Thinking about it now, if you're only dealing with one person, like a David Guetta, and you're the right age and you come with a distinctive sound—you're a commodity the label wants today. These DJs wear a t-shirt and jeans; they don't need all the stylists and fashions that the divas need. When I did the "I'm Gonna Get You" video, they flew someone in to do hair, then someone for make-up at $500 a day, a wardrobe person, etc. They don't have that expense with David Guetta; I'm quite sure. Financially, it's probably a lot easier to work with him.

I'm still very busy recording with many of these DJs today, such as "I'm on Fire" by Mark Masters & Funky Truckerz, "Crazy Love" with Osca Deep & Brent Anthony, "Never Give Up" by Mr. Vasovski & Kincses and, of course, making new versions of "I'm Gonna Get You." And it's interesting because these releases still say featuring Angie Brown, just like back in the day.

What goes through your mind when you think back about the '90s?

You always have a few regrets because you were young and silly and didn't think things through. But I have a lot of affection for the era because of the way people treat me *today*—as a result of it. I was there at that time, when it was all happening. That seems to mean a lot to people. And now they say to me, "Oh that's so cool! You were working with this one and that one." They are able to tell me my entire history, and all I can say is, "Did I do that?" People reminisce with me about these big names that I sometimes barely remember or didn't even know. The whole house thing from that era has really left its mark on me, though—it's in my bones now.

Are you happy with your life today?

Oh, yes. I'm a mum, and I'm 52. I had my boys when I was in my early 40s. My dad passed just two years after "I'm Gonna Get You," so I was glad he was able to see that happen. I also care for my mum now, who is 94. She's still healthy and in my boys' lives. She is able to teach them to be good, caring young men. I love my life. I work for myself and have no boss! "Angie, where's my sandwich! Have you cleaned that toilet yet?" None of that. I work for *me*. And I have a lovely partner, too, named Jay. [*She holds up a picture of her handsome partner, taken when they recently visited 10 Downing Street.*] We've been together for ten years.

What is dance music all about? In your view, what's at its core?

Well, especially '90s dance music, definitely it was all about joy, all about love. It wasn't gang-related, violence-related. Yes, some people died taking drugs. But there were thousands and thousands of people going to clubs and hearing and enjoying this music safely and happily, and they just had a great time. It was all associated with love. I think that's always been the core of dance music—love—and that is what has made it so unique and great.

"I have a lot of affection for the ['90s] because of the way people treat me today," says singer Angie Brown (courtesy Angie Brown).

Lightning Round with Angie

Diana Ross or Donna Summer?

Donna Summer! I love them both, but Donna just had this "take me as you find me" edge. She was cool, *really* cool.

Extended versions or radio edits?

Radio edits. I'm not a club person, am I? I guess you've gathered that by now. I don't need the extended version. I need that part where the singer is doing his or her thing.

Perfect hair or perfect teeth?

My hair is never neat. Perfect teeth!

Five good friends or one best friend?

Five good friends.

No more TV or no more movies?

No more TV. Since having children, I hardly ever watch it anyway.

Famous but poor or rich but unknown?

Oh, definitely, rich but unknown. I could buy fame if I wanted it.

Sannie Carlson, also known as Whigfield
"Saturday Night" (1994)

"I think, psychologically, if you give people something simple with a great hook, it sticks with them—even if they don't like the song."—Sannie Carlson

Few could have predicted that the remarkably simple, lively dance track "Saturday Night," sung by Danish-born Sannie Carlson, would become such an enormous world hit by 1994. But Ms. Carlson's debut recording, performed under the name Whigfield, had a few things going for it besides the singer's honeyed vocals, an irresistible beat and a relentless hook. Notably, it possessed the production expertise of Larry Pignagnoli. This maestro of Italo-disco had an ear for hits, and his résumé was filled with monster success stories by artists such as Spagna, Fun Fun and Baby's Gang during the '80s. But with a new era dawning in dance music, sounds and styles changing, and the talents of Ms. Carlson (a former model) still unproven, "Saturday Night" was far from a sure thing. However, when the song charged up the international dance and pop charts, reaching the number one position in Italy, Spain, Germany and Switzerland, not to mention a remarkable debut at the very top of the British pop chart, there was no doubt Whigfield was a star. Fast-forward, the now classic "Saturday Night" has become one of the most often remixed and re-released dance songs of the past 22 years.

Sannie had several follow-up hits in the wake of her gargantuan debut ("Another Day," "Think of You," "Big Time" and "Sexy Eyes" among them), and she remains an active singer-songwriter-producer today, collaborating with progressive modern-day dance favorites such as In-Grid and Benny Benassi. She continues to record her own adventurous new material (check out her recent singles "C'est Cool," "4 Ever" and her 2015 release "How Long" for a taste) while embracing the enduring and equally unavoidable legacy that is "Saturday Night."

Speaking from her home in London, this decidedly amiable and articulate virtuoso is extremely relaxed about her past. But she doesn't live in it. Carlson readily expresses great enthusiasm about her present and future, which she believes are every bit as important and engaging as her contributions to '90s dance pop.

Sannie, would you tell me a little about your early days?
I was born in Denmark, but my father had a lot of work in West Africa. So, in the 1970s,

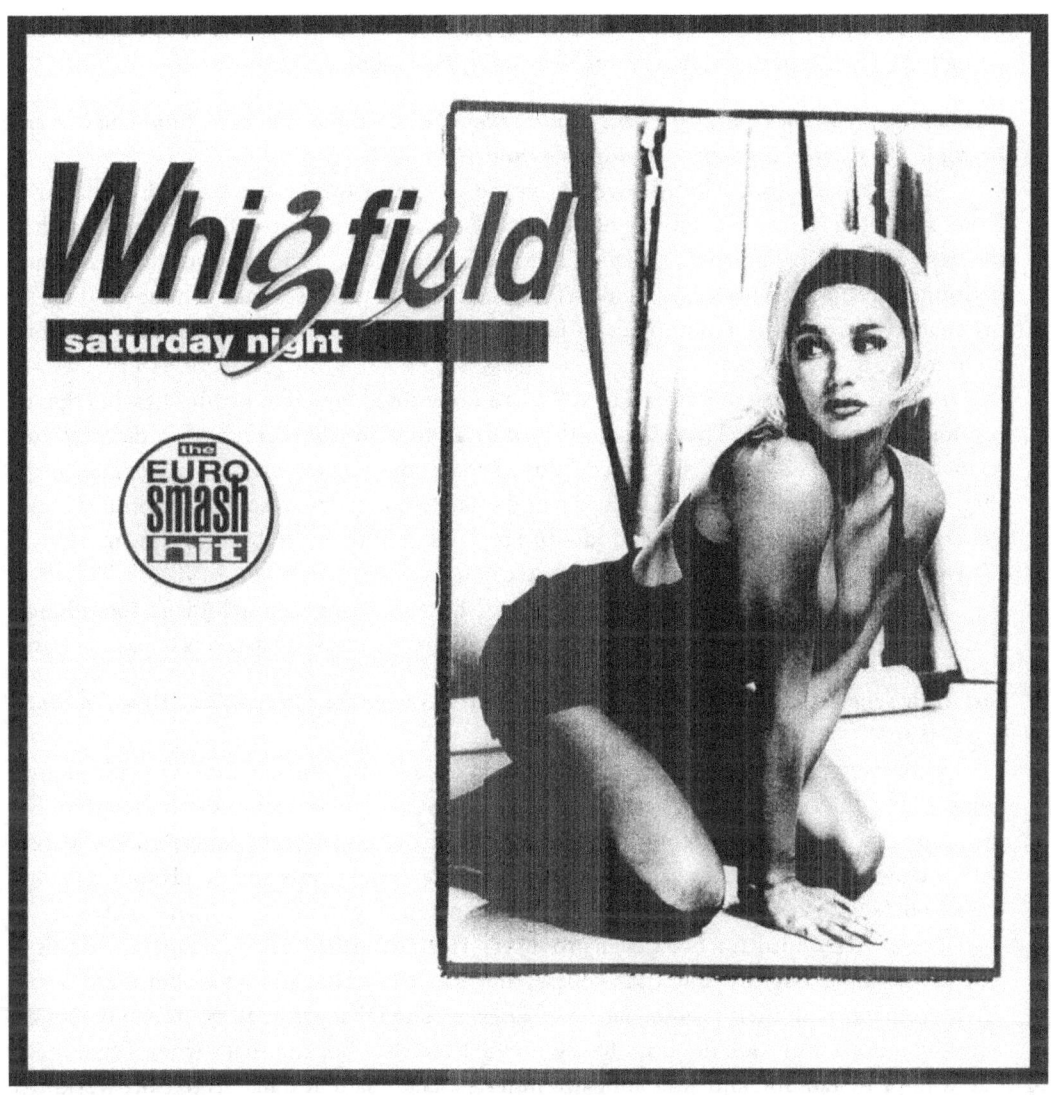

Sannie Carlson, performing as Whigfield, reached the top of the UK pop chart with "Saturday Night," seen here in its European seven-inch single sleeve (courtesy Off Limits Srl).

he thought it was a good idea to have the family with him. We attended schools there that conducted classes in the French language, and we traveled around to different countries, like Algeria and Ghana, during my early years. Then, at a certain point, my mother wanted my brother and me to return to Denmark to learn English. So we went to boarding school there for a few years, and that was basically my childhood. We still went back and forth to West Africa because my father stayed on there. My brother lives in the Congo now, so he's stayed connected with the region.

The musical influence in my life began when I was very young because my father was a bass player in a jazz band, and my mother was a trumpet player. My grandfather made violins and taught people to play the instrument. He built one for me when I was a child and tried everything to teach me to play it, but I just wanted to sing or play drums. When I became a little older, I began to think about what I wanted to do in life and, originally, I thought I was going to be an interpreter because I spoke so many languages.

Well, things turned out quite differently, didn't they? I understand your entertainment career began in the fashion industry working as a model?

Yes. Because I always loved anything in the arts and I was very good at drawing, my father suggested I become a clothing designer. So I actually ended up briefly becoming a fashion designer at first. There was a fashion awards show in Copenhagen. If you won the competition, you could win a year in an Italian fashion school, all expenses paid. I thought, "That's my chance." I didn't win it, but the dress I designed was in all the newspapers. So, I thought I'd better go to Italy anyway.

I ended up moving to Bologna in 1991, and I presented myself to Fendi, showing them my drawings and designs. They thought they were all very nice, but told me they didn't need anyone at the moment. Then they asked, "But what are your measurements?" [*Sannie laughs.*] Well, I was 21 years old, living in Bologna, and I had to pay the rent, so why not model? So, I ended up working in the day as a model and at night in different clubs, doing promotions. When you're 21, you have a lot of energy and can do it.

It was actually quite a boring time in my life because being a model wasn't something that really interested me. I never thought I was that pretty, so it was just a means to pay my way.

Just a few years later, your career in music received a tremendous jump-start. How did that come about?

It was very expensive if you wanted to live in Bologna by yourself. I didn't really enjoy living with other students or other girls. I was living alone in a small house on the grounds of a club called Les Bains Douches; quite a famous club in those days. I was very good friends with the owner and his wife, and they let me take care of the plants and do promotions for their club. I got to know the DJs who would come in. One night, I met a DJ who knew Larry Pignagnoli and Davide Riva, two Italian producers. He told me they were looking for a vocalist who could sing in English. In Italy, of course, they had a lot of Italian singers, but there were often problems with their pronunciation of English. The DJ suggested I go have a meeting with them both, so I took the train to see them at their studio, and that's when I first met Larry. I did an audition and after about 10 minutes, Larry said he'd like us to start working together.

Mr. Pignagnoli had a very accomplished background in Italian dance music, having helped create huge international hits for Ivana Spagna, Fun Fun, and many others during the '80s. Were you aware of his history at the time?

I kind of had an idea about his work, but I didn't really understand it until I was invited to his villa. It was an immense villa in the hills of Albinea, south of Reggio Emilia. I showed up in pigtails, shorts and ugly boots—I really didn't dress up that much. So I felt a bit intimidated when I showed up there. I remember Ivana Spagna was there; she came to pick up something at the house. I remember entering this hall with a huge white grand piano. I was like, "Yeah, I'd like some of this!"

I was never really a shy person, and I really clicked with Larry straight away. We had the same sense of humor. Whatever I said, he would laugh really loud. We were very much on the same page, and our working relationship was really great.

I do remember, though, when I first saw the contract [that he wanted me to sign], I peed in my pants. I wasn't sure what to make of it. I showed up to sign it with two lawyer friends the next day, and Larry just started laughing. "You didn't need to bring the lawyers," he said with his Italian accent. "I could have explained it to you." In those days, though, I didn't know that Larry was such a nice guy. We had just started working together, and people can start off nice and then become complete assholes the next year. I mean, in this business you have to be careful. You could sign a five-year contract and end up just sitting there in a corner, not doing anything.

So, where did the name Whigfield come from?

Oh, yeah. Larry and I were talking about my name. He thought I had a pretty name, but asked me if I could pick an artistic name, what would it be? I chose Whigfield. It was based on the name of a music teacher I had in Denmark. I thought it was different and quite a curious name. Larry agreed we'd stick to that. The funny thing is, later on in life, many people thought Whigfield was a group. I'd arrive at an airport, and the car driver would have a sign with Whigfield written on it, as if it were a band or something.

I'm curious, given your success, did you ever wish you'd just used your real name?

No, it's just a name. To be honest, I wasn't sure in the beginning if doing this music was even the kind of life I wanted. When you are young, you go a bit with the flow and just let life happen for you in a certain way.

After working with Larry and Davide, your debut single "Saturday Night" was a phenomenal success across Europe (beginning in 1993 and throughout '94). It first broke in Spain and then eventually became a monster in the UK and throughout the European continent. Tell me about the evolution of this very unusual song.

I basically took a train up every day to Larry's studio for the first six months to work on the song and came back home in the evening. That's how it all started.

In the beginning, when we were trying to look for a record deal for the song, nobody wanted to sign it. The labels didn't think it was a good track. When I first heard the final version, I didn't have any premonition it would be a hit—not at all. My brother listened to it, and he was like, "What is *that*?" He noted that it sounded nothing like the type of music that was being played in those days. A lot of songs came out and sounded like other hits, but not this one.

The first label to pick it up was a small one [Prodisc] in Valencia run by two completely out-of-their-mind guys. I remember I had to go to Spain to start promoting it at a club, and the guys just left me there! I was supposed to do a TV show the next morning, but they just abandoned me at this club. The beginning of my career wasn't very glamorous. [*Sannie shakes her head and laughs.*] It took quite a while for the song to get out there. But when the ball started rolling, it was pretty amazing.

What do you think made the song catch on so fiercely?

Ultimately, I think the reason the track became such a success was the fact that it was so different from anything else that was out there. It was a bit like a catchy lullaby for children, you know? I think, psychologically, if you give people something simple with a great hook, it sticks with them—even if they don't like the song.

Well, plenty of people liked the song, especially in the UK, where—

I know—the *Guinness Book of World Records*. Yes, I was the first foreign debut artist to go straight to number one on the British pop chart. I didn't know anything about it until my manager told me. She called me up when I was on tour and said, "Oh, I have some great news for you. You might want to give your grandmother a call." My grandmother was cutting out every article about me from any newspapers or magazines she could find. So my manager knew I'd want to share this news with her. It was funny.

What factors contributed to the song so quickly vaulting to the top spot in Britain?

The song was picked up by a Spanish DJ who was working at a major radio station. His show was called *World Dance Music*, and he'd play "Saturday Night" every Saturday. The track was then very quickly noticed by club DJs and those on holiday flying in from all over, especially the UK. The British vacationers flew back home and began requesting radio play this song that no one new about. A DJ at Capital Radio in London (called Dr. Fox) had never heard the song either, but after loads of intense requests by the public, he began playing it. By August of '95, "Saturday Night" went straight to number one and gained its place in the *Guinness Book of World Records*.

Today you seem rather casual about such a big accomplishment.

You know why? It was so long ago. I'm still in music, still singing, writing, producing today—it just seems like it was such a long time ago. There's just so much stuff that's happened in my life since then, and I don't stop to think about it often.

The song was released in the United States on Curb Records. Although it was a club and Billboard dance chart hit, it didn't fare as well on the pop side in this country.

I think it was a mistake being on Curb. I really wanted to come over to the United States. It was right after Ace of Base had been very successful there. They sold crazy amounts in the U.S. I don't think Curb was the right label for me. They were known more for their country music. They really did nothing to promote the record. I wasn't able to get great exposure there—I was asked to appear in San Francisco, but more on the gay scene. In the end, I was so busy going everywhere else that it was kind of okay. Hey, there's nothing to say I can't come over there now.

"Saturday Night" was followed by a series of very big international dance-pop hits for you, including "Think of You" in '94 and "Sexy Eyes" in '95. After such a tremendously popular global debut single, how difficult was it to find the right successors?

That's the problem you experience with the label you're signed to, especially when it's a series of independent labels, as I was. My music was released on many different record labels in different countries. They had different preferences for what they wanted to release. They used different album and single covers, different pictures. I ended up promoting different singles in different countries at the same time. Not everyone was on the same page.

I flew into Australia to do a one-month tour, and every time I sang "Saturday Night," the audience would look at me like I was crazy because nobody knew the song there. I don't think the Australians really understood the song. They only knew my later hits—"Sexy Eyes" and "Gimme Gimme." That was pretty weird. For my hits, though, I think "Saturday Night," "Another Day" and "Sexy Eyes" were probably the biggest, most popular among most countries.

One other thing I recall—the labels pressured you to do the same music, or the same type of music. They wanted us to do the same thing over and over—what I would call sort of cheesy bubblegum dance-pop music.

As a young woman experiencing this fame, what did you have to give up?

Oh, God—I gave up a lot. It was very hard to keep friendships going, and I never got to see my family. Sometimes I'd get to fly in and see them for a day—like my brother. He was living with me in Barcelona at the time. I'd see him one day and fly out again the next. Another problem was to try and have a relationship. I would have my then-boyfriend flown out to South Africa or wherever I was in the world. Otherwise, I wouldn't be able to see him. Relationships—they're very, very difficult if you're always on the road. My schedule was planned something like six months ahead. To have your life planned six months in advance was very hard.

My manager would tell me to let her know when I wanted a holiday. But I remember Larry Pignagnoli telling me—we had a discussion one day—and he said, "We don't know how long this is going to last. So it's up to you how much you want to push on." Well, you just end up continuing to take it in because you really don't know when it's going to end—the whole fairy tale. You can continue to work, but at a certain point you start seeing your songs going down the charts, and you start getting fewer gigs. So—you just keep on pushing.

You're from the last era where physical product sales were sizable, and you witnessed the dramatic change to music consumption via digital downloads at the beginning of the 21st century. What are your observations about that tremendous change in how we listen to music?

If you were lucky, you had hardcore fans that always bought your stuff. But I remember that in those days, buying physical product was very expensive. I think a CD album could be something like 25 euros—that was a lot of money for kids. I caught the last bit of those sales, but, for the audience, the change proved to be so much better. It became so much easier and less expensive to get the music. For artists, the new money had to come from live performances. It turned over to the other side.

It's hard for artists today. It is quite expensive for us to make new music. I'm producing a new project for myself right now. The studio, the video—and to pay for all of this, you need to sell a lot or get synchronization rights to make ends meet. It's really tough.

The truth is, everyone nowadays can make their own music—even young kids on their computers. You don't need the artists and record labels as much as in the past. The business also has a short memory. As an artist, if you are gone for weeks or months, nobody even remembers you. There's so much new music coming out. I see it here in the UK—it's hilarious how many new songs are released each week. You wouldn't physically have the time to possibly listen to all of it.

Another trend since the '90s was the change in focus from the artist to the producer or DJ. Fifty-thousand people screaming like he's Madonna. I even thought of maybe getting into the DJ side of things. Some of them collect a huge amount of money just for one gig. But then—I'll be honest—I don't really feel the urge to be staying out till five or six in the morning. That's not fun to me anymore.

Ultimately, though, in terms of technology and the way people listen to music, you have to go with what the public demands. You have no choice. You have to work your way around it and use your imagination to survive. That's what Madonna has always done—she just keeps renewing herself.

You were and are a very attractive woman in an industry that's been typically dominated by males on the business side. I wonder if you've encountered evidence of sexism as you've built your career.
It's funny, because I didn't see myself that way—you know—beautiful or anything like that. I felt I was more credible in the business because I didn't think I was that pretty. More of the girl next door—but thanks for the compliment anyway! I can't say I really encountered sexism in my career. The only thing I can remember thinking about was in terms of changing my image in a way, and I talked to Larry about it back then. Like maybe creating a girl group. The All Saints were out then, and it was kind of lonely always performing by myself. So I thought forming a group might be cool.

I was always the girl working with all these guys in the band and such. It's funny; I remember being at a restaurant in Sydney with my tour manager, and he didn't like the way I was handling my food. He told me, "Sannie, you're eating like a man. You spend so much time with men. You should get some girlfriends." [*She laughs.*]

Clubs in the '90s were infamous for their drug cultures, just as they were in the '70s and '80s. Did that atmosphere affect you in any way?
There was a lot of drug use in the clubs. I recall that ecstasy was everywhere—I remember that in Barcelona. Techno music was taking off in Germany, Spain and Britain, and that scene spawned a lot of drug use. I don't know which drugs went with what type of music.

As for me, I think all artists have had their bit of fun at some point, but if you were going to wake up and stay on schedule and make your money, it was impossible to do that and [party] all the time. The flights we took were often very long, and the schedules were really hard. The air on the planes would dry you out, and you'd have to drink so much water. In those days, people could even smoke on flights—do you remember that? Row one through row five. [*Sannie chuckles.*] You could be in Japan one day and have to fly out for an 11-hour flight for a sound check somewhere else, then an afternoon of interviews. You had to get sleep wherever you could, and if you were wired up, that was impossible.

The generation that first discovered your music is now into their middle-age years. How do you view mainstream culture's emphasis on youth, and how do you find your comfort zone with aging at this point in your life?
I take very good care of myself. I'm in the gym a lot, and I eat very well. I sleep quite a lot. I try to keep myself—well, I don't want to be the embarrassment you see sometimes. I dress stylishly and maybe a bit funky, but simply and without going over the top, like I'm trying really hard to stay young looking, you know? Or trying to have the look young people often have today. I think that's when entertainers become a bit silly.

I do look at young people today, and I do believe in freedom of expression. However, I don't think it's necessary to do what a lot of young singers do—the booty culture that's developed. I see a lot of American videos, and find it a bit sad the way women are presented in videos and the way the women let *themselves* be presented. Well, it's a new culture. It's like tattoos. Everyone has to have them. I don't even think they know why they're getting them, what it means. What is that thing on your chest going to look like when you are 70? I was walking through Soho yesterday, and there are 20-year-old girls with their arms, chests and legs completely covered in tattoos.

I know this—when you're young you tend to do stupid things. I did it. It was fashionable for a time to have your nose pierced, and I had this huge ring stuck in my nose. Now I have a hole in my nostril because of that decision. I know what it's like—you just do it. You're a kid.

When have you felt the most satisfied in your life?

Right now! The present! I think it's the advantage of getting older but still being young enough to be creative. You just know so much more. I'm lucky to still be making music. I love the project I'm working on now. I'm really proud of my ability to be able to do that at 45 years old. I think right now is my explosion. I don't see why I can't do it when I'm 50 or 60, too. Look at Debbie Harry. She's 70, and she's still touring the world. It's her party, and she can do what she wants.

"Saturday Night" keeps getting remixed, and it just seems to be immortal. How do you feel about your connection to this track today?

Right? There must be 500 remixes of this song out there. I did a performance last week in the Czech Republic with 20,000 people there. The song came on, and people went crazy, just jumping all around. That's the connection I get. The song gets the same reaction every single time. You know what I feel when it happens? It's just a very positive, calm sensation in me. It actually makes me sleep very well. In the old days, I would go back to the hotel after a show, and I wouldn't be able to sleep because of the adrenaline. Now, when I see people enjoying my music so much, it's a soothing feeling. Maybe the lullaby qualities of the song are starting to work on me.

Is there a highlight from your career so far that really stands out for you?

Oh, there are definitely a couple of them. I performed at the Bollywood Awards in Mumbai, and I was asked to do a duet with a Hindi singer. He had like 50 dancers—a massive production. I knew there must have been a billion people watching the show. That was pretty amazing for me. Another time, I was asked by the producers to be a host on *Top of the Pops*, which I'd been on a few times as a performer in the past. It was the week when Oasis was number one on the charts. It was so much fun and pretty amazing for me. I had a big party that night. I really got hooked on television—I wanted to be on it a lot! It's a bit like theater, with a lot of adrenaline and energy going on.

From the '70s through your era in the '90s, and even considering the present day, what do you feel has been the contribution, the value of dance music to pop culture and society?

Brilliant melodies. I think the value of real dance music can be seen in the music that comes out today. The sounds I hear on many of today's dance records here in Europe, many coming from America, are the same that we were doing in the '90s. The music some people said was "shit" back then just keeps finding a new audience. So that kind of shows the power it has. Dance music, even among musicians, gets a bad rap. Musicians often have a thing against electronic music. But it takes great talent to write a really good dance song—just as it does to make a good rock song or any other type of music.

Lightning Round with Sannie

Music or lyrics?
　Impossible—it's like choosing your favorite child!

Diana Ross or Beyoncé?
　Diana Ross.

Reality TV or fictional drama?
　Drama.

Extended versions or radio edits?
　Radio edits.

'70s or '80s?
　'80s.

Applause or record sales?
　Record sales. [*She laughs*]. It's an honest answer. People that say otherwise are bullshitting you!

Instagram or Twitter?
　Instagram. I'm not a big fan of social media though.

Perfect hair or perfect teeth?
　Perfect teeth.

Saver or spender?
　Spender, but I'm still very cheap.

Handbags or shoes?
　I buy so many shoes I never wear. Let's say handbags.

Tight fitting or loose?
　Tight, for as long as I can!

Saturday night or Sunday morning?
　Definitely Sunday morning.

Though Sannie Carlson enjoys the distinction of being the first foreign debut artist to go straight to number one on the British pop chart with "Saturday Night," she isn't inclined to dwell on the achievement. "There's just so much stuff that's happened in my life since then, and I don't stop to think about it often," says the singer (courtesy Sannie Carlson).

Marty Cintron, formerly of No Mercy
"Where Do You Go" (1996)

"The power of TV and videos made us the new guys in the '90s! That was important. We were kind of a macho group."—Marty Cintron

Marty Cintron says it's rare for his former group, the handsome three-man ensemble known as No Mercy, to receive accolades for helping popularize the Latin dance-pop sound that exploded in the '90s. But with widely embraced, Spanish guitar-fused smashes such as "Missing" (a dance-charged remake of Everything but the Girl's 1994 hit), "When I Die" and other hits under their belts, their influence can't be denied. Their international hit singles have reportedly sold over 10 million copies worldwide.

The group was developed by Cintron and renowned German producer Frank Farian, who had enjoyed enormous worldwide success with artists such as Boney M. and the Far Corporation in previous decades. Just a few years after the producer's infamous debacle with the mega-group Milli Vanilli, whose notorious lip-synching scandal rocked the music industry, Farian connected with Marty in Miami. From there, Cintron became the central figure of the group. The ensemble also incorporated the talents of Marty's friends, Ariel & Gabriel Hernández.

Enjoying massive success throughout Europe and South America, No Mercy became a pop sensation in the States as well, scoring a Top Five pop hit with "Where Do You Go" and a number one Billboard dance hit with a remake of Exile's "Kiss You All Over." They even made the leap to Hollywood when their music was featured in the Will Ferrell film A Night at the Roxbury (1998) and the ABC-TV series Lois and Clark.

Marty arrives at his spacious condo in the heart of Miami Beach, casually dressed for a typically hot, sunny Florida day. Still handsome and well built, he initially appears somewhat hurried and speaks of the day's chaos stemming from his business endeavors and a hectic schedule. But he quickly eases into the discussion, conjuring up memories readily and vividly with an invitingly youthful and earnest level of enthusiasm and positivity.

Marty, your story begins in New York, correct? Tell me about your youth.

Yes, I started life in the Bronx, New York, and then moved to a suburb called North Rockland at around the age of 13 or 14. My father wanted to get out of the Bronx and apartment life and live in a house. It was much cheaper to live in the North Rockland area, and a better quality of life. It's about an hour away from the city on the New York State thruway.

Marty Cintron (left) with group mates Ariel and Gabriel Hernández, as seen in an Arista Records publicity shot (author's collection).

But my father worked for Pan American airlines at JFK airport, which is further away from the city, so he had something like a two-hour trip back and forth.

My family life was okay. My dad had issues with alcohol—who wouldn't, with those kinds of pressures and commutes. It was a hard life for him, and I give him all the credit in the world for raising the family. I have an older sister, and we're doing okay, so he did his job. I lived in a cul-de-sac neighborhood, and I started playing guitar and drums there. We had a lot of garage bands going back then, but nothing serious. But that's how I started singing and getting into the whole music thing. I was taking music classes in high school, and I was into heavy metal like Black Sabbath, Journey and Rush—all those heavy groups back then.

You had an interesting career going before No Mercy. Indirectly, it paved the way for your professional music career.

Absolutely. Amazingly enough, long before No Mercy, I was a host for Chippendales in Vegas—part of the original crew working for an Indian-American named "Steve" Banerjee. Then in 1994, I started working in Japan. I was a musician and a host for a show there—it was kind of like another male exotic dance show. But it was choreographed by one of Madonna's dancers, a man named Alex Magno. It was a very tasteful show with these six foot five blonde guys, super ripped, and we did three shows a night in front of 100 Japanese ladies at each performance. During one of the shows, I tried to do a flip. It normally works, but this time it didn't, and I landed on my head and went into a coma. My dad had to fly out there and get me back to New York (after I got out of the hospital in Japan).

I still had to recover, but I didn't want to stay in New York, so I flew down to Miami and stayed on Ocean Drive at a friend's hotel. After I started getting my guitar skills back (I was a mess for a while), I started playing at a club on Ocean Drive called the Compass Café. This international music producer named Frank Farian happened to be staying next door at a hotel called the Casa Grande. He saw me perform my music one night and said he really liked the way I sang and played guitar. He thought maybe we could do a project together. I was like, "Okay, whatever; let's talk." I didn't know who the guy was at the time. He never said he was the producer of Milli Vanilli and Boney M.—nothing like that.

So we met again at another time and went to a Miami club called Glam Slam East, which was a club originally opened by Prince. I'll never forget this—we were about to go in, and he said he didn't have any money and asked me to pay for him. The guy was a multimillionaire! "I left my wallet in the hotel; I'm so sorry," he said in a heavy German accent. I kind of shook my head in disbelief and paid for him. Boom, next thing you know, he tells me he wants me to fly to his studio in Germany.

A few weeks go by, and he sends me the plane ticket. I go there and—oh my God—you see tons of gold records on the walls and the million-dollar console. That was the moment that I got it—I knew this was the real deal.

Frank thought the best way to go was with a group, so I brought in Ariel and Gabriel Hernández, twins who I had worked with at Glam Slam. They had toured with Prince and been in some of his videos. Although these guys weren't singers, they were great dancers, and I thought with my musicianship and voice and them dancing, it would be something really new and exciting. On the first recordings, I did all the vocals and harmonies, and Frank sang some of the low voices you hear in some songs. When the twins and I walked into the label and all the girls went crazy over us, that's when I knew we had the group nailed.

Frank (and a woman who was part of Frank's team nicknamed Millie—I think that's where Milli Vanilli came from) were sitting around a table with us in the offices he had, located a little bit north of Frankfurt, Germany. One of the first names for the group that got thrown out for discussion was No Mercy, and it ended up sticking.

The first song we recorded was "Missing," which Frank had gotten permission to record after hearing an unreleased Todd Terry remix version of the track by Everything but the Girl in Ibiza. That song got us into the business. We did two videos, one in Austria and another version in Miami. We made it to the Top Five in Switzerland, and it was a big hit throughout Europe. The clubs in the U.S. loved the song, too. It all happened very, very fast. The BMG/Hansa record company in Germany was behind us, and they were paying hundreds of thousands of dollars on radio and TV commercials. It just exploded from there. Rudi Gassner, one of the top executives at BMG (who passed away in 2000), loved the band, and he was the guy who really got us on the fast track. Clive Davis at Arista in America came along and flew us on the Concorde from England because he wanted to get us moving in the U.S. The *Concorde!*

Frank Farian has a long history of making hit records, and he's received his share of both praise and criticism. What was it like for you working with him?

Frank really knew what he was doing. Frank's a fucking genius. I know some say it was hard to work with him. Yeah, he's a controlling kind of guy, but I wonder if the artists who didn't get along with him just weren't open to working with him on his terms. He had so many incredible ideas. He was never disrespectful with me in the studio. Yeah, we'd get into a fight or argument sometimes in the studio, but if he would scream, I would scream louder. I'm from the Bronx, so I don't take any shit. A lot of people told me to be careful with him and warned me that he gave bad contracts. Actually, our contract wasn't amazing, but I wouldn't say it was terrible, and we had to understand that people who are producing and financing this music were taking the biggest risk. They were investing millions and the chances of you making it big were actually very small. You know what I mean? We made good money as a group, and I still make royalties from the music today—they aren't amazing returns or anything, but they have been significant enough that I was able to continue making music right up till today, 20 years later.

We're still friends, Frank and I, and, as a matter of fact, I just had dinner with him two days ago. So, after all this time, there's still this level of respect. In the studio, he has amazing ideas, and when he's excited about something and puts his power behind it, then it pretty much is guaranteed to be successful. Even today, he took this idea of a song called "Barbra Streisand" (with a loop from a Boney M. track), and it became a smash.

You mentioned the warning you received about Frank's artist contracts. Did you have any concerns working with Farian on No Mercy, considering his history of vocal controversies that swirled around groups like Milli Vanilli and Boney M.?

No. I should clarify that Ariel and Gabriel *did* sing on some of the records. Later on, we added their voices in. In the beginning, I handled all the vocals, but then we were able to bring them in for harmonizing. I worked with them on their singing. We wanted to make sure that all of us were singing, and that was especially important to Clive Davis after the whole Milli Vanilli scandal. He wanted to know we were an actual act and not some bullshit. The twins didn't sing so well at first, but then over time they started to sound really cool. We did many live, unplugged shows, and it worked out great. Check out the MTV unplugged sessions, and you can see we were the real deal.

The '90s saw an explosion of interest in Latin music in the U.S. and Europe. I remember No Mercy playing a key role in bringing the sound to the American pop and dance charts at that time.

Yeah. I don't think we get too much credit for it though. It goes to people like Enrique Iglesias, whose next album (after we came out) was a complete rip-off of our sound. Everyone started to copy our idea—bringing that whole Spanish guitar sound into the European dance flavor. We created that sound, with the Spanish guitar as the dominant instrument on songs like "Kiss You All Over," "Please Don't Go" and "Where Do You Go." It was something really different at the time. It was a unique sound. It wasn't programmed, and that's why those songs are still played today. There was real spirit in that instrumentation—the lyrics were great, too, of course.

You're a good-looking man today, and No Mercy was certainly considered an unstoppably sexy trio in the '90s. How did your sex appeal as a male group impact your success in those days?

The power of TV and videos made us *the* new guys in the '90s! That was important. We were kind of a macho group. Not that we had anything against our gay fans and friends, but we weren't a gay group, as some might have thought. I know a lot of people wondered back then if we were gay. We weren't—aren't. That's it. We had an amazing connection with the girls, and we treated them with respect. The twins and I are still friends, and we talk a lot about the past and the wild reaction of the girls. I remembered we'd be at our hotel or the airport and huge groups of female fans would be there—it was a pretty incredible experience.

By the end of the decade, it seemed as if No Mercy began to cool down. What actually happened?

Things started to really change with the explosion of the Internet, and people started to download music. I think the arrival of Napster was a big turning point. When that really kicked in, the record company seemed to stop supporting us. It was kind of like we were becoming a flavor of the month. We had come out, and then there seemed to be so many other groups to deal with. NSYNC, the Backstreet Boys,—they all blew up huge. After our initial big success, I kind of felt that Frank may have lost interest in us. He made tons of money with No Mercy; he had kind of redeemed himself after Milli Vanilli.

I'm not sure, but maybe he didn't want to keep killing himself in the studio, and the ideas started thinning out. He wanted us to do his songs, and not everything he was coming up with was a hit. You really needed a steady stream of amazing songs. NSYNC and Backstreet Boys had really great songwriting teams, and they consistently came out with great songs. I mean, we had great songs too, but other singles were like bullshit. They just weren't as good as the songs other groups were putting out. Frank would say, "No, no this is great," and since he was paying for it, we'd have to do those songs. For example, he wanted us to do a version of Boston's "More Than a Feeling." I was totally against that. Jesus, you can't beat the original on that song; some songs you just leave alone. He wanted to do a lot of covers, and that was a mistake I think. "Kiss You All Over" was another cover. "Missing" was a cover. I wanted to do more original material.

I guess we had about six or seven really good songs with videos, but the rest of our material didn't chart very well. It was all about the charts and timing and looking at *Billboard* every week. If it only hits number 70 the first week, then number 74, it was like, jeez, it's time to give up. Well, that's what the record company was saying anyway. There was a lot of pressure with those charts. We were always wondering what our position was. "Where Do You Go" was huge, but then they came out with another [similarly titled] song called "Please Don't Go," "Kiss You All Over" came out next, which was a great song, but it didn't do as well as "Where Do You Go." Once you don't top the previous song, it just starts getting weird, and the support starts to wane.

I think we were caught up in some bad strategies at the record label. They were pushing us in too many countries—Europe, South America—and not enough in the States. Clive was all set to get behind us, but BMG Germany wanted us more for their territories. Then they began to move on to other artists that they tested and thought would do better. And that's where they shift their focus and power. It's a lot of stress, a lot of politics.

I think our lack of proper management hurt us. Frank wanted to be the manager and the producer. We didn't know any better, so we went along with all of it. Frank was challenging to deal with in business. If he has an idea in his head, it's gotta be that way. Frank's interests came first, and that's just the way it was.

How does the band finally reach the end of the line?

We were still working, and our agency in Munich, Germany, was still getting us plenty of shows in the last years, months. That continued for a while. But we never did a proper tour. Other groups were doing traditional tours because they had proper management. I think that was another problem for us. We did promotion forever, instead of touring. That sucked—we'd be in three countries in one day—a radio show here, this and that—which were all designed to make them money from record sales. But it didn't help us to establish ourselves stronger as a group. And we lost out on money by not touring because of all this free promotion. As everyone started complaining about losing money, the group just kind of disappeared into the sunset, just like a lot of other groups. But over time, many of the songs proved they still have legs.

From your best days in No Mercy, was there an event that really stands out for you?

Oh yeah! There were actually a few moments and accomplishments I am really proud of. We were voted artist of the year in Germany. We had song of the year in Austria (for "When I Die"). We received an award at the same time the Bee Gees were getting a lifetime achievement award in Austria, so we were on stage with them at the same time. That was pretty amazing to me at the time. Just being on the *Live with Regis and Kathie Lee* TV show was cool. You pretty much knew you made it if you were on *Regis*. CNN did a piece on us. It was just magic. We all looked and sounded great in those days.

We had some really great times along the way. We were really tight with the guys from NSYNC. Justin [Timberlake] of the Backstreet Boys used to come up to me and ask for *me* autographs for his family and friends. Me! We were all part of the BMG family back then. We must have traveled on the bus with the Backstreet Boys about 30 times doing the same promotional events. Fergie [Stacy Ann Ferguson, later of the Black Eyed Peas] was in a band at the time called Wild Orchid, a three-girl group, and we'd do events with them as well. (The arrival of Christina Aguilera kind of put an end to BMG's interest in Wild Orchid.) We'd all run into each other at the same hotels too.

I saw Chris [Kirkpatrick] from NSYNC a few months ago. It had been years, and he still was super cool, very down to earth. He happened to be in Miami, and he got me tickets to the Justin concert. I never got to see Justin; he's too big now I guess, and it would be hard for him to just hang out, whatever. But I am very happy for him, and it's cool. Everybody is up his ass now.

Mark Wahlberg of Marky Mark and the Funky Bunch—another guy we used to do all these radio tours with. Now look at the guy! Some of these guys just had amazing management, and they chose to live in Los Angeles, which was the place to be if you really wanted things to take off. You know, I sometimes think about what would have happened if I had moved to L.A., like some of the artists did. I never really liked L.A., though. I wonder if I had gone there and gotten some great management, would more things have happened? Who knows?

You've been successful in real estate since then, but music still remains a big part of your life today. How has life treated you overall?

You know what? I like my little simple life now. I'm really very happy. I manage condos in South Beach, and it's pretty cool. I bought them at a low price, and they're worth a lot more now. That's the name of the game. I get to pick and choose who lives here and collect rent checks. [*He laughs.*] I have my studio here as well. Life is good—I go to the gym every morning, run the beach, do a lot of bike riding. I meet a lot of hot women—*a lot*! I'm single—every one of my friends got married and went through horrific divorces, lost all their material possessions, all that bullshit. Me—I've pretty much kept everything. I'm really having the fucking time of my life right now. I'm keeping life simple.

[*Marty gives a visual tour of his stylish, well-decorated but unpretentious condo and studio before returning to our interview.*]

What's your impression of the 21st century music business?

Music still means a lot to me. I still want to make it. I've been releasing new tracks, such as "Shed My Skin," and I recently released a new album called *Day by Day*. It's really important now to have somebody working your campaign all the time, blasting on Twitter and Facebook and directing people to iTunes and nomercymusic.com. I don't have time to be doing all that to be truthful. It's a full-time job. But the music industry is awful today. You gotta put up all your own money if you want anything to happen, and good luck trying to get it back. You can still have success, but you really have to get lucky with an amazing song and be an amazing artist. As tough as the competition was back in the '90s, today you are competing with *everybody*. If it gets that far, you gotta make sure your publishing is all in order and that you get a piece of touring revenue. For me, songwriting and producing is where it's at. With my studio, I get paid whether their record is a hit or not.

"I'm really having the fucking time of my life right now. I'm keeping life simple," says former No Mercy lead vocalist Marty Cintron (courtesy Marty Cintron).

How do artists make money? In my opinion, the only way is with live shows. But artists from the '70s, '80s and '90s—it's not like we all get shows every day. I'm in the process of putting together a "Best of No Mercy" show now and getting a tour going. People still love that '90s music. I just did a '90s event in Holland, and there were 10,000 people there. Unfortunately, in the United States it still tends to be more that "flavor of the month" situation I talked about. Generally, the masses here tend to gravitate from one person to the next. There are only a handful of artists that have kept a large fan base over a few years—your Taylor Swifts, Pitbulls, Beyoncés. It's like, Jesus Christ, what happened to everyone else? But I like the trend I see that the '90s are coming back, and that's why I liked the idea of this book and wanted to be a part of it.

What do you think is the public's biggest misconception about the '90s music industry?

Sometimes people come up to me and ask me what happened to No Mercy. They do it in a way like, you know, like our fate was entirely up to us. People tend to think it was kind of a breeze to be pop stars and keep the momentum going or that a band decides its own future. They don't realize how hard the business was and what it took to survive as long as we did—just to rack up a few classics that still get played on the radio today.

What do you think dance music has contributed to pop culture throughout the '70s, '80s and '90s?

Basically when people went out, they wanted to *move*. Dance music gave people a means to express themselves. From swing to disco to hip-hop, the rhythm affected people. It inspired them to dance. Dancing has been around for thousands of years, and it's a unique way we humans express our passion, energy—and I'd say our *humanity*. Dance music also blended great melodies and lyrics into the mix, and that was important. Yeah, rock music did that too, and you can bang your head to it, but dance music seemed to tap into people's souls in a different way than rock. And I think making people feel good, which is what dance music did, really mattered.

Lightning Round with Marty

Wallet or smart phone?

Oh, smart phone. Everything's in the cell phone—I mean *everything*! My whole life is in it!

Treadmill or StairMaster?

Treadmill—but on an incline! Much better for the knees!

Jeans or suit?

Ooh, I like both, man. It's so hot here in Miami, so jeans and shorts, but I like a nice suit at night!

Cocktail or beer?

I'm a vodka guy. But no sweet drinks.

TMZ *or* Entertainment Tonight?

TMZ—more juicy gossip.

Elvis or Jagger?

Oh, Elvis. I was never a Stones guy. Elvis was amazing!

Sports car or SUV?

[*He laughs.*] I love my X5, but for Miami, well, there are a lot of floods here. You don't want to be in a sports car on those days. So I'm gonna go with SUV.

'70s or '80s?

'70s man! You got the Eagles, Earth, Wind & Fire! You gonna go with the Eagles or Depeche Mode? Come on! I love Depeche Mode; don't get me wrong—those guys are awesome. But the Eagles are a whole *other* level.

Nance Coolen, formerly of Twenty 4 Seven
"Slave to the Music" (1993)

> "You work and work—you worked your ass off. You quickly realized that a show business life isn't all cocktails and fun."—Nance Coolen

Holland's contribution to dance-pop music was tremendous during the '70s and '80s, with such acts as Luv', Stars on 45 and MaiTai scoring chart-topping hits across the globe. During the '90s, the musical epicenter located on the western coast of the Netherlands continued to fan dance floor flames with yet another act that delighted Europe. The brainchild of Dutch producer Ruud van Rijen, Twenty 4 Seven first broke on the scene in 1989, led by rapper Captain Hollywood and an aspiring young singer and dancer named Nance Coolen. Though Captain Hollywood quickly departed the group to pursue a solo career, Ms. Coolen remained and teamed with rapper Stay-C. Together, they enjoyed nearly four years of tremendous success in Germany, Austria, Sweden, the Netherlands and several other nations performing an infectiously catchy brand of Euro-House and dance-pop. Among their most popular songs were "Is It Love," "Leave Them Alone" and their biggest high-energy stomper, "Slave to the Music."

Nance parted ways with the group in the mid–'90s and pursued other avenues in entertainment, including a very successful and ongoing career in television. From her home in Holland today, she expresses affection for the experiences she had as a part of Twenty 4 Seven and the great joy the era brought her. Dressed in white and looking most elegant with blond hair, a slim figure and youthful facial features, she shares her memories of the past with great warmth and directness.

Nance, would you tell me a little about your youth and how you came to discover music?

Actually, I was only 16 when I started in Twenty 4 Seven, so that was a big part of my youth. Before that I was in school, and I wasn't paying much attention in class because I hated it. My teachers always said in my reports that "she can learn, but she doesn't want to." I got the same assessment every year. I loved to dance, and I always kept busy with that. I also did a little bit of singing. My mom figured when I was around 14 I should have singing lessons. But the woman teaching me specialized in classical music. So I was only singing things like "Ave Maria" and Bette Midler's "The Rose." Nothing really hip. My love for music was in artists like Michael Jackson and Madonna, and when I looked at the magazines, that was the type of career I wanted.

The original 1990 line-up of the group Twenty 4 Seven featured Hanks & Jacks, Captain Hollywood and Nance Coolen, as seen in a BCM Records publicity shot (courtesy Nance Coolen).

How did you happen to become a member of Twenty 4 Seven?

I was going to a local disco (I wore a lot of make-up and pretended I was older). [*Nance laughs.*] It worked in those days, and it was a small village. They were really quite flexible at the door about letting me in. I would slip in there with my best friend, Barbara. One day, a DJ from the club named Ruud van Rijen asked me if I wanted to try singing a music track he was working on (after he heard about me at the disco). They had a lot of dance competitions there, so he had also seen me dance. He had recorded a song called "I Can't Stand It," but his original version had a rap and this robot voice as the vocal. He wanted a different sound for it and asked me to come in and try some of the lyrics. So, I went in one afternoon, did it and went back to school. I heard nothing for six months. Then, suddenly, the recording exploded in Germany. The song went to the top of the charts there, and that was the kick off.

Can you describe Mr. van Rijen and what it was like to first work with him?

In the beginning, it was a lot of fun. I was a young girl blossoming. He was this DJ at the club, and I think a lot of the girls there, including me, kind of looked up to him. We knew he was DJing, but he was also creating and mixing records, and that had its appeal. The "I Can't Stand It" record had been a local success, and everybody looked up to him a bit. So, when he asked me to come in to do some singing, to do a new version of it, I was flattered of course. People from the south of Holland are very trusting of each other. So, it was okay for me, as a 16 year old, to work with him. My parents thought it was okay and that he would look after me. So, I was allowed to pursue it.

Do you recall the recording session for the new version of "I Can't Stand It"? Also, how did the first official line-up of Twenty 4 Seven group come together?

I knew the "I Can't Stand It" original song and the robot voice, but I didn't pay attention to the lyrics that much. I knew the title was repeated as the lyric, and that's about it. I didn't listen to the meaning. When I went into the studio, Ruud let me hear a German dance song, but I don't remember who sang it or what it was called. He wanted the same kind of basic style and flow but with his "I Can't Stand It" lyrics. So that's how I sang it—in the style of this German song. [*Nance sings the refrain of the song.*] MC Fixx It [a rapper Ruud had been working with] didn't want to be a part of the new group, but the manager Ruud was working with at the time knew three people who would be a good fit. So, he called Captain Hollywood [Tony Dawson-Harrison] and also the duo Hanks & Jacks, who had done back-up dance work for C.C. Catch in Germany. When we did our first photo shoot [with famed photographers Esser & Strauss], also in Germany, that was the first time we all met—ever—and we became like brothers and sister at that moment. Hollywood recorded his part in Germany and brought a completely different rap to the song. That rap was about black and white, cultural differences. With the new song, Captain Hollywood and me, and our background dancers—I think that's what made us so big and special at first.

We were a very multicultural group. I was Dutch, Hollywood was from America (living in Nuremberg—his dad was in the army, I believe, and that's how he happened to be in that country), and our dancers, if I remember—one was Italian and one was part Moroccan, I think. I remember I got this big makeover—I got this platinum blonde hair, which was, at the time, image-making. I went along with all of it because I loved it!

"I Can't Stand It," with its message promoting anti-racism and powerful, high-energy melody, was a major hit across Europe and a Top 10 hit in the UK in 1989, and by the start of the '90s your group was well established as a hot new act. This kind of breakout success must have been incredible for you.

Oh yes, it was! We started touring right away, and that song lasted about a year. The strange part is that in the beginning it was so overwhelming. I can only describe it as a rollercoaster. You just step on the ride and don't think about it. Now, as an older person, I can really start to appreciate what happened to us. But at that point, you don't fully realize what's happening. You just do what you have to do. You work and work—you worked your ass off. You quickly realized that a show business life isn't all cocktails and fun. It was very hard work.

How did your life change as a result of this success? Did you have to sacrifice anything to begin this journey?

I didn't really feel that I was giving up anything to have this success. But after a while, my friends, who had been with me in school, didn't understand what I was doing. It's really hard to come home after six weeks and tell my friends that I was touring here and there. Or that I was meeting all these famous people who were so big at the time, like Snap! and Haddaway—you name them. I started losing friends because I couldn't keep up with their lifestyle, mostly because they were in school. (I was really in a somewhat illegal situation because I, too, was supposed to be in school—but we agreed to skip a bit of that, my mom, dad and me.) So that's what I lost—my teenage friends. That's the whole stupid thing with stardom. People think that *you* change, but often it's the fact that *other* people start looking differently at you. They sometimes make the changes for you—it's not necessarily your choice. There are some exceptions, of course.

Captain Hollywood and Twenty 4 Seven became my new friends and family. In the beginning, they looked after me. They promised my parents they'd keep me safe and keep an eye on me. They did a lot of things without me, but they did so on purpose. For example, if I would say, "Let's go out tonight," they'd suggest instead we'd all get to bed early. I would follow their instructions. I remember once I needed something and knocked on one of their hotel room doors. Well, they were all gone and out partying somewhere!

But they didn't know about some of the things that I did on my own. [*She chuckles.*] Sometimes I'd sneak out. You grow up really fast. Imagine being a 17-year-old girl, and you see an attractive older man—yeah, that's tempting.

You enjoyed great success with the follow-up single "Are You Dreaming?" and Twenty 4 Seven's 1990 debut album, Street Moves. Captain Hollywood dropped out of the team shortly after. What was happening with the group at this point?

We had signed a deal with BCM Records in Germany, but before that, Hollywood and his dancing mates, Hanks & Jacks (also members of our group), were trying to find fame on their own. Around the time our first album was released, BCM went broke as a record company. They closed operations. Twenty 4 Seven was very successful by now, and everyone knew Captain Hollywood's name. So he decided he wanted to go solo, and Hanks & Jacks left with him to pursue their own careers. I was left alone with our producer, Ruud. We had to find a new rapper.

We knew a rapper named Stay-C [Stacey Seedorf] because he had been one of our supporting acts in the past. We called him, and he agreed to become part of the group. At the beginning, Stay-C and I had good chemistry. Stay-C also began writing some of the raps—he also had a talent like Captain Hollywood's for doing that. He was very open and fun at the start. He loved to joke around, and he was fun to be around. He was very grateful to be in Twenty 4 Seven because we were a group he looked up to.

Our group changed a bit with the departure of our dancers. Even though dancing was their primary role, they also rapped a little bit, and they were very acrobatic. So we had a special kind of show. We had to change our presence a bit. I don't remember us ever feeling we had to be like any other dance artists of the time, like La Bouche or Snap! That was the producer's responsibility to determine how we would measure up to other artists. I can say we often were the last artists on the stage when we did shows. The last artist was always considered the best, and we were the best.

Did you have a preference for being in the studio or performing live?

Oh, it's hard to say because I liked both. It was really fun to be in the studio. I don't get in there as much these days, but recently, for a current work project, I was in the studio, and when I stepped in it I was like, "Oh yeah, I love this!" It was nice to be back in there. But performing live is great too. How do I say it? It's action and results—seeing people that like our music and hearing them singing along with our songs.

Your success was largely confined to Europe. Did the group have aspirations to be as massive in the United States?

Of course. We talked about it, and it was considered very important to try to be successful in America. But for us, it just never happened. I really don't know why.

Your electronic super-speed dance hits like "Is It Love," "Leave Them Alone" and "Slave to the Music," the latter said to be your biggest hit, were enormously popular throughout Europe, especially in Germany. As you amassed one smash after another, was there pressure to stay on top?

For me, personally, I didn't feel any sense of pressure. I think those feelings may have been more with the producer, the record company and our manager. At the time, our manager was a very important figure in Germany named Charly Prick (don't laugh). He was very confident. I remember him saying he could make us, but he could also break us as well. He knew Frank Farian, he worked with Boney M., Jermaine Jackson and Pia Zadora and many others. He had a lot of influence on our group. He knew which strings to pull to get airplay on significant radio and television stations, like MTV, VIVA in Germany and major stations in Spain and France. He knew exactly when to go there, when to call and who to call. He was vital to our success.

Stay-C was kind of a business guy as well. When he came to a new country, he would always shake the hands of executives and knew their names. He would always remember them. For me, I'd just say hi. Business-wise, I was just—*bad*. I admit it.

Let's talk a bit about the music industry back in those days. Were you treated fairly on the business end?

Well, probably not. I don't remember ever seeing a signed contract for any performance we ever did. So, if we had a gig and we got paid 20,000 German marks, it might have really been 40,000. I never knew if we were receiving the right amount of money or not. It was a lot of money for us to have at the time, whatever we did get paid, and it was nice to have. But it could have been double. I'll never know. I did get record royalties for three albums—that's important to say—but no publishing royalties, since I wasn't writing the songs.

The recreational use of drugs in the music industry and in dance venues has been observed throughout the decades. Did this affect you during your time in the dance-pop spotlight?

I have never ever seen drugs. I know we liked our Bacardis and Coke—that's what we did. I never saw my colleagues doing drugs, but I remember a visit to Sweden, I think. That's where I did a joint with Stay-C, in the back of a car. It was the best two hours ever because I just couldn't stop laughing. That was my first and last experience with drugs.

Why did the party with Twenty 4 Seven come to an end for you by 1995?

Oh, that's a difficult question for me. Looking back, I was a little too young maybe and enjoying performing in the group perhaps a little too much. I wasn't interested in worrying about what might be happening with the key people around me. In the beginning, I didn't notice what anyone was doing, perhaps behind my back. So, I think a lot of people disappointed me at the end.

When I was in Twenty 4 Seven, I met a man, and we were married within six months. This was a problem for the people around me in the group, who were already feeling he was too smart and seeing too much. The fact that I wanted to get married was a big problem for them image-wise. "If you're getting married, you're not the available girl for your fans anymore." My husband-to-be at the time was like, "What kind of an excuse is that? Look at Madonna. She got married, and she never lost any of her fans." That was his reference, but for me—I got a little bit scared that they didn't want me anymore. I think for [the members of the group], that was enough of a reason to start to get rid of me. I think they figured they could let me go, hire a nice girl who isn't singing for real, pay her a few bucks a month, and she wouldn't take that big piece of the cake (because I was into the royalties). Long story short, that's what I believe happened at the time.

When this happened, what direction did you want to take?

I left the group, and my husband (we later got divorced) knew I liked to sing and encouraged me to make my own music. We started creating some new tracks, and at the same time I was asked to do a Dutch TV show. I wanted to have my own song for the show, so we wrote "Love Is...," which was used in the program. My solo songs had success in Holland, but I wasn't hitting in Germany, which had been such a big country for Twenty 4 Seven. I didn't have much promotion in Germany, which I believe was a mistake on the part of my record company.

It was my luck to move into television. A lot of ladies, female vocalists from that time, lost their careers after their music ended and were stuck sitting at home. I loved presenting TV shows. I like to sing, too, but now it's at home in the bathroom.

I think it's important for me to say that I never really felt like a musician. You know, when Twenty 4 Seven performed on television for example, my voice was almost always on tape. The rap, most of the time, was live. So, I never had the chance to really practice singing live. That can make you very insecure. I don't know if other female singers will admit it was that way, but I think it was, even though these women also sang their original songs. I sang every song in the studio, but there was always a back-up track during performances. So, today I feel very insecure and am scared as hell when I am asked to sing live.

As a very attractive woman in the entertainment industry, then and now, how challenging is it for a woman to be in the business? I'm mostly referring to sexism and ageism.

I think sexism and ageism are supported by the media, thanks to Photoshop and whatever. I think you are as old as you feel. How do I say this? I have to be strong on my feet. If you are strong and confident as a woman, you can be whatever you want to be for as long as you want. Age shouldn't make a difference. Maybe I'm lucky. But I will say I would probably feel a little too old to be on stage performing as Twenty 4 Seven again. That's an honest statement.

About a year ago, I was asked if I would consider coming back to Twenty 4 Seven. I was really busy with my television work, so I declined. But sometimes I see my colleagues on Facebook, like 2 Unlimited, still traveling around doing '90s parties, and sometimes I get a bit jealous. For a moment I think I want to be there and feel the crowd and start singing "I Can't Stand It," just to see what happens. Sometimes I wonder if I were to go to Germany and be walking on a street, would anyone recognize me? I get recognized in Holland for my television work, but I never get recognized as the girl from Twenty 4 Seven—*not at all*. There's a whole generation here in Holland that only knows me for my television work. When they hear I was a singer in Twenty 4 Seven, they don't even know what I'm talking about. They'd have to Google me to know what I did.

Sometimes when I am out of the country and I am talking with people, I mention I was a singer. I usually try to get an idea of the age of the people I am with first. If they are 35 or older, they will probably know and recognize Twenty 4 Seven.

What motivates you, gets you excited, or gives you the most satisfaction today?

I'm going to get cheesy now. I have my own family today. I've had a wonderful boyfriend for 12 years now, and we have a gorgeous six-year-old son. He's the cutest. We have shown him my videos on YouTube, and though he's young, I think he understands his mom did something cool in the past. I've saved everything for him, and my mom used to collect everything about Twenty 4 Seven and me. She has albums full of clippings that I will share with him. My family is what I enjoy the most today.

I worked as a TV host with a very successful singer in Holland, Gerard Joling ("No More Boleros"). He is such a famous person here. When I was standing next to him, I felt like just an assistant. But I knew he needed me. People used to say I was jealous of him and his success. I would respond that I was in Twenty 4 Seven for a long time and had huge worldwide success. I know how it feels, and I don't need it anymore. I am happy that this is the person I am, and I don't need that kind of success today. I love the job I'm doing and my family.

I also had a really serious operation about two years ago, which made me realize health is everything. I know that's cheesy, too, but it's the truth.

What has been your greatest accomplishment?

If I look back on my career, I prefer TV hosting, but if I ask myself what I am most proud of, it would definitely be my work in Twenty 4 Seven.

In retrospect, what are your feelings about '90s dance music? What thoughts does it inspire?

In the '90s, it seemed that everybody was happier, and dancing was really the thing. It seemed like people were nicer and less violent. No heavy, offensive lyrics in dance music—now you can say anything on a record, and your child is hearing and learning it (which I think is really horrible).

In Holland, we watch VH1 a lot, and on the weekends they have a lot of those "Back to the '80s" or "Back to the '90s" shows. I put those on a lot, and I see all my old colleagues. I think to myself, "That's my time—when I was probably the most happy." It sounds stupid, perhaps, but I feel so comfortable when I think of that time. I feel so good about it. Dance music was such an important part of that time and that feeling.

Dance music was created by talented musicians. Somebody made it and put his heart into it. It was music from the heart. That's what we made. I think that's something to be valued.

Lightning Round with Nance

Diana Ross or Beyoncé?

I would say Diana Ross. I think she laid the foundation for Beyoncé. Always start with the original.

Reality TV or a drama?

Drama. Skip reality—it's way too much info.

"Sometimes I wonder if I were to go to Germany and be walking on a street, would anyone recognize me?" ponders Nance Coolen, who went on to enjoy television success in Holland following her tenure with Twenty 4 Seven (courtesy Nance Coolen).

Extended versions or radio edits?
Extended versions, please! I love all the extra stuff in them. I think of Janet Jackson. She had great extended versions of her hits.

Applause or record sales?
Both. They belong together. The more applause, the more records you're probably selling.

Instagram or Twitter
Neither. I love Facebook. It's an addiction.

Perfect hair or perfect teeth?
Teeth, please!

Saving or spending?
Saving. I had this big discussion about it with Stay-C one day. "Oh, when you have money, you have to let it go," he said. But I saved a lot of my money when I was with the group, and I was glad I did.

Five good friends or one best friend?
Five good friends because if one best friend disappoints you, you have nothing left.

Tattoo or piercing?
[Ms. Coolen raises her middle finger, which happens to be tattooed.]

Fred and Richard Fairbrass of Right Said Fred
"I'm Too Sexy" (1991)

"Any artist that tells you they know they've got a hit is probably lying. Music is so unpredictable, which is what makes it fantastic in a way."—Richard Fairbrass

"People thought we were a couple of gym queens who happened to get lucky with a song…"—Fred Fairbrass

Few songs from the '90s were as irresistibly infectious as the self-assured anthem for the masses called "I'm Too Sexy" by the British group Right Said Fred. When the song reached U.S. shores in the summer of 1991, it vaulted up the pop chart to the number one spot (just as it had in dozens of other countries). After going as high as the number two position in the UK, "I'm Too Sexy" remained an unstoppable global dance smash for several months. Today, it is still among the most vividly recalled and amusing of the era's hit songs.

The group Right Said Fred was originally embodied by brothers Fred and Richard Fairbrass, who had been performing together under various stage names for years, as well as with notables like David Bowie, Bob Dylan and Mick Jagger. Later, they teamed up with friend and fellow musician/songwriter Rob Manzoli. "I'm Too Sexy," the trio's campy yet inspired musical creation about the pros and cons of being overly attractive, ignited a firestorm of global popularity. (It's hard to find anyone who doesn't know this song.) The brothers parted with Manzoli in 1997, but their international impact was felt well into the next century. Though they never had another major hit in the U.S. (their first three singles all went Top 10 on the Billboard *dance chart, however), this lively, muscular, seemingly carefree and fun loving duo had no trouble amassing a series of British, South American, Asian and European pop chart and dance floor triumphs. Among them were the 1991 nugget "Don't Talk Just Kiss," "Deeply Dippy" in 1992 (another number one hit in Britain), "You're My Mate" (2001) and "Stand Up (for the Champions)" (2002), the latter two tracks particularly popular in Germany.*

Fred and Richard's hunky physical appearance (Madonna reportedly once named Richard the most beddable man in pop) and knack for fetching, tight-fitting, punk-meets-club attire branded them immediately with a unique identity that excited, perplexed and intrigued their audiences. As their videos raised eyebrows, the brothers' sexual identities were called into question for a short time, especially in label-obsessed America. But ultimately, it was their quirky, frequently clever and cheeky lyricism, upbeat melodies and distinctly "man's man" appeal that made the boys the pop stars they still are today. Recent singles like "Sexaholic," a German language version of "Stand Up (for the Champions)" called "Steht Auf Für Den Weltmeister" with singer Axel Fischer (the gentlemen never shy away from a challenge), and 2015's "Shoulda Been Me" have kept the Right Said Fred party going nearly a quarter of a century after their breakthrough hit.

Sitting beside each other in their London home, looking decidedly healthy and exuding a kind of rock star magnetism, Richard and Fred are, at first, a bit agitated by a frustrating business matter that's disrupted their day. But within seconds of our interview getting under way, they seem to forget their annoyance and our discussion is immediately frank and engaging. Richard's sense of humor and Fred's candor meld together well, and one can easily see the chemistry that's no doubt helped make their partnership so uniquely enduring.

I always like to know how artists got their start in the world. Fred, Richard, would you tell me a little about your early years?

Fred: We had quite a privileged family life, inasmuch as mum and dad were both very caring and loving. We lived about 30 or 40 miles out of London in a rural market town, and we got into music in our early teens. We weren't that close as brothers in our pre-teens, but by our teenage years we began to get closer through music. We bonded over playing.

Richard: Yes, exactly. There's a big gap emotionally between a 13-year-old and a 16-year-old. Your maturity levels even out eventually, and I'd say by our early 20s we were in the same place.

Fred: We were into writing songs right away. We were never content to have a band that would just play other people's songs. There were a lot of bands living in the area we came from called East Grinstead (mid–Sussex, near Gatwick Airport, maybe an hour's drive from London). Because of the ley lines, it was considered a town with energy. I never felt that energy, but you had a lot of artsy-fartsy bands and artists converging there. Plus, it was the headquarters for the church of Scientology and the Mormon church.

When you began making music in earnest, before you achieved fame, what kind of artists did you envisage yourselves becoming? How did you make ends meet during that time?

Richard: For me, the thing that defined it was watching the movie *Let It Be*. I thought, "How cool would it be with all your best mates, making music and making money?" That seemed to me to be a pretty cool way of living. Of course, you grow up and you realize that's not exactly how the business works. In those days, everyone went out live. You had to get your band together and get tight because you would then get a studio, and it would cost you a lot of money [to record]. So the quicker you were in and out, the better. In a way, it was healthier then. You learned a lot more. Today, I think there's something rather isolationist about sitting home on a computer in order to get yourselves out there. So, back then we just saw ourselves becoming a band. We never thought for a second it would go the way it did.

Fred: We did lots of part-time jobs in those days too. We worked in gyms; we were waiters. We even waited tables in New York for a while, around 1987. What happened was we both did a bit of session work here in England. Richard did some bass work with Bowie; I did some guitar work with Bob Dylan. We took that money and went to New York, and we got a deal with EMI-Capitol. We played a bunch of gigs at places like the Knitting Factory, little

Right Said Fred received the Ivor Novello Award from the British Academy of Songwriters, Composers and Authors honoring excellence in music writing for their smash 1991 single "I'm Too Sexy." The brothers are seen here in a publicity shot issued by Charisma Records in the U.S. (author's collection).

dives up and down Bleecker Street. Around 1989, we returned to the UK and got Right Said Fred started and began playing around with dance music.

How did you arrive at the name Right Said Fred?

Richard: Back in those days, if you were going to advertise your band in a key London music magazine called *Time Out*, you had to get your name in it by midday on a Thursday I think. The magazine came out on Friday. We did what Jethro Tull did—we changed our name almost every week. It's hard to hit a moving target, so if you change your name all the time, you're going to be pretty safe. At this particular moment, we didn't have a name. A friend of ours, Katie Randall, had heard the song "Right, Said Fred" on the radio, an old English comedy song from around '62 or '63 [by Bernard Cribbins]. She suggested we call ourselves Right Said Fred. We said fine and put it in *Time Out*. It was '89 or '90, and when we eventually took off, we got stuck with the name. I think if "I'm Too Sexy" hadn't taken off, we would have changed our name again.

You had a third member for many years, Rob Manzoli. How did Rob fit in the mix?

Fred: Richard and I tend work better with a third writing partner. We didn't immediately click with Rob, but we knew it was worth pursuing. Plus, Rob and my brother and I didn't have many options at that time.

Let's sink our teeth into your massive hit "I'm Too Sexy," one of the signature songs of the '90s. Please do share the story of how this song came about.

Fred: Richard and I were an acoustic duo and got very bored with it by the start of the '90s. I had been going to dance clubs and hearing the music. We kind of liked the idea of acoustic guitars with dance music. Even though there are none in "I'm Too Sexy," it kind of starts off sort of based on using an acoustic guitar, if that makes sense. We had gone to a programmer's house (Brian Pugsley—he worked with the band Shamen for a while) and had this song running around on his computer. Richard had a bass line, and he started singing the melody with the lyrics I'm—Too—Sexy. It was hot, and he took his shirt off. We were mucking around, and we started laughing that this was a mad idea.

Richard: The idea with the bass end was to play a traditional bass part. We just knew the bass part had to be the "I'm Too Sexy" vocal line. To be honest with you, I didn't really know what I was singing. I had no clue. We spent most of our time trying to be like the other artists we saw—Steven Tyler, Mick Jagger—you know. The bottom E I had to sing, well, I had no idea I could sing that low until I actually had to do it. The chorus about being a model—well, again, I had no idea what I was doing. I did the song pretty much section by section. We'd never done anything like it before.

After you finished the track, did you have any feeling for its potential? Or did you just throw the track against the wall to see if it would stick?

Richard: Any artist that tells you they know they've got a hit is probably lying. Music is so unpredictable, which is what makes it fantastic in a way. So you really have no idea. It was such a weird track. I wanted to sound like everyone else. [*He laughs.*] I don't know, like Salt 'N' Pepa. The only time I thought the track sounded kind of cool was when we put the live bass in. Phil Spalding, the bass player on the song, put the live bass in it—that's when it sort of began to come alive. I didn't think it would become a hit, but I thought, "I like it!" The same thing happened later with the song "Deeply Dippy." I was thinking, "How are we gonna get away with this?" All I know was—*I didn't know.*

So the song became this massive worldwide smash. What are some of the highlights you remember about hitting the stratosphere with this song?

Fred: "Sexy" broke very quickly, and so did our lives. I think the video had a lot to do with it. Because we took our shirts off and didn't look like musicians, the images were quite powerful. Radio was a little bit cautious at first in some areas. The label we signed to was a tiny music promotions company owned by Guy [Holmes]. Tug Records was set up to furnish "I'm Too Sexy." We were the only artists on the label. In Europe and Britain, America was the Holy Grail. So when the song hit the Top 40 there, that meant we had a pretty good hit. Top 10, then five, then number one—that's really impressive. But the problem with your first single going to number one in America is that there is pretty much only one way to go from there. People tend to want a song like that to be one of those here and now songs, but fortunately we were able to make other hit records. And I must say the longevity of "Sexy" has been breathtaking. It doesn't stop. It is quite amazing.

Richard: It sounds ridiculous now, but you can put anything after the title of the song. "I'm Too Sexy for my computer," anything. The power of that didn't dawn on us till further down the line. But when the song went to number one in America, it was quite scary. It was such a big, powerful market. It just has an awe-inspiring quality to it. So when we were flown over there to perform it, I personally was absolutely petrified. I can't tell you how frightening it is when your record label tells you 60 million people will be watching you on TV. I don't want to know that; it will freak me out! I only wanted to know two friends of mine would be watching—then I could relax.

Fred: It was very different being successful in America compared to the rest of the world. America understands the business side of show business. In Europe and England., the people in management don't always get that side of things. I think America is very good at creating "stars," and when we first took off with "Sexy," I think the management in that country understood the mechanics of making money from it. In Europe and the UK, they tended to misunderstand the power of the slogan; they screwed up the merchandise, messed up sponsorships. That didn't happen in the U.S.

Richard: We messed up too. I remember we were in L.A., and we were talking to the man who was creating the movie *Die Hard 2* or *3*, I don't remember which, and he was interested in us. I don't know what we did, but we were either too drunk or just stupid because we didn't even take his number and lost that opportunity.

Many artists have shared horror stories with me about their management or label ripping them off. Were you luckier in this regard?

Fred: We fared okay. We certainly got ripped off. Some of the advice we were given and took was breathtakingly appalling. We are owed money, and we're never gonna get that money. But we are luckier than most to be honest with you. We haven't written songs as big as "Sexy," but we have written other number one songs and high earning releases. So we never had to rely on just one track. For example, we wrote a song called "Stand Up (for the Champions)" in 2002, which has been used in a lot of big sporting events over here. We had more than one string on the bow. Overall, I'd say we were paid pretty well for "Sexy." I think it would be rather churlish of us to moan about that.

Richard: There were sort of ancillary areas like merchandise where we lost a lot of money, but the labels always treated us great. Yeah, you could find things to complain about here and there, but it wasn't one of those situations where somebody walked off with a whole pile of money. We were very lucky. A lot of musicians have a hit, don't make a penny, and become very bad tempered and bitter, and they begrudge those that do make money. I agree—it would be churlish for us to complain.

The aftermath of "Sexy" lasted quite a while from all reports, but you needed a follow-up. You released the Up album in 1992 and enjoyed some hits off it like "Don't Talk Just Kiss" with Jocelyn Brown and "Deeply Dippy." Would you expand on that phase?

Fred: "Don't Talk" did better than "Sexy" in some territories. It didn't do well in America, but it certainly did in South America. It got picked up as the theme for a TV show there and was used on a nightly basis for about five or six years. We gained some momentum with that. Then we did "Deeply Dippy," which was sort of an acoustic track, and what that did was take us to a demographic that was interested in buying albums. "Dippy" reached number one in the UK, and it was the kind of track you'd buy an album for, whereas "Sexy" was more of a single. It gave us more momentum, particularly in the UK and globally. These songs performed very well in the U.S. clubs, but not well on their pop charts. The album went on to do all right, not great, but okay.

"Sexy" just continued to sell in America. I know a station recently had to re-playlist it just because demand was still so strong. That's about 24 years after its release. It's mad! The song went on to be used on *The Simpsons*, *Family Guy*, *West Wing*, blah, blah, blah. The song really went on to have a life of its own. Three of us wrote it—Richard, Rob Mazoli and myself—but if just one of us wrote "Sexy," he could easily live off that song forever. You'd never have to work again. Two is a push, but three, well, you gotta keep working.

Can you tell me a bit more about the creation of the follow-up song, "Don't Talk Just Kiss"? It was kind of a unique pairing in that the song featured prominent background vocals by R&B/dance diva Jocelyn Brown. It was a sizeable hit throughout Europe, but missed the mark a bit in America, as you mentioned.

Richard: I thought it was a pretty smart move at the time. We weren't that clued up on PR and TV demands at that time, [and incorporating Jocelyn as a guest] was a bit of a mystery to us. Strangely, the PR folks sort of invented this relationship between Jocelyn and me. I mean really! [*Richard laughs.*] I'm sure that made me laugh as much as it probably made her laugh. I think it was all part of the plan—a company idea—and as it turned out it was good for the track. Funny, we met Jocelyn on a plane coming back from Germany just a few weeks ago.

I think the label had a difficult time with us. We were quite tricky to sell as artists. We weren't a boy band. We weren't strictly dance. We weren't really anything. All of our songs were quite different, and they were never sure what to release next. I think that's why they released the track with Jocelyn—just to grease the wheels a little bit.

"Deeply Dippy," your third hit and a number one in the UK, is a perfect example of the charm and individuality found on almost all of your songs. The track was kind of a bouncy, left-field pop composition that kept people guessing what you'd come up with next.

Richard: Yes, and it's another example of how the label didn't know what to do with us. I remember the conversation we had with them over that song. They wanted us to make it a four-on-the-floor dance track. Well, if you did that, it would have been running about 180 beats-per-minute.

Fred: They didn't understand it. It was a swing track. [*Fred briefly vocalizes the melody.*] We tried to explain that making it a dance track wouldn't work as a single. We had a real argument. We had to have our manager join us to beat the label up to release the song as we intended it. They weren't keen on that.

Richard: I don't blame them, really. I was in the waiting room at a major radio station about to do an interview about "Deeply Dippy." They were just about to play it. The track they played before it was Oceanic's "Insanity," which was a massive, big-sounding dance floor record. They played "Insanity," and as I walked into the interview they played the very simple intro to "Deeply Dippy." I thought to myself, "We're finished! This is it!" I figured it's all over as of this minute because it sounds like crap compared to "Insanity." But we went to number one with it, so what do I know? I'll just repeat that I know nothing! The less you know the better!

You're still great looking men today, and in the '90s you had a very hyper-masculine appearance that kind of shook people up. You were well-built and a bit ahead of the curve in terms of showing it off. That won you a lot of female fans, while at the same time generating speculation about whether or not you might be gay. How did you manage the challenge of your personal and professional identities?

Richard: [*Laughing*] "I remember they shouted at us in an airport, "Euro-fags!" I did have a ball gown on at the time, which, looking back, was probably a bad idea. [*He laughs again, and his brother smiles.*] The gay thing was weird. They made it a much bigger deal in America than in the UK. In the UK, I had maybe half a dozen—at the most—gay fans. In fact, in the early days, we ended up canceling a lot of performances at gay clubs because it wasn't working. It was mostly all girls, women and families who came to see us, completely. When we went to San Francisco, the gay image was played up a lot more. And I was more aware of it.

Fred: People usually assume I'm gay, which I'm not.

Richard: You're not?

Fred: Well, my boyfriend says I'm not. [*The brothers laugh and enjoy the humor of the conundrum.*] But people assumed I was gay because of Richard's—well, Richard is actually bisexual. People found that hard. They like to lump you into sort of one demographic, so, therefore, I must be gay. I think, in terms of publicity and such, they thought the gay thing was going to be big, and it wasn't. Our audience has always been, incredibly, mums and dads and their kids. We've always been surprised, but we've done millions of shows, and that's who turns up. We continue to attract a very young audience as well, probably because "Sexy" has been heard in so many movies and new generations are familiar with it. Right Said Fred was never a gay thing—it was just what some people perceived.

Did the gay community in America or abroad ever pressure you to represent them?

Richard: We didn't really get any pressure. We do get asked to do a lot of gay pride events now. That's it. I'm not in favor of songs or people getting boxed. I do think the gay community in general gets a little bit over-zealous in terms of who belongs to it and who doesn't. Nobody owns you. I think there is sometimes an issue with ownership. Once a song is out there, it belongs to everybody. And as far as sexuality goes, I don't want to be told by anybody what I am. When people do that, it precludes the possibility that you might fall in love with, say, a goat. Of course I'm being facetious, but don't tell me I'm gay, bisexual or anything because I don't know what tomorrow brings. So leave me alone.

Richard, you had been with your long-term partner Stuart Pantry from the early '80s through the early 2000s. In 2010, he succumbed to cancer. When intense life events like that have happened to you, how is your musicianship and creativity affected?

Richard: I think it just made me want to stop working for a bit. It didn't make me want to go out and write songs about it. I think we were just wrapped up in the event for a bit. I mean—we *did* work. The weird thing is, when you do a gig, you can kind of switch off. It's not like when you are creating a song and physically emoting and are filled with emotion. With a gig, and if you know what you're doing, you can get on a stage in all kinds of emotional states without necessarily impinging on the show. You sort of go into autopilot. But the writing, as I think back, was pretty difficult.

The '90s was the era of the mega-clubs and massive parties where your music was often played. Just as there'd been in previous decades, a hefty drug culture was attached to the scene. Did that culture have any impact on your careers?

Fred: Only when I snorted cocaine. [*He laughs.*] Which actually I did—a lot. You got into a club, you met these great looking women, she'd put some stuff up her nose, presto—

Richard: You got married!

Fred: Presto—everything is fantastic! Or you *think* everything is fantastic. I got into that quite heavily. But it wasn't necessarily just part of the big clubs. We were really only in the big clubs when we did Ibiza—places like Privilege, really big clubs—8,000 people, that kind of thing. I think we were sort of a burnout by the mid-'90s.

Richard: I was obviously with Stuart at that time, and I think we mostly just watched *Star Trek* for about five years. That was my drug! That accounts for a lot, really. I did drugs occasionally, but I never became really a part of it. Not as much as Fred. Fred was single at the time, and so it was a very different thing for him.

Fred: I was very, very lucky because I'd seen what happened to a lot of people I used to hang out with. With drugs, I was able to start and stop. I'd go on a bender for three or four days, then I'd stop for a few months, then I'd start again. Then come about 2003, I just pretty much stopped. I said, "Done!" [*snapping his fingers*]. I didn't really need rehab. Looking back, I just think I got really lucky. Something in my body, whatever my makeup is, I don't have that addictive switch. Many of my friends did, and they got pretty bad, needing recovery and rehab.

Richard: You know we broke into music late. We had a solid family base—mom and dad were great, we lived in the countryside, and we became popular in our late 20s, early 30s. I think if our success had happened when I was 18, I think I might have gone off the rails pretty heavily. *I think*. I think the additional maturity we had helped to contain it. Now, I don't even smoke. My only vice is red wine. Red wine and cheese. That's it!

All of the artists in this book transitioned from the era of physical music product to that of digital downloading. I'd like to know how you viewed that dramatic change in the industry.

Fred: Well, what happened was we signed to a record label based in Berlin in 2000. It was a satellite label of BMG called Kingsize. Interestingly, and even up to the present day, Germany still has a sizeable CD market. Because a lot of our sales at the end of the '90s and into the next century were based in central Europe, we didn't feel the transition that much. Our song "You're My Mate" sold about 500,000 physical CDs in 2001. The album, *Fredhead*, went gold and got very close to platinum at that point. I think the album sold a quarter of a million, maybe 300,000 copies. Physical sales were still strong. The digital avalanche was happening in other parts of the world, and we weren't working in those places as much.

Because of various health problems with Stuart and also some personal problems with me, all sorts of stuff, we became very much European-based.

Going back to song usage at that time, this was also the period where we wrote "Stand Up (for the Champions)." We were getting pretty large sums of money for synchronizations for that song (and for "Sexy" too). We only noticed synchronizations dropping off in terms of what we were getting paid around 2005–06. Before that we were still in good shape.

As selling singles and albums over the past 10 or 15 years has become—to put it mildly—increasingly challenging, many artists I've spoken with seem to feel that live performances are the only way to sustain their careers. Do you feel the same way?

Fred: People who don't know the road say that kind of thing. It depends on so many things. Not every artist is meant to be a live artist. They're just not. Some artists aren't even meant to do promotions. They're just entities. We were talking with a bass player we know the other day. He went out with some boy bands, and they were pretty successful. They have an entourage of 160 people. Now, you've gotta do some serious business to make that payroll. They probably did. But this idea that going on the road is this Holy Grail is very naïve. It does apply to some bands, but a lot of other bands are really struggling on that level as well. We've had more festivals cancelled this year, in 2015, than any other year I can remember. Lots of corporate shows being cancelled. I think what's interesting for us is that we're getting booked closer and closer to the time of the event. They used to book you a year in advance. Now it's two months. They wait until the final moment to see if they've got any money.

From our point of view, we're still quite lucky. We still do a lot of shows and are very proactive with song usage. Film markets, networking. We work with production companies. We don't go in heavy-handed asking for an advance. What we've found is that if the songs get exposure, it can lead to other things. We had a song appear in a film recently, and that led to the track being picked up for advertising in Italy. I think artists have to think more long term, more out of the box, although I hate that expression—but you have to. And I think they need to be aware of keeping your costs down on a recording level for any new material. We have a new track that we think has a lot of potential. But even so, we must keep recording costs as low as possible and develop our tracks much more cautiously.

Richard: If Apple invented the pen and paper today, everybody would buy it. They would sell it by saying it can't be downloaded.

Fred: The iPen and iPaper!

Richard: Yeah, yeah! Then you'd see a huge line waiting outside the bloody store on Regent Street all night.

Artists popular in the '90s are generally facing the challenges of middle age in a youth driven market. Do you have a philosophy that helps you manage the task?

Richard: It's funny—the aging thing. I hadn't thought about it at all until Stuart died. We had been together for 28 years, and that's when I realized a part of my life was over. It's not the whole thing, but it was still extraordinary to me. That was the point I started thinking about age. I think for men in this business it's not too bad. I think for women it's probably quite challenging. I'm sure it's true in Hollywood too. As soon as you hit the late 40s, 50s, you can only get cast as the bad tempered mother-in-law or the evil head mistress or the Queen of England. We definitely live in a very youth driven culture.

Our mother has Alzheimer's or dementia, one of those, or maybe both. There is a woman who cares for our mum when we're not there, and she gets a great deal of pleasure from talking with older people. If they still have their memories and the ability to communicate, she observes that their perspective on things is fantastic. I kind of do think it's a shame that all those memories, all the observations and experiences of older people aren't treasured more.

Well, we're all on the same train, aren't we; we're just getting off at different stops. You have to be philosophical about it; you can't do anything about it.

I would be tempted to do a facelift—I would be tempted—but I wouldn't do Botox. The idea of injecting your face with snake venom just doesn't appeal to me at all. But beyond that, I think we're aware of aging. The tiredness catches up with you a little bit. And the other thing is we're still doing gigs and the girls out front are screaming and shouting. I look at them thinking, "I am old enough to be your grandfather!"

Is there more pressure for you both because your images and performances have incorporated such a strong physical presence?

Richard: To be quite honest with you, we're quite good at letting go of stuff like that. I train at the gym when I can, when my body allows me to. We're quite physical on the stage still, but we don't dress like we used to. I wouldn't want to watch that.

Fred: I didn't want to watch that when we did it! [*The brothers laugh in unison.*]

Richard: Exactly!

Fred: I mean, we try to keep our weight down and hit the gym and are careful with our diet. But we don't have some kind of military regime. People thought we were a couple of gym queens who happened to get lucky with a song, but we write and play everything. So that's what's important to us. So if we can't train at the gym, so be it. We're no longer the gym junkies we once were, nor as fanatical with our physical training. We're more realistic today.

Richard: You just have to be aware of where you are in your life. You can't imagine you're 35 when you're really 70. Be happy with the fact you made it to 70. I think of Frank Sinatra on his last UK tour. I think he was 76 or something. I think he might have stamped his feet three times through the whole show, and the audience went absolutely mad! He barely moved! An older woman threw a rose on stage saying, "I love you Frank!" I mean—it took him 20 minutes to pick it up. But he didn't care. He was totally in touch with who he was. He didn't come on stage trying to be a young Frank Sinatra. I think if you are in touch with who you are, then aging is cool.

Do you see Right Said Fred going as far out as your 70s?

Richard: Right at this moment, I just see us going out for a glass of wine.

Fred: We had a horrible day today, thanks to some business bullshit that happened this morning. That side of the industry drives us mad, because we look after ourselves. We don't have people to take care of administration, bullshit, egos, and chasing money we're owed. That is exhausting. I think as time goes by, that will be what drives me mad first. Writing and playing—I don't anticipate I will feel too old for that. I think the key will be to keep like-minded people around us. We're lucky in that we have a little bit of a financial safety net, and we can make future decisions based on that. I think we'll just keep on doing what we want to do. Maybe we'll go on the road next year.

I will tell you one other thing about how we move forward. If we are dealing with someone and they piss us off, we're done. We don't say, "Oh, maybe they're having a bad day; let's try to make it work." Fuck them! We move on, and there will be someone else around the corner.

Can you tell me where dance music fits in pop culture history? What do you think has been its value over the past four decades?

Fred: For quite a few years, I think dance music was the only form of popular music that progressed. I think rock stagnated, R&B is in an appalling place, rap is struggling, apart from one or two artists. Dance music continues to evolve. It's very broad and experimental and the programming is often very progressive. I think the genre has contributed a huge amount to music in terms of its experimentation, the euphoria it can create in terms of the bonding that takes place in a club.

I remember the first time I heard Deee-Lite's "Groove Is in the Heart." I felt this euphoric moment. We were only just starting to work on "Sexy" at that time, and I heard this really loud tambourine from "Groove," and I thought, "Man, this is a fucking great record! We need to make a record like this." And there are certain moments, like when I heard "Gonna Make You Sweat" by C + C Music Factory, a big, big record, that are very, very exciting. I think the volume you usually hear dance music played at also adds to the experience.

Richard: Today, we've lost so much of that human connection that dance music inspired in society. You can now go into a super market and not talk to anybody. You can almost get through a whole day and not even say hello to anybody. At the gym, everyone's wearing headphones, playing with their smart phones. Nobody talks. I think that's really damaging. Once we lose our ability to communicate with your fellow human being, all sorts of other things can happen.

Fred: Yes, I think the sharing that took place in the dance clubs—not the drugs or drinks, but actual moments—is quite special. Not all clubs, of course, but many. Dance music gets a bad name sometimes, possibly for some good reasons. But there's load of crap rock bands and crap R&B songs out there, crap rappers. There's a lot of crap music from all genres—pop, rock, rap, R&B, etc., etc.

I think some DJs haven't done the genre any favors when they pull out their MacBook Pro, and everything they've mixed is pre-recorded. I won't say who it was, but I was up in a DJ booth with a really well known guy, and he's got his headphones on, and he's moving his arms all around—but he wasn't doing *anything*! He was sort of faking it! He was miming this whole DJ routine to other people's records, and I thought, "You fucking idiot!" He was getting his 20 grand for the night; he had his Ferrari parked outside. He didn't give a shit! There are some amazing DJs out there—I think, for example, Calvin Harris is a great guy—but the crap other DJs do doesn't help the dance music genre.

Richard: Going back to the music itself, you know I think anything that makes you feel good is automatically viewed as crap. If you make really depressing music, that's automatically considered artistically worthwhile. If you're a miserable, introverted band, that's kind of cool. But if you're a kind of upfront, in-your-face kind of fun thing, that's automatically rubbish. I remember when Dustin Hoffman made *Tootsie*, he said it was very hard to get an Oscar for a comic role. [If you portray] someone who's cut his leg off, pretend to be brain damaged, or portray a genius living under a bridge, you'll probably get the Academy Award. It is that weird thing we have in our culture that there has to be pain for a work to be worthy.

But ultimately, again, it's the power dance music has. There was the Northern Soul scene

"We're quite physical on the stage still, but we don't dress like we used to. I wouldn't want to watch that," says Richard Fairbrass. "I didn't want to watch that when we did it!" adds his brother Fred with a laugh (courtesy Right Said Fred).

in the UK. Remember the Soft Cell track, "Tainted Love"? In the verses, there was this double clap sound. So you'd have a club here in England filled with 4,000 people, and they'd all clap together at that moment. A DJ told me that it was the most fantastic feeling. I think dance music created that kind of feeling, that sense of community, and that's what makes it so special.

Lightning Round with Fred and Richard

Cardio or weights?
　　Fred and Richard: [*Voiced in unison.*] Weights.

Cocktail or beer?
　　Fred and Richard: [*In unison.*] Cocktail.

Giorgio Moroder or Nile Rodgers?
　　Richard: Moroder.
　　Fred: Rodgers.

Club or studio?
　　Fred and Richard: [*In unison.*] Studio.

'70s or '80s?
　　Fred and Richard: [*In unison.*] '70s.

Music or lyrics?
>Richard: Music.
>Fred: Ooooh, hmmmm. Okay then, music.

Applause or sales?
>Fred and Richard: [*In unison.*] Applause.
>Fred: That's an easy one.

Nicki French
"Total Eclipse of the Heart" (1995)

"I remember being in Brazil performing around 1996. The huge crowd there—they didn't really know the words, the English—but they'd sing them in unison phonetically. It was wonderful and so heartfelt. I almost broke down watching it happen."—Nicki French

In a 1995 Billboard *magazine article entitled* The British Invasion of the U.S. Charts, *the American music bible listed singer Nicki French as the third biggest British singles act in the U.S. (with Seal and Des'ree just ahead of her). Her massively successful dance version of "Total Eclipse of the Heart," the 1983 pop-rock classic originally recorded by Bonnie Tyler and now reinvented by famed British producers Mike Stock and Matt Aitken (Kylie Minogue, Dead or Alive, Rick Astley, Donna Summer), had recently reached number two on the pop chart and had become one of the most successful high energy hits of the period.*

Nicki won over audiences worldwide with her warm persona, bright smile and irresistible voice, winning many awards from the dance and pop music industry for her breakthrough hit. Though her subsequent single releases ("For All We Know," "Did You Ever Really Love Me?" and others) failed to chart quite as successfully as her high-powered debut recording, her popularity continued to remain strong in the years that followed. She recently released a zippy, electric remake of Diana Ross' "The Boss" and a retrospective album, One Step Further. *French also re-teamed with Mike Stock for the 2015 dance-pop hit "This Love," which reached the top spot on a number of dance music surveys. Meanwhile, she continues to perform live and has begun exploring theatrical performance opportunities in British productions of* Annie, Guilty Pleasures *and* Beauty and the Beast, *among others.*

Ms. French, dressed stylishly and looking brightly sophisticated, is a delightfully pleasant conversationalist. Her manner is quite modest and instantly ingratiating, and she speaks from her London home with great enthusiasm about her adventures in '90s dance music.

Nicki, let's talk first about your youth and how you discovered music.
  I was lucky that I grew up in a very happy and loving family environment. I am the youngest of four children. My first memory of growing up as far as the entertainment business was concerned was being six years old and listening on the radio to the chart rundown. I used to do that every week and sing along to all the songs on the survey. At one point, my godmother was walking by, observed me and said to my mum and dad, "She's going to be a singer when

she's older." It kind of stuck in my brain. I loved various singers from the olden days—the one I wanted to emulate was Lulu. She was my idol.

By the time I was 12, my older brother was part of a local band, and whenever he went to rehearsals, I would teach him harmonies to teach his bandmates. I always had a very good ear for harmonies. One week, when I was a bit older, he was headed out, and he said he was going to ask the guys in the band if they wanted a female vocalist. I kind of shrugged it off, and he said, "I'm talking about you." That was my first proper introduction to working professionally as "Nicola the singer." Weekends we'd play various places, some of them as far as two hours away. Sometimes it would be on a Sunday night, and we'd get back at 2:30 a.m., and I'd have to get up for school the next morning. It would be very tiring. I asked my mum if she was okay with me doing this, and I'll always remember that she said she was fine with it as long as it didn't interfere with my school work. I worked doubly hard at school, so that there was no dropping of standards.

I went to college and moved to London, and knew I had to find my way into music up here. I auditioned to sing at various places and eventually got onto a cabaret network. It escalated from there, really.

How did you come to be the vocalist of "Total Eclipse of the Heart"—the '90s dance reinvention of Bonnie Tyler's dramatic rock classic?
To start with, over the years I had been doing demo tracks for John Springate, the first producer and arranger of the dance version of "Total Eclipse of the Heart." The guys from a small record label called Energise had the idea for a dance version of the song. They approached John about doing it. They originally had another vocalist in mind, but they ditched her and asked John to find another singer. John phoned me up and told me about their plans. My first reaction was, "Oh no, you can't mess around with a classic like that." I wasn't that keen on it, but he played me a bit of the backing track on the phone, and I thought it actually might work. But I still wasn't sure my voice could manage it.

I went into the studio in 1993 and gave it a try, and my voice just sat right where I needed it to. We made a promotional 12-inch vinyl single of it, just to sell at gigs, really—pubs and clubs. Then in 1994, the guys from Energise and John knew someone who worked for Mike Stock and Matt Aitken—better known as members of the famous '80s production team of Stock Aitken Waterman. Mike now had his own production company, Love This Records, and he and Matt invited us all in to meet with them. I honestly thought they'd end up saying, "No thanks; we'll pass." They actually said they were interested and that they wanted to re-record my lead vocal. They ended up releasing the track in '94, and it peaked at the bottom end of the pop chart. That was that. But I was thrilled. I achieved a dream, and I'd worked with these music legends, and it was a great experience. And I just figured, "Okay, what's next?"

But, apparently, the buzz on the song would not die down, and the boys decided they were going to remix the song and put the slow start at the beginning back in. They planned to re-release it in January of '95 with two versions here in the UK (there was just one released later in the U.S. I believe). It just went mad! It went straight onto the charts at number 12 here, and up and up after. By the time it died down in the UK around June, we'd planned a trip to the United States and got a call from *Billboard* saying it had entered the charts there. By the end of my tour, it had reached number two on the American pop chart—ahead of even Michael and Janet Jackson!

Was it a challenge to forge your own identity with a song that was previously so closely identified with Bonnie Tyler? How did Mike and Matt guide you through the production of the track?

Because I'd already recorded it previously with the Energise guys, I kind of stuck to that direction. But Mike Stock was very particular in the studio about how he wants a song to sound—even a phrase within the song. If it wasn't what he wanted, you'd have to work with him to change it. He gave you very little leeway, but that was a good thing. What people may find surprising is that Mike was very big on diction. After a take, he would say to me something like, "Okay, you need to finish off that word," and things like that. I was surprised by that. But we didn't know each other well at the beginning, and they gave me a little bit of rope to adjust to their methods. We sort of discovered each other, who we were, through making "Total Eclipse," and that made working through the album *Secrets* less surprising.

For example, they discovered when I start a song, I like to begin quite small, so it can build. I change little nuances so the song can grow. It's a very old style of singing, traditional, but it's what I do. They allowed me to do that to a point. I like light and shade in a song and to start the verse by being very close to the microphone. Then you step back, especially for the bigger parts of the song. [*She laughs.*] I remember them often saying, "Can you step back a bit Nicki?" "Foghorn French" they jokingly called me. By and large, they let me sing in a way that was comfortable for me as well as them. It worked really well.

In regard to Bonnie Tyler, I don't remember them referencing her in any way. From the start, I knew I didn't have Bonnie's raucous voice, so I knew my version would be very different.

Did you find it intimidating in any way working with these producers, who had been such gargantuan hitmakers in the '80s?

Oh yes, I was extremely intimidated when I knew I was going to record in their studios. These guys were icons. But they make you feel relaxed very quickly, and after the first ten minutes or so, I realized they saw something in me that was worthwhile, so I had to show them that I was. I got over the nerves and told myself to just do what you do best and get on with it. They were very encouraging. Mike's very on-the-ball, standing by the mixing desk, telling the guys he wanted this, this and this. He makes notes on the lyrics where he wants certain things to happen. Then you had Matt [*she chuckles*], sort of leaning back on his chair, maybe doodling on a notepad or strumming on a guitar, doing his own thing.

They were keen to have success again, of course, but they were

Nicki French's cover version of "Total Eclipse of the Heart" became a monster hit in 1995, inspiring club goers to sing along as they filled dance floors worldwide (courtesy Nicki French).

still quite picky about who they worked with, and I think they were probably more relaxed than they had been in the '80s. They were doing what they wanted to do at their own pace. I think they were in control, sorting things out just between the two of them (without Pete Waterman) and without the demands of other labels. Mike was sort of the controlling one, though Matt was quite essential. They were very much a duo in terms of songwriting, just as in the '80s. (Pete Waterman was more the front man back then, selling the songs to the labels.) Matt would sit there sometimes very quietly, then suddenly make a comment that might change the whole direction of the project. Or you'd fall about laughing because he could also be a real joker. He was a bit more casual about things, and Mike was a bit more serious, but it was a positive way to work in their studio. I really loved to be there.

When I first heard the results of their work on "Total Eclipse," I was so excited. They just lifted the song so much, especially when they re-did it for the '95 version that became such a big hit. They completely transformed the song. I had been in Ireland when the song was released, and my manager was with me when we got the mid-week sales figures. I remember he got off the phone and turned to me and, somewhat stunned, said, "You're 14 in the mid-weeks." I said, "What? four-zero?" "No, no. One-four." I just burst into tears. We were performing with some other acts, and they all bought us drinks and were so excited for us. To be so high in the first week (and it went higher by the time Sunday came 'round).

Do you recall hearing "Total Eclipse" for the first time on the radio?

Oh, I do! There's a well-known DJ over here at a popular radio station (Capital Radio) who sent us a fax (remember faxes?), offering us congratulations and saying that he'd be able to now play our song. I was in a car being taken to do other interviews, and we asked the driver if he could turn to that DJ's station. Then we heard him play it, just at the end of the show. It was so exciting!

I also think being invited to *Top of the Pops* the first week of being on the charts; it was another major highlight. It's every child's dream to be on the show. I think every musician in the country was desperate to be on the program. I was married at the time, and my husband and I went into the studio. I recall that I was the only artist on the show that night to sing live. It was the most thrilling experience of my life at the time. I had spent the entire day drinking lots of coffee and rehearsing. Then I was at the BBC—*the* BBC, just amazing—and we did the show. As I came off the stage with all these people cheering, my manager said my cell phone was ringing and handed it to me. On the line was this dodgy old pub in London, not knowing where I was, asking if I was free on Saturday to do a gig for 50 quid cash. It was surreal. I was just on national TV, and they wanted me to do an hour show for 50 quid. It was hilarious. I was on 1500 quid for two or three songs by then! [*She laughs heartily.*]

My husband's brother took a bus to work following the telecast of *Top of the Pops* and overheard the conversation of two school kids who saw the show. They were chatting away, and they both agreed, "That Nicki French has a bit of a voice, hasn't she?" He wanted to lean over and say, "That's my sister-in-law!"

Are you able to describe your transition into virtually an overnight sensation?

Back then, the money suddenly went up and the gigs came quicker. One of the biggest changes was going from a 45-minute spot at pubs and clubs to really big clubs doing two or three songs maximum. I'd only just be getting into the set when I was finished. It was hard to get used to that because I have a strong work ethic, and the fact that two songs were considered fine was an adjustment for me. I noticed that most of these big venues were very surprised that I wanted to sing live, as well. So many artists just did track performances and mimed. I actually found it more difficult to mime.

Did you enjoy the experience of touring in the United States?

I had only visited America on a holiday once prior to the tour. Mike had contact with Critique/BMG Records in the U.S., who distributed the record there. They got the song on the Z100 station in New York. If you got played on Z100, you were set. From there, the song became a huge success in America. I did so many big outdoor summer shows and visits to other stations over the course of my visit there. I think I was number eight when I arrived. I literally went all over the country.

My first stop was in Louisiana—that was surreal, for all the wrong reasons. Our accommodations were over a truck stop, and the club was owned by a bloke with a name something like "Mister Big" that everyone was bowing down to. It was just a very strange experience, although the gig went just fine. Then we were whisked away to Buffalo, New York, then back down to Charleston, South Carolina—the geography, the route, was not planned very well. But it was fine, and I was living the dream. I was in this enthusiasm and energy bubble.

My biggest problem during the tour was trouble with my back due to a strain—bulging disc and such. I had to have quite a bit of therapy and was bed-ridden before the tour began. I remember I needed a wheelchair when I arrived at Boston's airport, and the label rep—I'm sure he must have been having a fit thinking, "Oh, God, she's supposed to be performing at discos!" But I was fine for all my performances.

One thing I can say about the U.S. was that the audiences were so positive and enthusiastic. I really loved that. I'm not just saying that—the U.S. was such an enthusiastic place, everywhere I went.

What does that do for you as an artist—seeing your audience respond so strongly to your music?

It's such a tonic. I remember being in Brazil performing around 1996. The huge crowd there—they didn't really know the words, the English—but they'd sing them in unison phonetically. It was wonderful and so heartfelt. I almost broke down watching it happen. That was also a moment where I felt like I'd really made it.

It's what you're there for. It's your role in life. When you get that positive reaction, there simply is nothing better. It can be an audience of eight or 80,000. If they are a good audience, a responsive audience, it's magical. I really mean that about the number of people. I've done gigs where there were less than 20 people out there. You go out thinking it's going to be soul-destroying. But because they are so into it, it suddenly doesn't matter. You can end up having a better time than if you've got 500 people in the room, and nobody pays the least bit of attention.

I remember a gig I did—I went out on stage (I don't think they even heard me announced), and I did a few numbers. The place was quite full and busy, and there was virtually no reaction to my performance. It was quite painful. They were very young people and had no interest in anything going on around them.

That could not have been a gay audience. The gay community is, largely, very supportive of heritage dance artists. Would you agree?

A large percentage of my work comes from the gay clubs here in the UK. When "Total Eclipse" came out, they kind of said, "She's ours!" because I had been performing for the community for a while. Back in the '90s, the mainstream clubs were keen to have you if your song was a hit on the charts. So while my song was hot, it was great. They weren't even that concerned with my voice—just that I had a current hit. The gay community tends to like a performer with a solid voice, a powerful voice, and I'm lucky that I do have that. They appreciate my work.

Did you experience what some might call the dark side of the music business or club life—the drug use that was quite common at the time?

I have never been into drugs at all. I never have, and I never want to. I love my glass of wine, but nothing beyond that. There were many times where I guess you would say I was in the vicinity of people either doing or offering drugs. You can tell how uncomfortable I am with the subject because I don't know anything about it. That was a dark side of the business. As far as the clubs would go, well, at certain times of the night you could see that people were just off their heads. That's the only way they could get through an all-nighter.

I can't even understand smoking. I was performing at a club with another pretty well-known singer, who was complaining that her throat was sore and bothering her. I gave her one of my throat tablets, and she thanked me. Then she pulled out a cigarette and started smoking. I just lost all sympathy. If you're going to be a singer—please don't smoke.

Please tell me a little about the album Secrets that followed in the wake of your debut hit.

We had started recording some of the tracks by the time I was touring, and Mike really wanted to get it completed with the U.S. success being so strong. With my back problems, I staggered into the studio to finish the work on it. Matt Aitken was great because he had also experienced back problems, and he and Mike were very accommodating. We got the album done quickly, but that began what you might call a bit of a downward slide. In the U.S., after "Total Eclipse," the next single was "Did You Ever Really Love Me?" Mike thought Critique was going to pay all the promotion costs, and Critique believed it was up to Mike to pay. So nobody paid anything. This caused the single to kind of disappear, which was a shame.

In the aftermath of your success, was there a great deal of pressure to have another hit or to release more songs in the vein of "Total Eclipse of the Heart"?

To be perfectly honest, there *was* pressure. You always want to pick the right material. I might have chosen a different song to be the second single. Over in the UK, what tended to work was to release a ballad after a dance track. That kind of cements you as a credible vocalist and keeps you from being associated with just one genre. In the States, I thought "Forever and a Day" might have worked better as a second single. Although I'd been working as a singer for a while by then, I really didn't know how the recording industry worked. So I was happy to leave things in the hands of Mike and Matt. They also remixed "Did You Ever Really Love Me?" and changed its flavor, which I felt unsure about. I felt the version from the album worked really well. They made it sort of—I don't know—it just didn't have the same instant effect. Perhaps it didn't matter because without the money for promotion being settled, nothing we released was going to go anywhere. It's a shame because, to this day, "Did You Ever" is still the best song I have ever had the honor of recording. It's funny because Mike says he wrote that song in 15 minutes. [*She lets out a hearty laugh.*]

The second single in the UK was "For All We Know," which was released as a tribute to the Carpenters. People liked it, but there was a problem with the barcode on the physical single. It should have registered the artist, the name, etc., but came up as "unknown–CD sale." So we lost loads of chart points because of that. I think it made it to number 41 on the charts here, and it disappeared. Radio was in charge, and by the time the third UK single arrived ("Is There Anybody Out There?"), well, things were challenging. Mike had an independent label and didn't have big money to throw at the radio stations. So each single got a little bit more lost each time. I didn't have the best of luck with any single releases after "Total Eclipse."

I never really looked at making a lot of money from my records. I never really have. I mean, look at "Total Eclipse." It sold something like 5.5 million around the world, but I didn't get much at all because it's just the way the business worked—you'd always lose a lot of the money you thought you would make. I always worked on the premise that my money comes from live shows. Eventually, it was time to discuss a new contract with Mike and Matt, but we realized it wasn't going to work for either side, and we parted ways. Interestingly enough, we started working together again about two or three years ago, Mike and I, which has been really great.

You've also now been working in theater, singing and acting. Does that bring you a different sense of satisfaction than singing dance music?

Yes, I must say it's very different. You're doing the same thing, night after night, but each time with a different audience. So, it's never the same experience twice, and it's really quite thrilling. There's something about being backstage in a theater that I've always gotten that thrill from. There's no feeling like it. I originally wanted to do musical theater exclusively. I moved off the path when I started doing the dance-pop music. An unfortunate reality of aging in the pop and dance music world is that generally the gigs eventually get quieter. And I don't think many people will want to be seeing me try to jump around on stage in my 70s singing "Total Eclipse." So I decided to try and move into theater a bit more. I've managed to be pretty successful with it, and I have a ball. One gig in a night club pays me probably double what I get to perform in these productions for a week, and yet there's just this satisfaction from it that is so wonderful.

That rather nicely brings us to the topic of so-called middle age. How do you view yourself at this stage of life and the music business in the current day?

It's true—the mainstream is into youth—young, vibrant looks. Here's a weird little known dream of mine. Musical theater was one aspiration I've had, but I also wanted to be a newscaster, believe it or not. I love news. Being a news presenter would be so great. But they generally want young, pretty reporters with tiny figures—the right side of 25. It galls me at times, but then I say, "Hey, c'est la vie."

For a while in the music business, longevity was viewed as a great thing, something cool. By the '90s, it was starting to be a bit more image and youth led. Then this sort of sense of ageism took hold. I just think it's so different now. People don't seem to be bothered whether a young person can or can't sing or how much work has been done in the studio to make them sound better. They are focused on the image. Singers mime and people are screaming for them. That really upsets me. But it's the change that's happened, and performers like myself have to cope with it and manage, don't they?

It's interesting to observe some of the changes that have occurred in the music business. I'm well aware that it's very difficult to make money selling digital music by streaming or on iTunes. Mike Stock was very reluctant to release our new song, "This Love," on iTunes, saying once we did, we'd never make any money (because iTunes takes such a huge portion of your sales). But there's something else that's happened, too. People download the track and just dismiss it after a few days. There's a lack of concentration in regard to music. In the '90s, you devoted yourself to going out and buying a CD by an artist. You wanted to read the liner notes and hear all the tracks, 10 or 12 songs. That's vanished.

"It can be an audience of eight or 80,000. If they are a good audience, a responsive audience, it's magical," says singer Nicki French, who continues to perform her hits and record in the present day (courtesy Nicki French).

In your mind, what's been the value of dance music to pop culture over the past few decades?

Oh, goodness. For starters, you'd hear a track like Chaka Khan's "I'm Every Woman," and you'd have to get up and move. People who are rooted to their seats suddenly are inspired to get up and dance. Dance music has that kind of power—it gives you a sense of freedom. How can I explain it? I believe it has an artistry that is under-appreciated. It has so much variety. There are so many forms, like my "poppier" brand of dance music or the heavier styles. Dance music offers something for everyone, and that feel-good factor has made it invaluable in society. When I see people singing and dancing to my music, I just love it, and I know they do too. You know it's something special when people start cheering seconds after just the first beats of a song start!

Lightning Round with Nicki

Cats or dogs?

Dogs. Always dogs.

Music or lyrics?

[*She gasps.*] If I had to pick one? Oooh—I can't choose! I love gorgeous chords, but I am very much a lyrics person. I'll choose lyrics, but—ohhh—that's so hard!

Radio edits or extended versions?

Here's a surprise for you, being a dance artist—radio edits.

Diana Ross or Donna Summer?

[*Another gasp.*] I own more albums by Ms. Ross than Donna, but I do love Donna's stuff. "Last Dance" is a favorite, but I also recently recorded my own version of "The Boss." I'll pick Diana Ross.

Five good friends or one best friend?
I'm lucky that I have a few amazing friends, so I must pick five good friends.

Never use the Internet or never watch TV again?
Oh, these questions are so hard! I am a TV addict, but now I can't disconnect from the Internet. Wow! Never watch TV again because I'll just find it all on the computer, won't I?

Saver or spender?
Saver. I can't tell you how often I tell myself I should go out and have a splurge, but I end up looking for the best investment for my money instead. "Just spend it," I tell myself. But, no, I'm a saver.

Nestor Haddaway, also known as Haddaway
"What Is Love" (1992)

> "It was shocking—the size of show business in the U.S. It was like the difference between visiting the top of the Empire State Building and going on a Ferris wheel at a county fair."—Nestor Haddaway

Before he gained global fame, he was known as Dr. Nestor Haddaway, a man with a PhD in political science listed among the highlights of his résumé. Dropping the formalities, he plunged into dance-pop music, became known simply as Haddaway and unleashed his monumental 1992 debut single "What Is Love" upon the world. To this day, it has remained one of the most popular dance songs to ever come out of the era. Working with his musical comrade at the time, Alex Strasser (billed as Alex Trime on his recorded work with Haddaway), and German producers Tony Hendrik and Karin Hartmann, Haddaway's "What Is Love" topped the charts across Europe (while just narrowly missing the Top 10 in the United States). The song exemplified the commercial power of the Eurodance style and synth-pop movement that was sweeping the world during this period. The track (with its pounding beat and easy to sing lyrics) was given a second lease on life in America thanks to its prominent inclusion in a Saturday Night Live *TV sketch and in the film* A Night at the Roxbury *near the decade's end.*

Though often branded a one-hit-wonder in the U.S., Haddaway's career remained a solid one in Europe, Asia, South America and Eastern bloc countries throughout the '90s. Among his most popular follow-up dance singles were "Life" (1993), "Rock My Heart" in 1994, "Fly Away" (1995) and "Who Do You Love" in 1998. In more recent years, he teamed up with fellow '90s stalwart Dr. Alban for the Euro-house novelty "I Love the 90's" and the Mad Stuntman for "Up and Up." Haddaway still maintains what seems like a non-stop touring schedule today.

Enjoying a rare late summer break from his concerts, the artist speaks from his home in Austria with great candor, humility and a refreshing sense of humor as he reflects on his music career.

Please tell me a little about your early years, Nestor.

My bloodline is Trinidadian and Dutch. My father was a marine biologist, constantly on the move. My mother didn't play a great role in my life, and my father was the most important thing. I don't usually get too personal with discussions about my private life, but it's okay

The deceptively calm image on the jacket of the BMG/Coconut/Arista single "What Is Love" gave little indication of the high energy contained in Haddaway's smash debut recording (author's collection).

to say that. I grew up listening to Foreigner, Led Zeppelin, Journey, Steve Perry and all this amazing, emotional rock and pop music. Later, I made a little money in the military. If you were the type of person who was unsure what you wanted to do in the future, the navy was the ticket to help you decide. You won't see my military service mentioned [in my bios] anywhere. It was kept away from the press because some people viewed it as a bad thing. But I'll tell you it was an excellent career move because I learned so many things that I'd never have experienced in a nine to five job, and it was very good for me. But after about four and half or five years, I discovered being "the robot," if you will, wasn't something I was comfortable with any longer. It just wasn't right for me to continue. I finished my higher education in the Washington, D.C.–Bethesda (Maryland) area.

I found I really enjoyed being in the United States, but I discovered that being in Europe was more my tempo—more me. I just couldn't fully identify myself in the U.S. I think it was maybe because of my multi-cultural background. Thinking of this reminds me how in the U.S., for example, if you were a black singer, you had to be R&B or hip-hop—something other than mainstream. No one really saw you as a pop artist. That wasn't as true in Europe.

There was a German band in the '70s called Kraftwerk, Howard Jones in the '80s and Thomas Dolby also struck a chord with me. I was a fan of the techno sound that was being born early in the '90s. I was completely blown away by these sounds. I just decided to take what I could from all this music I enjoyed and tried to put it into music of my own. I tried to find something that was mine.

How did you get your professional start in the German music scene?
After banging on a lot of doors and eventually meeting the right people (like Tina Turner's husband, Erwin Bach, who was directing EMI in Cologne, Germany) and a few other German producers, things started happening. It was a period where people were there for you and very hungry to make something happen. You had every bloody international band coming there. Donna Summer even got started there in the '70s. It was truly the place where a music movement was happening. It wasn't like today. Today, the German music industry is, unfortunately, dead, and it doesn't really influence the international market anymore. But back then it was amazing. I started doing so many things—productions and remixes—together with Luca Anzilotti and Michael Münzing, the original producers of Snap! We were all in a clique, you might say, and very good friends. We learned from each other what you could do. Michael was a hardcore businessman, and I saw myself to be exactly that way. I felt like more of a businessman than a musician. But I had to have something that I could truly feel was mine (in a creative sense). I had made enough money with Michael and Luca to go ahead and start looking at doing my own thing.

Unfortunately, as my luck would have it, for a time I just kept being asked to team up with the wrong people—people who just gave me a stomach ache. I turned down about the first five contracts offered to me. I was doing well in the fashion industry. I was doing a bit of dancing and also playing some football for the Cologne Crocodiles. I was a good looking boy, you know—the girls loved me, and the fashion companies loved me. Also, very important at that time, the gay community was really growing. So you couldn't be homophobic and run away from it. All this is to say that it was crazy at the time—you had to have a flair for fashion, fresh new music, an open mind and a good voice (and a brain to go with it). You also needed the tenacity to push and make it all come together.

With its distinctive a cappella opening, "What Is Love" was an instantly recognizable monster of a song that reached the number one spot in numerous countries and number two in the UK and Germany. Some reports indicate the single had sold close to three million copies within two years or so of its first release. What are your memories of making this iconic track?
I was with my [music] partner, Alex Strasser, and we were in a little studio owned by Germany's Coconut Records. Tony Hendrik and his wife and partner, Karin Hartmann [both producers of the popular '80s German group Bad Boys Blue and Chyp-notic in the '90s], came to us with a song they had written that was almost like the familiar "What Is Love," except it sounded more like the Yardbirds. [*He laughs.*] They wanted me to try singing it like Joe Cocker. Well, I love Joe Cocker, but I'm *no* Joe Cocker. I stood my ground, and I told them that Alex and I had an idea of how we could do it. They let me try it our way. That became the first creation of "What Is Love."

I have to admit, Tony was a very good producer (he and Karin produced the track using the names Dee Dee Halligan and Junior Torello). We could have settled for our version in the beginning, and it still would have been a good song, but Tony locked himself in the studio, and eight or nine days later [he came out with] the song you know today. We all collaborated with great ideas, but I have to give "What Is Love" to Tony. He was amazing. To this day, we still get along well.

"What Is Love" is really a signature sound of the '90s. Why do you think it had such strong appeal on a worldwide level?

Its simplicity. I think we kept it light and didn't try to act like I was the greatest singer and the song was all that. You have melody occurring in all aspects of the song, the rhythmic verse, the "whoa-whoa" sound in the lyrics. It's simple, but it works. What made the Beatles' "She Loves You" work? [*Haddaway sings a few seconds of the Beatles' hook.*] Or a disco song like John Paul Young's "Love Is in the Air"? [*He sings that song, too.*] The melodies made you happy. I wanted to keep "What Is Love" happy. You know, this world is so full of trouble today, and people just want to be happy. We felt the same way back then.

How did it feel to see your audiences getting so into this song?

Very, very good. Look, I don't do drugs; I don't do alcohol. I don't need any of these stimulants. But I am like a sponge soaking up the energy you get from an audience that is clearly enjoying your music. I soak it all up, and then I squeeze it and give it all back. That's the best thing you can really do. I left Copenhagen yesterday after doing a '90s festival for an audience of something like 20,000 people. The anthem of the festival was "What Is Love." I could have sung the track five times—they do not let me go. That feeling—it's so good for you. It's a wonderful thing when they scream for more. I'm an adrenaline junkie when it comes to that.

You mentioned that you didn't do drugs, but it appears recreational use of various substances was a significant part of the club scene and music industry during the era.

I actually think the '90s was the beginning of the cleaning up of the drug influence in the music industry. But let's stick to the world of alcohol. It's still there in that a lot of artists still need to whet their palate before they go on stage. In the past—I've seen it myself—there were artists who could kill two bottles of Grey Goose before and after the show.

I wasn't an angel, but my biggest vice was beautiful women. Oh my God—it was a disease. I had about three years where I was hopelessly drawn to beautiful women until I discovered something. It may sound like a sad generalization, and I don't wish to insult women (because they are the greatest creatures that ever walked the earth), but until you find that partner you can trust—well, I think you understand what I mean. I was a juvenile until I was about 33 or 34, if you understand what I'm saying. From 27 to 32, man, a beautiful body and a lovely face was—oh my God—I was in *serious* trouble. That was my kryptonite. [*Haddaway laughs heartily.*] I was like a kid in kindergarten with unlimited piles of Playdough in front of me. I'm being very honest.

How would you describe your relationship with the record labels at the time?

Coming to America with the song and being around Clive Davis and all the rest at Arista Records who really pushed for us was amazing. Unfortunately, they didn't stick to their guns with the rest of the singles. I was very drawn to Europe and the world territories, countries such as Russia and the Ukraine—very important big new markets at the time. Many shied away from them, but I knew there was a great deal of money to be earned in these areas. Follow-up songs like "Life," "Rock My Heart," "What About Me," "Who Do You Love"—

most westerners don't know about these tracks. They all went to the top of the charts in these other areas. But you must understand that these countries aren't reflected on *Billboard*. "Life" was big in Europe, but because it was not pushed in the U.S. by Arista, it had very limited success there (it only made it to about number 41 on the *Billboard* pop chart).

Let's look at "You're Taking My Heart" and "Who Do You Love." The beautiful ladies of Moscow and Tel-Aviv, places like that, they love those songs because their radio bombarded them with them. These areas followed up Haddaway very well. The European-American collaboration didn't really believe in these songs—I have no idea why. But they dropped the ball with them.

But during those peak years, Arista (I should say BMG/Arista/Ariola), Clive Davis and his boys treated me extremely well. It was the largest team I've ever seen in my life. In 1994–95, Annie Lennox and myself were Arista's number one European artists. For North America, Toni Braxton and Whitney Houston were their [domestic priorities]. [*He starts laughing.*] I remember Whitney Houston showing up at an event that I was also performing at, and she would arrive with a posse of 50 or 60 people, and we would show up with maybe four or five people.

Here we were—the European side of things—in this massive American entertainment machine. It was shocking—the size of show business in the U.S. It was like the difference between visiting the top of the Empire State Building and going on a Ferris wheel at a county fair.

But that whole excitement—by the end of the '90s, these things were eroding because there were new sounds and new artists in the air.

It must have been a bit frustrating to have been unable to further penetrate the U.S. market after "What Is Love."

I've played concerts in more than 83 countries around the world. The U.S. market, because of publishing, has been a great thing. But for live audiences, the U.S. has, unfortunately, been one of my lesser markets. I toured in the U.S. for maybe four years, but that was back in the '90s. I have not been back since. I have had a few offers, but I will be honest, the pay is just too little. However, the rest of the world, from Chile to Columbia, from Australia to Norway, I still do 130 to 230 concerts every year.

The U.S. immediately put me on that one-hit wonder list because they didn't know the rest of my songs. I can't blame them. Remember when we thought the planet was flat or the sun rotated around the earth? When you're a big market like the United States, you're kind of acting like that. There are many international artists who deserve a lot of credit. But for them to make it in the U.S. market, they need major millions. You need that constant marketing push and a never-ending campaign that costs millions annually. Your music can be good, that's fine, but your campaign needs to be *way* better. I think we spent maybe just half a million promoting "What Is Love" during the first three years. So I guess I got lucky.

How much did "What is Love" change your life?

The first few years I couldn't go anywhere without being spotted (or even harassed). I was on TV a lot, billboards, everywhere. There are still countries where I can't even go for a walk without being recognized (like Russia, the Eastern bloc countries). So with the success, I had to sacrifice some freedom. You also lose friends that you don't have time for. If they were true friends, they were still around; if they were kind of superficial, you lost them.

You gave up a lot of things and realized you had to handle things in certain ways. In some countries, for example, it was best to be very close to an international airport so you could immediately just leave after the event.

You also had to deal with people literally camping outside your door. I had a long talk with Jon Bon Jovi about it, and I was complaining about dealing with it for three years. [*He laughs.*] "Three years?" Bon Jovi smiled. "I've been dealing with it for 20."

Speaking of camping outside your door, you had a great deal of sex appeal as a '90s pop star, and your promotional images and videos appeared to take advantage of that.

[*Haddaway smiles.*] Yes, well, I was always getting propositions. My ex-wife was *not* fond of that. She was always like, "What are you looking at that bitch for!" or asking me why I was taking pictures with another beautiful woman. I was like, "Stop it. This is my job." It wasn't irritating because I knew the rules of the game. But having a partner and a private life made it difficult.

Then I had this other problem that was really weird. Many people thought I might be gay because I was dressed well and had a good body. I was like, "I'm not homophobic, but I'm not gay." At the end of the day, I didn't care who bought my music, and I enjoyed gay audiences very much. I don't care how anyone swings their hammer. It's their hammer and their business.

"What Is Love" attained some cult status by being featured in the "Roxbury Guys" sketch on NBC-TV's Saturday Night Live, featuring Chris Kattan and Will Ferrell, and in their 1998 feature film, A Night at the Roxbury. Does something like that diminish the integrity of the song in any way or is it just a check mark in the plus column?

Sometimes you just have to be thankful that you get advertising of any kind. No matter if it's a joke, or a novelty, or a one-off, you just have to be thankful. This industry is ridiculously hard. In Europe, I have about seven or eight singles that the crowd will start singing whether I open my mouth or not. But it's nice to have fans in the U.S., even if it's because they heard "What Is Love" on a funny TV show or in a comedy movie. Some of those fans may have explored my other music because of it. You must accept the way this industry is. You're a hot potato for three, four, five, six years, if you're lucky, and then someone decides this potato is cold. You are suddenly in a wasteland. There are so many artists, bands and solo artists, and you expect them to have incredible longevity, but it just doesn't happen. So, something like my song appearing in a film, if it extends the life of it and me as an artist, it's a blessing.

Following such a successful debut, you must have experienced a lot of pressure to keep the momentum going.

The first three years after "What Is Love," I put that pressure on myself. That pressure was so bad that my marriage, my private life at the time, went to shit. About 1999, I put myself into a divorce, and I started to rethink things. I ran away basically—I took about half a year off. I came back wanting to make music again, enjoying what I did. Since then, I truly enjoy what I do. Before that, I was making it a job. I was putting myself under so much pressure because of the success with "What Is Love." Everyone was looking at me for another album and another release. I'd say, "Yeah, but there's lots of stuff [to still be heard] on the first album." They'd say, "Yeah, yeah, but when's the *next* one coming? It's gonna be greater than 'What Is Love'!" Hello? Calm down. It's a stupid cycle, but that's just the way it was.

You shared the stage with so many great stars of the era. Any interesting memories of working with those people?

There are so many. Annie Lennox, the Eurythmics—she is truly one of my favorite world artists. She is really just the best. In the '90s, I was on the stage with Justin Timberlake and with Backstreet Boys and NSYNC. We were in so many events together. Even Will Smith and Mark Wahlberg. We did so many events around 1993 through '95, hanging out backstage, you know? Oh, Bonnie Tyler—the list goes on and on. It was just madness!

I remember Robbie Williams throwing temper tantrums backstage. I remember upcoming stars like Lenny Kravitz—he'd just appear—his godliness—and just walk past us, not saying anything to any of us. We were like the little un-popped kernels at the bottom of the bucket, and he was the big, tasty popped popcorn at the top. [*Haddaway laughs vigorously.*] And Whitney Houston. I'm sorry, but the moment the cameras went away, she was *not* your friend. Ouch! [*He laughs again.*]

It was a good time, mostly, and I never looked at other artists in the '90s as rivals. I did something different, and so did they. I always appreciated their strengths. The only time I remember feeling a little bit of envy was around the time of Whitney Houston's *The Bodyguard* soundtrack. "What Is Love" was number two in Germany, and she was number one. For 26 weeks I was number two [*another hearty laugh*], and she spent 28 weeks at number one. I just wanted one week at number one in the bloody country where it all started, but, unfortunately, I never got it. I have no animosity or regrets, truly, but it was, at the time, like—"Can't you just slide over for a minute and let me be number one? Please?"

You've lived with "What Is Love" for nearly a quarter century. Is it a blessing or a curse?

"What Is Love" is a blessing, definitely, and I'll explain why. Without this song I'd have ended up as maybe a local artist just doing his little local thing. Or I might have pursued political science, doing some kind of judicial work. To be realistic, I am extremely thankful for it.

It's a challenging time not only for heritage artists to create new music, but all artists. The industry has undergone massive changes and artists are dealing with the monetization challenges of free downloading and streaming. How do you view all this turmoil?

I think that's it, right there—that people often can get and expect their music for free. To me, it's one of the greatest insults to artists around the world who try to put their product out there. It's lovely for young people who do their thing on the Internet and hope that people will just download their music—hope that someone will discover them. But for the established artist that's already there, it's a bad situation that's developed. It's also quite sad that vocalists have been relegated to "featuring" status on the recordings of DJs and that they get a very small piece of the pie. I'm so glad I'm fully in control of my work.

Every year or two I turn out a new track or album. In 2013, I did a project with the Mad Stuntman [of "I Like To Move It" fame] called "Up and Up." I've always tried my best to serve the market, but I must admit, from 2007 until today, I've kind of serve my own ego. I haven't really cared what the market wants. [*Haddaway chuckles.*] I make music to please myself now.

When I go into the studio, I like simplicity—a good beat, a good melody, a good hook line. Sometimes I am more emotional and want to make something for the heart. But you can't always write a song like "The Greatest Love of All" or "The Rose." My fans, they want to shake their asses and have a good time. They don't want to hear a ballad from me. You're caught between a rock and a hard place.

What changes have you observed in yourself as you travel through this period of so-called middle age.

At this point, life makes more sense than it did before to me. [As you mature], you're more responsible in a social manner. You care about your community, the young people that will follow you, social issues, things that you didn't tend to pay as much attention to when you were younger. You tend to feel like you want to leave not only a legacy of success, but also you are aware of something more than your own pockets. That's how I feel today.

I did a TV show not long ago called *Hit Me, Baby, One More Time* (I think I was taping with the Rembrandts and Men at Work possibly; I'm not sure). But we were having a deep conversation about this topic backstage. It's funny; these bands meant a lot to me in the '80s and '90s. Bands like these made such inroads into pop culture, and you can't brush that off. Look, I don't want to insult today's music, but it's forgotten so quickly. Bands of the '70s, '80s and '90s—they're like gods and seem to be here forever. You remember what you were doing when you heard their songs for the first time.

It gets me feeling quite sad about the European music market today (the Americans have a bit more electrical current, so-to-speak, behind their music). In the last 12 to 15 years, it just feels like Europe took their foot off the gas.

But back to middle age, or shall I say becoming "a cultured one"—it doesn't disturb me. We must understand the basic fact of life—one day you must die. People always say, "You only live once." No, you only *die* once. And when we finally comprehend that, we start to live better. Many people in my business use Botox, hair dyes, blah, blah, blah. I just go with the flow. I'll bloody well just shave my head and partake in a bit more sports to trim my belly and keep moving so that I remain stage presentable—or I'll just get off the stage and stop. Aging is a natural thing.

I'm going to keep on doing what I do. I have two very sexy girls dancing and a lovely singer on stage with me in my shows, and we have a lot of fun. I'm just so bloody happy that the machine for "What Is Love" is still turning so well. I'm a very optimistic individual, and I have a lot of energy. I don't see that changing anytime soon.

Can you explain the power of dance music?

You truly understand the power of dance music when you go to a club or a festival and everyone is jumping up and down, waving their arms and dancing. There's usually no aggression, and everyone is celebrating together, brought together by this music. It's an amazing thing. To know that you are one of the key figures bringing these sounds to them, as I have—that's really incredible.

Picture this: you've pulled up next to someone on the highway, and they're blasting a dance tune from their car. It's like they are losing their minds as you watch them sing and shake. You can tell they want to jump out of the car. *That's dance music!* I love that feeling it creates—it's magic.

Lightning Round with Haddaway

Diana Ross or Beyoncé?

That's unfair! I can't pick between them. I love them both. There wouldn't be a Beyoncé without Diana, but no, I'm sorry, I can't pick one. I must take both.

"At this point, life makes more sense than it did before to me," says Haddaway today (courtesy Haddaway).

Giorgio Moroder or Nile Rodgers?
   Nile Rodgers.

'70s or '80s?
   Oh no, that's unfair too! I am not going to pick between them. From 1975 through 1985, it was the greatest period in music—ever!

Applause or record sales?
   Record sales, please. Oh, record sales, *pl-e-e-e-ase*! You gotta sell some of the damn things for them to love 'ya!

Five good friends or one best friend?
   Definitely one best friend; the closer the better.

Tight fitting or loose and breezy?
   [*He laughs.*] I'm all about tight. I don't do loose and breezy very well.

The chase or the conquest?
   The chase is much more interesting. The conquest—game over.

Famous but poor or rich but unknown?
   [*He laughs again.*] That's funny, too. It depends on your ego. I'd rather be rich and unknown.

Sten Hallström, also known as StoneBridge, DJ, Producer, Remixer
"Show Me Love" (Robin S, 1992)

"...you can't go through the whole process and be intimidated by the artist or their fame. You take on the remix because you think you can do something with it—and then you don't have to worry."—Sten Hallström

Sten Hallström launched his professional career as a DJ/production maestro working with Sweden's SweMix team in the late '80s. As an independent artist called Stone Bridge (two words), his name first appeared on the 12-inch single "Spank Beats" in 1987. Throughout the '90s and beyond, StoneBridge (one word) ranked among the world's most in-demand remixers, producers and DJs, standing beside the likes of such greats as David Morales, Tony Moran, Junior Vasquez and Roger Sanchez.

StoneBridge's remixes helped take some of the planet's biggest international artists to the top of the charts, including the Eurythmics ("Here Comes the Rain Again"), Robin S ("Show Me Love"), Shaggy ("Boombastic"), Britney Spears ("Gimme More"), Cher ("You Haven't Seen the Last of Me"), Debbie Harry ("Two Times Blue"), Lily Allen ("The Fear") and Taio Cruz ("Dynamite"). He's also produced numerous crossover hits under his own StoneBridge moniker, including "Put 'Em High" and "Take Me Away" (featuring Therese), both top singles on the UK pop chart in 2004 and '05. StoneBridge enjoyed big club hits most recently with "Believe It" in 2015 and a pulsating number one smash update of "Put 'Em High" during the summer of 2016.

From his home in Stockholm, Hallström speaks about his life and success with, ironically, the same kind of fast-paced rhythm found in many of his productions. Swirling in the deep well of his energized personality is a tendency to be quite candid. He is, at other times, a man with a great deal of gentleness in his observations, as he warmly discusses his gift for musical reinvention in a demanding business environment.

Sten, please tell me about growing up in Sweden and your introduction to music.

I was born in the early '60s. Sweden was not affected by World War II, and by the '60s the country was making shitloads of money, and the middle class was enormous. This is like a cliché, but I grew up in a musical home. My dad was playing the piano for fun—these kind of burlesque tunes—and he would invent his own lyrics. My family and I would gather around and join in. My parents got divorced sometime later, and my father started seeing a woman who was a bit younger. She was really into the Rolling Stones and the Monkees, so my first impressions of music were the pop and rock sounds of the late '60s and early '70s. I remember the covers of those albums—there was a lot of flower power and LSD influence in the artwork. The first seven-inch vinyl record I ever bought was "Tumbling Dice" by the Rolling Stones. I also was into the David Bowie *Ziggy Stardust* album—I got it from a cousin who said I needed to listen to it—"It's the future." The production, chords and depth really made an impression on me. I was really into those rich chords and never favored minimal beats. You can hear that in my dance productions—I love that big chord flavor.

New York became the home of disco. I became a disco boy and was lucky enough to be in the clubs when the Chic songs were first played, "Ain't No Stoppin' Us Now" by McFadden & Whitehead, all of those hits. I loved the strings of Nile Rodgers and all that stuff. Music education in Sweden was free, and my dad forced me to learn the clarinet. I tried it for one term, gave up, and then I swapped to a guitar. Most parents also bought their kids computers. I remember having the Sinclair ZX81, or something like that. You spent a day building code for it, and then it calculated 10 times 10—amazing. [*Sten laughs.*]

Swedish dance music producer, DJ and remixer Sten Hallström, better known as StoneBridge, is seen in his studio during the early years of his career (courtesy Sten Hallström).

Atari started coming out with sequencer programs. Avicii probably started when he was seven years old with an Atari, creating simple melodies. So our musical educations and early introductions to computers helped make creating music second nature. I had been playing in crumby bands, playing in people's basements and things like that. I played rhythm guitar, but I was bored and left. I learned the piano, keyboards, how to use synths, and I bought a lot of 12-inch vinyl.

Here's the defining moment—my sister's graduation party in 1983. My dad looks at the budget, and he sees DJ $50. He says, "No, no, no. Stone, you're playing." I never played records for people in my life, but I had plenty of them. I took the job really seriously. I called a friend, who actually was a DJ, and he had a Technics turntable I could use. I had to buy the other one. Then I borrowed a mixer. I did the party, and it was so much fun. I ended up doing about 30 other graduation gigs as a result. After that, I was hooked.

[My friend and I] started a club. We knocked on the door of this restaurant in central Stockholm and told the chef who answered, all covered in sauce and dirty looking, that we wanted to open a disco there. He asked us if we knew anything about running a club, and we said we knew everything, lying of course. We opened a club called Fellini. I even wrote to the famous director asking permission to use his name. I got a handwritten letter back saying it would be an honor. Miraculously, we kept that club going for three years.

You helped launch the SweMix production and remix house in your country during the late '80s. What were those days like?

I started to meet a lot of DJs, mostly at record shops, so we set up this DJ company called SweMix. I had some basic equipment, and a bunch of friends pulled their stuff in, and we started doing remixes, usually reel-to-reel, editing tracks, and adding samples. A lot of rappers started coming to us. We didn't need to write anything. They'd record a rap, and you'd have a little hook in the chorus, and that was it. One of them was Dr. Alban, a dentist from Nigeria. He had a song called "Hello Afrika," and I remember saying, "That track is the worst piece of shit I've ever heard, and it's not coming out on our label." Well, Dr. Alban ended up licensing it to another label, and it became a massive smash. A corporate guy came in and started to run our label. We took the "Hello Afrika" song back and mixed it, and we made so much money out of that. It paid to upgrade the studio. I wasn't involved with the Dr. Alban track or the album because I still thought it was shit, but I wasn't about to say no to the money. My friend Denniz PoP [aka Dag Krister Volle] produced it, and he went on to produce NSYNC and Backstreet Boys.

We ended up splitting up. He went pop, and I remained house music. It was always a fight. He thought anything that didn't have potential to be a pop hit was completely useless, but I thought some tracks were just great music anyway. But if it wasn't charting, he was like, forget it. So we couldn't work together anymore. In the mid-'90s, I set up my own company called StoneBridge Productions.

Why the name StoneBridge?

Sten means stone in English. Bridge refers to a mixing tool we used to use, and when I put them together—StoneBridge—ah, I knew I had it.

Robin S's debut release, "Show Me Love," which eventually became a '90s classic, had been pretty much languishing at a UK label until your remix helped thrust it into the spotlight. Do you recall how the project fell into your hands?

The Robin S remix I did is an interesting story. I had licensed tracks to this English label, Champion Records. We had moderate success on a club level. I asked them if they had any old shit in the basement that I could remix. They said, "We do, actually." They had this track called "Show Me Love" by Robin Stone. I thought with the name Stone and StoneBridge, it was meant to happen. "Hell," I said, "send me that tape!" I still have it. It was produced by the guys who did Jocelyn Brown's massive hit "Somebody Else's Guy." "Show Me Love" was like that song—a New York boogie type of thing. So I did a mix with my classic bass line sound, but using the preset "Pick Bass" on an M1 keyboard.

The UK guys didn't really like it, and I got really offended and angry. I had four hours before going to a gig on a Saturday night in 1992, and went back in to try again. I changed the bass sound to Organ Two, the next preset on the M1. I liked the sound—"That's hooky, man! That's a record!" I thought. It was just one of those amazing moments when I heard it. I added two chords in the chorus, I took a little cowbell loop from a David Morales dub, and the last thing I added was that "dah-duna-duna" sound—a distortion from a Yamaha keyboard. I mixed it all down, and sent it off to the guys. I had to re-edit it a few times. Then I didn't hear anything for a while. Sometime later, I got a fax from DJ Joey Negro saying, "Stone, your record is like the biggest thing in London." I didn't know which one, because I had made quite a few. "You know, that Robin S thing," he said.

In May of '93, I visited London and watched *Top of the Pops* on TV (on a Thursday I think it was). I see Robin S performing the thing, and it was Top Five UK pop. What? I called the label and asked why they didn't tell me it was a hit. "We didn't want your remix fee to go up," they said. [*He laughs.*] They kept me in the dark for like eight months while this song was getting really huge.

Then it was released in the U.S. in '94. It was unique there because it hit the Top 10 *Billboard* pop chart *and* the R&B chart, which was unusual. The phone didn't stop ringing after that. It was mad. I got offered some crazy projects after that, remixes back-to-back for at least four years at something like $25,000 a pop. I was, "Oh yeah! This is the life!"

Would you give us an idea of what your particular remix process involved?

The process in the '90s was—and technology has made it so much easier now—we worked with two-inch tape (a 24-track tape). So we got kick drums, snare and everything lined up. We worked with the original track and the elements from it that we liked and would program our own drums. Today, it's so much easier to grab parts of the original song and do something creative. I analyzed the records I worked on—was there a big moment in it, something I could turn into the "event," so-to-speak, of the club mix? Take Sia's "The Girl You Lost to Cocaine" in 2007. There's this massive orchestral vibe going on with classic piano in the original version. I thought that had to be part of my mix. I think that's the key to my process, and I still use it today. Because I'm a writer and a producer as well, I'm not like a DJ just mixing loops. I understand the songs.

Was there ever any hesitation on your part to take on a project? Did you ever receive resistance from an artist when you delivered your mix?

I don't take on everything that comes my way. For example, I said no to [Youssou N'Dour and] Neneh Cherry's "7 Seconds" in 1994. I didn't get the African chanting thing at all, and it was really slow. Well, I regretted that decision, as it was a huge hit. For commercial reasons I should have said yes, but I just felt I wouldn't have been able to do a good mix of the track. This has been true of my entire career. I have turned down those types of songs that sounded like the artist deliberately went into the studio to create a Top 10 hit (in the worst possible way). I know when the song won't translate well into a club mix, and if I can't bring a really good StoneBridge vibe to it, I will pass on it.

I've been rejected as well, where an artist had pride moments—like if I ditched the bridge they wrote. I've had labels come to me and say, "What the hell? You knocked out the whole bridge, and that's the most important part of the song." Sometimes they understand, other times not so much. There are very powerful artists, like your Madonnas, that when they say no to what you want to do, it's no. (Actually, Madonna was very happy with my mix of "Living for Love" from her *Rebel Heart* album.) But others, speaking through their managers, tell me they want this and that changed. Some A&R managers want a draft from you first, outlining your ideas before you do anything. Or you must send them a sample before you finish it. Nine times out of ten, I am told to finish it.

I would imagine you must have experienced some anxiety or pressure working with artists who were extremely popular—making sure your mix lived up their reputation and past work.

You just listen to the song, and you just go with your instincts and the way you envision it. Usually it works. One time I did a Lenny Kravitz remix. He was very hands on. I had to call him one day. "Mr. Kravitz, this is StoneBridge from Stockholm. I have your—." "Okay, play it; play it," he jumped in. I had to hold my phone up to the speaker and play the mix. It was a tough five minutes. I was shitting my pants. At the end, he said, "It's cool," and that was it. I had so much respect for his work, and I was so nervous playing my piece of shit remix for him. I got through it though.

But you can't go through the whole process and be intimidated by the artist or their fame. You take on the remix because you think you can do something with it—and then you don't have to worry. That's another reason why you should pass on something that you know you won't be able to create something good with. For example, even though Axwell and Ingrosso are huge right now, and they are friends of mine, I would have passed on their [2015] hit "Sun Is Shining." It is very hard to do a remix of a song with that kind of shuffling waltz tempo.

You created club-friendly mixes for many artists who were not traditionally a part of the dance genre? Did you have to approach these projects differently?

No, I didn't approach them any differently than established dance artists. Sia is again a great example. It was a live recording of a band and a very bizarre record. At that time, she was an English singer-songwriter type of artist. I took it on as a challenge, and I knew I could do something with it. They were very surprised with the results. After my remix, she did a lot of dance stuff and ended up on "Titanium" with David Guetta.

I think of Tori Amos with the Armand Van Helden remix of "Professional Widow." She was a singer-songwriter of weird, folky stuff. The remix opened her eyes, and she got a Top 10 hit in the UK with it. I embrace unusual artists and songs, as long as the track doesn't have a weird time signature or stage vocals or a strange structure (though I'm not excluding everything that's weird or different). If it's soft-sung, I'm not going to try to make a banging, noisy remix. I will match the sentiment of the song. You have to think about these things.

Describe the difference between creating a successful club mix and a radio version.

Up until five or six years ago, you'd make a radio mix, bring the vocal up, soften a few things, and bring a hook in right away. (Radio One in the UK had this thing that if there isn't a hook in the first 20 seconds, they wouldn't play it.) There were these unwritten rules. But in the last few years, the kids decided they didn't want to hear some watered-down version. They want to hear what's in the clubs on the radio—that same version. So the club mixes just got cut down. Now it's evolving so that the club mix is about four and a half minutes. That used to be a radio version.

We have massive ADD going on now; people don't have the time or attention span to enjoy longer tracks. They want to hear the thing [*StoneBridge quickly slaps the palm of his hand a few times*]—"Okay, next?" In the '90s and early 2000s, we had these eight, nine, 12-minute mixes. People would fall asleep with that now. Nobody can take that. I see it when I play live too. If there's too much groove, people get nervous. They want explosions. I think it's an instant gratification thing—the world of social media, etc. They are used to getting rapid blasts of information and sensations all the time. People can't handle what we did in the '90s. I guess it's full circle though, isn't it? The Beatles' songs were so short. Please don't bore us—just get to the chorus, as Roxette said.

It's been said of every era in dance music since the '70s that recreational drugs played a significant role in the acceptance of a track on the dance floor. Did you experience this in the '90s?

I'm such a geek. I never did drugs. I remember in the '90s people talked about E moments. What the hell was that? I soon realized when people were on [the drug] ecstasy (aka E), they loved a breakdown with big fluffy chords or emotion. Everyone loved each other, and they were always hugging—an E moment. Same thing in New York. You had a ketamine problem there. It was really dark, and people were leaning against the walls of the club drooling—the Ketamine funk or k-hole. The atmosphere of the club, as a result of this, definitely dictated the type of music played.

Tell me about your career as the '90s drew to a close and how you approached the new millennium.

Around 1996, I started to feel things were getting a bit formulaic. I was getting tired of the same thing all the time, the same type of chords and mixes. I was offered an opportunity to play a show with Todd Terry at Ministry of Sound [a nightclub that eventually became a record label and media company] in London. I initially said no, but a friend of mine said, "Are you crazy? When Ministry of Sound calls, you say yes." I started out playing gospel-house, and these E'ed-up English kids were looking at me like, "What the hell is he playing?" I realized the club scene had moved on a bit since '92, and I went on a mission to rebuild myself. I started my own record label, Stoney Boy Music, and started going harder, a bit more banging. Not trance or techno, but a lot clubbier. It confused some fans with that because I had been the sweet piano strings guy.

By 2000, I was back in form again. I had big success with a mix of "Inner Smile" for Texas. Then I met this guy from Hed Kandi [a label and event creator from the UK], who had featured a lot of my '90s stuff on his compilation albums. He asked me if I wanted to play their Miami party during the Winter Music Conference [a gathering of dance music artists, DJs and label representatives that began in the mid-'80s and attracted thousands annually]. He gave me a residency after that, and I played all over the world with Hed Kandi.

He asked me if I ever thought of doing an album. He basically gave me a bunch of cash to go and do my thing—it was like a dream. I had freedom to create songs like "Put 'Em High," and it was a big hit in 2004. I had two Top 10 UK hits at that time—the other was "Take Me Away" in 2005. By then I had a niche—when labels had a sweet R&B or house track, and they wanted to keep the song intact, they came to me. That was always my thing.

I never messed with a song. I think it's important. Say they have a little guitar sample or sax or special chord or stab—they give the song a stronger feel, even in a club mix. It's a smart thing to preserve the essence of the original song. A lot of young guys today just take the a cappella and ignore the music. Sometimes they even change the timing of the vocal.

I was remixing Britney Spears, Sophie Ellis-Bextor and Ne-Yo's "Closer," which got a Grammy nomination. Then I got the Taio Cruz track "Dynamite" in 2010. It was a dance record—distorted stabs, heavy bass lines—and I was wondering what to do with it. I polished it, softened it maybe, but I knew inside I was seeing a change in the business.

By the end of the 2000s, EDM (electronic dance music) came in, and the DJ became the artist. It's not a bad thing. It may be a little bit overheated. Before, [people] went to see a band or vocalist perform; now they go to hear a DJ like Avicii. They expect him to play all his hits, and they want to see the guy play their favorite records that he mixed. The change for me has been that I now make most of my money touring. I get booked in the U.S. a lot (having a mix show on SiriusXM contributes to that), and I really like it. But it wasn't like this in the '90s. I mean, back then, if you didn't play the right stuff you got beer cans thrown at you. And making new music is easier today. You don't need a record label or to pass a certain filter they (the A&R, managers, executives, etc.) imposed on you to get a record out. Now you can make a record and post it on SoundCloud or Spotify the same day and reach hundreds of thousands of people, theoretically.

How quickly do styles and trends generally emerge in dance music?

I would say every year. Trends developed a bit slower in the '90s because the only way to hear new music was in the record stores, which also had a social function. You met other DJs there, and we asked each other about how we felt about records, which led to a consensus of what's hot. Now you listen on your own; you don't discuss it much with other DJs. And you are exposed to much, much more music.

Let's say you listen to the biggest summer club record of 2014, and then you listen to the biggest hit a year later. You will hear certain things changing. I get about 800 promo tracks a week, and I get a really good grasp of what people are doing. For example, last year we started to notice the disco-type "high hat" sound creeping back, the big clap-clap. The sound was banned for five years; no one used it. I've noticed an upward trend in future house, which is basically EDM with a funky beat. It's really a retro sound. They went back to electro-2005. We're really waiting for an aggressive format now—an angry sound. Angry kids will come up with something bombastic.

Wow. How do you keep track of all these sub-genres and categories?

You know, you really can't, and you shouldn't. It's all just music at the end of the day. I'm never bleeding edge. If everybody goes to one type of music, like electro, I won't necessarily follow the herd. I will make a note of it and maybe make my bass line slightly more aggressive, but I will keep putting music together the way I like.

There have been a number of dramatic changes in the world of dance music over the last ten years, not the least of which has been the diminished billing of the vocalist, as the DJ takes preeminence. This appears to have especially impacted heritage artists, who have expressed frustration over the change in their role within the genre they helped create.

I understand that, and I agree with those vocalists who feel this way. They are right in many ways, aren't they? I mean, it's the song and the singer that people remember in music history. And they've earned a level of respect for their contributions. I try to be careful about using that term "featuring" in regard to vocalists on my records. I prefer "StoneBridge and" the vocalist. But look, as much as I understand how singers feel slighted by being demoted, if you will, there is a reality about the situation. Times are changing.

I think for a vocalist to stay relevant, they have to try and work within the system and keep creating new material, not just relying on their past hits and past lives. I think doing remixes or updated versions of your past hits all the time just keeps you old. I think that's a mistake. You continue to live in the past. Yes, it's true your old fans may not like your new material, and they may want you to stay in the past. But [with new material] you may get heard by younger listeners, who may say, "Wow, what's that?" I think you have to try and project a positive attitude and have the courage to do that.

Madonna may have been too defensive throughout her campaign for the *Rebel Heart* tour, fighting back about being 57 and trying to still be in it. It was almost like she was prepared for a massive critiquing that she would be too old. But she's great proof of what you *can* do. She has made relevant music throughout her whole career. I think the last campaign was too desperate, instead of leaning towards her natural abilities as a performer and writer. She's an extremely good hook writer. But she's still out there working. Whereas other singers from the past have given up. You have to push the envelope to show progress.

How are you coping with the other dramatic changes in the business, such as streaming and dismal digital sales?

Here's what people don't get. New dance music in the '90s was always kept very secret, very exclusive, and then they wanted a tastemaker to say that the new record was the shit. And then a lot of people would follow that advice and buy the record. The CDs cost the label next to nothing to manufacture, and they made indescribable profits from these sales. That is gone. Over. Now you need to make as many people as possible hear your music—that's the key. If you put out an album, [people] download one or two songs off it or add them to their playlists.

I realized about a year or two ago, running my labels, that the sales were constantly declining. DJ promos are leaking everywhere—it's unreal. If you send out promo tracks to a few DJs, a few days later you see that your entire set of promo tracks are online. There are so many pirate sites that give it all away.

You can't spend all day trying to stop these things. It's better to look at it as promotion, which was Napster's original argument. To an extent, they were right. Now it's gone so far that it's really hard to get paid for music—it's down to streaming only. The challenge now is to get your stuff out there to as many people as you can so that they become interested in seeing your live shows. That's how you'll get paid. Once a million people have streamed your songs, then Hollywood, ad agencies, etc. start paying attention and might offer to use your track for a decent amount of money. That can only happen if the song becomes popular and is heard by the masses. That's the mind fuck—instead of trying to protect your song from downloading, strive for getting a million people to listen to your song, even illegally or through streaming, and maybe 2,000 of them will show up when you do a show in New York, and they'll pay $20 or $30 for a ticket.

The record industry of the '50s through 2010—rest in peace. Finished. That's the reality; that's the challenge.

How do you view your future in the dance music industry?

I have had many bitter days, like some of the singers we've discussed, but instead of complaining about my labels or agents or changes in the industry, I realized I had to take things into my own hands and make it better. What do I want to do in the future? I want to just be able to sit in my studio here, work on a track for three weeks, get paid and pay my bills. There are many times when you go, "What the fuck?" When you see that record sales are nothing, you know your budget to make remixes will be less and less. But I refuse to lie down. I have increased my live shows, I do my radio shows, and I do my singles, which still bring me good feedback.

"That's the mind fuck—instead of trying to protect your song from downloading, strive for getting a million people to listen to your song, even illegally or through streaming," says Sten Hallström of current music industry challenges (courtesy Sten Hallström).

I'm actually pretty happy now. I've made that leap from the old record industry to the new reality (it took me about three years). But I have a good presence out there, and I never do big rants on social media, as many of my peers do. Who needs to see that? You have to keep that shit to yourself. Singers who complain about the new generation of singers, the old "back in my day" thing—it's the same thing. It's just bitterness. We all just need to do *something*. Not waste time complaining. We need to figure out what's going on, why some things aren't working, and do something about it. It's not easy.

Look, when I'm 65, I don't want to be in a club entertaining 20-year-olds. I don't live in the clouds. I understand that there is an expiration date. I don't plan to be Rolling Stones, wheeled out on stage, performing my old hits. I will look to expanding my horizons, though. Maybe scoring a film with that StoneBridge angle—I'd love to do that. I just want to continue writing, producing, making my music because *I want to*—and that's where I plan to go.

When you think about dance music from a pop culture perspective, what comes to mind?

I think it's true about dance music being underrated in pop culture history, until about 2010. Now, unquestionably, dance music *is* pop music. It's the biggest pop music format out there today—it's massive. We didn't get that respect in the '90s, but I think dance music has been vindicated. I don't think you'll hear too many people saying dance is a shitty niche format anymore.

The world of dance music is different today, though, that's for sure. You won't go to a club and see turntables anymore. That's finished. (I've bumped into one or two stored on the floor at some places. You go, "What the hell is that?") The styles and formats will continue to change. And I think as more time goes by, the respect due '70s disco and the dance music of the '80s and '90s will continue to grow. The musicianship of disco, especially—all the players involved, singers and musicians—they contributed to that sound. You can't just go to a computer and create what they did. It was unreal. That's why it will have a lasting quality.

I wonder, 20 or 30 years from now, when they look at the music of 2015, what will they say? [*He laughs.*] "Oh, that was when they did all the 2015 versions of the '70s, '80s, and '90s hits!"

Lightning Round with Sten

Diana Ross or Beyoncé?
Diana Ross.

Giorgio Moroder or Nile Rodgers?
Nile Rodgers—he's the funky man.

Applause or record sales?
Applause, fuck yeah!

Five good friends or one best friend?
Five good friends.

Music or lyrics?
Music because I'm Swedish!

No more TV or no more movies?
Oh, Jesus. That's really hard for me. I couldn't live without movies, so no TV.

Meet your ancestors or meet your descendants?
Descendants. You can't dwell too much on the old shit—you have to move forward.

Nosie Katzmann, Composer, Lyricist
"Mr. Vain" (Culture Beat, 1993)

"I'm a singer-songwriter. I always write whatever comes out of my head. I'm mainly influenced by what is going on in my life. Life is my biggest inspiration."—Nosie Katzmann

(Jürgen) Nosie Katzmann began his music career in the '80s serving as a musician and vocalist in a series of German rock bands. A chance encounter with producer Torsten Fenslau in the early '90s opened the door to a new stage in Katzmann's career and an unprecedented series of international dance-pop hits. As the songwriter of such high-energy, floor-filling classics as "Mr Vain" by Culture Beat and "Right in the Night" by Jam & Spoon, Nosie became one of Europe's most in-demand composers and lyricists of the period.

With his background and influences steeped in classic rock, one might expect Nosie to have been a bit reluctant to fully embrace the dance music culture in which he found fame. Instead, he plunged head first into the genre, and his songs sold millions. He speaks with a great fondness for these special years in the '90s, expressing appreciation for this exceptionally creative and successful time in his life.

Nosie, please tell me a little about your youth and early musical influences.

I was born in 1959 in Bad Neustadt an der Saale, which is in Bavaria, Germany. My parents were very poor, and I spent my early years on a farm with cattle, pigs, sheep and horses. I lived on this farm with my mother Rosmarie, my sister Renate and my younger brother Ralf. My father worked about 300 miles away from where we lived, and he had a little flat in the city of Darmstadt. We joined him there when I was five years old. He was a Johnny Cash fan, and my mother loved Ted Herold, a famous German rock 'n' roll singer who sang in the German language. I loved Johnny Cash, and my favorite album of his was *Showtime*. I still play "Folsom Prison Blues" in all of my live sets when I perform today.

When I was 13, I started getting interested in watching music bands and singers on German TV. Through TV, I was introduced to the Beatles, Kinks and Stones. I also loved T.Rex and Slade. While on a journey with my schoolmates to a summer camp, I learned about the songs of Bob Dylan and Neil Young (and I really fell in love with his music). I became hooked on singer-songwriter music and rock and started buying magazines like *Bravo* (the biggest music teen magazine in Germany at the time), *Melody Maker*, *Cashbox*, *Billboard*, *Rolling*

Stone, etc. The next big musical thing for me was Creedence Clearwater Revival, Bread and John Fogerty, whose raw and energetic guitar playing and songwriting I loved. The movies *Woodstock* and *Monterey Pop* introduced me to still more artists. I learned to play acoustic guitar and formed my own bands, trying to sound like my heroes.

While learning to develop as a songwriter, especially in the '80s, I admired Hall & Oates, Curtis Mayfield and, above everyone, Prince. He inspired me more than anyone else, besides Jimmy Webb and Robert Palmer. (I must admit, though, Jimmy Webb, to this day, is my greatest songwriting hero.) But Prince combined everything—singing, playing, performing, songwriting—on a level never seen before by anyone else.

My first semi-professional band was called Head Over Heels (with roadies, fans, etc.) which was inspired by the music of Poco, Eagles and Buffalo Springfield. From there, I also played with the Balloons and then Pirates of Pop, both of which were influenced by the music of Hall & Oates, Palmer and Prince. My first [official] band had the name the Noses. We had three-piece harmony vocals, just like Crosby, Stills & Nash. We played my own material mixed with cover songs of my heroes. I was the main "nose" of the band, and soon my nickname became "Nosy." I didn't like the spelling, so I changed it to "Nosie."

How did you come to begin making dance music with fellow producers Torsten Fenslau and Jens Zimmermann?

Torsten Fenslau and I had a favorite cafe where we happened to be every day at noon without knowing each other. I was the big local music hero, and he was the local star DJ on the rise. We had heard of each other, but we never talked. One day in 1989, we were standing next to each other, and he heard a conversation I was having with a friend about the record company (ZYX Records) that was going to release my Pirates of Pop single, "Shake It"/"Change." He had a record about to be released by the same label called "Out of the Ordinary" [performed by the Dream]. Torsten asked me something about my experiences so far with ZYX, and then he asked if I was interested in writing a song to a playback he and his production partner, Jens Zimmermann, were about to record. That same evening I wrote the lyrics to "Alone (It's Me)" [later credited on the recording to a concept called Abfahrt]. We recorded the track the next evening in Torsten's little one room flat. He asked me if I could sing the song and then just speak the words in a low voice. I did it, and that was it.

A few weeks later, he called me and asked me to come down to the club [Dorian Gray] where he was the resident DJ. He played the track with my voice on it, and the crowd went wild! It was thrilling and flattering, and I liked the sound, vibe and groove immediately.

This was definitely your baptism in dance music. But before we delve further into your extraordinary career in the genre, can you tell me a little about the process a song goes through, from creative inception through production? How did the extended dance versions of songs play into that process?

When a song is first created, composed, it's recorded on a ghetto blaster cassette recorder (to this day, in many cases). All of my original ideas are recorded on a cassette recorder. My songs are 95 percent written with an acoustic guitar, 5 percent with a piano. When I think a song is written and the lyrics and melody are finished, I do a studio demo recording with a rough arrangement (which normally includes guitar, bass, keyboards, groove and vocals). The vocal line is exactly the way it should be recorded later—the rest of the playback is just to support the demo line melody.

When it's clear who the artist will be, the track will be arranged in the style of that artist and recorded in the studio (sometimes beginning, again, with a demo recording, but most times as a finished product, with clear, obvious vision of how it should sound in the end). Tempo is always important, but it should always fit the song and not the "tempo of the day."

Working with the vocalist was always easy for me because the songs were always in the right pitch for his or her voice. I was a singer myself, so I always knew what was the best key for a singer.

As far as record label involvement, well, they just picked the songs [to be singles] based on what they liked. [As we became] successful (and as long as we continued to be successful) they just took everything we gave them. A song could be a big radio hit and a flop as a club hit and vice versa. Radio hits weren't usually as big in the clubs and needed those extra remixes and extended versions, which sometimes had little to do with the original song. The writing of my songs was my main interest. Torsten, or whoever was the producer, had to think of the remix or extended versions. I hated thinking of longer than necessary versions. They were not my cup of tea. I had no interest in these things and trusted others to handle them. Most extended versions are just boring and unnecessary.

This newfound connection with Torsten paved the way for your breakthrough Top Five German hit with Culture Beat, "Der Erdbeermund" ("Cherry Lips," as it was known in the U.S.)?

Yes. Torsten asked me if he could listen to some more tracks I had written, and so I played him some more of my tunes. One track caught his attention—a song called "423211." He asked Jens if he could re-record my demo with a more club-oriented bass drum. They pumped up my groove a little bit and "Der Erdbeermund" ("Cherry Lips") was born.

When the instrumental was recorded, I didn't have time to record my vocals on the track, so initially Torsten used a reading by German film star Klaus Kinski of the poem "Der Erdbeermund" by Francois Villon and used it as a substitute voice for mine. It sounded so cool that we kept it and just later re-recorded the spoken poem with Jo Van Nelsen, an actor from the Frankfurt area. The song became our first big success and worldwide club hit in 1989 and 1990.

The gay audience, or better said, the gay clubs, first noticed "Der Erdbeermund," and they helped it a lot to become a big hit. Jo Van Nelson was well known in the Frankfurt-based gay community, since he was gay himself.

Your partnership with Torsten and Jens led to a phenomenally successful string of hits in Europe, the UK, Canada and the U.S. Would you describe how you felt about the partnership and the tremendous demand that rose within the dance music industry for your sound and expertise?

Well, meeting Torsten and Jens was a very exciting experience for me. In my eyes, they were more than just talented in what they were doing, and they thought the same about me. We had a great creative chemistry, and we felt that we were far better at what we did together than most at the time. We felt we had the ability to create some really innovative and exciting music together. Everything that probably shouldn't have felt normal felt *very* normal with them. For example, it felt totally normal to become *very* successful with them. It felt very normal that doors just opened and everyone wanted to work with us. For a while, everything we did hit the mark.

Dance music at the beginning of the '90s was becoming new and exciting again with the arrival of techno and house. I loved and admired Lil' Louis and all the house records coming out of Chicago and Detroit. Musical boundaries were being torn down, and everything seemed possible—mixing "black music" with "white music," rock with jazz and folk with acid. And all with a four on the floor bass drum. We tried to combine as many elements as possible; we didn't care about anything except that we liked it.

It was very cool that these danceable tracks were coming out of my singer-songwriter tunes, and I loved what they did with my songs. I envisioned we would become the Stock Aitken Waterman of '90s dance music. It looked to us that we had the same Midas touch as those gentlemen with every song we recorded. The only ones that seemed close to us were [the production team behind] Snap!. We felt Snap! were the Beatles of dance; we were the Rolling Stones. Later, 2 Unlimited came along, and I saw them as the Kinks of Dance." [*Nosie smiles brightly.*]

Between the first Culture Beat album in 1991, Horizon, and the follow-up set in '93, Serenity, the partnership between you, Mr. Fenslau and Mr. Zimmermann became unstable. What happened?

The split of our Culture Beat team as a creative trio involved some personal issues with Jens in those days. Also, I believe Jens felt the pressure of staying successful and keeping up with time schedules and release deadlines. He couldn't stand that pressure. I loved to work my ass off in the studio. I loved the pressure of having to write three to four songs more for an album.

Tensions got stronger when Torsten became the star DJ and main head of Culture Beat in the public eye. He was our chosen frontman for the public, and more and more, Jens took the perspective that Torsten had forgotten that he didn't record the tracks alone. Most tracks were recorded by Jens and me—*without* Torsten. Torsten mixed the songs and sometimes asked us if we could, for example, record another bell melody for a chorus—the typical things a producer requests. Sometimes Torsten would change our arrangements for the better, but he wasn't the musician in our creative team. However, to the world it was he who did almost everything—although for a lot of songs he did almost nothing. Yet his name was mentioned the most. Frankly, this bugged Jens more and more.

To regain more creative influence, Jens wanted to record a solo masterpiece, and he wanted me to become his partner in this new project. The project was called Tyrell Corp., and the song was called "Running." Well, I believe Torsten may have become jealous, and he didn't like the fact that Jens and I were going separate ways without him, so he forced himself into the project, much to Jens' disapproval. He couldn't say no, but with this move, Jens lost total interest and creative energy in what we were doing. Torsten mixed the track and called it finished because he felt Jens was taking too long to complete it. "Running" became a huge club hit, and everyone said it was Torsten's masterpiece.

Because everyone talked about "Running" as the great new Fenslau track, Jens decided to split, and he quit the trio. He wanted to gain creative freedom again and step out of Torsten's shadow. I also didn't like this side of Torsten's personality so much, and creative tension began to come up between us as well. I, however, was very successful with my side projects. Torsten and I didn't talk for a few weeks, for no obvious reason, but one day he came to my house. We talked about everything that had happened and cleared up all unclear matters between us. We decided to record a new Culture Beat album together—*Serenity*.

You mentioned earlier that you'd been doing well with your side projects. One such success was the Captain Hollywood Project and the hugely popular electro-Euro-house hit called "More and More" in 1992. This project fell under the umbrella of a rising studio team called Dance Music Production (DMP). Can you tell me about this experience?

One day, Michael Eisele (from DMP) called me and asked if I could write the lyrics for a dance instrumental they were working on. I agreed, and that was the beginning of a very successful collaboration. I wrote "More and More," and he loved it. He invited me to his studio and introduced me to the DMP team. He also gave me more tracks he wanted me to write songs to.

I was working on the new Culture Beat album and a lot of tracks for other people. In the beginning, it was just another job for me to write for DMP, but I liked the team and got more and more involved in the working process of their songs. For a while, I also did the vocal recordings for them because I wanted them to understand that every single note should be sung exactly the way I recorded the demo vocals. If they didn't follow this advice, I couldn't guarantee a hit. It happened that I would get very angry with them if they didn't record a song exactly the way I had done it on my demo.

I was pleased with our very successful commercial collaboration and enjoyed being their main (and only) song and lyric writer. However, to them the situation was not so pleasing after a while. With our success came a lot of output they wanted to release, but (because I wanted to maintain a high level of quality) I gave the thumbs down to a lot of the material they sent me. Ultimately, I became too powerful and too problematic, and they couldn't have control over me.

"More and More" became a worldwide hit for the Captain Hollywood Project, but "Mr. Vain" for Culture Beat [from the *Serenity* album] became even bigger, and this game between DMP and I went on and on. They were depending on my creativity and needed to keep me in a good mood, while at the same time they looked for someone that could take my place—someone that they would have more control over.

One day, I just quit. I didn't want someone I didn't respect as a writer to be part of the same team I was on and weaken our quality level. There were no tensions or bad vibes. I just left and never looked back.

One listen to your repertoire and it's easy to understand why your skills were so highly valued. Can you describe the process of creating a dance song like Culture Beat's "Mr. Vain"? From where did your inspirations come from?

I'm a singer-songwriter. I always write whatever comes out of my head. I'm mainly influenced by what is going on in my life. Life is my biggest inspiration. I always just wanted to create something I liked, that my girlfriend would like, my best friends would like. I don't make music for any specific group of people, but I'm glad for every person who likes to listen to my songs, no matter what genre they fall in. I don't think of genre when I write a song. I just want the lyrics to fit the melody.

Creating a dance song was like creating any other kind of song. You think of the bass drum that will fit the vocal vibe. You think of a high hat pattern that enhances the groove of the words that will be sung. You think of the synth pattern to underline your main vocal melody line—and everything should come in a constant creative flow.

Were there essential elements that had to be in place for a song to be a successful dance record? How did you keep track of new sounds and trends emerging in the clubs, on the radio and with music consumers in the '90s?

The "mood of the day" or the "style of the week" told you to add this and that flavor to your arrangement in order to keep it sounding up-to-date. I was almost carefree when it came to this, but, of course, I was a child of my time and was influenced by the new sounds and creative ideas of that period. There were also certain chords (Am-F-G) that appealed to the masses and were more promising in terms of success than other chord sequences. But at the same time, there was always room to add something totally new. I always loved that which was new, provocative and not so obvious.

When everyone copied my style of writing dance choruses/dance hooks, I changed everything to a non-chorus—the verse became the chorus. Whatever came to my head felt right. As soon as you make up rules, just forget them and try something totally different.

The writing of my songs was my main focus. DMP, Torsten or whoever was the producer had to think of the remix or extended versions. As I said, I hated thinking of longer than necessary versions.

I always listened to new artists, new tracks, sounds and variations of songwriting. I am a music lover, and I am nosy. [*He smiles.*] It's a natural thing for me to keep up with latest in music, style, fashion and trends—to this day. I don't need to like everything, but I love to be surprised by new sounds, new artists and new ways of expressing one's self musically.

Many of your songs were extremely successful on the U.S. and international pop and dance charts, and they were often considered ground-breaking representatives of the '90s sound. They include Captain Hollywood Project's "More and More" (1992), Jam & Spoon's "Right in the Night" (1993) and Scooter's "Break It Up" (1996). Can you tell me your impressions of working the artists that represented these acts?

Captain Hollywood [Tony Dawson-Harrison, formerly of Twenty 4 Seven] was a big star in the Netherlands when he was introduced to the DMP team. But the record company [handling DMP output] told the team they needed a hit record from Hollywood or they were going to drop him due to declining sales. I don't think he trusted the DMP team too much because the first time he and his manager showed up for a meeting at the DMP studio, [Hollywood] waited in his car and had his manager speak for him. I was a bit stunned by this. This was for the "More and More" project. I don't think they expected a hit, but when it happened things changed for the better. Hollywood was a very nice person, always very kind and polite. Very professional. What I liked most about him was that he was a very soulful person (and still is).

I loved working with Jam El Mar [aka Rolf Ellmer, producer of Jam & Spoon], and I still do. At the time of the Jam & Spoon hits, he was at the top of his game and a great musician and engineer. I always felt "Right in the Night" was one of the best songs I've ever written, but the record company and A&R people who came to my place to listen to new songs for the project just thought of "Right" as being average. Some other individuals from A&R asked, "Where's the hook—the punchline?" I really hated to play the song for the record company, and a week before it came out I thought for sure it would be a flop because the label people just didn't hear the hit in it. And just like most times, the label people were wrong.

I met Scooter at an award show. I happened to be talking with [frontman] H. P. Baxxter, but he didn't know who I was. We just talked and had a great time. When he found out who I was, he asked if we could do something together. He told me the band needed a song that would really break them on radio. Two weeks later, I visited them at their studio in Hamburg, played them 14 songs on my acoustic guitar, and they picked two—"Break It Up" and "Don't Let It Be Me." "Break It Up" did exactly what they hoped for and paved the way to their radio and TV presence. It became a big hit, and they still play it in their live shows.

As a hit songwriter, how did your life change after you began to achieve mainstream pop chart success?

Success came so fast. We were constantly working in the studio, day and night. We invested almost all our money in new recording equipment, studio time, etc. There was no time for parties or things like that. However, with the huge success came bigger checks and, of course, bigger apartments, better clothes and new cars. But, all in all, we were the same down-to-earth people—just living better than we had before. We worked so hard that we didn't notice much our lifestyles had changed. It was just part of the flow that none of us questioned. We had the same friends as we had before and went to all the same places and restaurants. We'd already been "local heroes" in the community, so no one in our neighborhood treated us differently than before the arrival of success.

I felt pleased, honored and blessed that songs like "Right in the Night," "Mr. Vain," "More and More" and many others received so much recognition. I gave up a private life for a life in the studio, but I didn't regret anything. It was great to work day and night with many wonderful artists, great musicians, engineers, managers, photographers, etc. I guess the most difficult thing was not to completely lose track of real life. I had an assistant who provided me with everything I needed. I was in a working frame of mind day and night, disturbed only by award shows and short visits with the record labels. Life became unreal, and for a while I didn't mind that.

How did you handle the pressure of having to create a steady flow of hits?

I didn't feel any pressure from anyone. I always thought [my latest hit] might be my *last* hit. But after more than 30 hits on the charts, I didn't worry about it at all. I just wrote songs and recorded them. I was focused on pleasing myself and other people, but I felt no sense of business competition. I just looked at the others in the industry—some of whom were not as successful as us, others who were more so—as simply colleagues.

In 1993, Torsten Fenslau was tragically killed in car accident in Germany. I'm sure this was a profoundly sad time for you.

I have thought of Torsten every day of my life since his passing. I had great times with him and not so great, but I've always liked him and respected him. I admired him for his guts and ability to actually do things instead of just talking about them. And I am grateful for the time we had together and thankful for the doors he opened for me.

How would you describe the integrity of the German music industry in the '90s? Did they treat you fairly?

I think they treated me okay. Fair might be a little bit too much to say, since it's a crooked business. But I guess as far as proper financial compensation, I can't complain. The business is tricky for everyone involved as a musicians or businessmen—and for vocalists as much as anyone else.

Did the AIDS epidemic or the rampant use of drugs in the music industry or in the clubs during this period have any direct impact on your life or work?

They didn't affect my life so much. I saw a lot of people having major problems with drugs, and I saw musicians taking a downward spiral, totally passing out and ruining their careers because of drugs. Personally, I didn't drink alcohol, and I didn't smoke or take any pills, substances, etc. I didn't allow any alcohol or drugs in the studio, and I did not allow people [who indulged in them] to surround me. So, fortunately, [substance abuse] was never directly an issue in my life.

By 1996, your musical output seemed to taper down. What was happening?

I slowed down because I diagnosed myself with burn-out syndrome. I prescribed a rest for myself and planned to take as much time off as my head, body, heart and soul needed. Well, it took almost 10 years until I fully recovered. During that time, I did a lot of soul-searching, a lot of research into finding the true meaning of being here in this life. I read a lot of spiritual books and tried to regain happiness and joy in the smaller things of life. I took care of my relationships, my friends, my parents, my siblings, my health, body and soul. I enjoyed this trip to myself very much.

One day, a spiritual guide asked me what I would enjoy most about making music. I replied, "Sitting together with friends, playing my music live and unplugged—just for good spirits, just to celebrate music in its pure and innocent form. Just being with friends and having a good time." My guide said, "Well, why don't you do this?" I then called up some of my favorite musicians and recorded (totally live in my favorite German studio) my 2008 album, *Greatest Hits 1*. I had a really good time recording the songs, as they were performed as they were originally written and arranged. On this album you can hear all of the influences I felt from the great songwriters who first inspired me.

I followed this album with *Songbook 1*. I told the engineer of this project to roll the tape and that everything that would come out of my mouth and guitar would be the song. Period. It was a challenge to write a song and immediately record it with only one take. I invited musicians to also listen to the songs once and record their first take. The end results were amazing, and with that way of writing and producing I found myself feeling back on track, enjoying music again.

Have you been thinking about what you'd like to do next in your career?

I think the question is actually, "What do I want to play tonight?" I might find even that question difficult to answer. I perform many sold-out concerts today and my audience seems more than pleased and happy. That makes me very happy. I go with my audience and the energy that certain songs create and then decide what the next one will be, without any set program. It's great fun for me, my musicians and the audience.

The playing field for producing music for the commercial market in the 21st century has changed quite a bit from the '90s. What are your thoughts about this?

Creating music now is no different from any century before—only the way in which it is done has changed. The biggest challenge is always how to express one's self as a creator and succeed in one's achievement. If you don't learn the craft and have the skills to express what you want to say, you will fail, no matter if you have the hippest equipment or the most modern computer. You need to learn creativity, talent, personality. You need to have discipline,

Nosie Katzmann, who penned the lyrics to Euro-dance classics such as Culture Beat's "Mr. Vain," performs live in Darmstadt, Germany, in 2014 (courtesy Nosie Katzmann).

a clear vision of what you want (or at least what you don't want), and you need the strength to cope with failure.

If you want to make a living out of music, it's easier than ever—and harder than ever. In the '70s, we had two or three TV shows with only 15 or 30 acts to be seen. Tabloids gave you the idea that maybe there were 30 to 50 more, and the clubs gave you the impression there were about 100 to 200 more out there. Today, thanks to the Internet, it's *not* a billion more acts. No, there's *trillions and zillions* more acts out there. They all want the same venues, the same TV slots, the same positions on the charts. The day your record comes out, about 1000 other records will be released. The sheer mass of music songs available now—acts, bands, singers—makes it almost impossible to see the forest through the trees.

But still, it boils down to one thing—*have an idea*! And getting that idea noticed is the same challenge we had in the '50s, '60s, '70s, '80s and '90s. It's the same problem artists face today.

I believe we can agree that many dance music innovators have had some brilliant ideas. When they were received by the masses, the effects were astonishing. When you think of the power of dance music, what comes to mind?

Dance music has developed from being just a kid's niche music to becoming radio compatible and mainstream, just like rock 'n' roll became mainstream in the late '50s and early '60s. It went from noise and teenage crap to becoming an accepted genre with big commercial impact. In Europe today, dance music and local rap is the sound of youth and dominates radio, while rock is more or less tolerated on radio, transforming into an adult/old school niche. Dance music is the sound of today and influences almost every genre connected with youth, energy and hipness.

And your thoughts about the era in which you enjoyed so many hits?

As for the '90s, I can tell you I enjoyed my dance years very much.

LIGHTNING ROUND WITH NOSIE

Frank Farian or Dieter Bohlen?
Frank Farian—he is a very nice person and more my cup of tea. Frank is my choice.

One number one pop chart hit or five number one dance chart hits?
One number one pop chart hit.

Producing/composing your own music or producing/composing for other artists?
I like the mix, but I'd place producing and composing for others first.

Seeing a packed club dancing to your music or hearing your song on the radio?
Hearing my song on the radio.

Donna Summer or Beyoncé?
I prefer Beyoncé, but I have to say I loved Donna's *On the Radio* album and the song. I also loved her superb album *Cats Without Claws*.

Grammy/Echo Award or sell a million copies?
Sell a million copies.

Sybil Lynch, also known as Sybil

"The Love I Lost" (West End featuring Sybil, 1993)

"'If a man does not keep pace with his companions, perhaps it is because he hears the sound of a different drummer. Let him keep pace with the music he hears, however measured or far away.' I always loved that quote."—Sybil Lynch

New Jersey native Sybil Lynch, best known to the masses as simply Sybil, is all about duality. The singer/songwriter was a pro at jamming on both sides of the Atlantic during the late '80s and well into the '90s (with hits like "Don't Make Me Over" and "The Love I Lost"). She skillfully eased into the role of an American R&B/house diva with the same seamless effort that made her a hip UK dance-pop/soul star, and, through it all, the artist proudly says she maintained her integrity and sense of self.

Allmusic.com describes her as "an excellent vocalist and one of the finest among disco divas." But there is much more to Sybil than her sultry vocal resonance and stylish beats. Mentoring young people in her role as an educator provides the artist with a positive new direction as she continues to pursue a recording career and perform in clubs and at festivals and concerts worldwide.

Finishing up a series of late summer showcases in London, Sybil speaks in great detail and with an earnest verve about her most unique experience bridging two of dance music's most progressive decades.

How did your recording career get started, Sybil?

Music for me really began in earnest after I graduated from college. At that time, I thought I was going to be an attorney. I don't know what I was thinking! [*She laughs.*] I was studying for the LSAT exam, and on the weekends I was singing in a band with Ce Ce Rogers (who had the big house record "Someday" in 1987). I was the only one with a real job at the time. I was an editor and a proofreader at a publishing company, believe it or not. It was my first job out of college at 21 years old. I'd tell Ce Ce to just give me gas money, and I'd come to the gigs.

A friend was always trying to get me to go into the studio to do some vocal work, but I was never interested. I wasn't interested in being a singer, but entertained the idea of maybe being a songwriter. I got talked into going to the studio under the notion I'd be there to write songs for a girl group. The producer there, James Bratton, wanted to hear me sing, but I didn't want to. He said something like, "Well, you must not be able to sing then." I didn't like that challenge, so I let him play me the song he was interested in having me sing. It was "Falling in Love." I thought it was simple enough and sang it in one take. It ended up being my first record, which was signed to Next Plateau Records in New York in 1986.

The back story was they had been shopping this record for a long time, and Next Plateau told them if they could get someone good to sing it, they'd think about releasing it. It ended up being a nice marriage between the record company and me. I ended up recording "My Love Is Guaranteed" and "Let Yourself Go," which became big songs for me and ones I had the pleasure of co-writing. These tracks also introduced me to the UK market.

Eddie O'Loughlin was the co-founder of Midland International (Carol Douglas, Silver Convention, etc.) and Next Plateau Records, labels with a long and rich history in dance music. What was your professional relationship with Eddie like?

Eddie was about making sure Next Plateau was what he wanted it to be. He had a great deal of passion for music. I have a lot of respect for Eddie. He always joked with me that I was different from most of the artists he worked with. I think that stems from the fact that singing wasn't all I could do. I think he realized that. I was fortunate enough to have had parents who stressed education, and as a result I wasn't as "hungry" as other artists—I didn't have that back-stabbing, desperate way that other people in the business sometimes had. I didn't feel I had to compromise who I was for the sake of making a record. Eddie respected that about me. I remember him saying, "Sybil, the one thing about you is that you are going to maintain your integrity." Looking back now, I realize there were things I could have done to have stayed in the genre longer, but I refused, and I have no regrets. I'm passionate about the creative process in music, and if I had to comprise that in any way, it wouldn't have worked for me.

Sybil, seen here in a U.S. publicity photograph issued by Next Plateau Records, scored a top UK hit with a remake of Harold Melvin & the Blue Notes' "The Love I Lost" in 1993 (photograph by Next Plateau, courtesy Sybil Lynch).

I'm going to tell you something about Eddie—I had some issues with the song "Don't Make Me Over," which became one of my most well-known hits. They were telling me it was going to be a big record for me. (Little did I know just *how* big it was going to be, come 1987.) But I was getting frustrated because I had been working really, really hard and had some successful records behind me, and I hadn't seen any money. I was in an awful production situation—I was being paid by the label, but not by the production team that I was part of. I decided I wasn't going to promote "Don't Make Me Over" until it was straightened out. Eddie stepped in and got me a new contract, getting me out of the deal I had with the production end. So, I have a lot of love for him. He showed me that I was bringing value to Next Plateau, and he made sure I was properly compensated. We ended up having a great deal of success with "Don't Make Me Over" and "Walk on By." We were able to then get a licensing deal with the popular PWL label in the UK and did very, very well.

"Don't Make Me Over" and "Walk on By" were huge hits both here in the U.S. and abroad. They came at the twilight of the '80s, when dance music styles and tastes were once again shifting. It's also a time when your popularity in the UK began to swell. What do you recall about this period?

During the late '80s, I saw a real change in what was deemed to be a really cool rhythm. Soul II Soul, a lot of the British soul sounds, were having a major impact on the U.S. market. Initially, when I did "Don't Make Me Over," it didn't sound like the song we know today. It was transformed by Tony King and the team at PWL in the UK, and it took on a whole new life. It now had a real Soul II Soul–esque vibe. We were right on the pulse of that trend. Dance music, by then, had to have a really good lyric and very strong melody over a cool, soulful groove. You had to have that hot dance rhythm, but you also had to have solid lyrics. I was a dance music artist (that's how I was categorized—all my hits were on the *Billboard* dance chart in America), but then with "Don't Make Me Over" I started charting on the R&B and Top 100 charts. The shift in sound really kicked in by the early '90s when I did "The Love I Lost." These hits came at a time when there was a demand for singers to be at the forefront again.

You were working with Stock Aitken Waterman at PWL, a team of gentlemen other artists I've spoken with described as being very strong-minded. What was your impression?

I started out working with Stock Aitken Waterman when I first signed with the label. But then I ended up working with just Pete Waterman and Mike Stock. They really took a chance on me because I did not fit their traditional PWL image. I think it came down to the fact that they just liked my style of singing. Although I was a black singer, my voice wasn't so ethnic sounding—and I'm gonna say that for lack of a better term because I've heard that description before, and it's not necessarily derogatory. The voices of some artists of color had a style that appealed to a limited audience, and radio didn't always embrace them. I had the kind of voice that pop and R&B radio seemed to be comfortable with, and I think the PWL team knew I would interpret their songs without going too far to church or being too sappy. They had done Kylie and Rick Astley on the pop side and were looking for something different, and I offered that.

And yes, as many of the artists who worked with the guys may have told you, they were very nice gentlemen, but they *were* very controlling about what they wanted. That's not necessarily a bad thing, but it is where we bumped heads sometimes. I came with my own distinct sound, and they recognized it. They were familiar with my voice and image. They may have wanted to tweak those things to work better within their system. However, they were dealing with someone who was really clear about who she was. So it was difficult at times and sometimes frustrating, especially during the recording process.

I'll tell you the story of "The Love I Lost." It illustrates some of the challenges we had. There was a version of that song [we did] with Eddie Gordon of West End with PWL that had background vocals that were way too thin. I didn't like it at all. It wasn't as up and festive as it should have been. I knew it needed more body in the background. So, when the track went over to Eddie O'Loughlin, I told him we needed some girls in the background that have been in a church. The track was redone by Tony King and Eddie Gordon and the backgrounds were beefed up. The slow intro was gorgeous, too. That's the version that was a hit, and I wish the proper people (including the people that sang these background vocals) had gotten credit. That's always bothered me because the song was made better by going back in the mill and worked on by people who understood how it needed to sound. PWL ended up using Eddie Gordon's revamped version; they kind of absorbed it. They had to—I think Gamble and Huff, the creators of the song, would have recognized this as the better version.

Did the joint partnership between Next Plateau and PWL run smoothly? How challenging was it for you to work in two very distinct markets, the UK and America?

I think the teams got along as long as they both were making money. I'm being very candid. We definitely had two separate markets. The way I was perceived by fans in each market was very different. In America, I was more the R&B/dance/house girl, and they had to make an album that was going to meet the demands of my U.S. constituency. In the UK, I appealed more to a soul/pop market. So, in the early '90s we ended up with two different albums—*Good 'N' Ready* in the UK and *Doin' It Now* in the U.S. It was kind of weird. I had this battle with myself, multiple personalities—and I'm a Gemini, so you can imagine! It was challenging for me to figure out who I was in each market.

The songs that initially made strides were "You're the Love of My Life" in the U.S. and "The Love I Lost" in the UK. I'll put it this way—I think it would have been nice if cooler heads had prevailed and everyone had been on the same page, working together. Had that been the case, I think we could have jointly done some wonderful things globally. Egos sometimes get in the way, but on top of that Eddie O'Loughlin was going through a label transition at the time. I think we needed more cohesion, but I do believe each team, Eddie and his guys and gals in the U.S. and Mike Stock and Pete Waterman in the UK, thought they were each doing the right thing.

I'm always curious to know how an artist felt watching his or her songs climb the pop and dance charts, especially when they reach the Top 10, as your hits did.

You know what? I honestly didn't realize how big things would get. I remember that at the end of 1992, once again, people told me I was going to have another big record in the following year with "The Love I Lost." When I say I had no idea—*really*, I had no idea. I had been on *Top of the Pops* with "Walk on By" years before, and suddenly I was back on the show. Then I followed it with "When I'm Good and Ready." There was a time when I had two records in the top part of the chart—one coming up and one going down. It was an amazing time for me. I had done really well by PWL, and they had done really well by me.

During this period, you also created some inspired works with one of hip-hop/dance's most popular early innovators, Salt 'N' Pepa (most famously comprised of Cheryl "Salt" James, Sandy "Pepa" Denton and Spinderella). Would you tell me about that experience?

We were label mates, and I'd say we were both the shining stars for Next Plateau at that time. I was slightly older than they were. Cheryl and I probably connected the best. I was close to all of them though, and we got along really well. Cheryl and I were doing a benefit for Texas Children's Hospital, and on a break we were doing some shopping. I was going to run back to this store to buy some shoes I'd seen, and, unexpectedly, she kind of stopped me to say, "Sybil, you know when I met you, you were so cool. You are the same now as you were then. I appreciate that about you. If someone ever says anything bad about you, I'd have to fight them." It caught me by surprise, and I was touched. It was a time when label execs wanted to pit artists against each other, especially in hip-hop, I wasn't having any of that. I respected these ladies, and I was thrilled to work on their projects like the *Blacks' Magic* album, doing background vocals on their single "Independent." They were featured on my single "Crazy 4 U," which was a big hit on the U.S. R&B chart. I still get royalty checks for those projects! [*She lets out a laugh.*]

Being an American, did you have a personal preference for finding success in the U.S., even though you were achieving higher chart positions in the UK?

I think this concept I'm going to discuss came from the idea that prophets often weren't recognized in their own lands. It was sometimes challenging as an artist to be recognized in your home country. I understand now (more than ever) why so many singers and musicians end up taking residence in countries outside of their homeland.

I would have loved to have been embraced with the kind of fervor and zeal that the UK audience gave me. Don't misunderstand—I'm not saying I don't get a lot of love in the U.S. It's just a different level. The reality is this—we in the U.S. are very much driven by what's current. We don't seem to have a lot of love and respect for what's deemed as old school. Outside of the U.S., people seem to have a stronger regard for those who set a precedent or are viewed as icons in their respective arenas. I have been in this business for nearly 30 years come October of 2016. (I'm only 30 years old—how did that happen?) [*She chuckles.*] Like everyone, you want to go to your job and know you are appreciated and respected for what you're offering. I perform where people feel that way about me. If it's across the Atlantic, that's where I have to go. I have to pay my bills, I have to have my healthcare, and if I have to go to the UK or Europe to do that, that's what I'm going to do. If this book is more popular outside of the U.S., will you tell the publisher you only want to make it available in the U.S.? No. You'll embrace your readers wherever you find them.

It would have been nice to have been able to stay closer to home during the '90s, but it also afforded me a chance to make friends and establish relationships with people I might never have otherwise known. Like meeting my friend Angie Brown [of Bizarre Inc]—we did a UK *Sisters of Soul* tour together—something I wouldn't have been able to do had I not had hits in this country. I'm glad I've been able to travel and see the world—I appreciate that deeply.

Would you give me your take on '90s club life as a performer whose hits were so essential to the playlists of DJs in these venues?

Oh my God! Well, at that time, you realize how popular you are by the size of the clubs you performed at. I was doing some huge clubs and big tours, working an awful lot—to the point where I was in the UK at least three weeks of every month. I lived in a flat in London, rather than hotels, because I was there so much. The clubs were great. The energy was amazing. I was doing gay clubs, straight, black—all kinds. It was a beautiful time. At times it was overwhelming. One thing that stands out for me with these clubs was the need for me to take care of my voice. I was a live singer—it's difficult for me to lip sync. I also had to physically take care of myself because of the rigors of the road and the late hours of the clubs. It can do a lot to you if you're not careful. I surrounded myself with positive people. I was fortunate because I had a great team around me that helped me keep my footing.

It's funny—I recall that in our contracts with these clubs we were very specific in our riders that the sound quality had to be on point. We were very specific. We went to this one club, and they just didn't have the sound right. I tried three times to get it worked out with them (at soundcheck), but it was just awful. I literally walked off stage and threw a boot. It went right into the bar and everything, all the bottles of booze and glasses, came flying down. My friend reminded me of the incident not long ago [*she laughs*]; they remember it, too!

You must understand, I was so frustrated that I was unable to present my craft—not because of something I was doing wrong. I had contractual safeguards in place, and they weren't there. I'm a perfectionist and a stickler for things like that. And then they acted as if *I* messed up. I got so aggravated, and I lost my temper. That's why you need people around you to keep you calm.

In what ways did the AIDS epidemic that was raging during the '90s affect your career?

I remember when the AIDS epidemic was first starting, and I think it was *Lifebeat* magazine in New York that ran a story about how many artists were scared to admit they were going to support AIDS fundraisers, shows and dances. They were concerned about being identified with the gay culture or the disease or something. I never felt that way. I think it stems from the fact that my mother was a buyer in retail for years, and she would be interacting with the gay community often in her fashion work. So my exposure to gay culture came early. I found them to be really good people. I never knew them as anything but loving and kind. They were just who they were.

I recall so clearly being with my parents in the village in New York as a little girl. We were going to pass a jazz spot, and my dad was (and still is) a very good looking man. I remember another man passed us and gave a compliment to my dad. [*Sybil lets out a hearty laugh.*] I thought he was giving it to my mom. My mom got a big kick out of it. My parents were very comfortable in their own skins, so being exposed to gay life wasn't a big deal.

When it came to music, I went where I was supported. The gay community embraced me at the time when the DJs were really becoming stars themselves. Larry Levan—I absolutely adored him, and he was a very big supporter of mine. I had no real clue what gay life was really all about, but I knew the community was embracing me. When the HIV and AIDS epidemic came in, all I knew was that my friends were being hit with it. I knew people I personally cared about were going to die. I remember hearing a good friend of mine, the manager of a club on 57th street who I adored (a beautiful blond man), had become ill. Then, shortly after, it hit home again. My uncle was diagnosed as being HIV positive. When it hits so close to home—[*Sybil becomes emotional and pauses for a few moments. She wipes her tears away and continues her thought.*] When it hits close to home and you see people falling victim to something so terrible, you just become consumed with the desire to raise money to educate people and empower the community to fight back. I never thought for a moment that this *couldn't* happen to me, so I never stopped being involved. I tried very hard to help where I could. I still try to help with causes that serve those with and those who care for people with cancer, Alzheimer's and HIV. I'll do that until I take my last breath.

I think when our humanity stops and we start thinking that things like HIV, Parkinson's—any dreaded disease—can't happen to us, that we are somehow immune or above any of it, then we cease to have compassion, and we cease to progress.

You've given a lot of yourself as an entertainer. What did you sacrifice to have this career?

Having my career, I sacrificed being married earlier in life (I tried it later) and having a family and being—well—*still*. In order to be in a relationship you have to be still sometimes or very lucky to be with someone who gets what it's like to be with an artist 100 percent, someone who gets the nature of an artist. I wasn't with anyone who understood that. Sometimes I wish I had tried all that a bit earlier, but at the same time, I gained a lot. I don't have children of my own, but I've had other children and other people come into my life in a way that's really impacted me. I have nieces and nephews, a goddaughter—I'm very fortunate and very proud of the young people in my life. I've been able to impact young lives, and had I [raised] children of my own, I'm not sure I'd have been able to give back as much as I have.

I am a real proponent of arts-based education, and I work with young people and young adults today who want to do some of the things I've done. I want them to be prepared for what lies beyond an entertainment career. Because of my education, I had much to fall back on when recording, gigs, and the music thing slowed down. Thanks to my parents, I had a mind. That's what I aspire to do now. If my songs haven't made it into your heart, I am putting other good things into the universe. All of us have a song in our hearts. We all may not be able to literally sing them, but we all have something that is very rhythmic about who we are, and we all have something that is cause for celebration in our life to sing about.

I don't take my success for granted. The sacrifices I may have made have all been worth it. The rewards have been really great.

You released one more album during the era, 1997's Still a Thrill. **Afterward, you largely stepped out of the recording spotlight. What was going on in the years that followed your peak success?**

To be truthful, I went through a period where I felt I didn't want to do this anymore. I didn't stop singing; I just didn't want to have to keep traipsing all over the world for my supper. I didn't want to have to dance to the beat of someone else's drum. I was physically and emotionally drained. I also saw the music and the industry changing. I didn't see room for someone like me. I felt they wanted me to sell my soul to be in the business. I'm not going to be scantily clad, and I'm not going to sing songs with explicit lyrics. I didn't feel I had to align myself with a hip-hop artist to be viable. Don't get me wrong—I respect that genre. But I didn't feel I had to do that. I did that already with Salt 'N' Pepa. I got it; I understood what they wanted. But I realized I wasn't getting any younger, and when that happens, I think you start to look at yourself and think about what else you want to do.

I wanted something else. I made a decision. I sold my loft in New Jersey and moved south. A mentor of mine, the director of a program at a college, offered me the chance to be a lead instructor for an initiative called "Highways to Success." It was a program that helped young adults to do great things with their lives. I received master's level certification in research and marketing, and I was able to use those credentials to try something new, something else I felt some passion about other than singing. I always wanted to work with young people who didn't have made-up minds. So, that's what I did. I started in the early 2000s.

As time went on, I also started writing again (entertainment pieces for a newspaper), a few music gigs now and then, and in 2003 I got married, as I mentioned earlier. I tried the marriage thing for almost nine years, and though it didn't work out, it was a good experience for me. No regrets, and I learned a lot about myself over all those years. I found out I am a really good instructor. (I even won a few awards for my work in North Carolina and a few national awards for my work with foundations). I discovered—and I'm sure my music work contributed to this—I have a knack for thinking outside the box. I'm really appreciative of that.

I'm in a very peaceful place in my life. I expect things will change again at some point, as they always have, and I will move on to something new again when the time is right.

You seem very comfortable with what we generally refer to as middle age.

I embrace being my age. On a daily basis, I come in contact with people who say they are inspired by what I've done and what I do. I'm inspired every day to get up and make a move and strive because of them. I think people who are considered underappreciated, underprivileged, underserved—they need to be empowered. I'm always looking for ways to do that. The songs I sing are often a reflection of my life, and maybe people will find that empowering.

"Don't Make Me Over"—Burt Bacharach and Hal David were ahead of their time when they wrote that, whether they knew it or not. They empowered people with that song—women, that gay man or woman, that person who is different in any way. Accept me for who I am and what I do. Don't make me over. If nothing else, there's a saying I learned in school long ago [*credited to Henry David Thoreau*], and I'm a firm believer in it. It goes something like: "If a man does not keep pace with his companions, perhaps it is because he hears the sound of a different drummer. Let him keep pace with the music he hears, however measured or far away." I always loved that quote. Live and let live. Let me dance the way I want to, without persecution.

How do you view the state of the music industry today?

What has happened is quite sad. We have watered down music so much that we have made it acceptable to have lackluster production, limited musicality, lyrics that say nothing (and if they do, the messages go ignored), and where the visual is so important that our senses are becoming dulled. I'm bothered by it, but I'm hopeful there will be a turnaround. I've seen it in the past, where there was a breakdown in the quality of music followed by a period of the greatest music you've ever heard. I think we have to teach and foster the art of good songwriting. Where are our James Taylors and Carole Kings? Where are the Stevie Wonders and the Barry Whites? Where are the Gamble and Huffs?

I don't know what is happening in dance music. I hope and pray it will get back to where singers and musicians get the stage back—not a remixer or DJ being the exclusive star. I'm not putting down DJs, but what I am saying is that anytime a DJ is taking the spotlight from a singer who gave life to the song—and you become a featured player after 20 years of success—to me that's not right. But that's the current reality. I have to be honest; I don't think it's cool. *I do not think it's cool.*

Dance music has never received the widespread accolades bestowed on other genres of music. I'd like to know what your thoughts are about dance music's value in our society.

The value of dance music can be seen in the fact that it has probably been the most globally accepted genre of music—ever! Anytime you have mainstream pop, rock country or R&B artists doing dance records or dance mixes, it's not because of anything other than the fact that they *know* there's a market for them. Dance music is more prevalent than some will ever admit. There has been a stigma attached to this genre for decades. However, what they've done is taken dance elements and just called it pop. I think it's funny because the truth is that dance music has had more impact on other genres than anything else. They'll never admit that because they don't want the once red-headed stepchild (who languished in the corner of the room waiting to be heard) to take the driver's seat.

Go anywhere in the world, and you will always hear dance music. You won't always hear rock or country or any other style. But you will always hear songs you can dance to, resonating from somewhere. From Spain to Africa to Russia to Asia. I've performed in countries where they don't speak a bit of English, but there they are—people dancing and singing the words to my songs and feeling great. Dance music makes you celebrate life. It is and always will be the voice of a global community.

"I had the kind of voice that pop and R&B radio seemed to be comfortable with, and I think the PWL team knew I would interpret their songs without going too far to church or being too sappy," observes singer/songwriter Sybil Lynch (courtesy Sybil Lynch).

Lightning Round with Sybil

Money or fame?
Money. The idea of fame scares me. I don't know what that looks like. Money—I can manipulate that!

Donna Summer or Diana Ross?
Donna Summer—all day, every day. I loved her. I wish I could have done a duet with her.

Live performances or in the studio?
Live performances.

Perfect hair or perfect teeth?
Perfect teeth. I can always buy hair. I could buy teeth, too, but it's a lot more expensive.

Saver or spender?
Oh, gosh. I used to be a spender. Today, I'm much more a saver.

Taco Bell or McDonald's?
Eeew to both! Well, I kind of like McDonald's coffee, so I'll have to go with them.

Fabulous nightlife or the great outdoors?
[*Sybil laughs heartily.*] Oh, fabulous nightlife. The great outdoors? Oh no, no—I don't rough it. Me and a tent? Oh, no!

Robin Jackson Maynard, also known as Robin S
"Show Me Love" (1993)

"To be on that stage and enter with the first notes of 'Show Me Love'—and Bobby Brown and Whitney Houston and all the other huge artists of the day enjoying the music—it made me feel like I belonged."—Robin Jackson Maynard

One need only take a quick look at YouTube to discover what fans really think of Robin S's signature smash "Show Me Love." You'll see numerous comments echoing the posted sentiment, "This song will never die!" It's an accurate statement. The track, a smoldering, soulful house anthem that incited millions to bump and grind on the dance floor, began to find its worldwide audience in 1990 with its original UK release. By 1993, it was a monster in the U.S. and across the globe. Since then, the song seems to have lost none of its appeal.

The jam uniquely belongs to the divine Miss S, whose brilliant interpretation was surprisingly created during a bout with illness. Still, despite the less than ideal conditions under which she recorded, Robin managed to breathe a long life into one the most revered dance-pop house tracks of the decade. Nearly a quarter century later, "Show Me Love" continues to be covered and sampled by the 21st century's hottest acts. (Early in 2016, the singer proved her continued relevance when she returned to the upper echelons of Billboard's dance chart with the hit "Shout It Out Loud," performed with DJ Escape.)

Robin S (born Robin Jackson and sometimes billed as Robin S.—with a period at the end) basked in success on the dance charts with a number of follow-up singles, but "Show Me Love" remains her defining moment. It's something the dancer, singer and songwriter doesn't take lightly, and she is quick to express her appreciation for the lofty ranking she enjoys in club music history.

From her home in Atlanta, Georgia, Robin reflects on her journey with the song, a house anthem that became the groove for millions who experienced the era.

So, Robin, how were you introduced to music in your early years?

I grew up in St. Albans, Queens Village, New York. My father was a professional boxer named Stonewall Jackson. Growing up, I always had music in my life. I've been singing since the age of five. I think that's all I ever wanted to do. I wanted to entertain. I started off in a children's church choir, and I was a Michael Jackson fan from early on. I think I might have been influenced by my father because of his popularity in the ring. My mom was very supportive of me and did all she could to help me pursue my dreams. She didn't live to see it happen, but I know she was smiling down on me when it did.

I had to work really hard and prove myself. It started when, as part of the choir, I was somehow heard on the radio by Berry Gordy. They'd record our morning singing at the church for broadcast later in the evening. I took singing lessons with an accomplished teacher for a couple of years, and Motown paid for it. They were interested in me. When they approached my mother with a contract for me, she was very cautious about signing my life away. As a kid, I didn't understand all that—all the logistics—nor did I care. I just wanted to sing. She declined their offer. So, I just kept taking singing and dancing lessons. My mom couldn't afford both, so it was two years of one, then two years of the other, back and forth. My mom arranged my first concert. She booked a club and hired a band, and that was her way of showing her love and support for my dreams.

How did you come to cross paths with Allen George and Fred McFarlane, the songwriters and creators of "Show Me Love," your smash recording debut?

I started singing with bands when I was 15, with the permission of my mother. I used to sing at colleges, weddings, everything. I learned how to truly become an entertainer by singing with these bands. Interestingly enough, I never sang dance music with them. The closest I came to dance music was singing Michael Jackson's "Don't Stop 'Til You Get Enough." I always sang R&B and jazz. Time passed, and I was once again singing with another band when a young lady named Shirley Goban, out of Brooklyn, heard me and wanted to introduce

U.S. label Big Beat/Atlantic Records issued this photograph of Robin S upon the release of her massive hit single and album called *Show Me Love* (photograph by George Holz, from the author's collection).

me to some people. These gentlemen [*referring to Allen George and Fred McFarlane*] said they were working on a record that they wanted to try me on. Me, not knowing the business at all, just said, "Alright; why not?" I developed a friendship with them and started hanging out at the studio. "Show Me Love" was recorded in New York, and the writers then partnered up with the Champion label in the UK to release the song in 1990.

Do you remember the recording session for the song?

When they brought me the record "Show Me Love," I was really unsure how to sing it. I liked the song, and, you know, I liked Donna Summer, and I liked those types of songs. But I never imagined me singing that style. They told me to just try it. The weekend I was to record it, I had the flu. I walked into the studio, and I was all stuffed up in the head, and it was just like, well, we'll see what happens. In the beginning, they had all the lights on in the studio, but I just wasn't feeling anything. When you sing in a club, the lights aren't full blast; they are dim so you feel the atmosphere. So they turned off my lights in the booth and dimmed their own, and then it was much better for me.

I sang the song, and they were like, "This is fine! This is exactly what we were looking for!" I was like, "*Really?*" I could not stand to hear the playback because I didn't feel I really sounded like that. To this day, it's hard for me in the studio because I am more comfortable as a live singer. Recording me at a show—that's fine. I feel the vibe from the people. But in a studio, it feels so desolate and isolated to me.

I really didn't think the song was that great. I took the recording home and listened to it over and over. All I kept saying was, "Yuck." But I think the secret of the song was the fact that because I was sick, I had to really *sing* this—push it from the gut, you know? I wasn't screaming or yelling, but I had to reach deep to make it sound like I wasn't sick. I think that's what made the song so believable. I also kind of took the song apart and thought about what parts fit in with my own life. Did this song actually apply to me? I had to find that, relate it to what trials and tribulations I have faced. Anytime you sing a song that you yourself did not write, you have to sort of go into character to perform it. A song is just a song until a singer breathes life into it. I was ready for it, and I got sick. But I decided we couldn't keep rescheduling the session—I had to just go in and do it. When people heard it, I think they were able to feel what I was singing.

They certainly did. "Show Me Love" was a remarkable success. It took some time to build momentum, but after a 1992 remix of the track by StoneBridge and Nick Nice, the song began to really get noticed in Britain. Eventually, it crossed the pond and became a Top Five pop hit in the U.S., reached number one on the* Billboard *dance survey and sold well over half a million copies in this country alone. It quickly became an anthem of house music and an iconic song of the era. How did you react to having a hit of this magnitude?

This is the thing—"Show Me Love" came out overseas first. I got a phone call saying the song had hit number 10 in the UK. I wasn't excited at all—not a bit. I just figured I'd have to head over there if it went to number one. I said, "Okay, call me back if it gets to number five." I said it just like that—completely disinterested. A week later, I get told it was number eight. I had the same response. Another week passes, and I get a call saying I better pack my bags; it's number five. So I said, "Call me when it hits number one." Well, a short time later, I got told it reached number one on the *Top of the Pops* show in London. I freaked out, but not in a good way. I had never been overseas before, and I didn't want to go. They told me I *had* to go to support the record. Well, of course, I went, and that was the beginning. But despite a big thing like that, it still didn't hit me that the song was going to be a monster.

I lived in the States. Nobody was playing it here. So to me, it was just a record. Overseas it was becoming huge, but that didn't affect me over here. There was a U.S. DJ who flew over to the UK sometimes to do some shows, and he and his crew brought the record back here. Mind you, we had been trying to get it signed to Atlantic Records, but nobody would take it. No one. It was said that I couldn't sing and that it wasn't an interesting record—a lot of negative things like that. It went platinum really quick in Britain, and then the DJs started playing it here. That's when Atlantic finally became interested in it. That explains the delay in releasing the song in the U.S.

Where did the name Robin S come from?

When my song came out, you had all the members of the Jackson family releasing music. You also had Keisha out there, Millie Jackson's daughter. They thought there were too many Jacksons on the market, and I'd get lost in the sauce with Robin Jackson. I was asked to think of a name that I'd like to be called for this record. Because my father's name was Stonewall, I took the name Robin Stone. From the time the record was with Champion and the music was redone for the American market, I couldn't get used to the idea of being called Robin Stone. I wouldn't even respond to the name. So I said (as the new U.S. version was about to come out) what if we just make it Robin S? They were okay with that.

When did it finally hit you that you had achieved something significant?

Once the record came out in the U.S., I started to get more excited. Now you're talking home. I remember driving on Long Island's Southern State Parkway. I was tuned to KISS FM on the radio. "Show Me Love" came on. I turned it to WBLS, another huge station, and it was playing there as well. A little while later, it was on KTU. That's when it became clear to me that some serious stuff was going on. I pulled my car over because I got so nervous and couldn't believe it. It was the moment I realized that, wait a minute, that's me! This thing is for real! It was cool because I was still kind of unknown at the time; a lot of people I was in contact with didn't know I was Robin S. So when I would hear them say, "Oh that's a cool song"—hear them react—that was really something.

I can still remember some performances I did like they were yesterday. I remember performing at the Hippodrome in London, on the stage, by myself. It blew my mind because the stage lifted up from the floor, and I was surrounded by all these screaming, cheering fans. And I was the only person on the stage. When you're up on that stage by yourself and people are vibing with you and feeling your music, you can feel their energy, no matter how far away they are. It is overwhelming.

Then I did the Apollo Theater in New York, which was televised. Home is different. When you do a show where you live, in such an historic place, people running down to the stage to be closer to you and a part of what you're singing—wow, it's totally overwhelming. That is something I will live with for the rest of my life.

I also remember well receiving two *Billboard* awards, and I did their show with a lot of hip-hop artists. To be on that stage and enter with the first notes of "Show Me Love"—and Bobby Brown and Whitney Houston and all the other huge artists of the day enjoying the music—it made me feel like I belonged. I felt so good. It does all happen so fast—you're whisked from one event to another—but I've tried to hang onto those special moments and cherish them deep, deep within me. I refuse to let it all be a blur because that was my life and legacy—that's what I leave to my grandkids, you know?

I still have moments like these that feel surreal to me. I'm thankful. I'm blessed. I try not to take things for granted. I don't forget where I came from. I still feed off that vibe people give me when I sing. I still perform at clubs, and I see kids there my children's age and younger. I tell them to go home and thank their parents for playing my song around them. They're 23 years old—that's how old the song is. [*Robin laughs.*]

You scored a powerful follow-up with the similar-sounding "Luv 4 Luv," which was a number one hit on the U.S. dance chart and quite successful across Europe. Was there pressure to keep the hits coming?

I didn't feel any pressure because we had done the entire album by the time "Show Me Love" was up and running. So it wasn't up to me to decide what singles would follow. It was up to the producers and the label. I still didn't know too much about the business to be honest with you. Even though I was in on some of the label meetings, I really didn't take anything seriously. I was just enjoying the situation so much.

It took almost four years to release your follow-up album, From Now On, released on the U.S. Big Beat/Atlantic label in 1997. It featured the top dance single "It Must Be Love." There were a number of different producers involved in this project (Todd Terry and Tony Moran for starters) but none from the original production team. What was happening at this time?

It took a long time to launch the *From Now On* album because I was parting ways with my original producers. It wasn't a very amicable parting; let me put it that way. I felt it was better for me to [work with new people]. The vibe and feeling was gone. It took me a while to get going again, and I was playing catch-up.

Todd Terry was to produce a song I was going to put on the album, but he came to me with another song that he wanted me to hear. I said no problem. I listened to the music, and I started ad-libbing [some lyrics]. He said, "Keep going; keep going!" We were able to write that song, "Givin' U All That I've Got," in less than 20 minutes. The song was also featured on the *Space Jam* soundtrack. We ended up working together on that track and on "Shine on Me."

I can never put the blame for difficulties I experienced [in the business] on any one person or persons. It was my job to learn this industry. I entrusted my life to other people's hands. Rule number one—*you don't do that*. You learn that by experience. I didn't take the time to learn the logistics of the business. I was a green bean, and I placed too much trust out there. Eventually you learn, but sometimes it's too late to change a situation. So directly after my first album, I sat down to look into things and made some decisions. I guess you could say my partnership with my original producers started out as a good marriage, but it was time to get a divorce.

It cost me. I never saw any of the royalties I earned from the *Space Jam* soundtrack because I bought my way out of that situation. It was just money, right? You can't miss something that you don't have, so I just let those royalties go. I wished everybody well, but it wasn't a healthy situation for me. I didn't want to reach the point where I didn't want to sing anymore. If I had stayed in that situation, I can tell you I would have never sung again.

The clubs were into the new material on your second album, but the project, unfortunately, didn't fare as well (on the pop charts) as your debut effort.

From Now On didn't get a lot of support from the record label, for whatever reason—I don't know why. I couldn't get a tour arranged for it. I had a very successful album release party in Miami that went over well, but the actions of the label didn't match what they were saying to me. They just didn't push the album and were dropping the ball. I think they just didn't want me anymore. I was okay with that. My voice was a God-given talent—it had nothing to do with the record company. I'm still not connected to a label. That's fine for me because I have the freedom to sing wherever and whatever I please. I admit it becomes challenging when you try to release a new record in terms of support—distribution and radio support, things like that. But other than that, I'm okay.

You have a very enthusiastic following on both sides of the Atlantic, but many American artists feel there is a greater sense of loyalty overseas. Do you share this opinion?

I've always said that Europeans seem to embrace the past a bit more than Americans. When the *Show Me Love* album came out, there were only particular songs that the U.S. would play, like the title track and "Luv 4 Luv." I'd go overseas, and they'd know the whole album. People over there still request songs that I haven't sung in years because they weren't hits here in the U.S. Europeans seem to know my entire album, and back in the day, they'd play the entire album in stores and cafes. When I come home, there's only the one or two songs that they'll play. I don't think it's so much the public's memory as it is that the labels and system fed you what they wanted to feed you back then. So if you're not the type of person who explores an album on your own, then you'll know the one or two songs, and that's it. Overseas, they explore. That's why album sales were always much stronger over there.

As the '90s began to wind down, what trends did you see developing in dance music, and how did they affect you?

By the time of my last album, hip-hop was really on the upswing. If you didn't have that hip-hop flair about your music, it wasn't flying. So sometimes—and it happens to most artists—you have to step back, clear your head, look at what's out there, and decide *not* how you fit in, but rather how you *re-create* yourself to join in. Not to fit in—because that leaves you vulnerable to being pushed out.

"Show Me Love" has been recreated a couple of times, and people ask me how I feel about it. I say it keeps me relevant. I don't have to always like it. Jason Derulo did it with "Don't Wanna Go Home." The only thing I don't like is that I'm available to reach out to for my blessing, and they don't always do that. Or they could say, "Hey, would you like to be a guest on it?" Something like that—I think that's proper respect for where the music came from. When Kid Ink and Chris Brown did "Show Me," I didn't mind that. It keeps people talking about the song. But it would have been nice to have been a part of the project.

Where do you see yourself taking your career in the future?

It was never all about the money for me. It was about doing something that I loved. It paid the bills, yes, but that wasn't the focus. I'll be happy if God continues to bless me as he has in the past. I have a lot of records out there on the Internet—if you throw one out there in today's market and it sticks, then everything else that you've ever done will follow it. So, if you love making music, you just keep doing it. That's what I'm going to do. When it doesn't work out the way your mind says it should work out, you won't lose your love for it. You do it because you love it. I often have to ask myself, "If you never get another record deal and never have another hit record, do you want to still keep doing it?" The answer for me is yes. I'll never again let anyone or anything take my passion away from me. I'll never second guess my passion.

Have dance music artists received their props in pop culture history?

Here's the funny part. Dance music gets shoved to the back of the bus when it relates to the artist who is primarily associated with it. But now we have all these new R&B and pop stars and artists from different genres creating dance versions of their songs. Explain that to me. That's considered fine, but the artists who directly helped create the genre and nurtured dance music are often ignored. I'm very confused by that.

LIGHTNING ROUND WITH ROBIN

Perfect hair or perfect teeth?

Perfect hair. I've always been a stickler about everything to do with my hair being on point.

"I still perform at clubs, and I see kids there my children's age and younger. I tell them to go home and thank their parents for playing my song around them," says Robin Jackson Maynard today (courtesy Robin Maynard Jackson).

Meet your ancestors or meet your descendants?

Ancestors. You need to know where you came from in order to know where you are going.

Donna Summer or Diana Ross?

Wow, that's difficult. I can't choose. I have great respect for both.

Rich and ugly or poor and good looking?

Poor and good looking. I think I'd be alright with that.

Personal chef or personal fitness trainer?

Chef. If I have the chef, I won't have to worry about my weight, and I'm less likely to need the trainer.

Five good friends or one best friend?

One best friend. Truthfully, I don't really need a whole lot of people around me.

Extended versions or radio edits?

Oh, extended versions! More to love. The extended versions give you an opportunity to hear the artist let loose.

Lane McCray of La Bouche
"Be My Lover" (1995)

> "Most people see an artist get a hit record like this and think it's just luck. But I think the best records are written from a very honest place—reality."—Lane McCray

For a time in the mid–'90s, the duo known as La Bouche ruled the pop and dance charts of the world. Based in Germany, the act was comprised of two eager young performers named Melanie Thornton and Lane McCray. To say the pair once dominated radio and clubs across the globe with their frantic and irresistible brand of electronic Euro-house music is an understatement. "Sweet Dreams (Hola Hola Eh)" and the blistering "Be My Lover" (the latter track written by the duo) are widely regarded today as indispensable classics of the decade.

Though initially determined to stay on track with their musical vision, the momentum of La Bouche's high-speed ascent wavered soon after the release of their second album, as Melanie's solo career aspirations began to take root. A short time later the world received the news that the 34-year-old singer had lost her life in a horrific plane crash that killed a total of 24 passengers. The loss of his friend and partner was a severe blow for McCray, who largely withdrew from the music scene following her death.

Fortunately, Lane's story didn't end there. A few years ago, he returned to the industry and his musical roots in Germany, pursuing a new career as a solo artist and re-envisioning La Bouche. His recent singles "Heartbeat," "Angel of My Life" (featuring Tanja Geuder) and a 2015 revisit of "Sweet Dreams" performed with Djane Monique show smooth vocals reflective of his renewed sense of confidence and energy, backed, of course, by ferocious beats. He's also working on a new La Bouche album that will further revamp some of the group's signature hits.

In this interview, he is a laid back and soft-spoken man with a solid memory of his '90s glory days. On a stopover in New Mexico, he discusses his career and the all-too-human experiences that have kept his reality very much in check.

You have a somewhat unusual background in that you had a military career before becoming a pop star, Lane. Tell me a bit about these early days.

I was born in Fort Bragg, North Carolina, so I was an army brat. My father later retired in Alaska, and that's where my family ended up. I joined the military after I got out of school, and that took me away from Alaska, thankfully. There is *nothing* to do there, unless you like

The cover of the 1995 U.S. version of La Bouche's debut album *Sweet Dreams* on RCA Records features American vocalists Lane McCray and Melanie Thornton at the pinnacle of their recording careers (author's collection).

to fish and hunt and that kind of thing. My father said I was the one kid who went wrong because I joined the air force and not the army, as he had. That was his running joke with his friends. But I just forged my own path, and I was kind of an independent thinker. I joined the military to get my education. One enlistment followed another, and before you knew it, I had served 15 years. (I remained in the Air National Guard after that, and that's why I'm here in Santa Fe, New Mexico, at the moment.) It's interesting that as a musician in the air force band I did go into areas like Iraq, Afghanistan and Kuwait, areas like that, and we boosted the morale of the troops there.

How did you start your professional career in recorded music?

Interestingly enough, when I was on active duty in the air force I was involved in entertainment by being a part of *Tops in Blue*, which was a cast of about 30 military personnel that were selected for to perform in a show. We flew around to different bases to perform for about a year. I did that for four tours starting in 1988. Initially I was a dancer. This whole entertainment thing intrigued me, and I wanted to do more. I started singing, but I can't say I was really a bona-fide rapper. I was reassigned to Germany and met Melanie Thornton, and we began singing together in a cover band called Groovin' Affairs. I started rapping and doing covers of Sir Mix-a-Lot, Sugarhill Gang, Prince and Michael Jackson, and Melanie would do standards by Chaka Khan, Whitney Houston—all kinds of different sounds.

Melanie had started working in the studio with producers and DJ Ulli Brenner and Amir Saraf, and she asked me if I'd be interested in coming in to do some raps. Of course, I said sure. I went in, and the rest is history, as they say.

Can you describe the chemistry you had with Melanie at the time?

Well, you know there was another young man, a buddy of mine, singing in the cover band with Melanie before I became a part of it. Actually, I was asked to cover him for a couple of gigs. So I went in and did my thing, and the band really enjoyed my energy, as did Melanie. They asked me to stay, but I said they'd have to clear it with my buddy because it was really his gig. It turned out he couldn't continue in the band, so I stayed on. There was a real kinetic energy between Melanie and me, maybe because we were both from the south originally. She was from Charleston, South Carolina, and I was from North Carolina. We definitely had good chemistry.

Even at the beginning of our work together as La Bouche, people thought we were dating. We didn't have any issue with people thinking that, and we became this little dream team of the dance-pop world, especially in Germany.

Melanie was so sweet—caring, giving. Silly, too—we laughed a lot. If I miss anything about her being gone, it's probably that laughter we had and my memories of situations we had on the road. So many silly stories—oh man, I have a plethora of silly stories.

How does your producer at the time, Frank Farian, come into the picture? When you first met him, were you aware of his background in the music industry (Milli Vanilli, Boney M., etc.) and the controversies surrounding him?

I wasn't aware of Boney M., but I was certainly aware of Frank's connection to Milli Vanilli. I kind of found out about him because Ulli and Amir were renting studio space from him in Rosbach, Germany. When I was asked to be a part of this musical project with Melanie, I was introduced to Frank. I thought to myself, "So, you're the guy from Milli Vanilli." The whole issue about other people's voices being used in recordings went on before Milli Vanilli, and it certainly still goes on today. You can't take anything away from Frank's music though—it was great. It just would have been better if they had gone about it legitimately.

So, when Melanie and I came into the picture, we were definitely not going to be puppets. We were so involved with everything and had so many opinions, it reached the point where Frank would get annoyed with us. When we were trying to come up with a name for us, he said it should be "The Mouth," because we had so much to say all the time. [*He laughs.*] Well, of course that didn't sound that great, so what about the French way of saying it—"La Bouche"?

How did La Bouche break onto the music scene?

Our first hit, "Sweet Dreams," was done around the same time as Melanie recorded "Tonight Is the Night" as Le Click. Both records were being shopped around in Germany, but Logic Records picked "Tonight" up first. Nobody wanted "Sweet Dreams." Ulli and Amir sent it to [Henri Belolo's] label in Paris, Scorpio Music. Nobody there wanted it either, but one of the guys at Scorpio sent it to a DJ in Italy, and it started getting club and radio airplay there. Next thing you know, it was all over the radio, and it became the number one song there. Nobody knew what we looked like or anything. We started working in Italy first. Once we started gaining momentum, Frank Farian came in and decided to sign the song to his label, MCI, a subsidiary of Hansa-BMG at the time. From there came our first album, *Sweet Dreams*, which went gold in several countries.

How would you characterize Frank Farian?

I would say he was definitely controlling in that he knows what he wants. They called him the pop genie because he had an ear for what works—Boney M., Milli Vanilli, No Mercy, etc. I think maybe Melanie and I had a different relationship with him because—how can I say this—we weren't 18 or 19 year olds. We were educated, and we weren't looking for fame and fortune at the drop of a hat. We were willing to work for it and be a part of the process that would get us there in our recordings.

Melanie, I know for sure, always stood up for what she wanted to sound like in the studio. There were a couple of times I was in the studio, and Frank wanted me to sing something in a particular note or with a chord structure that I just knew was wrong musically. I just couldn't support that. But that's typical of the ups and downs that happen in the studio when you sing someone else's song with limited input. I remember he said to me, "Well, Lane, I can't guarantee it's going to be a hit unless you sing it like this." At one point he thought I sounded "too Broadway." I said, "What exactly is that?" He said it was singing too phonetically correct and not giving way to Ebonics and that sort of thing. Well, that just wasn't me, and what you see and hear is what you get.

I can't say he was annoying to me. I mean, Melanie and I were two people with zero experience in the industry, and he was hugely successful and willing us to lead us on the path. He was very generous with us. We got a great advance on the records, which indicated he believed in us. I think most new artists at the time generated one to three points as royalties at the time. We received 12. After the Milli Vanilli thing, I think he wanted to be free from scandal, and perhaps we benefited from that. He let us write quite a bit on the records, which was also a really good thing.

The single "Be My Lover" from 1995 is regarded by many as one of the quintessential electro-dance-pop songs of the '90s. The track reached number one in Germany and Sweden and was reported to have reached the Top 10 in as many as 14 countries. It has sold, by some estimates, six million copies worldwide. You even earned top ASCAP honors in the U.S. as "the most played song in America" at the time. What details do you recall about this extraordinarily successful song?

Most people see an artist get a hit a hit record like this and think it's just luck. But I think the best records are written from a very honest place—reality. "Be My Lover" was a *real* song with lyrics by Melanie and me. We were at a gig in Germany, and in between sets she says to me, drying herself off with a towel, "So, how do you feel about mixing business with pleasure?" I responded that it was my experience that it doesn't usually work. I had dated a young lady who performed on the tour, and when she was mad at me she'd bring that on to the stage. But, then again, never say never. We continued doing the shows, and when we got into the studio, she said something like with all the time we had spent together, I should know if I wanted to be her lover. My response was that I heard what she was saying, but I needed to know more about her. Well, that's where that song came from.

The hook of the song, the la-da-di-da-dah, came from being unable to create the right lyrics to fill that portion of the music. So we just kind of ad-libbed that portion, and it stayed. It became the hook that everybody knows.

We never dated; we never took it there. She was interested, and I kind of was, too, but I knew how it would go. I know me. [*He laughs.*] It was cool the public was thinking we were dating, but it was an illusion. She started dating someone else, one of her security guards, and that took some of the pressure off. I started dating Kim Sanders from the group Culture Beat. Everybody was happy.

In those days, if you had a hit of the magnitude of "Be My Lover," especially when you were the songwriter as well as the performer, were you pretty much set for life?

I wouldn't say life. We were compensated decently. When I used to look at shows like *MTV Cribs* and I'd see artists that sold maybe one or two million records and they had these palatial homes and cars, I'd be like, "hmmmmm." La Bouche sold over ten million CDs and singles, and I sure didn't have all that. But I'll tell you what I *was* able to do. I bought my mom and sister's homes. That was bit of a relief not to have to worry about my parents. I took care of a few people. I never wanted that much myself. I still need to work today. Our success didn't set me up for life. I also made dumb choices and blew quite a bit wining and dining women who left me for someone else. "I want that ring back! I want that dress back!" I'd say. [*He smiles and shakes his head.*] My mom would always say, "Baby, just let it go." So, I did. I have no regrets. I was able to live comfortably and travel, so no complaints.

Other than financially, how did your lives change in the '90s as a result of La Bouche's success?

Once we had our success, things *did* change. I remember I was driving, and I heard our song "Sweet Dreams" on the radio. This was before cell phones, so I couldn't call anyone. I just pulled to the side of the road and freaked out for a minute. It's not like I never heard the song, but on the radio it was kind of cool. I didn't know how big we were becoming until we did a big music event in Italy called *Festivalbar*. At the time, it was a huge event. When Melanie and I got there, we had something like 30 security guards at arm's length around us because there was a crowd of about 50,000 people at the stadium. I was trying to understand why there was such a need for so much security, as nobody really knew who we were. I thought maybe it was because somebody huge like Michael Jackson or Madonna was there. Well, the guards escorted us to the stage, and when I heard the crowd roar when they announced La Bouche, it was total pandemonium.

So, one of the changes we had to get used to was the loss of anonymity. Where you were used to doing your own thing, now you were dealing with people recognizing you, wanting an autograph, etc. This was way before the paparazzi became what it is today, but it was still intense. Even so, I wanted to try to stay as grounded as possible and be accessible—not to become like some of the artists I knew who really believed the hype about themselves and stardom. It's just an illusion, and I don't think it's a good idea to start buying into the "you're all that" mindset.

I guess the other thing that changed about me was my look. If you look at the earliest photos and videos of me, I was wearing baggy pants and a style cap. That gave way to the

Gucci look—you name the designer, I had it, you know? I had a sponsorship with Gucci for a while. The more money you had, the more you could do. I think, for me, I became a bit more of a clotheshorse. Melanie was a bit more practical. Her mom was a seamstress and made a lot of the things she wore. People were coming out of the woodwork to dress us for events—like Dolce & Gabbana for the *MTV Awards*.

Were the vices of the time, the prevalence of drugs in the music business for example, a problem in any way?

I knew what I was getting into. I think being a part of the Air Force entertainment thing helped me to stay grounded. I had no problems with sex, drugs or alcohol when we hit it big. Neither of us lived that sex, drugs and rock 'n' roll lifestyle. We talked to kids a lot about HIV and abstinence. We were part of an organization in Germany that helped those in hospice and living with HIV and AIDS. We read to people, listened to music with them, whatever was needed. So, I think Melanie and I were just grateful for the opportunity we were given, and we didn't want to mess it up.

How did you view yourselves in comparison to other dance-pop artists hitting the European charts?

We hit at a time when acts like 2 Unlimited, Snap!, Culture Beat, Twenty 4 Seven, E-Rotic, and Mr. President were very popular. They were driven a bit more by rap, and the hooks were sung. Our songs were a bit more melodic. I think La Bouche changed the game a bit because we really crossed over to mainstream pop radio, sporting events and movies. I think we were more of a dance-pop act rather than strictly a dance act.

I remember we decided we were going to put a live band together to support our act. The label said we couldn't do that because we were a dance music act. We told them to sit back, relax and just watch. We put together a showcase for the executives in Berlin with a seven-piece band, five dancers, and three background vocalists. They found it so strange that we were able to reproduce our sound in a live setting. Dance music was traditionally track driven.

Was success in the United States on your radar from the beginning?

I don't think that America was someplace we were looking to conquer. I remember writing and calling home to my family in the U.S. saying that we were on TV and doing this and that. They'd kind of say, "That's cool," not really believing it. But when our music first hit in the States, I think it was 1995 for "Be My Lover," it was—of all stations—BET [Black Entertainment Television] that first played our video. Then we performed at Spring Break down in Florida. Then people started seeing La Bouche.

I can truly say it was the gay community, the gay clubs that picked up on the record first, from the Limelight in New York to the Copacabana in Ft. Lauderdale. They really supported us.

I don't think we ever thought of any country or had our sights set on any place specifically, outside of Germany. We were very big in South America, and we sold two or three million in Japan. Everywhere but England (at first) picked up on the record. Subsequently, when we did hit the States, we probably lost out on a lot of money because the record company had us do so many promotions there. We lost out on what might have been a big two-week tour of Japan because we had to do promotional visits to radio stations like WBLS in New York. That was cool, but we were never pushing that hard—as if making it in America was the true mark of success.

Ironically, in the United States, you're only as big as your last hit. Well, ours was over

20 years ago. Overseas, however, I'm still actively working. I wouldn't say we don't have loyal fans in America, but the Europeans are extremely steadfast and gracious.

What went wrong with the second album, 1997's SOS *(also known as* A Moment of Love*), which didn't fare as well on the charts?*

Yeah, it was pretty much a flop. I think we had a few too many cooks in the kitchen. Most of the hits off the first album were because of Ulli and Amir. By the second album, we were bringing in Diane Warren, Christopher Applegate—people who could create great music, yes, but weren't a match for the type of artists people knew us to be. So I think we changed the formula too quickly. But we also did the *All Mixed Up* remix album and a greatest hits set, which did pretty well.

Shortly after signing a solo deal in 2001, Melanie was tragically killed in a plane crash near Zürich, Switzerland. She was just 34 years of age. May I ask you to recall this difficult time and the aftermath?

Going back to that time, Melanie had begun to feel possibly too controlled by Frank and wanted to branch out to a solo career, as probably anybody would. Melanie wore her heart on her sleeve, so when I heard her songs, I was never sure if she was talking about me or maybe somebody else. She did a song called "Back on My Feet Again," [that contained lyrics about being better off alone] which I took kind of personally (though it could have been about anybody). We talked on AOL (remember that?) and had two or three very brief conversations on it over the course of 2001. She had gotten married and divorced, and she was dating again.

I was out at my dad's house in Las Vegas around Thanksgiving. I got a call from singer Crystal Waters, and she asked me if I had heard anything about a plane crash in Switzerland. A friend of mine in Germany then called me and told me there *was* a plane crash. Another dance music group called Passion Fruit was on this flight, along with Melanie. At that point, we didn't know who had survived. I remember I thought if anyone was going to walk away from something like that, it would be Melanie. Just about the time I got off the phone, there was a blurb on CNN that singer Melanie Thornton died in a plane crash. Honestly, I was so numb [when I heard] the news. You talk about having spent 24 hours a day, seven days a week with someone—you are pretty much married to that person. You know so much about them. I was dumbfounded. I was glad I was at my parents' house at the time. It was a little bit of a safe haven for me.

Eventually, the label contacted me, and they asked me to do something for the memorial service they were having in Berlin. I will tell you—I didn't go to Berlin or the funeral. The reason was I had some ongoing legal litigation with our management at the time, which was essentially Melanie's sister, and it was rather serious. I didn't want my presence to disrupt this service for Melanie. I had friends who told me I should have gone anyway, but I knew Melanie knew my heart, and I was of the belief at that time that she would have understood my reasons. I heard it was a beautiful service in Berlin.

I backed away from everything for a couple of years after that. I can tell you I have thought about it every day since. I still find it very hard to believe she's not here. There are days when I'll listen to some of the records we did, and I'll start bawling. During our last performance together, one of the last songs we performed was called "In Your Life," which we wrote together [and it was commercially released in 2002 on the anniversary of her passing].

The message of the song was that tomorrow isn't promised, so we really have to live our lives like it's our last day on earth. Tell people you love them and quit sweating the small stuff. Life is short.

I admit for a couple of years after Melanie passed, I deliberately tried to numb myself. I probably drank alcohol too much—to get rid of the feelings. Once again, my mom came to the rescue. She again helped me to let it go. She reminded me that I'm still here, and I had to keep going. So, I called our agent and told him I was ready to get back to work. Unfortunately, he responded by saying, "La Bouche died with Melanie." That was a crushing statement to me—and very damaging to my ego. I wasn't recognized as a singer, as part of this group? I parted company with that manager and reunited with a manager I had worked with previously, Ruben Martinez. We just started rebuilding things from the ground up.

There was an attempt to bring in another female vocalist for La Bouche following Melanie's passing, correct?

Yes. I should take a few steps back at this point and mention that in 2001, as Melanie was moving on to a solo career, Frank Farian had discovered another young vocalist named Natascha Wright [also known as Natascha Rekelhof], a beautiful girl. We did one song together. Now you would think that if I had co-written a couple of Top 10 hits, you would include me in writing the new La Bouche record. Well, this young lady kind of wrapped her fingers around Frank and [co-wrote] the song "All I Want." However, I was not involved. I think the video, filmed in the Florida Keys and South Beach, cost something like $350,000 to make. The song entered the German charts around number 98, and the next week it was gone. So much for that.

So, that's who I started working with after Melanie. Her range was kind of limited. It didn't work out too well working with her; I just didn't approve of her methods of getting ahead. I worked for a bit with Kayo [Shekoni] who lived in Sweden. But it wasn't going well with promoters, who didn't want to pay for her flights to gigs. Eventually I started working with Dana Rayne, and we've been performing together for the last eight or nine years. Great energy, great singer, and she was happy to be a part of this phase of the La Bouche journey. I recently started working with Kayo again, as Dana wanted to start a family.

You seem to be fully immersed in La Bouche again. Has it been a comfortable transition back into the groove?

Now that I'm living in Germany again, things are moving a lot quicker, and La Bouche is being booked quite heavily. I'm back in the thick of things. I'm really happy to be back in Germany. I went to the German version of the Grammy Awards [the *Echo Awards*] in February of 2015. I was a little nervous to be there because I hadn't been in Germany since Melanie passed. It was a little surreal. I was wondering if anyone would even know who I was. I got out of the car, and the cameras were going off. Then some girl in the crowd starting shouting, "Lane! Lane!" People started realizing I was Lane from La Bouche. I ran into many people from BMG I knew there—they were like a family back then. They really seemed to care for us at BMG in Germany. They made us feel very special. We didn't experience that feeling as much from the United States label, RCA.

It reminds me of a funny story. Back in the day, we were flying from Germany to the U.S. I had acquired miles or points and was able to upgrade from coach to first class. So there I was on the plane with my Louis Vuitton bag and my shades. When I landed in New York,

I see Bob Jamieson, who was head of RCA Records at the time, and Dave Novak, the A&R guy. They actually asked me what I was doing in first class! [*Lane laughs.*] I have to say, though, when we were at our peak, a lot of times the German airlines would give us these courtesy upgrades from coach and business class to first class. But that never happened in the United States. You were just another worker bee.

How is middle age treating you?

Who's middle aged? [*He smiles.*] Because I'm still doing the military thing right now, I can have a moustache but not a goatee, and a goatee makes me look and feel a lot younger. A lot of people don't believe I'm 53 years old, but, really, it feels pretty good. And when I'm performing, I really still feel like a kid. I don't really handle things differently; I just try to keep as much negativity out of my life as possible. I try not stress over things and do my best to remember to be kind, to be nice.

I'm a grandfather now. My grandson will be seven months old in a few days, and I waited a long time for him to come along. I told my daughter I was glad she put one out for me. But I insisted I was not going to be grandpa or granddaddy. I'm gonna be *glampa*!

Life is good, and I have nothing to complain about. To be able to still be doing music is such a great thing. I'll be retired from the Air Force at the beginning of 2016 after 24 years of service, and I'll be able to really focus on the music. I plan to try and enjoy the fruits of my labor.

Ironically, the days of La Bouche were also the last days where physical music product sales were meaningful. Since then, the landscape for the business has changed dramatically and monetization of music is a real challenge for artists today. What's your take on this?

I'm always gonna try to stay creative and put out great music. But yeah, we've gone through some big changes since the days when you'd go to Tower Records to thumb through the CDs and read the liner notes. I remember when Napster came along and everyone started downloading digital music. So, here we are today. Do I want my music out there, being available by whatever means is used today? Or should I have my music never heard by anyone? Today, it's sort of damned if you do, damned if you don't. I still try to navigate the best ways to release music today. Do you really need a label anymore? There's a lot more to think about. It's a different time, different vibe now.

"When I'm performing, I really still feel like a kid," says Lane McCray, who continues to sing the hits of La Bouche worldwide (courtesy Lane McCray).

As La Bouche, you brought dance music to the top of pop culture's music charts. What do you believe is the value of dance music?

I did an interview not long ago, and I remember observing the many eras of dance music—jazz in the '20s, the swing era in the '40s, the pop-dance of the '50s and '60s, '70s disco, you know, every music form had its time. As I look back at the last 20 years, I believe the '90s was really among the biggest eras synonymous with dance music. I think when you listen to pop music today, your Chris Browns, your Rihannas, and Nicki Minaj—they're all doing dance music. And they're doing it in the style that was created by artists like La Bouche. I think a lot of artists are scrambling to find a sound that will keep people interested, and dance music is doing that again. I can't even tell you how many '90s festivals are springing up now. And I'm glad to see dance music becoming so mainstream again. La Bouche was nominated for best new artist by the *Billboard* Music Awards in '96 I believe. "Be My Lover" won an ASCAP award, as you said earlier. I think that speaks to the power of dance music.

Dance music has the power to transcend religions, ethnic backgrounds, sexual orientation and politics. Bringing people onto the dance floor, it lets you know how much more *alike* we all are, rather than drawing attention to our differences. Dance music has a power to make people feel good about who they are, which is probably its greatest value.

Lightning Round with Lane

Giorgio Moroder or Nile Rodgers?
Nile.

'70s or '80s?
'70s.

Performing live or in the recording studio?
Can I say both? I love performing live and the creative process in the studio equally.

Applause or record sales?
Applause. If you're getting applause that means someone came to see you, and that usually translates into a financial benefit, as well as a feeling of personal satisfaction.

The chase or the conquest?
The chase.

Meet your ancestors or meet your descendants?
Ancestors. I say that because my grandmother used to share with me all these African proverbs. One was, "If we stand tall, it's because we stand on the backs of those who came before us."

No more movies or no more TV?
No more TV.

Sports scar or SUV?
Sports car.

Famous but poor or rich but unknown?
Probably rich—I'm being honest.

Rozalla Miller, also known as Rozalla
"Everybody's Free (To Feel Good)" (1992)

> "When I got on stage, I could see this sea of fans so tightly packed together that, from my vantage point, they looked like a massive swarm of bees moving side to side."—Rozalla Miller

Everybody's Free (To Feel Good)" is the euphoric stuff of which classic dance music anthems are made. Infused with the impassioned vocals of Rozalla Miller, the Zambian singer who delivered the song to the masses using just her first name, the track reached number six in the UK and became a Top 10 smash throughout Europe in 1991. In the United States, the song made it to the top of Billboard's dance chart and gained especially strong support among the gay community, who embraced the track's empowering chorus. Melding elements of rave, acid house, disco and electronic dance-pop, the song has remained the high point of Rozalla's career, enjoying numerous remixes and reinterpretations over the years. (A testament to the artist's longevity, a version of "Everybody's Free (To Feel Good)" by Global Deejays, featuring Ms. Miller as a guest vocalist, reached Australia's Top 10 in 2008. In 2016, Florian Kempers' version with Rozalla reached iTunes Top 100 in Germany.)

Rozalla enjoyed more upbeat hits during her '90s breakout, including "Faith (In the Power of Love)" and "Are You Ready to Fly," which earned her the "Queen of Rave" title among pundits for a time. Miller's success also won her the coveted position as the opening act for the European leg of Michael Jackson's Dangerous tour. It is history that any singer would be proud to call his or her own, but Rozalla seems especially grateful for her experience. In 2016, Florian Kempers' version of the classic featuring Rozalla reached iTunes' Top 100 in Germany, and the singer scored a hit in the clubs with Allan Jay called "Breaking My Heart."

Rozalla, you were born in the Republic of Zambia in Southern Africa. Can you tell me a bit about growing up there and how your musical talent got noticed?

I was born in a city of Zambia called Ndola. I always wanted to be a singer. I was about 10 or 11, and my aunts used to write me the lyrics to Diana Ross and Aretha Franklin songs and have me sing them for friends when they had parties. "This girl can sing!" they'd all say.

So from a young age, I was being told I had a talent for singing. I guess it stuck. People were saying things like that, and I pursued it. I appeared on children's television programs in Zambia, and when I was 14 my dad got me a two-week performing stint at the Hotel Intercontinental. I was under age, so they didn't advertise it. They might have gotten into big trouble, but they obviously believed in me.

We moved to Zimbabwe (where my dad was from) when they got independence in 1980 or '81. I joined a band called Grab, and we went around performing cover tunes. That led to me entering a talent contest called *The Golden Voice*. By this point, I was thinking I wanted to record new material, maybe in the western world, not to just keep covering other people's songs. But I was wondering how that could ever happen. Well, I entered the contest, and I won it, and the prize was a recording deal with a local record company. I did some songs and videos with that company and sort of became a starlet of Zimbabwe. I was called Rozalla Miller at that time. An English producer named Chris Sargent was in the area and saw my videos. He was a friend of a DJ named John Matinde, who was a big champion of mine at a major station—ZBC Radio 3 I think it was. That's how we got connected. In late 1988, he invited me to the UK, and his team put money together for me to fly there (I sure had no money) and record with them.

The material we recorded was released in South Africa, and we sent the cassettes around to other labels trying to get me a deal. A major label, I can't remember if it was Atlantic or Arista, said yeah, yeah, they'd love to sign me up. I was so excited—I had a record deal! But at the 11th hour they sent a letter saying they decided they were not interested. That was my first big brush with rejection, and I'd quickly learn that the business was full of it. I suppose that's the way life is when you are involved in the world of the arts.

Epic Records in the U.S. issued this publicity shot of Rozalla in conjunction with the release of her 1995 album *Look No Further* (author's collection).

The rejection must have been a great disappointment, but it set the stage for some even greater developments.

That's right; we didn't give up. We kept sending out the tapes, and that's when the Band of Gypsies (Nigel Swanston and Tim Cox) heard my voice and loved me. They said they had the perfect songs for me, songs that would be written specifically for my voice. I told them I wanted to make songs that would get people on their feet and make them dance. Strong bass lines, drums—all the elements that would have people dancing with their hands in the air. They took that idea—they believed in me, and they saw my passion for wanting to do up tempo dance tracks.

We started recording at a studio on Denmark Street in London's West End, a very famous street for music. Nigel told me to go into the studio and just keep practicing, singing the words "everybody's free," over and over, round and around. We didn't have any verses, chorus, or anything of the sort yet. It was friendship, first and foremost, that made it all work. You have to get along to do good work together. Tim and Nigel were such strong songwriters, and we felt each other's passion. We had great chemistry.

So, tell me about the recording session for the single "Everybody's Free."

Well, from what I can remember, the Peer Music studio where we did the recording was in a basement on Denmark Street. I must say it was quite dingy. That's what I remember. But I didn't think too much about that. I was hoping I was about to record songs that might have some kind of international impact. Nigel gave me the song to sing, or at least the chorus, but I should mention that I couldn't sing any song *exactly* the way the writer or producer might necessarily have wanted me to. I always had to personalize it. Well, I went in and sang the chorus over and over until we had a sound that everyone loved. We played the chorus on the studio speakers, and we just knew we had it—our hook. That put Nigel on the next level to find the verses, the storyline so-to-speak, to go with the chorus.

"Everybody's Free" was such a positive song. That's exactly what I wanted to do. If you listen to that album, practically every song on it has that same uplifting spirit.

The game really changed for you with the release of this song. Tell me, what was it like as the momentum of "Everybody's Free" began to build?

Well, we actually released a track called "Born to Luv Ya" first [retitled on the *Everybody's Free* album to "Born to Love You"], and that became a club hit. They called it my "club song." It didn't go Top 100 or anything, but it was successful in the dance clubs. But still, I wasn't sure we were going to succeed in Britain—I had to keep traveling back and forth from Zimbabwe. I was worrying I wasn't going to have enough money to buy my next air ticket if something didn't happen soon. I was doing club dates and not getting paid a single penny. Fortunately, they really believed in me and managed to get the money together to keep flying me over. I was living with my cousin, living here, living there—a real struggling artist.

But I was passionate about our music, and I believed in it. Then we released "Everybody's Free." I don't know what stuck about the song, but something definitely did stick, and the song just started racing up all the charts. There was a TV show called *Top of the Pops*, and whenever you did this show, you were almost guaranteed your single would move several notches up the charts. Well, that's what happened. "Everybody's Free" peaked at number six in the UK and went Top 10 in several countries. It also hit number one on *Billboard's* dance chart in the U.S. So, yeah, I wanted to grab every moment and do every possible club date.

I remember I appeared at seven clubs in one night in Scotland, singing two songs at each place—straight out to the car and on to the next club. I started with the teenage clubs at seven in the evening, and my last gig was at four or five in the morning. I'll tell you; I was so tired—I put some serious work into that song! It wasn't easy, but my passion was strong. It still is!

Was there any difference in how people reacted to the song in clubs across different nations?

It was very uniform. The feedback for "Everybody's Free," anywhere in the world, was absolutely phenomenal. I can't say any one place reacted more enthusiastically than another. It was just one of those songs. In America, I can say artists like myself were treated like royalty. The respect I got there was amazing.

I remember I did a gay club in or around Miami, and there was a massive, beautiful drag queen there who was a big fan of mine. I was performing, and it was jam-packed. People couldn't even move. Coming through the crowd—I could see above their heads—was this gigantic vase of roses making its way towards me. It was the drag queen trying to bring me this big heavy vase of flowers! The security guards were all over her, and she was calling out my name, unable to reach me. Wow!

The song resonated strongly with the gay community. How did you feel about this connection your song had fostered?

Very proud. In fact, I'd go as far as to say that I think it was my gay fans that made the song as big as it was—and is. I believe that in my heart. So many gay people have told me things like, "Your song inspired me to come out of the closet!" It's just been wonderful. But the song had the same empowering effect on straight people. It's one of those songs where everyone has a story to tell about how the song added positivity to their lives. It gave people the encouragement to make changes—whether they were stuck in a rut, in a bad relationship, were afraid to come out, whatever the problem.

I've even heard a few times from people that "Everybody's Free" was played at funerals. They played it in churches during the services. That kind of shocked me, and I felt kind of honored by that.

I'm curious. Back in the '90s, did any record label decision-makers ever try to distance you from the gay community in order to broaden your appeal with the mainstream market?

To be honest, I never experienced that. My record label, Sony, didn't have much involvement in my club dates. That was my own personal choice and how I earned my living. They promoted my records, but they never suggested I disconnect in any way from anyone. The majority of my agents were gay.

I can tell you that when I perform at a gay club today, I know I am going to get a great reaction. In fact, all my friends who are professional vocalists sing hallelujah when they get booked at a gay club. We just know they will react positively. I'd say they are absolutely among the most loyal people as well. I'm appearing at two gay clubs this weekend, and I have a few Gay Pride events lined up. I can't wait!

One of the highlights of those days must have been your selection as the opening act for Michael Jackson's European Dangerous tour. Would you share memories of that remarkable accomplishment?

I had just signed a deal with Sony, and I just had some of the biggest dance singles across

Europe. Michael was about to embark on his *Dangerous* tour, which was, as we know now, going to be his last. They were looking for an act that had major dance hits out at the time to open his show. Sony put my name forward. I was in New York at the Sony offices when I heard that Michael had personally chosen me. He had seen my videos and heard my songs. *I could not believe it.* I had to rush back to the UK to start rehearsals.

The tour was something like 43 dates over a three-month period. It was the most unbelievable highlight of my career. I will *never* forget it. We were doing all these venues across Europe and the smallest was a stadium that held 25,000. I remember when we were in Paris there were about 100,000 fans at the stadium, and they couldn't wait to get in. They smashed the gates down. The guards were afraid to stop them. When I got on stage, I could see this sea of fans so tightly packed together that, from my vantage point, they looked like a massive swarm of bees moving side to side.

In London, we did a few dates at the Wembley Stadium. At one of them, Michael was having some vocal trouble. I went on and did my set, and as soon as I came off the stage, I was grabbed by security, and they rushed me into a car. They told me we had to leave right away because at the 11th hour Michael decided he couldn't do the show, and they were afraid the fans would riot when they made the announcement. Fortunately, they didn't get that reaction.

I had the pleasure of meeting Mr. Jackson himself. He was a really lovely man. The first time I met him was in this room where he was taking pictures with people. He hugged me, and I thanked him for the opportunity to support him. He was so genuinely lovely and very shy. He said he was happy to be working with me. He said whenever he drove into the stadium, he heard me singing and the fans screaming. This was when he was starting to have some voice trouble, and he asked me what I did when I had problems. I was like, "Look who's asking me for advice!" It was crazy! I told him I knew it would be hard, but the only thing he could do, really, was rest. When the hell could he do that?

The way the press made fun of him was terrible. He honestly was a normal human being. He was the most talented and magical performer I've ever seen in my life. Every time I finished my performance, if I didn't have to jump in a tour bus to get to the next city, I stayed and watched him from backstage. The tour itself—it's like a moving village. It's surreal. Catering, buses people could sleep on, moving houses, massive trucks with equipment. You become very friendly with the crew, like family. I became very good friends with singer Siedah Garrett, who had done a duet with Michael in the '80s. We remain good friends to this day because of the tour.

Many people might think you interacted with Michael on a daily basis, but this wasn't the case?

Oh no; not at all. Any meeting with him had to be arranged in advance. Keep in mind the tour was very demanding and tiring. It does things to your body and mind. You had to be at your peak condition. Why would he want to meet me every day? I wouldn't want to meet with him either, to be honest. Often, I wanted to just stay in bed. [*Rozalla laughs.*]

Were you intimidated in any way by performing in front of such massive crowds?

The biggest crowds I had performed in front of prior to this were probably at the raves with 10,000 people. To now be in front of audiences that were three, four, five, maybe 10 times bigger was phenomenal. But I just kept saying to myself that I have a golden opportunity, and I can't mess this up. This was everything I had been waiting to do. It was so nerve-wracking. But there were great people on Michael's team that helped me tremendously. They taught me how to warm up, which was something all new to me. I learned that it was so vital to do those warm-ups.

The fans were incredible, but I have to tell you—out of those thousands and thousands of fans that were there, there certainly were some *crazy* ones. I'll tell you a story. There was an article in a newspaper called *News of the World* that said something like, "Rozalla says she never sees Michael Jackson, and he's like a ghost, two ships in the night." It wasn't true, and it wasn't a very flattering or nice article. I thought, "Oh no, Michael will fire me from the tour." I sent him a card apologizing for the situation. He sent me a note back saying something like, "Don't worry. I'm used to journalists trying to stir up trouble."

That article caused about five or six fanatical—and I do mean *fanatical*—Michael Jackson fans to hate me. I'm telling you, Michael had some seriously over-the-top fans. So, I found out that the minute the gates to the stadium opened, these crazy fans would run right to the front of the barrier and wait till the show started. Because of the article, when I'd go on stage they'd give me the middle finger and swear at me, shouting really nasty remarks and threatening to throw stuff at me. I couldn't believe it. They even painted some derogatory things on my tour bus, although this was kept from me at the time and cleaned up by the staff. It was so scary. I remember their antics were putting me off from performing because they were so close to where I was singing.

I told the security guards about them, and they assured me not to worry. There were four huge guards, each about six foot five inches tall. Well, they watched the crowd closely, and, sure enough, these crazy fans started up again. The guards jumped into the area just beyond where these fans were, and I don't know what they said to them, but they must have scared the shit out of them. From then on, they never looked at me. They looked down when I looked at them and never said a word. The guards were like the godfather or something. They told me I wouldn't have any more problems, and I didn't.

A while after the tour, I was doing a pride event, and this young guy came back stage, came up to me and said, "I have an apology to make." He said he was a cop now and that he was one of the fans swearing at me on the tour. He said he just wanted to say how sorry he was for acting as he did. You know, after all this, I kind of realized why Michael might have been so reclusive. I can't blame him.

Hopefully the good experiences outweighed these unfortunate incidents. Did you meet any other celebrities on the tour?

Oh yes! I spotted Gianni Versaci, who was staring so hard at me. He was probably thinking, "What the hell is she wearing? I should be dressing her!" There was a VIP section at most concerts, and sometimes I'd watch Michael's show from there. At one concert, Liz Taylor was sitting there with her husband at the time, Larry Fortensky. She looked amazing with her big black bouffant and wearing a leather jacket. She decided she wanted to leave at one point, and I thought I would follow behind them to get through the crowd more easily. She stepped into her limo, which was right in the stadium, and I don't know what I was thinking—I just followed them through the crowd and got in their limo. Oh my God! They looked at me like I was crazy. There were so many people around, I guess I didn't grasp that we were getting into a car. I quickly left it, and they didn't say anything. It was too funny.

I have a Diana Ross story as well. I loved her growing up—she was my idol. Still adore her music. I did a performance at Michael's show in Norway, I believe, and after I left the stage, I once again stayed to watch him. In the next area of the special seating section was Diana Ross with her long, flowing hair. The people I was with—we were all saying, "Oh my God, this is all too much!" I had just come off stage, and she recognized me. I asked her for a picture together. She agreed but asked me to hurry because Michael was about to come on. We got it, and that was that.

The very next day I was in the airport, and I was in the duty-free shop. Well, I see this woman with long hair. I thought, "Surely this can't be Diana Ross." She turned around and faced me—it was, indeed, Diana. I said, "Oh Miss Ross, how nice to see you again. We met yesterday. I support Michael Jackson on his tour. I'm Rozalla." She completely ignored me, as my hand was held out to shake hers. [*Rozalla laughs vigorously as she recalls the awkwardness of the moment.*] Like a fool, with my hand still outstretched, I continued to follow her around. It was like, "I'm not leaving till you shake my hand." I asked her if she was flying back to America. She then quickly took my hand, gave it a tap, and said, "yes," quickly rushing away. And that was my last meeting with Diana Ross. She wanted nothing to do with me. [*Rozalla laughs again.*]

I grew up wanting to be Diana Ross. As a kid, I remember singing "The Boss" all the time. I have to say, this encounter dented my image of her a bit. A *big* dent. That's how the business is at times, but it got under my skin a bit. Oh well; that's life. However, I came away from it knowing how important it is to treat my fans well and be respectful of their enthusiasm.

So, after such an extraordinary run with your colossal hit "Everybody's Free," were there any self-imposed or external pressures for you to live up to your initial success?

There was a period some years ago when I didn't have a record label deal, and all these companies wanted was another "Everybody's Free." So, in some ways, I was pigeonholed by the song, and it was so frustrating. I mean, I did have several other Top 20 or Top 30 hits in the UK. Please understand, I love performing "Free," but I went through a love-hate period with it. I was more than just that one song, and, well, I believed I could also deliver a killer ballad. I think even today, many people want just "Everybody's Free," but hopefully enough time has passed that if I release a new dance track, it will be appreciated on its own merits. In fact, I just recently released a single called "If You Say It Again," and it made it to number five on the *Billboard* dance chart in the U.S. That was very encouraging.

You recorded "I Love Music" for the soundtrack of the 1993 hit movie, Carlito's Way. It was also featured on your follow-up album, Look No Further. You must have a few interesting recollections about that.

Well sure! I got to meet Al Pacino, one of the greatest actors of my time. I was due to fly to New York to appear at the premiere for the film; I think it was the Ziegfeld Theater. Let's say the day is Sunday. I was due to perform at the event on that Wednesday. I went with some friends to an Italian restaurant here in Britain, and on the way I told them I would be appearing at this premiere in New York. Well, as we walked in the place, there was Al Pacino, with 14 of his friends at a long table. How crazy is that? They were having so much fun. I couldn't believe it! I thought I *had* to introduce myself, so I struck up my nerve and went up to him at his table. I apologized for disturbing him, and told him I had recorded the song "I Love Music" for his movie and that I would be appearing at the premier. He looked at me and realized I couldn't be lying to have that information. Oh my God, he freaked out! He was so wonderful, and he introduced me to his whole table. He said, "Let's have a dance!" He twisted me around on the floor so much I thought I'd get squashed like a tomato. It was unbelievable. For the life of me, I can't believe nobody had a camera to take a picture of it!

So, come Wednesday, there I was, walking up the red carpet in New York like a celebrity. It was so surreal to see so many famous faces. Jellybean Benitez was there—he produced the song—and we sat at his table. I sang "I Love Music" on stage, and the reception was fantastic. Afterward, I was taken to Mr. Pacino's table and asked him if he remembered me. He was all like, "Yeah! Yeah! Yeah!" He hugged me as people were flashing cameras. But still, to this day, I can't find anybody who has a picture of that event either [*Rozalla laughs profusely*]. Not even one! My husband is a big fan of Pacino, and he always asks me to tell that story again.

Let's look at some of the challenges of the industry and the '90s era. Did being a woman of color ever create any issues for you?

I've been fortunate in that I never experienced problems like that first hand. I remember a journalist once asked me if I thought I'd have been a bigger artist if I had been white. I can't answer that.

The '90s was an amazing era for mega–dance clubs, circuit parties and large-scale dance events. Did the drug culture connected with these environments have any impact on you?

No, it didn't. Coming from Africa as I did, with very strict parents, it was instilled in me that drugs were very bad. Plus, I grew up in a household where my father, who has passed, was an alcoholic. That was a tough thing on the family, and I saw that. When I came to England, I performed in a lot of those massive warehouse raves I spoke of earlier. People were high off their rockers, taking a lot of drugs. But I naively thought at the time they just loved my music. I remember being in the dressing room, and these guys were taking some kind of white substance. Somebody told me it was cocaine or heroin. It was the first time I'd ever seen it. It shocked me. I never took drugs, never drank alcohol, and I never smoked. I saw what it did to people, and I never wanted to be involved in that. I steered completely away from it.

Would you say the music industry of the time compensated you properly and treated you well?

Oh, no. I got ripped off, as most of my artist friends would say. I always joke that "Everybody's Free" was so massive, I'm sure I must be a millionaire, and I just don't know it. The label I was signed to, Pulse-8, in my opinion, did a lot of artists wrong. I remember I had my accountants do an audit back in those days, and they found the label owed me at least £100,000. I remember speaking to a member of the group Urban Cookie Collective ("The Key, the Secret"), who were also signed to the label, and he said they owed him something like £365,000. Who knows what they really owed us, because they ended up liquidating the company. It was a really sad state of affairs. Greed. Some people have success and handle it the right way. Others get greedy and want to keep it all for themselves. My personal opinion is that if the label had maintained the success and relationships with their artists, who knows [what heights] they could have reached.

Human beings are complex. I often wondered how these label executives expected us to eat, to pay our bills. It's what we did for a living. When you work hard and create a really good successful song, the royalties are like your pension. We depended on that.

My parents taught me to save. I saved money from my club dates and whatever money I got from royalty checks, if I was lucky. I put money together so I could buy a flat, a home, and have something to show for myself. In the end, I was okay because I sold that flat for double what I paid for it. And my clubs have been good to me; my fans have been good to me. People continue to believe in me, I'm lucky to say. Throughout the past six or seven years, my club dates have been excellent. It's been amazing.

When the boy bands and girl bands started taking over later in the '90s, there wasn't really a place for me. I was lucky if I had one club date in two months. The label dropped me. I wasn't flavor of the month anymore. I started to think this might be the place where my career ends. So I decided to take up a beauty therapy course. I can give a mean massage. [*She laughs.*] I did it as a sort of an insurance policy in case I needed to do other work. You know what? It showed me again that I had to believe in myself and that life goes on.

The downturn also gave me an opportunity to meet and get to know my husband, Alan (who is not in the music industry, thank God). If I had still been traveling around the world, I would have missed that chance to be in a good relationship.

Digital downloading changed the entire music business with the arrival of Napster at the dawn of the 21st century. You mentioned your single "If You Say It Again," and you recently released the song "Breaking My Heart" with Allan Jay. So you're actively out there in the digital marketplace. I wonder how you are coping with the challenges of releasing music today.

The truth is I can't depend on digital music sales. That's why so many of us must latch on so tightly to live work. Really, in some ways, it's the same as back in the '90s. Getting paid for your music has never been that easy. Getting our royalty checks then was such a struggle. I keep recording new material because I really enjoy creating and working with good people in the business today. But there are realities that I—and all artists—have to face. It's a learning curve in the music industry today, like most things in life I suppose, and we'll see how it goes.

We're definitely all on a life-long journey of learning, and it requires a lot of energy to stay positive through some of the challenges of aging. What's your philosophy about maturing?

You know, I admit there have been moments where I've asked myself if I should get out of this industry and wonder if I'm too old for it. But I keep getting these great club dates; people want to work with me after 24 years. In itself, that is telling me something. It keeps me motivated, encouraged. I've mentioned my concerns to my agents, and they've said to me, "Excuse me, you're *Rozalla!*" [*She laughs.*] That keeps me going—that there's still a place for me in the world. I love performing, and when I go on that stage and I get that audience reaction—that is what tells me I am still allowed to be me. As long as I get that feedback, baby, you're gonna hear me singing! I'm in a good place now; I'm happy.

Wow, it's amazing that it's been 24 years since "Everybody's Free." It seems like yesterday that I first heard it. What is your relationship with this song today?

I just say thank you for it. Thank you so much. It's given me such a long career. It's allowed me to get paid to sing almost a quarter of a century later—how many people can say that? This song is my passport.

What would you say has been dance music's value or contribution to society and pop culture over the past few decades?

I feel that for me, personally, dance music—how can I say it—I've seen it make people feel incredibly euphoric and positive. Hands in the air! You wanted to get off of your chair and *dance*! What other form of music has done that to the extent that pure dance music has?

When I came to America, to get "Everybody's Free" to be played on the radio was so hard. There were different stations for different styles of music—R&B, country, rock—but not dance. I found that so odd. It just wasn't a genre to which a station could devote itself.

But in the last few years, I think that's changed in the U.S. The sound of the Top 10 now is pumping the music style we did in the '90s. So now it feels like stations *are* devoted to dance music. I think that speaks volumes about the enduring power of this genre.

Lightning Round with Rozalla

Perfect hair or perfect teeth?
Perfect teeth.

Money or fame?
Money. It gives you the freedom to take care of yourself and help others.

Meet your ancestors or meet your descendants?
Ancestors. I'm of a mixed background. We are known in Africa as coloreds, not blacks. My grandparents were coloreds, but their parents were dark black and white (from England). I had a great grandfather who was white, and I'd like to go back and meet them and see where I come from.

Donna Summer or Diana Ross?
Donna Summer.

'70s or '80s?
'80s.

Day or night?
Night, so I can sleep!

"I keep recording new material because I really enjoy creating and working with good people in the business today. But there are realities that I—and all artists—have to face," says Rozalla Miller (courtesy Rozalla Miller).

No Internet or no TV?

I'd much prefer to never use the Internet again. There are too many programs I need to watch on TV!

Rich and ugly or poor and gorgeous?

Ooooh, that's very hard. Poor and good looking. I could work my looks to get rich. Hmmm—but if I was ugly and rich, I could buy plastic surgery. [*Rozalla laughs.*]

Tony Moran, DJ, Producer, Remixer
"HIStory" (Michael Jackson, 1997)

"I want to be the Anderson Cooper of DJing."—Tony Moran

As the list of distinguished artists he's worked with attests (Gloria Estefan, Cher, Annie Lennox, Jon Secada, Donna Summer, Beyoncé), native New Yorker Tony Moran (of Colombian descent) has shared his formidable remix and production talents with some of the biggest stars in pop and dance music. It's tempting to name-drop a few more celebrities: Mariah Carey, Cyndi Lauper, Barry Manilow, Deborah Cox, Ne-Yo, Amy Grant, Jennifer Lopez and Rihanna have also benefited from his expertise. They've all turned to the two-time Grammy nominee to transform their songs into masterpieces of energy and positivity, and for many years the results of his efforts have packed dance floors worldwide.

He first gained fame in the mid–'80s as part of the Latin Rascals, a production team and musical group that helped launch the freestyle genre with artists like the Cover Girls. Despite experiencing a temporary career slowdown as the popularity of freestyle waned, his success grew exponentially in the '90s as more and more top artists of the period enlisted his skills to remodel their latest productions.

As a production maestro and songwriter, Tony has enjoyed the Midas touch when it comes to creating sounds that inspire the soul, move the feet and stay locked in the heart and mind. Likewise, his artistry as an accomplished DJ, playing for tens of thousands in prestigious clubs and at events held throughout the U.S., Europe and beyond, has made him one of the most in-demand spinners on the planet.

Moran continues to create chart-topping hits in the role of producer, recently reaching the number one position on Billboard's dance chart with "Free People," a song he released in 2015 with dance music icon Martha Wash.

Shortly before leaving for a DJ gig at a massive Australian event, Tony sat down to reflect upon his life and accomplishments as a premier figure in dance music culture.

I'd first like to hear about your youth and growing up in New York, Tony.

I was born in Brooklyn, in a ghetto, pretty much a welfare situation, though my parents worked very hard supporting five kids. I grew up in a tough neighborhood, Brownsville—right near where Mike Tyson was brought up. It was comparable at the time to *New Jack City*, like the movie. It was a melting pot of cultures and everyone was "ethnic" on some level. My parents worked hard for us and sent us to Catholic school so that we would have something to rely on—faith. It was good having that as a starting point and having faith in something (not just in God but in a power that is instilled in us). I joined the folk group at church and really liked that—it was good to be part of something rather than worrying about being caught in a shoot-out. I was subjected to a diversity of cultures—black, white, Cuban, Puerto Rican, Dominican—and not all of it was good. You were subjected to prejudice on a daily basis.

I was a small, scrawny kid, and I was limited in my options to try and be cool. I went to an accelerated high school called Brooklyn Tech. All I wanted was to get a job. That was my simple dream at the time. My older sister had a full scholarship to Brown University, and I felt a lot of pressure to excel. But I noticed every time I was around music, I was really drawn to it. My thinking was as long as I was doing well in school, my parents couldn't complain if I started doing DJ work on the side. It was the period that followed the disco craze, at the dawn of rap. I loved listening to disco records late at night on the radio—almost like a closeted disco queen—and then I started getting into rap.

When did you realize you needed to make music your primary focus?

In college. I remember my girlfriend at the time (I'm gay, but I had a girlfriend back in those days) was being taunted by a group of guys. I asked the guys to give me a break, and I got pounced on by all of them. I ended up getting stabbed in the back with a hunting knife. The incident gave me (at a very young age) an epiphany of sorts. I was a teenager given a second chance to live. So I thought, "What am I gonna do? Am I gonna do the regular stuff or seek out music, something that constantly fills me with energy and positivity?"

I decided to start DJing, buying used or even broken equipment. My education gave me the skills to fix the stuff, and I taught myself how to spin records. I started throwing block parties and became very entrepreneurial. I started charging people to come and listen to me. Scratching, a DJ technique of the mid-'80s, was very popular, but for me, I had a different feeling for how I wanted to blend songs into each other. Instead of scratching, I started blending dance and rap records together, and I gained a bit of a reputation for it. I started hearing from a lot of rap DJs, and suddenly I had my own rap show on 98.7 KISS FM in New York. I got very good at editing songs in a way that worked very well for a 30- or 40-minute set.

No doubt this laid the foundation for your emergence as one half of the Latin Rascals production team.

Yes. I was a very determined person in my early 20s, pushing industry people to listen to my tapes. They'd end up saying, "Oh shit, this is really good." My popularity kept growing, and I happened to meet another young Latin named Albert Cabrera (he was Puerto Rican), who was also doing well along the same musical lines. He was doing work similar to mine, and so we partnered up. We were very young, and people were looking at us in amazement because of the high quality sounds we were producing. Everyone seemed to be astonished by this music we were making on our little $99 reel-to-reel. Once we were dubbed "The Latin Rascals"—well, things took off. Everything revolved around timing, I guess you could say. Timing, skill, determination, devotion, risk-taking, insecurity, security—they all started blending together. As the Latin Rascals, we were doing edits of popular songs that others in the industry had no idea how to accomplish.

We became sort of these representatives of success that the Latino community began to admire. It's pre–Gloria Estefan and Ricky Martin. The Latin Rascals became these cool DJs, and people were really falling in love with what we did. We started doing more and more re-edit work, and then producer Arthur Baker asked us to try our hand on Diana Ross's "Swept Away" in 1984. He was a true pioneer in the whole electronic transition between disco and the sound of the '80s, and he really gave us a break. Where I had been doing these unique but straightforward edits, Arthur said to me, "Don't pick pieces of the song that people are picking for you to create this maxi-single; stay in the studio, and create the pieces that *you* want." Well, I asked to stay in the studio overnight, telling him I wanted to absorb what I was doing. Instead, I pulled out every single manual for all the equipment because I didn't even know where the on and off buttons were. But I have to say, the electricity that flowed through me at that time went beyond the fatigue of having to learn quickly. I didn't learn how to do everything in a day, but very quickly I did learn how to do things in that studio that nobody else could do back then.

From there, I ended up working on Bruce Springsteen's "Born in the USA," projects for Duran Duran with Nile Rodgers, Simple Minds and many others. They were top level projects. Things were really moving so fast.

The Latin Rascals produced and mixed the single "Show Me" by the Cover Girls, a Top Five Billboard *dance hit that really brought the freestyle genre to the mainstream in the latter half of the '80s. This must have been a very significant step forward for you.*

It was. I had been working with a man named Andy Tripoli, and we had written the song "Show Me." We decided we wanted to create a group that featured all Latin women. I was already producing a popular Latin group called TKA, and this freestyle sound that I had helped create had really taken over the Chicago, New York and Miami radio and club scenes. The Latin Rascals were signed to Polygram Records, and I sang on many freestyle hits that crossed us into the mainstream even further. [The freestyle sound] dominated for several years. We had the encouragement of Arthur Baker and Nile Rodgers on the Cover Girls project. I had Daryl Hall of Hall & Oates helping me fix harmonies on some tracks. These guys were walking around, in all the studios of the building we worked in. It was amazing.

But I'll tell you—I didn't have time to think I wasn't worthy. These guys never felt sorry for me or treated me like I was less than them. They were like, "You got a spark, dude!" I didn't have to live up to anything; I just had to keep myself open to learning as all this was happening. I was able to ask the advice of extremely prestigious artists and producers. That doesn't happen anymore in the business because everyone is so into protecting their own domain. But at that time, it was a great experience, and the Cover Girls turned out to be a huge success.

As the '80s drew to a close, what changes did you observe in the dance music industry and in what direction did you want to take your career?

Once I sold a million albums with the Cover Girls, I sat with my partner and talked about investing in ourselves and learning how we could do what we do better—from a technical perspective. I wanted us to be able to analyze the work we were getting and be able to discuss projects and ideas more fully. I stopped DJing and started buying new equipment and building a staff. Because I was surrounded by people like Mick Jagger and the Pet Shop Boys, I really wanted to be able to pitch ideas and take things a step further—not just coast our brand. Opportunities kept coming, but Albert was content with what we were making (financially) and what we were already doing. I explained I didn't want to stay in this place; this was just step one. I understood why he wanted to stay where he was. For someone who never had money before and all the rough stuff we'd gone through coming of age, I could understand his desire for stability. But to me, everything was about potential. So, we disbanded the Latin Rascals.

I detoured for a while to do a show on MTV (*2nd Generation* in 1991) and was a consultant at Telemundo [the American Spanish language television network]. It was cool, but it wasn't easy at times. After a TV deal with the Fox network fell apart, I decided I wanted to get back into music. I hit a tough spot because nobody wanted to hire me for a while—freestyle was absolutely dead by then. I left music as a king, and I came back as a pariah. I felt a little like a has-been for a while, but I knew it wouldn't break me. I just started working on my own new music and paying for it myself. I offered to do a remix for Gloria Estefan of "Everlasting Love" [Moran's Marathon Love Mix] for free to re-establish myself. It was a big success. I just rebuilt myself from there and was able to start commanding good fees again for my work with Janet Jackson ["Together Again"], Barry Manilow and other artists.

I was being embraced again so strongly by so many people from so many communities—Latin, black, white—I couldn't be a fuck up now, you know? I can't die of a drug overdose or get caught up in a shootout. I really put it on myself to not let people down. It didn't mean I had to achieve anything; I just had to really do my best. With the '90s, I entered a new phase of development in my career where I was able to go beyond what I thought my best could be.

You were responsible for a plethora of hit records that defined the entire period. You refer to it as going beyond your best, and I imagine working with Michael Jackson might have been an example of that.

Oh, absolutely. Michael had worked on an album called *HIStory—Past, Present and Future—Book I* in 1994. In 1997, I worked on his *Blood on the Dance Floor: HIStory in the Mix* album, which was a remix set with some new songs. This was kind of a reinvention for Michael because he had gone through so much controversy prior to it, and the original *HIStory* album hadn't done quite as well as Sony had hoped. This album was extremely important to him. Keep in mind, this is all just my view of the project, based on what I experienced and know. I sat in the Sony offices through many meetings about this remix project, and I sat in a room directly with Michael. Sony told me they didn't want to hire me just to tweak his songs, they wanted me to help elevate his level of work, visually and audio-wise.

Michael was a very hands-on person, and I'll be the first to admit there were things I did that he wasn't too crazy about sometimes. We'd go into a meeting with him, in a room filled with many people, and basically there'd be an interpreter between Michael and myself. So, Michael would lean to this interpreter and whisper something like, "Can you please tell Tony that I want to change this part of 'Billie Jean.'" I said something to the effect of, "Michael, I speak English. I want to do what you want, but just talk to me. I'll be able to just tell from looking at your eyes what you want to happen. You don't need to have someone else tell me. You're Michael Jackson. Believe me, every possible sense of my being is going to be focused on understanding what you want." He stopped using the interpreter and told me what he was looking for.

I was a little nervous working on this project, but I wasn't intimidated. I just felt I had to get my words out fast enough so that Michael would know what I was feeling and trying to say. I was aware that I had to respond in the right way. Then he asked me to remix "HIStory," and afterward he requested that the track be labeled "HIStory (Tony Moran's HIStory Lesson)." The response to the album in the UK was tremendous, where it went to number one. My mix of "HIStory" was a number one song throughout Europe, and it turned me into what I guess you'd call a "remixing superstar" at the time. I also became this star DJ without having to even get near the turntables. Basically, Michael instantly upgraded me to this whole other level.

That led me to my work with Céline Dion, creating the dance mix of "My Heart Will Go On" and other songs for her. (I remember being in the studio with her, and she was dressed up in Versace leather—that's the point in the '90s where I thought, "Oh my God, that is *fierce*; that is glamorous!") I was being accepted as a remixer *and* as a producer, and that propelled me into a world where I was able to diversify. I was able to give music my own interpretation, not just put a spin on somebody else's stuff. I was trusted to make their material better—kind of like someone who redecorates a house, only this was with songs—and to create original material.

Though it's probably not as instantly recognizable as your many other '90 hits, I personally remember being completely captivated by your remix of the Wes (Madiko) single "Alane" from the summer of '97. The song reached number one in France, the Netherlands, Belgium and Austria. I'd love to hear your reflections about this record.

I remember when I started working on that song, I thought it was a bit weird and exotic sounding. It had this unusual African style. When I finished remixing it, it became so organically popular that I didn't mind that it didn't reach number one on all the charts. When I'd spin in clubs, people would ask me to play that song, even before I'd get asked to play Céline Dion or someone who was better known than Wes. I guess I captured something in "Alane," and it was kind of amazing. I tried to make the song my own, as all of us who remix records try to do, and I was inspired by the results.

How were you able to balance your personal life with such an intense career moving ahead at high speed? Was it challenging in any way to be a gay man during these years?

Well, you know, I have always wanted to be a person who is appreciated for the music he makes. I'm not afraid of being who I am—a gay man. I've never felt inclined to hide it or say, "That's not me." I was extremely lucky that as a young man I was physically and personally considered attractive to many kinds of people. Sexuality and seduction revolve around the sum of the parts. But I don't think people ever looked at me when I entered the room and thought I was "dressing gay," "he looks gay" or "he sounds gay." I didn't witness anyone making an issue about anything like that. And in my music, it was never being gay that propelled me to be better. It was just one part of who I am.

I had my social life in those days, and I remember being in gay bars when I was starting to be a big name in the business. I remember I wanted to be accepted as just a person there, not as this important DJ or whatever. I wanted to be able to just say hi to someone, and it was like a luxury for me to have them *not* know who I was. I didn't want to be someone who acted conceited; I wanted to blend in. It was so great to have them like you just because you looked cute and sounded like a nice guy, funny and charismatic. It was also difficult because many people would assume I was some kind of player or that I had a guy in every city.

So, when it came to dating, I didn't worry about things like age. I would date a man of any age or background or income—they could have been 50 or 60, whatever. I remember Gloria Estefan was kind of surprised that I was seeing a much older guy at the time, and I guess it wasn't what people expected of me. I chose to be around people that tended to have a moral compass, if you know what I mean, and people who were my biggest cheerleaders—but didn't want to take control of who I was. They were just supportive, and I was lucky in that, throughout my whole life, I've really been surrounded by people who made me feel special and loved me. And I loved them.

Those I had relationships with—sometimes it would be overwhelming for them. I was so wrapped up in what I did all the time, and it would reach a point where they would say, "Hey, can't you stop for a minute?" It was challenging for everyone—me and them.

Do you still have the same enthusiasm for music today as you did in the past?

When I work on a song with someone today, it's like the day I worked on my first Cover Girls song. I still have that level of emotion and excitement. But now I have this knowledge and experience behind me that allows me to embrace it in a much more intense way than I was able to in those days. I think whatever power there is running things in the universe, if it gave me a talent of any sort, I have to appreciate it and respect it. I think that's what has brought me back into DJing at the clubs over the last several years. For so long, people would tell me the songs I worked on were so special and such emotional experiences for them. I started to wonder what that really felt like, because I was sort of in this studio bubble all the time.

In the '90s, what was the one thing you noticed most about the fans of your music?

All those songs I did in the '90s just made people so excited. And they looked at me in this special kind of way—I guess I was the next best thing to having the artist in the club with them. When I served as a DJ, they saw me and these great artists like Gloria Estefan, Donna Summer, Cher and Janet Jackson in the room with them. That's the impression I got. It was overwhelming for me.

Thinking of this, it reminds me of a boyfriend of mine who had died of a drug overdose, and it really hit me hard. It made me very confused about the world, and I lost my sense of balance. What rescued me from that was being with these people in the clubs. To feel the honor they were giving me made me want to honor them, and it was a very cathartic experience to be with my fans.

There's been a lot of change in the dance music industry since the '90s. One such development has been a shift in focus away from the vocalist (and over to the DJ/producer). You've worked closely with some of the greatest divas in the history of dance music, but they often seem to be relegated today to the background. What's your take on this rearrangement in ranking?

The regime changes over time, and we are in the era of the superstar DJ. He or she is the attraction. There are still the Madonnas and Rihannas of the world, but there are so few of them compared to the DJs, like David Guetta and Tiesto. I'm not a personal fan of every big DJ that is out there today, but I am totally respectful that they upped the game for our part of the industry. As a DJ today, you need to command that kind of star performance and treatment these guys are receiving. In the process of this happening, the vocalists did get drowned out.

Let me say this. Throughout my career, I've hit points where I wasn't at the top of my game, where I wasn't producing a Gloria Estefan or a Madonna. But instead I wrote a number one dance hit for Kevin Aviance and songs for Deborah Cooper. Those successes came when I was 40 years old, and they fired me up. I had to look at my life and ask, "Where do I go from here?" Dance music and being a DJ gave me the opportunity to find a sense of satisfaction and excitement—in a different way from, say, the studio and production work I did in the '90s. You become who you are supposed to be under the circumstances you are presently living in. Yeah, it's scary because it may be different from what you did before. But you roll with it and you build on it.

I know how hard change can be. When digital downloading took over and as technology on personal computers advanced so quickly, you could have a guy producing a track that sounded every bit as good as one produced in a mega-studio. The difference was he didn't need that million dollar studio. He did it on a $2,000 Mac. Yeah, that's scary. All of us found ourselves confronting the new age of doing business in this industry. (I sold my studio and began working on equipment that was a lot less expensive, but it was giving me the same excellent results.)

I do feel that many artists, especially the heritage vocalists, have been short-changed by these trends in the dance music industry. But where you once had record companies spending tons of money on all these singers (and, yeah, they do great work), there's now this whole new world where this one guy can produce 20 hit remixes. So they take the chance on him. I also think the DJs decided to invest in their brand. They chose to elevate themselves. When I make a new song, I pay for the making of my videos. I pay to do my social media. I don't wait for a record company to jump in and do it for me. I create my own image. When I work with vocalists, I make sure my brand is incorporated into the product we are releasing.

I have found that some of these vocalists, who sometimes have a nicer car or more money than I do, won't invest in a video or a new photo shoot. There are a lot of fans out there who may know their work, but they don't have any idea what they look like. To be honest, I don't get that. I think they do themselves a disservice by not understanding the relevance of a brand. If they don't work on these things and push their brand, then guess what? The DJ/producer will.

I try to feature the artists on my releases as best I can. But it is their responsibility as well to do the kinds of things that someone like Kristine W does. She's out there and makes sure she's seen. It costs her money, but she gets the value and importance of it. To me, it makes sense to invest in yourself, rather than waiting for that big paycheck that may or may not come—to make what you do count.

What is your personal goal for the future as a DJ and producer?

You know what? I have gray hair. I ain't dying it. I want to be the Anderson Cooper of DJing. I want it to be cool to be my age, have gray hair and to be comfortable and secure in my own skin. It's a challenge for any artist to mature in this business. I want to be a person that can display a level of grace to his audience, even when a 22-year-old DJ might have gone on right before me. You can feel you're old, or you can feel, "I've earned this." I feel like I've earned the right to be exactly who I am up there.

You've had an intimate relationship with the genre for many years. In your eyes, what has dance music contributed to the world?

Tony Moran shares a moment of pride with vocalist Martha Wash following the success of their 2015 number one dance hit "Free People" (courtesy Tony Moran).

Dance music (because of its tempo and the energy that it is infused with) doesn't allow you the opportunity to analyze yourself. By that I mean things are moving fast, you're shaking, and it's easier to break free of your personal restraints. You get overtaken by it, and you stop being self-conscious. There are other styles of music that people dance to, like salsa, but people have to generally think about their moves with those forms. They're thinking about being sexy and skillful on the floor. But when a disco classic, a '90s dance hit or a contemporary dance song plays, you just get enraptured by it and you don't care about anything. Many people think about the drug enhancements that helped make that happen, but, truly, drugs have never been a requirement to enjoy great dance music. People listen to it at home, in the gym, and in their cars on the way to work—drug free.

Record companies today recognize that dance music is probably the most popular of all genres. Every major pop, rock, R&B, hip-hop (even country) artist today, with few exceptions, has to release at least one dance track off their album. It is part of pop culture now. Dance music has made people move, and it allowed them the opportunity to feel another level of personal intimate sensuality. When you're into a dance song, you close your eyes, and you go into another world. It makes you sweat, and it gets your blood pumping, almost like sex.

I don't like all the dance music that comes out today, but I respect that it is still such a powerful force. It has become so technical now that often it seems like you can pretty much exchange any one of 10 singers to handle the vocals. The music has a lot less personality today. (However, there are some great songs, too, like "Clarity" by Zedd—I was like, "I'm gonna start crying any second with this song.") So, it is the responsibility of me and all the producers, songwriters and artists out there now to make the kind of dance music that will be as memorable in the future as that Barry White, Donna Summer or Michael Jackson song of the past.

Ultra Naté
"Free" (1997)

"'Free' felt like this culmination of experience, time, effort, blood, sweat and tears finally coming together and validating everything."—Ultra Naté

Nightlife in the '90s owes a debt to singer and songwriter Ultra Naté, whose fiery hits stirringly melded R&B, house and electro-pop energy. She provided the era with a rich and diverse soundtrack that was extremely popular in both the United States and Europe. Britain has held the artist in especially high regard. She's been a mainstay of world dance floors ever since her full-fledged arrival in 1990, and the always stylish entertainer is proud of her longevity in the business.

Ultra's edgy, hip persona and innovative, powerful vocal prowess cemented her standing on the club tip, resulting in five number one Billboard dance chart triumphs, including 1993's scintillating and triumphant "Show Me." She was back at the top with the heated signature anthem "Free" in 1997, "Found a Cure" the following year, "Desire" (2000), and "Get It Up (The Feeling)" in 2001. In 1998, she teamed with fellow crossover artists Jocelyn Enriquez and Amber (collectively known as Stars on 54) for the hugely successful "If You Could Read My Mind," lifted from the soundtrack for the movie 54.

Never one to rest on past accomplishments, she remains a highly in-demand performer today. Driven to keep creating intoxicating musical experiences for her legion of fans, she is as comfortable writing and singing new material as she is running her own indie label. She released a new album, Hero Worship in 2013, as well as the timely single "Everybody Loves the Night." Ultra unveiled the single "Alive" late in 2016. She looks casually elegant as she sits comfortably in her Baltimore home, hair pulled back and hands elegantly adorned with well-crafted bracelets and rings on this warm early summer day. Ms. Naté speaks with the firm voice of a seasoned pro who has witnessed first hand the many changes the dance genre and music industry have undergone over the past two and a half decades.

Ultra, please tell me a bit about your beginnings in Baltimore and how singing and songwriting became your focus.

I moved to Baltimore when I was about eight years old. I lived in the inner city. My mother and my stepfather left me alone (in that they let me be who I wanted to be). By that I mean I never felt like they had their thumbs on my neck to do or be something. I was a positive kid and very curious. I had the room to be that way and that was pivotal in my decisions later to choose my career. I used to write plays and did artistic things in school, but I never realized how that would play into my life later on.

I actually planned to go into medicine and become a doctor. I attended Paul Laurence Dunbar High School, which had a really great college-prep curriculum. As you got into your later grades of high school, you were actually doing work in the medical profession. You went to school half the day, and the other half you'd work in a medical facility. That was my great plan, and I really loved the path I was on. Once I graduated in the mid–'80s, however, I started going to a club in Baltimore called Odell's, one of the few clubs that had a Richard Long [a popular sound engineer of the era] sound system. That was the thing to have—the sound of Paradise Garage in New York and all the epic marquee venues from that era. Needless to say, clubbing at Odell's created a whole lifestyle of its own, and people still hold that club in very high regard (even though it's been closed for a million years).

The moment I stepped into that venue and experienced the energy of nightlife, the sound system, the lights, the music and the people—it set me on a new path. For lack of a better term, I was swept away. It really became all encompassing, and I literally *had* to be there all the time. I had a lot of gay friends who did the drag thing and were into makeup, and they inadvertently taught me about being on stage and what people wanted to see. Being in that environment, I started to meet people in music and became sort of a club kid of that period. Around 1987-ish, I met Teddy Douglas, Jay Steinhour and Tommy Davis of the Basement Boys, a budding production outfit at that time. Back then, I was singing in my church choir (though not in any lead capacity)—a second soprano, an alto kind of position. I think I may have shared that information with Tommy, so he may have known I sang a little bit. It wasn't something I was pursuing at that point. They had just done a record on one of the small independent house labels called Jump Street—a remake of Rose Royce's "Love Don't Live Here Anymore" [retitled "Love Don't Live Here No More."] It was a big hit for them, and their A&R person was a lady named Cynthia Cherry. She became pivotal to my career as I began to go into the studio with the Basement Boys (just for fun, hanging out, writing stuff).

As the Warner publicity shot for Ultra Naté's 1993 album *One Woman's Insanity* suggests, the multifaceted artist was able to deliver a variety of sounds that filled dance floors (photograph by Eric Johnson, author's collection).

The very first song that I ever wrote was "It's Over Now"—we wrote it in the kitchen area of the basement where the studio was located—literally in Jay's basement. Before we called it quits that night, the boys wanted to get something down on tape. They had a little closet of DAT tapes (remember those?) and pulled one random instrumental track out and sent me to the vocal booth (which was literally the bathroom) and played the track. I had the lyrics of "It's Over Now" in my head, so on the fly I started singing them to this track. So fast forward, they finished putting the song together, and it started getting great traction in Baltimore. The boys brought it to DJ Tony Humphries in Jersey, who was integral to the era of the Zanzibar club. Tony was taking a lot of underground records from people making recordings on four-tracks in their basements and getting the attention of major labels. This was basically the result of the backlash of the disco era. Technology was now enabling these young producers to create dance music productions much more cheaply and without having a whole orchestra. Great music like this was coming out of Chicago with Ten City, Jomanda out of New Jersey, and now Baltimore. Tony played a lot of this music on his radio shows here and in the UK and at Zanzibar, and "It's Over Now" quickly became an anthem—on both sides of the Atlantic.

Meanwhile, Cynthia Cherry joined Warner Bros. Records as an A&R director in the UK to start a new dance imprint there. She took my "It's Over Now" track as one of the records she wanted to sign. I received a two 12-inch record deal, so all I had to do was come up with a second song. I started charting in the UK and was on *Top of the Pops*, and the label was convinced I'd be a good candidate for an LP. This was all crazy for me—I was living my normal life at home and doing this cool underground music here in the U.S. But then I would get on a plane and go to Britain, and I'm all over the radio with mainstream dance-pop artists like Adeva.

You must have experienced quite a rush of excitement suddenly finding yourself in the spotlight in the UK and launching your first album.

Oh, I did! I was like, "What are they hearing?" This was my first attempt at song writing, and I'm not a singer by trade—I kind of winged it. Now it's catching on, and I'm in the UK being offered a major record deal. And shooting a video and doing shows like *Top of the Pops*. And all this was happening like within a matter of months between 1989 and '90, when the track came out officially and became a Top 20 British pop hit. I was kind of a silent observer in all this as we began work on my first album, which eventually was called *Blue Notes in the Basement* (1991). We wrote whatever came off the top of our heads—there was no structure; there was no anything—it was just a very raw, authentic effort. We didn't worry about right or wrong. We just followed our vibe.

Warner UK didn't pressure you to deliver a commercially viable sound?

No. We had that luxury at the time—that's what garage music was—it was very organic. It could be weird and quirky, and we had this complete carte blanche at the time to make an album on our own terms. I have to credit Cynthia Cherry again—she really believed in us as artists and appreciated our authenticity and individuality. She wasn't interested in turning us into some kind of cookie cutter act or making me into the next Janet Jackson. That probably was the plan of the label because their primary interest is in how they are going to make their money back. But having Cherry, as we called her—and we nicknamed her "The Godmother of House Music" (as she's done this with a number of artists)—as the buffer between us and the label gave us that room to grow throughout that first album.

The demands of commerciality didn't really happen till the second album, *One Woman's*

Insanity (1993). The reason why it happened then was the British dance imprint label we were on called Eternal was moving to the U.S. Cherry moved to the U.S. with the label. Being out of the UK now was the bug-a-boo. Britain was a lot more open to various musical styles and individuality. You would hear a Michael Jackson record played after a Billy Joel song, followed by a house record—it was more of an even playing field. America—we were in a very different environment. We went into meetings with the head of the label, Benny Medina, and the big executives, and the demand was for a more commercial, radio friendly record. This meant we had to come out from the underground and the garage sound. The music was changing at that point too—music was starting to evolve and wasn't so loose and minimal. It needed to have a fully produced sound, and we needed to rise to that challenge.

Would you describe how you approached your second album, One Woman's Insanity, under these circumstances?

We tried to meet in the middle—having our underground club credibility while still satisfying the label's desire for radio-ready records. My manager at the time, Bill Coleman, was instrumental in broadening my base as a writer and artist during this period. He brought in other producers besides the Basement Boys, who represented the comfort zone that I had been in. He felt it was important for me to stay on my learning curve, so he brought in producers like D–Influence, Nellee Hooper, Cutfather—all successful in dance music but completely different in styles. We ended up creating a very well rounded album.

I'm the first one to say I've had a charmed experience. Now, in hindsight, knowing what it *could* have been like dealing with the labels, executives, management, etc., I know everybody really had my best interests at heart. That's how I feel about it. They really wanted the project to succeed, and they really brought their A-game. Bill really had a knack for honing in on where I was as a singer and writer and knowing where I needed to fill in the blanks and how to take me up a notch. And that's really a manager's job—not just handling the contracts (although that's important too). When I think about the work I did with this team and I look back and listen to this album, I'm amazed. This collaboration allowed my art to flourish. But nobody ever came to the table with an ego or ever tried to devalue what I brought to the table as a songwriter or vocalist. Everyone came to the project with respect and the goal of making this the most amazing work that they could. I had the best of experiences during that period.

I was involved in every part of the process, and that, absolutely, was vital to me. There is a certain level of trust you place in the others who are involved. It's a give and take of ideas and vibes, like a tennis match. I may hear something go a certain place and whoever I was working with would try to fine-tune it further or maybe take it to another place. Or they put down some keys, and I was able to take it where I felt it needed to go. It was a beautiful process and a great way to work, whether you are creating dance music or working in any other genre.

There was a lot of inter-label politics going on, unfortunately. One of my singles from the album was "How Long." It was a dance record, but an R&B dance record. The dance department needed the R&B department to cooperate with the record. But the R&B department didn't really feel the dance department. If they aren't all on the same page, it becomes a bottleneck, and nothing moves forward. Or it becomes the blame game, with departments blaming each other if the track doesn't catch on. So many layers of craziness; it's a wonder how anything ever got done. Sometimes a label can be its own worst enemy.

The 1998* Situation:Critical *LP, your third album, was widely acclaimed and included your landmark hit "Free." Tell me about this project and the move to the independent New York label, Strictly Rhythm.

Moving to Strictly Rhythm really came about because of the shift to Warner U.S. I didn't leave Warner by choice—I was dropped. What they wanted from us just wasn't happening at the time. Nellee Hooper was having amazing hits with Soul II Soul, but the connection wasn't being made in the same way with my album. Warner needed to see reaction and response right away—there's no time to build. Your first single doesn't hit the target, okay, we'll try another one. It's a numbers game, and you had to hit the target they had set. But you only get a certain window in which to accomplish that.

I think they let me go in '93, and Bill and I spent a couple of years working on where I wanted to take my music next. I didn't necessarily feel (and Bill definitely agreed) that signing up with another major label was the right way to go. The music was weird here in America. The labels didn't know how to market dance music. The label was always confused, saying, "Who do we sell your sound to?" Well, I had a broad fan base. But they needed specifics—is it black, is it white, what age, etc. When you appeal to a broad base as I did, it makes it harder for them. But how can you say a song is only going to appeal to one group or another?

Anyway, I knew Gladys Pizarro, the co-founder of Strictly Rhythm, from the dance scene. She always had top-notch energy and really believed in her records and worked her ass off to build them. She courted me for a long time to do a record for her label, and I was writing (for my next album—always looking to the future) quite a bit in New York. The chemistry was right, and I worked with them until about 2001. Strictly Rhythm also had the financing—which was important to me. After being on a major label and having a charmed experience, I understood how important it was to have the financial backing to build your profile and support your records. It is what it is, and I felt Strictly had the means to do that. Not to the same degree as Warner, but sometimes you didn't need to spend what Warner would lay out—with less money you spend smarter and are more focused.

You've had some tremendous success in the dance genre, and "Free" really exemplifies the power of your work. It reached* Billboard's *dance chart summit in 1997 and then crossed to the pop chart. How did this uplifting track come to be, and how did it feel to see the track hit number one?

"Free" first came about from the writing I was doing in New York, without a deal. Bill Coleman had the idea of working with the producers Mood II Swing, a New York outfit that was putting out a lot of great records. We felt that would work for me, and we did our brainstorming session with them. I remember I wanted to come up with something that didn't sound like anything else out in the dance market. It had to have its own identity—it needed to have its own voice and story. I was very inspired by "Losing My Religion" by R.E.M. and wanted a lot of guitar work—that bittersweet, melancholic guitar story being the root of what the track would be about. There was another collaborative give and take. They took these elements, and Mood II Swing's creative process came up with the backing track that became "Free." It was like, okay, we got the guitar sound, and we need the angst to be pumped up—to get the rhythm pocket ride. Kind of structured—but not. I always wanted to do a rock record, and that's how it was first built—as a full-on rock record. I was totally crazy. When it was almost finished, I knew it was where it needed to be, but yet a little too far away from the dance floor. I felt we needed to reel it back, just a hair. We needed to give the drums, that signature Mood II Swing sound, so it would connect on the dance floor level. Concept wise—"Free" was writer Lem Springsteen. He came up with the "free"—kind of the Seal tip. So you took these elements, and we took that call to do-what-you-want to-do concept and connected them. All these crazy little things came together.

The other secret sauce was a gentleman named Danny Madden. He was brought in to work with me as a vocal producer. I had written two different versions of the song with two different verses, B-sections, etc. We started cutting up the best bits of both versions. And in the end, we put it all together, and you have the final version of what became known as "Free."

It's hard to put into words what it means to hit number one, especially with "Free." I had been successful before in the UK, and "Show Me" had hit number one on the U.S. dance chart. With "Free," it felt different because it was after my work with Warner, when the label came swooping in and putting out all our underground stuff and not really knowing what to do with it. "Free" felt like this culmination of experience, time, effort, blood, sweat and tears finally coming together and validating everything. When we finished the song, we were like, "yeah, it's done" and we loved it. But it was quite different from other songs of the time. So we didn't know if it would catch on. You only know *you* love it—that's all you got! After that, there are so many other elements that come into play to determine if it will hit. So Gladys began making her plans to release it. Then to see people affected as they were by the song was wonderful.

Right before it was to be released, I remember we sent bits and pieces to the Winter Music Conference in Miami to key DJs. It was still the era of "what's the record of the conference?" If that were your record, your song would be built almost instantly around the world. DJ Louie Vega crushed that record for us at the conference, and a bunch of major DJs took the baton as well.

We spent a lot of money on the *Situation:Critical* album, which featured the track, and I have to thank Strictly Rhythm's founder Mark Finkelstein for kind of giving us a blank check to get the record produced. It cost probably more than the first two albums I did—we spent a boatload of money on all those producers, the live instrumentation and top-notch production. Mark could have put the brakes on it at any point, but he never did.

The Gordon Lightfoot soft rock classic "If You Could Read My Mind" has been a disco staple since 1980 when vocalist Viola Wills transformed it into a number one club hit. You sang the song on the soundtrack to the Miramax motion picture 54 in 1998 with a collective known as Stars on 54 (which included Amber and Jocelyn Enriquez). The song once again brought you to the top spot on Billboard's dance chart and was another significant pop crossover success for you. Can you tell me about the experience of making this track and working with the ladies?

The original version and Viola's dance version were great—a great song *is* a great song. If you can bring your own vibe to the song without sacrificing the integrity of the original, you can't really lose. I became involved in this project following my success with "Free" and "Found a Cure." The movie was being shot and Tommy Boy Records was going to release the soundtrack. They wanted to include a song that was slightly original, in addition to the classic disco songs they'd be featuring on the album. Tommy Boy wanted to bring me into the project along with their two major artists, Jocelyn and Amber. They decided on a reworking of the Gordon Lightfoot song, and they brought in the Berman Brothers to do a work-up. They called us all into the studio, and we sang it from top to bottom and went on our separate ways. A week later we heard Miramax loved it and decided to rewrite the ending of the movie to make "If You Could Read My Mind" the theme song and to include us in the film. All this kind of happened out of nowhere and turned into a huge thing.

I knew Jocelyn and Amber, from a distance anyway, because we all had chart records at the time, and in the States we did many of the same circuit parties. We did a lot of gay pride events as well together. We weren't strangers, and we just kind of got on with it. All of us recognized that this was a great opportunity—don't trip, you know what I mean? Nobody had time to come to the table to be a diva. We were all winning—hello—and that's how we all approached it.

I was really on this crazy run at this point. It was all about timing. It was all about preparation meeting opportunity, which, for me, always equals success. I was doing what I needed to do so that I was able to take advantage of an opportunity like working on that film.

What has given you more satisfaction—performing in front of a crowd at a club or event or stepping back and watching a dance floor catch fire as your song blasts through the sound system?

For many years, performing was the most enjoyable aspect of my career. There's a give and take between an artist and her audience. There's a certain level of love and validation that you get from the crowd—you know, that energy. As you're performing in front of them and people are affected by it, it all makes sense—all the nonsense that led up to that moment. In later years, I've been able to stand back and just enjoy the records the way the people do. For a lot of years I didn't enjoy the records the way the fans do because I was so in my head in one way and in the record in a different way. I didn't get to hear what the fans were hearing. I think I've gotten better at doing that now. I can watch people enjoying the records, and I get great satisfaction from that. It reminds me that this is exactly what I'm supposed to be doing.

Just like the '70s and '80s, the mega-club environment of the '90s was well known for its drug culture. Did that aspect of the business and nightlife affect you in any way?

I have always been kind of a granola head—a bit of a health nut. Smoking or doing anything harder never really interested me—an occasional cocktail, but always within reason. I think I was always more concerned about my body as a temple, taking care of myself and preserving myself. I didn't need to get high on substances to get high on the music. It just naturally happened for me; maybe a lot of people aren't blessed that way—I don't know. But I didn't need drugs to get to the next level. You just give me a good beat and cool people, and I'm good. But obviously I was around and exposed to it. Fortunately, nobody that I knew in my camp was ever involved with that to my knowledge at all. Not my management, not anybody. It was never an issue for us. But maybe other artists, label people were.

Our industry was built on a social setting. It is what it is. People did party favors to get elevated, but whatever drug they were doing usually didn't put them in a bad space. So the energy was usually never bad—it was positive, fun energy. Yes, I noticed that sometimes the music in a club seemed to be dictated by the drug of choice and the people who used them. If there was a lot of angst or anger, it was because of the drugs that people were using. House music was built on happy vibes, and so that's what people wanted to feel—by whatever means necessary, I guess. But I don't feel during the '90s and during my exposure to the music that the sound of the era was completely driven by drugs.

I don't think it's really fair to say that dance music was a catalyst for drug use, as some might like to suggest. It's not fair to the artist. Music is the backdrop to people's lives; it defines a moment in time. If you're in the dance music culture, it's a social environment. As a dance music artist, I don't think you have any control over that—unless you want to switch genres.

We don't see dance music getting the kind of applause and recognition other forms of music typically receive. Why is dance music's value in pop culture history so hard to acknowledge today?

I think the reason dance music is kind of the bastard child of pop music is that people find it hard to define who it appeals to. This has been true since the '70s. The appeal is so massive, and the music itself draws from so many other genres, like rock, gospel and R&B. There are rules with those other genres that don't apply in dance music—how you write a song, produce it, etc. I think *not* having those rules kind of makes dance music this little wild child.

Dance music also has so many sub-genres, and that's a blessing and a curse in itself.

I think another reason it's hard to define its contribution to pop culture is the change it underwent from being a genre about artists to a genre about producers and DJs. You removed that person—the man or woman that the consumer used to buy into. This didn't happen in other genres. The energy of that artist was what the consumer bought into. When you think of dance music, this nameless, faceless wild child becomes vague and unidentifiable. "It has a great hook, but I don't know who it is." I think that's the reason I've survived—by being with a major label it established me as a clear entity, an artist, something for a listener to gravitate to. This is missing today, and I think it perpetuates the notion that dance music is a less than respectable genre.

Did you encounter any personal challenges with racism or sexism in the industry?

I'm sure it's there, but I can't say there's been anything that's directly, overtly happened to me along those lines. I think in later years it has possibly been more prevalent than in the early years of my career. Signed with Warner, I was kind of in a very protected environment—safe, sequestered. Since then, and having my own label now, the industry has changed dramatically, and doing what we did then has become obsolete. But that's a whole other story.

So let's talk about the changes in the music industry since the '90s. You enjoyed life as an artist when there were still physical product sales, and you've seen the digital revolution that began with Napster. Give me your take on the evolution of the business, especially as it relates to dance music.

File sharing pretty much obliterated building records in the way we used to before. The game shifted, and we have had to readjust, like it or not. The necessity for songwriting got so dialed down, however, so dumbed down during the 2000s. It's starting to shift back a bit today towards songwriting, but there was a very long period where I felt there was this massive outbreak of what I call "diva syndrome." [*Ultra laughs.*] The people producing the record want the screaming black diva vocal for a riff or two, just to give a bit of substance to the song. But they don't want the full spectrum, a real body of work to give dynamics and resonance to a song. The music got so dialed down and redundant that they feel like if you, as the artist, put any real depth into it, it's overkill. They feel that people don't have the attention span anymore for a full song. You get put in this box. Well, we want Ultra Naté for the name value and the authenticity, but we don't want her full spectrum. They just want to perpetuate the black diva syndrome. They just want enough soul to get it over the hump—a four-bar loop with minimal instrumentation and a hook.

It's been this way for a long time, and I feel it's diminished the music industry. They underestimate the musical acumen of the listener. I didn't grow up planning to become an artist; that this was my calling. I grew up listening to the radio and listening to wax by Chaka Khan, Earth, Wind & Fire, George Michael, Madonna—that was my school. Music with meat! A whole flurry of emotions and memories goes with their songs, and they go into perpetuity. When music became my career, that's the music I called on to navigate myself as an artist. Kids today aren't getting that meat. People are expecting so much less now—the same songs over and over, the same keys, every artist starting to sound exactly the same. In dance music, there's nothing to anchor you to the floor. Vocals anchor you to the dance floor, and that's been lost. You aren't hearing [commercial dance music] records today that will be timeless 20 years in the future. You're hearing records made just for that moment, a quick set of digital downloads, a quick buck and a promo tool to put the DJ/producer on the road at clubs and festivals.

In an age where, in many cases, you can no longer earn a living from the recorded music directly—when people have come to expect their music for free or, at best, very cheaply—how does an artist survive today and manage to remain creative?

It's a very real problem, and everyone has been feeling it for well over 10 years. Fortunately, I've always been performing live, and I've always been on the road here in the U.S. or Europe. That's really key now. You really can't make a living if you're not a live performer. And having name value becomes even more important. Venues and booking agents are buying your brand, your name, not necessarily your music. As artists we *have* to make music, but the music has become more of your promotion card because it's so difficult to sell.

I really wonder where this train is going. If it stays on this track, it's definitely going to end in disaster for artists trying to make a living from their craft. And it's going to allow for a lot of sub-par music to inundate the world—the chain and cycle keeps going. Fortunately, for me, I had hits before all this began. So I still have royalties coming in, and publishing and writing create a different revenue stream. My managers have been very active at getting my music placed in commercials, film and TV as well.

I really hope the consumer is going to come to a place where they ask themselves if they are going to be a part of the problem or the solution. Right now, the perception by the consumer is often that their one-ripping of a file is not going to affect anything. But everybody has to start feeling that sense of accountability. When that happens and the value of the work that goes into music is appreciated again—that it's how people put food on the table and feed their kids—then possibly things will become better. But the Internet's not going anywhere so—it remains to be seen.

Where do you want to take your career in the years ahead?

I really do love being an independent artist and having my own label, and being able to work with who I want (which has always been the case—knock on wood again). [*She chuckles.*] You can't do it without a big support team, and I've been lucky that way. Sometimes as an artist, it can take away from your creative energy thinking about the administrative side of things as well. It can be overwhelming at times. But when it all comes together and your project is successful, that's when you feel the gratitude. I've been very lucky to be able to sustain my career. There are many from the '90s who have not, whether it's from lack of support or financial stability to continue. Money affords you freedom and creature comforts.

I've had a very loyal fan base as well. Another blessing. The gay community is one of the most loyal fan bases you could ever ask for. That's been pivotal for me.

The problem with being in the business for over 25 years and starting in a time like the '90s is that I have the memory of what *used* to be. It can really drag you down if you keep thinking about "well, back in the day." I love that I had that experience, and it set up an amazing platform for me to be known and respected. I try to be a realist where things are now and try to keep it in balance with my—I guess you'd say "dreamier" goals of what I'd like to be happening. I'm on the right path. I've invested my whole adult life in the music business, and, for much of it, it's been on my own terms. That's a blessing a lot of artists haven't had.

I spent a lot of time in Ibiza over the past few years and met all the top dogs now, the who's who of electronic dance music DJs. When they meet me, there is so much respect in their eyes and admiration. I really appreciate that because I can tell they get it and respect the roots and foundation of this music. I love being a part of that, being a champion of dance music and moving it forward.

"I've invested my whole adult life in the music business, and for much of it, it's been on my own terms. That's a blessing a lot of artists haven't had," observes singer Ultra Naté (courtesy Ultra Naté).

Lightning Round with Ultra

Wallet or smart phone?
　　Definitely smart phone.

Treadmill or StairMaster?
　　StairMaster.

Fried or sweets?
　　How about sweet fries?

Own or lease?
　　Clearly, own!

Movie theater or Netflix?
　　Movie theater.

Spandex or cotton?
　　Spandex!

Sports car or SUV?
　　SUV.

Heat wave or snowstorm?
　　Heat wave, without a doubt!

Music or lyrics?
What? I can't—I just can't!

Facebook or Twitter?
Facebook.

'70s or '80s?
Can't deny those '80s synthesizers, but I'm gonna lean with '70s.

Alban Nwapa, also known as Dr. Alban
"It's My Life" (1992)

"If I tried to be like other pop stars, to be somebody I was not, I would have had a problem—I'd have ended up with a complex."—Alban Nwapa

In the early '90s, Nigerian-born Alban Uzoma Nwapa's career as a dentist (practicing in Sweden) was sidelined when he became a world-renowned innovator of a unique and highly charged form of dance-pop music. Yes, you read that correctly—dentist. As unlikely a success story as that may seem, Dr. Alban (the rapper and songwriter's stage name) and his production partner, fellow DJ and then rising producer/composer Denniz Pop, created a hugely popular hybrid of dance, reggae and world music that topped the international pop charts. Songs like "Hello Afrika," "It's My Life" and "Look Who's Talking" resonated powerfully with clubs and radio, sending sales of his initial releases soaring in Germany, Israel, Austria, Switzerland, the UK and many other nations, including his Scandinavian proving ground.

He views his past success with a kind of casual nod, effortlessly acknowledging that, as he says, what once was hot eventually cools down. He is a grounded, realistic artist today, but that doesn't prevent him from having an upbeat sense of purpose. Dr. Alban has found a balance with his past, present and future, as evidenced by the release of his well-regarded current single "Hurricane" and an ongoing schedule of performances that nearly rivals his '90s heyday. He was featured on the Basic Element single "Good To You," released in the summer of 2016.

From his home in Stockholm, the artist gives spare but revealing answers to the questions posed to him about life then and now.

Alban, please tell me a little about your childhood and growing up in Nigeria.

I grew up in a family with 10 children. My mother and father promised all of us a good education, every one of us. They kept that promise. They were good parents and really believed in the power of education. I listened to a lot of Fela Kuti and James Brown when I was young.

You started off your professional career as a dentist in Sweden. That's a bit unusual for a pop star.

It all started because my uncle was a United Nations ambassador in Sweden. I visited him there, and I ended up staying. I started earning my dental degree in Sweden when I was 23.

How did you go from being a dentist to a major Euro-dance chart-topper?

It really wasn't as difficult as it may sound. While I was working towards completing my dentistry degree, I had to do something to make some money to supplement my studies. So I ended up being a DJ on the weekends in Stockholm (at a club called Alphabet Street) and making my own music. I tried mixing in some of my own rapping and singing as a DJ, and it was very popular. I opened my practice as a dentist, and (for a while) I kept doing the DJing on the side.

What made Sweden the right place for you to explore the club, rap and dance music recording frontier?

It's funny; I'm not sure it was Sweden so much as it was luck. I came here to study; I became a DJ to make some extra money, and by a stroke of luck we made a dance track, and it went to the Top 10. I was never thinking Sweden would be a great place for me to make music. It never came into my head. My success in music was a combination of luck, destiny and a good track.

Alban Nwapa, better known as Dr. Alban (and seen here in a Logic Records publicity shot), moved from Nigeria to Sweden, abandoned his dentistry practice and became a leading '90s pop star in Europe. His hit songs combined electronic dance, hip-hop, reggae-pop and house music (author's collection).

That first track you are referring to I believe is "Hello Afrika," a tribute to your homeland that featured singer Leila K., which became a huge hit across Europe in 1990. You created this record with producer Denniz Pop (real name Dag Krister Volle), who also started out as a DJ and later worked with many popular artists of the day, including Ace of Base, Backstreet Boys, Robyn and Britney Spears. How did you happen to come together?

We met through the DJ channels, as he was working as one at the same time I was. We just started working together on "Hello Afrika," and it all came together. We had a good chemistry, and we just thought, "Come on, let's go in the studio and see what we can do." It was hard to get the song initially released, but the thing is that other DJs (who we gave it to before we had a record deal) played the track and liked it. That built demand for it in the clubs, and then it started to hit radio. That later paved the way for our deal with [Logic and Ariola Records].

You created this very unusual mix of Euro-dance, pop and dancehall styles that was unlike most music of the time. Why do you think your sound caught on so strongly?

It's very simple. It's just what you said. It was really different. When you try to copy or sound like someone else, people start saying, "Oh, I've heard that before." We tried to do something that was different and original, and I think we really made something out of it. Denniz and I were DJs, not musicians. They are two different types of people. As DJs, we knew what people liked to dance to, and we knew how to arrange the beats and what would get people moving. We saw what affected the dance floors every night. We created something we knew would be popular on the dance floor, as well as on the radio. And then, of course, we tried to make sure it was as catchy as possible—but still had that African influence. I never took out that African influence—I kept the accents, the African drums in the background and all that. All this together was the secret.

Did you encounter any resistance from the mainstream or music industry because your music was so heavily influenced by African themes? Or perhaps because you were African?

Well, there was never anything like that I was aware of. You know it's stupid for C to try to be D and B to try to be C. You have to be what you are, who you are and do what you want to do. If I tried to be like other pop stars, to be somebody I was not, I would have had a problem—I'd have ended up with a complex. You always have to be who you are, be the best you can be and try to do whatever you do a bit differently.

Did you focus your attention on the club dance floor and let the pop market catch on from there? Or did you have to consider both audiences as your success grew?

Since Denniz and I were both DJs, I can tell you at the beginning we never created records with the intention of having pop crossover success. I never knew it was going to blow up that big. I never thought about fame. We kept our heads down and made music that we thought people on the dance floor would like.

Once our songs started hitting the top of the charts, I can say it *was* incredible. In a way, however, somehow I was not surprised. We knew we were original; we weren't copying anything else. It made people curious and want to hear more, and they spread the word about it. "I just heard this great track in the club!" I still say it to people today—to people who ask me how to make it in the music business. Be original. When you sound like everything else on the market, it's not interesting anymore.

You speak of the importance of originality, and you certainly were able to deliver that in multiple world hits. After the success of your first album (Hello Afrika) you and Denniz released the LP One Love in 1992, which surpassed the sales of your first album. It contained one of your biggest hits, "It's My Life," a number one smash in Germany and a number two hit in the UK. Then came "Look Who's Talking" and another successful album by the same name. Was it difficult to maintain your originality as you racked up these successes?

No, because I never approached my music like, "'Hello Afrika' worked, so let me do another song like that." "It's My Life" and another hit off the second album, "Sing Hallelujah!," had totally different sounds, which I wanted to explore at the time. I left the "Hello Afrika" sound and did "It's My Life," which had more of a pop, catchy style. Keeping things fresh was very natural for us.

Another trademark of your music was its very powerful, socially conscious lyrics. How important was the message to the impact of your songs?

Sometimes dance music artists didn't put much emphasis on lyrics. As I said, I decided early on that I shouldn't be doing what everyone else is doing. "Get up and dance," "get up and boogie," blah, blah, blah. I wanted to make dance tracks that you could listen to and get something from. I decided to make songs like "No Coke."

If you listened to any of my songs without the lyrics, you'd probably say they were crap. I wouldn't probably even be known today—nobody would remember me. I'm remembered because of what I said in my songs.

Do you remember what type of process you and Denniz developed to create your sound with when you entered the recording studio?

We never went into the studio really thinking hard about what we were going to do. I remember the songs were all different in terms of how long they would take to record and release. For example, "Hello Afrika" took about two months to record. "It's My Life" took just five hours. It all depended on the vibe and feelings we had when we were in the studio. Truthfully, sometimes you might be in a bad mood, and that can affect your ability to get the right vibe on a track.

You were able to conquer Europe and other parts of the world, but the U.S. was less receptive to your music. Your American releases on Arista Records didn't fare quite as well. Did that matter to you at the time?

It was important. When you have success in one area, of course you want to conquer the next. Everybody wants more. But there was a lot of politics going on in America with my songs. For example, "No Coke" was an anti-drug song, and they said nobody can be singing about that in the U.S. music business. They wanted me to re-record the song.

In 1998, Denniz Pop died at a very young age from cancer—he was just 35. You had already been working with other producers for a few years before his passing, but I wonder how you felt at the time about the tragic news.

He was a genius, you know? He was a great guy. He understood the dance floor, and he knew how to create a great song, even though he wasn't technically a musician. He did some amazing work with other artists besides me. His genius was really based in the basics—he created simple melodies that people could connect with.

It was huge setback when he died. But life has to go on. None of the artists he worked with, myself included, could stop making music because he died—but it was a difficult setback to deal with. I think the only way [to pay tribute] to what he was doing was to keep making our music.

Did the record companies in the U.S. and Europe treat you fairly?

Yeah, they did in the '90s. I was treated very well. But you know how it is. When the records are hot and selling big everything is great. When things cool down, it gets bad. [*He laughs.*] That's the way it is.

Was there a highlight from the '90s that really stands out for you?

I would say my visit to South Africa, when the apartheid system died. I wanted to perform for the people in Soweto—the poor people that didn't have any money to pay to see a concert—and I got the chance to do that. Meeting Nelson Mandela in 1993—that was another big highlight.

Shortly after the end of the decade we have the arrival of Napster in full force and the beginnings of digital downloading, making the music business a tougher terrain to navigate. How did you react to the change in music distribution?

It was very difficult. That was probably the most difficult thing I experienced in my career. In the '90s, I was lucky. Physical records and CD sales were still significant. Suddenly, people were on the computer downloading music for free, and all that shit that was going on. Sales dropped drastically, and very little money was being made. You went from selling thousands of copies to literally nothing. This was a great shock.

But you know, there are also other factors that affect sales. I think there has always existed—the '70s, '80s, '90s—a limited time span for [the popularity] of most artists. You know—like Kool & the Gang, Earth, Wind & Fire. They were big in the '70s but not as popular in the '80s. Madonna is not as big now as she was in the '80s and '90s. That's how it is. Anything that's hot gets cold after a while. It's like cooking food—it starts off hot and then gets cold. [*He laughs.*] Like food, you can't expect to stay hot with your sales and career. Ten years of having hits—that's good. But you have to expect that things are going to change. I even thought that way when I was younger and having success. I was very aware that things change. Things come and go.

Those who can't anticipate that, who can't accept that things are not going to be the same year in and year out—they are the ones who turn to drinking alcohol and end up in drug abuse.

How does that reality you describe—that the music you are releasing today may not find as big an audience as you had in the '90s—affect your self-esteem as an artist?

Well, you always hope for the best, but you have to just believe in what you do. You have to face reality and know that, over time, your material isn't going to reach the top of the charts. So you have to take it the way it is and just continue doing what you're doing as long as you are inspired to do it.

It's interesting that you came from the DJ culture and today dance music is so producer and DJ-focused, with vocalists having a less prominent role. Why do you think that trend evolved?

I think it's just that—an evolution. Each era has been different, with changes in the music evolving. It's a trend, just as the disco sound ended in the '70s and the euro-pop sound took off in the '90s. I think we'll see something different happening in dance music by 2020. This DJ thing is the trend now, but we'll see how long it will last.

You give the impression of being very grounded as a middle-aged man. How do you feel at this stage of your life?

I do a lot of thinking and have a lot of ideas. I think I am comfortable with where I am because I've experienced so much. I also had my family later in life. I didn't get married until I was 45. Experience is the best teacher. This is the best time of life, your 50s and 60s, to use your experience. It's a good age—you're not too young, and you're not too old.

Where do you see your music career going in the future?

I find I am touring a lot more now. Every week I'm appearing somewhere new. I want to keep recording new tracks—they keep me in the marketplace, and I think creating new music reminds people of what I did in the past and keeps them curious about what I am doing now. I plan to keep people aware that I'm still around and that I'm doing new things. I've found that, yes, it's true, people want to hear the old hits. But because that's true, does that mean I should lie down and stop trying to do something new? I believe people are open to hearing something new as well. So, as I said before, life goes on.

I think of that song back in 2000—Carlos Santana's "Maria Maria." He hadn't had a big hit in years, and then this song went to number one for something like 10 weeks. I'm sure at that time people wanted to hear his old hits, but they were also open to something new from him. And look what happened.

What would you say has been the primary value of dance music in society?

Well, I can say the entire club industry is based on this genre, so I'm not sure where it would be without this music. There would be no clubs. I think dance music created its own culture (within the broader pop culture). Now that may not sound important—having clubs and a dance music culture—but without it, people would never have been able to release their energy, their emotions, in such a physical and positive way. This is something many people *need* to do—just to get out and shake it and go home.

Says Dr. Alban of life today, "I do a lot of thinking and have a lot of ideas. I think I am comfortable with where I am because I've experienced so much" (courtesy Alban Nwapa).

LIGHTNING ROUND WITH DR. ALBAN

Giorgio Moroder or Nile Rodgers?
  Nile Rodgers.

'70s or '80s?
  '70s—I like the old songs.

Diana Ross or Beyoncé?
  Beyoncé—I like the old stuff, but Beyoncé, well, she's something else!

Applause or record sales?
  Record sales. [*He laughs.*]

The chase or the conquest?
  The chase.

Meet your ancestors or meet your descendants?

Ancestors—originality, as I always say.

Sports car or SUV?

I love sports cars!

Extended versions or radio edits?

Radio edits. That gives you the whole thing in a nice compact version. Anyone can extend a song, but not many people can create a nice, creative track in three and a half minutes.

Brushing or flossing?

[*Alban laughs again.*] Both, but if I have to choose—brushing!

CeCe Peniston
"Finally" (1991)

"'Finally' was exactly what it was supposed to be at that particular time. I can try to create something that's close to it, but can I reproduce it? No."—CeCe Peniston

By the end of 1991 and into early 1992, there were few club goers and pop radio listeners who were unfamiliar with the name CeCe Peniston. Her blistering debut single "Finally" peaked at number five on Billboard's Hot 100 singles chart, reached number one on the dance survey and won song of the year honors at the '92 ASCAP awards. Quickly regarded as a classic of house music, "Finally" also played an integral role in the success of the celebrated film The Adventures of Priscilla, Queen of the Desert and its long running Australian, London and Broadway stage adaptions. Peniston is credited with writing the lyrics of the famous song, an ode to the joys of being lucky in love, which reached number two on the British pop charts. Unsurprisingly, the song was a hit once again in the UK thanks to a 1997 remix that soared into the country's Top 30.

During the '90s, CeCe released three albums on A&M Records, her American label, including her 1992 debut set Finally (which reportedly sold over half a million copies in the U.S. and three million copies worldwide). Though pop hits were harder to come by following her triumphant breakthrough, the singer was a frequent visitor to the number one spot on the U.S. dance charts with tracks such as "We Got a Love Thang," "Keep on Walkin,'" "I'm in the Mood" and "Hit by Love." She was named Billboard's number one Hot Dance Music/Club Play artist in 1994, according to Joel Whitburn's Billboard's Hot Dance/Disco 1974–2003.

Since then, CeCe has continued to be an in-demand performer, undaunted by the challenges of an ever-changing music landscape. She has released numerous songs over the years that cover a wide spectrum of styles, including R&B, gospel and dance, as well as a popular 2011 Paul Oakenfold adaptation of her perennial hit. Most recently, Chaos featuring CeCePeniston scored a major club hit in 2015 with the single "Believe." The artist was in between shows when we reminisced about her days in the spotlight and the journey she has taken since.

CeCe, I'd like to know a bit about what life for you was like growing up and how you discovered your talents in music.

I was born in Ohio and grew up in a military family. We eventually moved to Phoenix,

Arizona. My mom was also a dancer at one time, and my father was great at writing poetry. That's how he got her. He wooed her with poetry, and they were together ever since. [*CeCe laughs.*] I was always that one kid in the family who is a curious little being. I took the required music classes in elementary school. I played the piano and never even thought of myself as having a voice. But one of my teachers heard me sing while playing, and she was like, "Oh, I didn't know you had a voice," and I was like, "I didn't either!" She encouraged me to try out for a play, *H.M.S. Pinafore*, when I was 11 years old, and that was the first time I stepped on a stage. That's when my mother and I really discovered I had a talent for singing. It was funny, because the moment I did that, it put something in me, and I began thinking that singing would be something I'd love to do. I remember coming into the house and saying, "Mama, I'm gonna be a star someday." She said something like, "Yeah, right. I hear you. Go play." My parents knew I had something though, but they knew kids were little dreamers. But they never put pressure on me about it. Their feeling was if this was something I wanted to do, they just wanted to make sure it was genuine—they would work hard to try and help make it happen.

I would perform in those parks and recreation reviews and karaoke shows. I started doing pageants, and I'll tell you that was one of the best things I've ever done in my life. It taught me about poise and how to do interviews and things like that. There was a lot of competition in them, don't get me wrong, but the beautiful thing was I was able to get what I needed out of them. From that, I did supporting vocals on records. The first time was for a rapper on A&M Records called Overweight Pooch. Then they started asking, "Who's that fierce diva in the back?" I was asked if I had any songs of my own, with just my vocals on them. I told the label I had this one song, which ended up being my hit single "Finally."

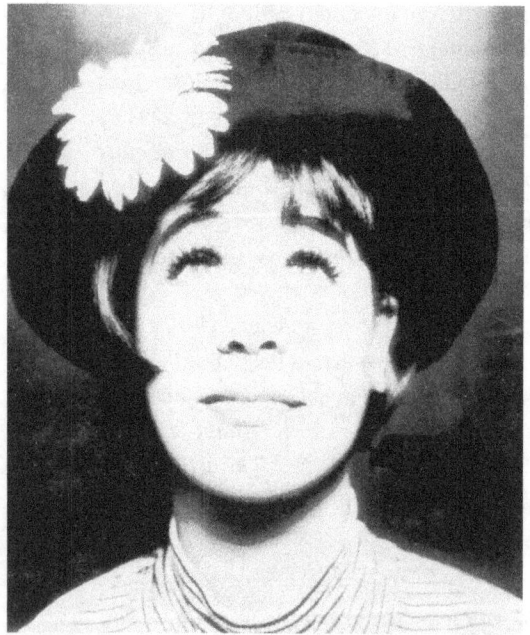

Things are looking up for CeCe Peniston, seen here in the 1992 A&M Records "flower power" publicity shot that was also used on the cover of her debut album (author's collection).

What a song that turned out to be. Do you remember any of the details of recording the track?

It was a great experience making this song. I remember being in the studio with producer Felipe Delgado, and we didn't have the second verse written. I had forgotten some of the lyrics and just ad-libbed some of them—that "yeah-yeah" part. They ended up sampling that, and it became a big part of the song. It's amazing how those raw moments happen. The song was sung with my natural delivery, my natural interpretation and what came out of me, my soul, at that time. I had never been in the studio like that before. I had done some of the work in bits and pieces on the Overweight Pooch material, but I had never sung a full song in the studio before.

I remember when I first heard it on the radio, and I was like, "Oh my God, my song's on the radio; my dream's come true!" It was the beginning of great things for me, because anything I put my mind to after that—I did it.

What is it about "Finally" that made so many people connect with the song?

I'm so thankful for that. It was such a blessing. I think there were a couple of elements that made "Finally" catch on so big. One was the bass line [*Peniston vocally recreates the bass sound*], and the other was that "yeah-yeah"; it was so different at the time. Vocally—this is what people told me—I didn't sound like anybody else. It was an easy song to sing. A young child of three can sing it; older people can sing it—the words were easy. It was an easy concept and so upbeat—and I think that's what made people gravitate to it. It was incredible for me because people were enjoying and singing a song that I wrote.

Really, I remember this song exploding on the market, and it seemed like overnight your name was everywhere. How did things change for you?

I thought about having success as a child, but you can never imagine that it will take you to Chicago and then Paris, London and Europe. All of a sudden, you're walking down the street, and people know your face and voice and song.

I went from working at a clothing store—Jeans Land—and I was still getting an allowance from my father when the song came out. You know what I'm saying? I was a normal girl living in Arizona, and I went from that to becoming a star. I started traveling everywhere. I was able to buy what I wanted to buy, I was on TV, and in *Billboard* and other magazines. I would sometimes do interviews from nine to five, grab a quick nap and have to do a show that same night. I'd get tired from traveling and the different time zones. I'd be like, "Where the hell am I at?" Overnight, people knew who I was and what I had accomplished at that point. At the same time, I had to give up my normal life and privacy. All of a sudden, I had to be "on." You gotta act like a star, you had to dress like a star, you had to have your hair and make-up done and look like a star, your voice has to be on all the time. And if you were having a bad day, guess what? They don't want to hear about your bad day. You had to learn how to adapt very quickly. That was the biggest change that happened to me.

Also, I had to grow up quickly because I soon saw that many people just wanted to be around me and my success. I started making all this money, and I had to keep track of everything. There was a lot going on.

"Finally" received many awards, and you performed it throughout the world. Was there a highlight for you from all that you experienced?

I remember being in Africa and thinking, my God, I'm in the motherland—the beginning. It was a full arena of people, and I was doing a band show. "Wow, okay, here we go." It was a euphoric moment for me, and I had to take a moment to just appreciate that.

I think it's definitely true though; I didn't really appreciate or realize how much I did until later on. When I was featured on the show *Unsung*, you get a chance to review what you've done, and you get to see it for yourself. But as it was happening, man, all you wanted to do was catch some sleep. Then you'd do the whole routine again in the next city. I was on that kind of schedule on a regular basis, so I didn't get to appreciate everything as it was happening.

***"Finally" made significant inroads into gay pop culture by also being prominently featured in the film and stage show adaptations of* The Adventures of Priscilla, Queen of the**

Desert. *The 1994 soundtrack for the film placed your track among disco classics such as Gloria Gaynor's "I Will Survive" and "I Love the Nightlife (Disco 'Round)" by Alicia Bridges. How did you react to your inclusion in this project?*

There have been many different people that wanted to use the song, and I would usually think, "Okay, someone wants it again." And that's what I initially thought about *Priscilla*. But then when I saw it, I was stunned. The film caused a resurgence in popularity for the song, which was great. Seeing the show in London and on Broadway, I remember saying to my mother, "What were the odds that a little girl from Arizona would be watching her song performed in London and on Broadway in *Priscilla, Queen of the Desert*?" You know, I've always felt that no matter where you are in life, good or bad, that's where you are supposed to be. My song being featured in those productions was definitely a transformative moment of mine.

Was there pressure on you to deliver a follow-up as strong as your debut hit?

Can you duplicate something that was as organic as "Finally"? People were always saying things like, "Can you do this song like 'Finally'?" The answer was no. "Finally" was exactly what it was supposed to be at that particular time. I can try to create something that's close to it, but can I reproduce it? No. I've had other songs that I think were good and were successful, but "Finally" has been my baby. It was my favorite song from that album; I've had other songs I've liked from [my follow-up albums] *Thought 'Ya Knew* and *I'm Movin' On*, but "Finally" is my baby.

To answer your question, yes, absolutely, there was pressure. I could have given them another "Finally" and called it "Suddenly." I could have done several variations like that, right? Same beat, same melody, different lyrics. But I didn't. I've had that one song that's lasted over 25 years, and I have no regrets about it. It's taken care of me, I have my royalties on it—I even have a commercial [using the song] on national TV here in the U.S. that has paid me very well. I'm blessed to have had that one classic song.

You are considered dance music royalty by many. Does that pose any problems for you?

You know what? As far as categories, I've always been flattered to be called a dance artist or house diva. How can I even be mad at that? But what I wouldn't like is to be given props *only* for that type of music. It would have been different if dance was the only type of music that I sing. But because I sing a variety of styles and genres, I don't see myself in the same way that others sometimes see me. But I love a challenge. So, okay, is that all you think I am? Okay then, let me show what else I can do. I am [singing and recording] a lot of styles beyond electronic dance music. But I realize sometimes there's one thing with music—[the public] wants a certain thing from you. You give them what they want and try to do other stuff as well. I've learned to try and mix it up, some of what I want, some of what they want.

Female artists in contemporary pop and dance music have to really rock it in terms of looks and image. Did you feel this pressure in the '90s?

Having that "look" is absolutely part of the business we work in. They always want you to look lean, even back when I came out. But it's really gotten tough now—they want you to be a size two. You can follow that or fall off. If you don't want that pressure, there's always another artist around the corner that wants it more than you.

The fact that artists can be their own entity, their own business, does make it easier—at least they don't have to worry about some record company's demands or standards.

Throughout the course of my career, I found out how to avoid food allergies and eat healthier. I work out, and last year I entered my first bikini fitness competition. I lost 30 lbs., and I'm getting ready to do another one. I did have liposuction performed about six years ago, but I lost weight on top of that and worked out very hard to get where I am today. In the process of wanting to live a more healthy life, I really got addicted to fitness.

How about the music business itself—were you treated fairly?

Well, I've certainly had my problems with the business. I had someone steal over a million dollars from me—that's a lot, and it caused a lot of complications for me.

But what it also did was make me a better person, a grateful person. At the time, I was very angry about it, vowing nobody will ever take from me ever again. Eventually, I took that negative energy I was feeling and channeled it into making myself an entrepreneur. It taught me to be very aware of what's going on around me and in the details of my own business. It taught me to be resourceful. I'll give you an example. There was a time I needed to get a new outfit to perform and rather than spend a lot of money (which was short) on a new wardrobe, I was able to look at what I had and figure out how I could make it look different. So I cut a sleeve off, added rhinestones, made the skirt shorter—things like that. It taught me to appreciate what I had and not be so quick to throw things away.

I now have my own clothing line, and I'm getting ready to start moving my designs into boutiques. So, from being an artist who was forced to make adjustments on her wardrobe because of a major financial setback, I'm now an artist with a unique fashion line.

You seem to have a very positive attitude. Has that always been the case?

As I have matured, I've gotten better at being the type of person who can rebound after a setback. There were periods in my life where I was very unsure about what to do in certain circumstances. I spent a lot of time being angry about negative situations, until I said, "Well, what are you gonna do about it?" I remember viewing a DVD called *Secrets*, and it suggested that it works against you to say things like "I can't do this," or "Damn, I hope this happens." I feel like when you say things like that, you give those words power. It took me going through some periods of depression, anger about the loss of money, and career changes (not understanding where my place in music was) to start looking at my life and handling it differently.

One thing I don't do is think of myself as old. I'm young at heart, I work out, I take care of my body and spirit. Am I mature? Yes. Do I think I have to act in some kind of "old" way? Absolutely not. I can find happiness in little things—it doesn't always have to be about money. I try to get out and enjoy life and stay in the moment. I love laugher—I think it takes a lot more energy to concentrate on the negative things of life. I just keep moving. I'm not saying I don't go through bad times and bad feelings—of course I do. You go through all kinds of moments in life. I just try to find the good in life, not just complain. Nobody wants to hear you complain.

Another thing I try to do is not to hold onto things—like people's opinion of you. That's not my problem. I just try to treat people the way I would like to be treated. That's the best way I think you can live your life.

We've seen a lot of dramatic changes in the music industry over the past several years. The focus in dance music itself has shifted quite a bit from the vocalist to the producer or DJ.

Yes. That's one of the reasons I started doing all the side lines. You have to diversify—

physically sell products, like my clothing line. I'm also the face of an energy drink. I'm even working on a workout DVD based on "Finally." What could be better than the "Finally" girl being in shape and doing a workout video to the song everyone says they love to hear when they work out? That's just the way it is in the business today. As an artist today, you're not really gonna make any money on record sales. You have to tour. People aren't buying music anymore; they're streaming. Because pop artists have gotten a lot younger, that's changed the business as well. So you have to really work harder to get yourself out there if you're not in that demographic.

When have you been most satisfied in your life?

I know you'll think this is crazy, but actually—in this moment. I feel like I know what I want, and I know where I'm going. I'm more confident today about who I am as a woman and as an artist. I still love singing, and I feel my voice is even more powerful now than when I was younger. I'm not afraid to try new things. You know, when I was younger, or let me say in the middle of my career, I was very much an "I don't like that," "I don't want to do that" type of person. Now I'm more open to trying things, and if they don't work out, that's okay. I move on. But I am open to trying, which I wasn't so much before.

Would you give me your take on dance music—its value and place in pop culture?

I've got a good answer for that! I think the reason people, in general, didn't treat dance music with that much respect or appreciation is that they thought the beat was what drives the music—not so much that the person singing it that added to the song. I think that was unfortunate. The great dance songs were all driven by the singer's vocal quality, how well they rode the beat, the things they sang about, their tone, inflection and interpretation. All these elements drove the song to be what it was.

If dance music had no value, why would contemporary artists like Chris Brown ever switch over to this genre? Or Usher or Kelly Rowland? But they recognized the value of a music genre that brings fun to people—the power of a form of music that can turn a bad day into a good one.

If you're looking to see what the value of dance music is, look at the longevity of songs from the '90s. You can't go anywhere without hearing Robin S's "Show Me Love" or Snap!'s "Rhythm Is a Dancer," for example. The music from this era is still all over the place, and it's still making people feel good. Even with "Finally," after two and a half decades, I am still traveling the world. Dance music was and *is* the life of the party—and it makes the soul feel good. That's its value—simple.

Lightning Round with CeCe

Diana Ross or Donna Summer?

Donna Summer. Her catalog speaks for itself. There's nothing I need to say or add.

Music or lyrics?

Music.

Extended versions or radio edits?

Extended because then you get all the great stuff that radio won't play.

"'Finally' was exactly what it was supposed to be at that particular time," says CeCe Peniston of her landmark hit (photograph by Angelique White, courtesy CeCe Peniston).

Meet your ancestors or meet your descendants?
Ancestors—I just think they are the history within you.

Performing live or in the recording studio?
Live.

Applause or record sales?
Oh, I'd have to pick record sales because you need that money in your pocket.

Famous but poor, or rich but unknown?
Rich but unknown. You can hire people to follow you around and make it look like you're somebody!

'70s or '80s?
'80s. I liked that music. But wait; let me take that back. The '70s had so much great dance music. That's a hard one. One of my favorite singers is Evelyn "Champagne" King. Oh, but she had hits in both the '70s and '80s. Forget it—I'll have to be a rebel and say both!

Frank Peterson, formerly of Enigma, Producer
"Sadeness Part I" (Enigma, 1990)

"We started to wonder if we were on drugs or something that we thought this could be a hit."—Frank Peterson

Frank Peterson was formally introduced to the world of dance-pop music stardom when he was invited to play keyboards for Sandra ("(I'll Never Be) Maria Magdalena"), one of Germany's most popular singers of the '80s, during a TV broadcast. But it was his immense contribution to the creation of a rather mystical international smash single called "Sadeness Part I," credited to a curious studio entity known as Enigma, that cemented Frank's high ranking in dance-pop history. This sensual and intoxicating track, which incorporated Gregorian chants and a rhythmic beat as its unconventional foundation, reached number one in dozens of countries and earned a Top 10 position on the U.S. pop chart. It also reached number one on Billboard's dance chart early in 1991 and stayed there for nearly a month. The song is widely acknowledged as one of the most unusual, inventive and hippest musical creations of the '90s.

The unexpectedly behemoth worldwide response to "Sadeness" caught Frank and the track's producer, Michael Cretu, by surprise. Disputes arose between the innovators, and the two parted ways (following the release of the project's highly successful debut album, MCMXC a.D.). Peterson, however, lost no momentum and quickly moved on to a celebrated career producing his well-received spin-off concept, Gregorian, and hugely popular releases by such esteemed vocalists as Sarah Brightman ("Time to Say Goodbye," "A Question of Honour").

Frank, speaking from the den of his home in Hamburg late one evening, doesn't quite see himself as a purveyor of uncommon '90s dance-pop music, however popular his hits may have been in the clubs and on the charts. Nonetheless, he is proud of his accomplishments and enjoys reflecting on them with a grounded perspective—one that clearly reflects the industry's long-held sobering realities.

Frank, I'd first like to know a little about your formative years and the path that led you into music as a young adult.

I was born in Hamburg in 1963, and my parents had me when they were very young. My father was a musician who was also into developing public address and sound systems

Frank Peterson works his magic in the studio, which led to tremendously successful recordings by Marky Mark, Gregorian, Alannah Myles, Princessa and famed classical crossover soprano Sarah Brightman (courtesy Frank Peterson).

and things like that. I grew up with the piano, and I had an opportunity to try many things. My mother had a younger brother who was just about 10 years older than me, and he introduced me to new music. I started to really show an interest in music by collecting records at the age of four. I spent all my money on buying records when I was young. I even sang very well in English in kindergarten—at that time hardly anybody spoke English at that age in Germany. By nine years of age, I was seeing big stars in concert like Gary Glitter, Alice Cooper, Santana and Grand Funk Railroad. In the Germany of the '60s and '70s, it was safe for me to go to see a matinee show at a music club at a young age. (Today, I wouldn't let my daughter go out of the house at the age I was doing these things.) I received professional drum training and started in my first bands when I got a bit older.

In Germany at the time, you finished your studies and went on to become an academic person, or you received training for something. I made absolutely sure I joined the coolest company and became a trainee. In Hamburg, there was a shop (called Logic) that sold minimoogs, Gibson guitar and Fender amps and so on. They kind of liked me and gave me an internship there. They became one of the coolest and best known shops in Germany for this kind of equipment, and I was their first trainee to become a businessman in that industry. All the biggest stars came in to get their drums and sound equipment there. I remember Howard Jones coming in, and I remember working on the very first small club date of Sade. I delivered all her equipment. It was all quite glamorous for me, and I was quite lucky to get the job. Plus, they paid me like a real employee. It was wonderful.

I received many opportunities there. The shop owners teamed up with program developers who came up with one of the first programs to run sequencers on a Commodore computer. I was finishing up my training, and I was offered the chance to run the company that would sell this program (that was later sold to another company for something like 15 million dollars). I think something like 70 percent of all music at the time was created from this software, and I felt very proud to have set it all up.

While working at Logic, you received another lucky break that moved you firmly into Germany's burgeoning dance-pop scene, did you not?

I certainly did. One day, a person from Virgin Records contacted our guy in the [sound] system rental service department asking if they had someone who could perform on a TV show with one of their new artists. The artist was Sandra, the singer from the group Arabesque, now gone solo. So I showed up at the TV studio with a guitar and a remote keyboard, and there I met [her producer] Michael Cretu. I introduced him to one of our brand new emulators at that time. He was quite intrigued by it. Sandra had been a little known solo artist up until that TV show, but the song she sang ["I'll Never Be (Maria Magdalena)"] ended up going to the top of the charts. Suddenly I had two jobs—running around with Sandra, playing guitar in the background on many TV shows and at her concerts, while also working for Logic. There were many female singers at the time (C.C. Catch, Lian Ross, etc.), but the record company wanted to give her a little more credibility by putting her with a band. They put her with three musicians, and I was lucky because I lived in Hamburg, and they usually didn't have to worry about hotels and flights for me.

Michael and I met on what you might call equal terms because he hadn't really become famous yet with Sandra or his other work (like Moti Special). So Michael, Sandra and I traveled together for the next five years as she became very, very big in Europe, and we all became friends as well. A few of my songs were picked for Sandra to record, including her hit ballad "Loreen." I kissed my job at Logic goodbye and moved to Munich to work with Michael and Sandra. After five years of this, I began to want to be in more of the situation Michael was in. By that I mean not so much running around, but pulling the strings, producing and creating the sounds. Around the five year mark, it was felt Sandra needed a change, to be seen by herself on TV, and that was perfect. I was able to move away from the band and the TV stuff to work more with Michael and Sandra in the studio. I got more and more involved in arranging her songs, production work and doing the remixes. I even had the chance to co-produce some of the tracks from her *Paintings in Yellow* album in 1990. Sandra became one of the three or four biggest artists in Europe of that time.

Would you tell me a bit about what it was like working with Mr. Cretu?

Michael was really in the driver's seat as the producer. He wasn't a very social person, and when it came to teamwork, he might be best described as introverted. He was bit of a loner and wasn't very outgoing. He saw himself as—and that's how he described himself—sort of an alchemist, mixing things together. He was very much into the technical side of productions. He has a very high musical pedigree—he studied music as a conductor, a concert pianist, and his studies in the conservatory set his mind in a certain way. For example, when we first got together, we talked a lot about music and influences. For him, the music of Yes was an influence.

Michael had luck as well as talent. In the early '70s, Richard Branson founded Virgin Records, and he started opening little offices all around the world. He built up an international company, and he needed people to run it for him. He hired someone to create domestic (German) product for Virgin. Well, it was just through some kind of weird connection that Michael, too, became part of this office. He wore funny glasses and had a really left field, progressive look—like a German version of Mike Oldfield. The basis of Virgin Records' success had been Oldfield's "Tubular Bells" for the movie *The Exorcist*. So Michael had the right funky image, and they said let's hire this guy. It was all innocent at that time, not the corporate suits of today. They liked him and wanted to hire him. Michael became sort of an in-house staff producer for Virgin, though his first records didn't work too well.

When Michael launched the solo career of Sandra, he just teamed with the right people. The song "Maria Magdalena" was [co-composed] by Hubert Kemmler (also known from the group Hubert Kah). At that time, Hubert was past his peak in his solo career. He was a big star early in the '80s when Germany was first beginning to make pop and new wave hits in its own language that influenced the world. When his wave came down, Hubert wanted to try to reinvent himself. Michael picked him up, and they began to write songs together. "(I'll Never Be) Maria Magdalena" was the first song to come out of it.

I remember Sandra had problems pronouncing the "th" sound, and it took a lot of great work on their part to come up with songs that didn't have a lot of that sound and yet still sounded great to Europeans, without having masterpiece lyrics. I think that's another reason why these songs didn't hit bigger in the English-speaking territories. At that time, it was more important for us to have great *sounding* lyrics rather than *genuinely* great lyrics. Klaus Hirschburger was another songwriter for Sandra, and he was a very intellectual person. Sometimes his lyrics were a bit of a tongue-twister and would have to be re-written for Sandra. So, often her songs were stripped down to the essence, and the words that were used had to have impact. However, in a very commercial sense, maybe this was the way to go—keep it easy, simplistic. That's what pop music is all about. But, in the case of "Maria Magdalena," it's a great song with a unique production. However, lots of lucky coincidences were necessary to make it happen.

My story is no different—a lot of funny coincidences where I was in the right place at the right time. It's all luck. If I hadn't been where I was at the time, I'd probably wouldn't be in this book today. Who knows?

Do you recall feeling a sense of competition with other German producers of the period?

Well, let's say I'm glad I worked with Michael and not some of the other producers who were out there. Some of these gentlemen weren't very concerned about lyrics. Grammatically, the lyrics of some songs were horrible. Fortunately, Michael would still work with people like Klaus, who wouldn't let a song get too ridiculous. We wanted to sell pop records, but we didn't want to be on the tacky side. We wanted always to create a bit of sophistication. In the end, I think our team managed very well with Sandra.

In terms of competition, some producers make outrageous claims to have sold hundreds of millions of records. It is *not* possible to sell hundreds of millions of records in continental Europe. And they never sold records [in large quantities] anywhere else. It tends to be hype. For example, a producer can potentially have in his contract a requirement that he get four gold records for any one gold certification he receives—one for him as a lyricist, one as the producer, one as the composer and one as the artist. They often include compilation albums and multiply them by the number of roles the producer performed on the record. It all adds up. One gentleman in the industry wrote a book that had a sticker on the cover saying he had sold one billion records. That's more than Michael Jackson and ABBA combined—more than Mariah and Whitney together. He may have even included estimates of pirated sales in those figures. They can get away with it because people don't really check it. Sometimes it just irritates me because it undermines everybody else's success, including my own.

Then the credibility of many singles sales figures, especially in the dance genre, may also be suspect.

Well, it's true [dance music probably] generates more single sales than album sales. But I suppose you can say in the "old school" way of tabulating, the single was just a publicity tool, and the album was the focus. I guess I just look at things from the original perspective.

I stopped measuring my success with these numbers anyway. I just consider myself lucky that before the arrival of Napster and downloading and streaming, I managed to ship 50 or 60 million *albums*. It doesn't matter anymore. Everyone knows what the real story is.

Why did you part company with Sandra after her Paintings in Yellow (1990) album?

For one thing, musically it wasn't my cup of tea. I wasn't embarrassed by it; don't get me wrong. She was very lovely and pleasant, and I am totally thankful for the opportunity I had. It got me started. Most of the business contacts I have today I met through her. I flew in business class, stayed in great hotels and went all over the world.

This is a difficult thing to explain—but running the whole enterprise, as Michael Cretu did, you have an amazing responsibility. For the first few years I spent running around with her, I didn't have any responsibility; I was just enjoying it. Even as I moved more into production, writing, arranging and mixing for her, I *still* didn't feel that sense of responsibility for it. (I finally started to feel that sense working with Sarah Brightman in the early '90s.)

Lastly, towards the end with Sandra, her priorities began to change, and that made departing from the team easier. Three or four years ago, she contacted my attorney about possibly doing some work together again, but I didn't feel that I wanted to go back there. But, again, I am very grateful for the experience I had with her.

How did the Enigma project come about?

I saw the 1986 movie *The Name of the Rose* (featuring Sean Connery), which was basically a medieval James Bond movie. I was fascinated by that and had a great love of choir music. I was married to a Spanish woman at the time and living outside of Madrid. They have a very famous cloister there. For about two years, I suggested to Michael Cretu that we do something with Gregorian chants. He always questioned who would buy this music (because he had studied this form of music). In other words, it was like me suggesting we do math or Sudoku just for fun. He wasn't interested because he felt it wasn't commercially viable. I heard a rhythm coming from someone's Walkman while taking a guided tour of the cloister, and it hit me that the sound might work with the chanting. I went to a department store and bought all their Gregorian chant music. They had a small pile of records that were all dusty because nobody had ever bought them.

Michael was in the studio working with [co-writer] David Fairstein on a sophisticated French project, and they didn't know what to do with it. Then I came in with CDs of these chants I'd made and asked him to put on one of the drum tapes, like a Soul II Soul sound, and it really started to groove. Michael started playing chords with it. We just knew this was it. It was funny—we put in that first CD, we started playing around, and, fuck, it was just so in your face. We couldn't believe that it had been so easy to create something this magical. We went through all the CDs, but we stuck with the first one and put the others aside. This was it. Basically, overnight we finished the whole track "Sadeness."

That was followed by some doubt. You expect to put in so much effort usually to create a hit (nothing really came by accident in the five years with Sandra). We started to wonder if we were on drugs or something that we thought this *could* be a hit. We tightened some things up. (One of the effects on the record was just the result of a synthesizer crashing and creating a weird sound). We lifted the chanting from one of the records (and later on that resulted in a law suit where Michael had to give them a share in Enigma).

Ironically, when I was at Logic I had sold Michael a sampler that could handle a great deal of storage. That kind of opened things up so that were able to create something like this. So this song was a combination of pure luck, me insisting that we do something with Gregorian chant and putting Michael's nose into the shit that this could be great. And on top of that, we had a state-of-the-art computer system that allowed us to do it technically. "Sadeness" is the result of sampling a choir that follows hundreds of years of tradition and taking the best pieces of the melody and matching chords to them and adding loops—that was the longest thing for us to figure out. Everything else came in a flash.

Michael came up with the name Enigma for the project, and we later realized it was the same name of the Nazis' secret coding machine. So we thought that worked. I came up with the title "Sadeness," working in the whole Marquis de Sade element. I'm telling you, it just gave us goosebumps as it happened. We were in an amazing mood after coming up with something so outrageous.

How did you react to the overwhelming popularity of this project, which extended far beyond the continental success you had enjoyed with Sandra (whose whispering vocals were also used in the background of "Sadeness")?

Well, we finished the song, and we were in total awe of ourselves. Michael's manager, who also managed Sandra, came out to Ibiza with us for a weekend, and we played him the track. He was sitting there listening and said, "That's heavy going. You'll never get that on radio." We started thinking, "Oh shit." An hour later, our contact at Virgin tells us his secretary and other people at the office are fucking amazed by the song. He said he didn't get it, but everyone else seemed to love it. So pretty quickly the song came out. We all used pseudonyms on the record credits (Curly M.C. for Michael, F. Gregorian for me), so nobody knew who it was. This is what I totally believe—the song combined so many things. It was culture, it was hip, it was new sounding, and people couldn't tell where in the world it came from. American, French, Italian? They had no idea. It sounded so familiar, but yet so foreign at the same time. I think that was the key to its success.

The Catholic church was upset, calling it blasphemous. So we had the scandal attached to it. That made it front page news. It went so wild in just three or four days. Record shops were selling out almost immediately. It went to number one so quickly that demand just increased and increased. So many people started to congratulate us.

Michael would get the most accolades, and, in the beginning, he would say, "Actually, it was Frank's idea." Then Richard Branson called and said the idea with the monks was awesome, and Michael just said thank you. That's when I realized that he was starting to take all the credit. We were under pressure to get an album together before Christmas—we had something like two weeks to finish it. Michael had to get to Florence to shoot the video, and I started putting the first tracks together. He came back and basically said he was sorry, but he thought the tracks were shit and suggested I take myself off the project, and he would finish it himself. Some of my ideas were used, but that was the beginning of the end of our business relationship.

I did some checking and found out the name Enigma had been registered. I asked him what my share was going to be because, clearly, the song would not have been conceived without me. I can't tell you what he came up with—it was ridiculous. But he felt it was his studio and his financial investment. I did finish the album with him, but it was done very quickly. How can I put it? I thought if I went to a lawyer, I'd just end up kicking myself out of the whole thing. I wanted to see if I could contribute to the album, which I kind of did. I was really hurt though. I had sampled my entire record collection on CD, and the entire album was made from those samples. I can tell where each song came from. Also, I knew the song was so successful and the album had to get out before Christmas, and I didn't want to be the asshole to slow down things. I believed once the record was done, we'd find an amicable settlement.

We finished the album (*MCMXC a.D.*—I believe it is certainly among Germany's Top Three bestsellers of all time), Christmas came, and I left for Hamburg. I realized my time in Ibiza was over. I knew I wasn't going back there and had a bad vibe for it now. I only met Michael two more times. The first was to settle things out of court—[the settlement] was alright, and it helped me to finance my own work. I didn't regret doing that. I probably would have if my career had died down, which, thankfully, it did not. The second time I met him was when I received an Echo award for my work with Sarah.

You know, they hadn't taken Michael that seriously before Enigma. Suddenly, he did something super cool, high brow, sophisticated and super hip—it was being played in the best clubs. It wasn't all that danceable, but it was almost too cool *not* to be played. He took the credit for it—I don't think it was so much about the money; I think he wanted or needed that credibility.

Was this experience something you have to chalk up to working in this business? How do you view it in hindsight?
There is no black and white to it. I have worked with so many people in my life and—[*he pauses*]—unfortunately, now that everything is about income and all that kind of stuff, integrity and attention to ethical values have declined. But there are still some people out there that you can deal with without ever signing anything. Generally, there are far more assholes running the music business, but there are people I've worked with for ages and have never experienced a ripple with. I think about the situation with Michael—maybe I did something wrong, too. Maybe I should have come into the studio and presented this really cool idea, but signed a contract that if we did it, we'd share 30–70 or something. If I had done that, maybe we'd still be friends. I don't know. Maybe the whole thing became too vast and too successful too fast. Everyone dreams of something like this happening, and there it was. It had never happened to either of us before. Yeah, well, that's just the way it is.

Twenty-five years later, is Enigma still a meaningful footnote in your professional history?
To be honest, I don't think if I were to go around saying I was involved in the Enigma

record that people would go, "What? Wow! You did that?" I think the reaction, if they remember it at all, would be more like, "That's interesting." People who grew up with the record, or had sex with it, maybe remember it. I use the record as a door-opener, but it's not like something that changes the game after all these years. It's more like, "Okay, but what has he done lately?"

You were responsible for some beautiful productions in the '90s that enjoyed a powerful response on the dance floor, among them many magnificent projects with Sarah Brightman. Please tell me about collaborating with this acclaimed vocalist.

When I came out of this whole Enigma thing, I had offers to go to Italy, America and Japan to work. People would ask me if I wanted to work with such-and-such an artist. I felt like I just wanted to go back to Hamburg and start my own studio because I realized if you control the whole deal with your own studio—like in the old days of Hollywood—you had the power. I felt really hyped up about being in the center of things. I could do whatever I liked. I bought some really great equipment, thanks to my connections with the shop I used to work for, and I came back to my hometown as a super successful writer and producer. I felt like king of the castle at that time. I instantly got a record label and publishing deal for a significant amount of money—and that helped me not care so much about what had happened with Michael. Despite the situation, this was the best departure I could have asked for. I learned to separate the personal hurt from the amazing developments in my business.

I worked on some records with my Gregorian concept that were very successful. Two of the songs I had worked on were sent by my publisher (without me knowing) to a former disco singer named Sarah Brightman (of the Broadway and London cast of *Phantom of the Opera*—I had no idea about her involvement with that show until the day before I met her), who, at that point, was viewed as an artist with pop potential signed to A&M Records, one of the coolest labels around. But their A&R department didn't know what to do with her. She was sitting there for more than a year with her deal, trying out songs. They couldn't get a formula for her. She heard the Enigma record and liked the classical sound presented in a modern way. "That's what I want," she said. At the same time she received my Gregorian cuts. She realized that all of this music was coming from the same source. We connected, and she came to Hamburg. Her taste in music was completely different from what I expected—she liked the Cocteau Twins, John Cale and all these underground artists. I told her that's not what I do, and we couldn't agree at all. I wanted to do another international album and suggested she sing rock classics in a classical way. She said something like, "Nah, that's a bad idea."

Well, despite that, we still agreed to work together. I suggested to Sarah and A&M we do a concept album. But the truth is, when they asked me what the concept was, I didn't have one. I just came up with a theme about the travels of Magellan, which evolved into a theme about water. I started looking for appropriate songs with that theme. I loved the word "dive" (not knowing in the English culture the term could also mean a flop or a low-end bar). I was thinking of the Swedish electronica band by that name and the song "Captain Nemo." I named her album *Dive* and picked a bunch of songs that kind of evoked the theme of the sea. It took two years to get this record together. Sarah was used to singing as one would in a live theatrical setting, and she wasn't prepared to sing with the fixed rhythm, the fixed timing of a drum. It took a long time to work with her to get a pop vocal, and I feared it wasn't going to work.

She had to get it done or the label would let her go, and I had to get it done because I couldn't send her home. Quite honestly, I needed the money from the deal to launch my studio. We were basically bound to each other, and that actually made us grow very close—and we fell in love after about a year. We were together for almost 15 years.

The album went gold in Canada, but nowhere else, and Sarah was dropped anyway. Around that time, I also worked with Prince Ital Joe [a reggae vocalist also known as Joseph Paquette] and Marky Mark [Mark Wahlberg], who were hugely successful in Germany with their euro-dance hits like "Happy People" and "United." Thanks to being successful with that project in my own country, I was able to get Sarah a new record deal with Warner.

This deal led to an important track in 1995, Sarah's brilliant melding of modern classical music with Euro-dance energy, "A Question of Honour."

Yes, it was her first hit in many years. But I have to tell you—everybody in America calls that song a "dance" track. You know what it really is? A European trying to imitate Journey. Obviously, I failed miserably. [*Frank laughs.*] The song "Running" (2007)—the same thing. In your face American stadium rock. Because that type of music isn't really in my veins, and German electronica is, songs like those, to American ears, sound like European dance music. To me, I'm almost trying to create American metal. Listen to "Separate Ways" by Journey, and listen to the rock part of "A Question of Honour." It's the same rhythm, the four-quarter bass. It's like doing Journey with a computer. That it turns out to be electronic dance music comes from the mix by Tom Lord-Alge. Dance mixes are just created to get the song played in the clubs. It's not an art form for me—we fuck up a song [with a remix] to get it played in discos. But, as I noted before, the true version is the album version.

It's interesting how we can both appreciate the song from completely different perspectives. It's really a testament to your work and how it can be enjoyed on different levels.

True. The song was a very unique piece (there really wasn't anything like it around), and it certainly started Sarah's solo career. Because it was so unusual, I never worked with a reference point. I ended up creating a reference point. We set a standard. It was a very rewarding experience for us. By that time, we had already worked together for almost four years, we were a couple, and suddenly things started to get off the ground. It was especially gratifying because it combined her work, which was based in years of classical training, and my personal tastes—plus the fact that everybody misunderstood it. [*He laughs.*] You know? It's very funny to me that I'm trying to do "Journey meets Puccini," and everybody thinks of it as a dance track.

Did having a romantic relationship with Sarah make creating music together easier or more difficult?

I think it's natural that you both put in a few more night shifts. It can be really overwhelming because not only do you share your professional lives, your share your private life. It worked quite well for us for many years, though. I was in the studio, and she'd go off to do concerts. She left everything involving the production up to me. She was, like many artists, never fully happy with the end results. She couldn't help it—she was just never fully satisfied with anything. I think maybe two or three times she said, "Yeah, it's good." I know she appreciated everything, the success—all of it, and that she knew working with another producer she wouldn't have had the freedom that our partnership gave her. When you are engaged so closely with each other, you have more patience. It was a great relationship and one of the best points in my life where everything went smoothly. I never got bullshit from the record companies where they'd say, "We don't like the mix. Do it again." It was all no questions asked, and I got handed my paycheck. Total bliss.

Sarah's 1996 duet with Andrea Bocelli, "Time to Say Goodbye (Con Te Partirò)," was a monumental achievement for all involved. How did it come about? (Also, the song has been covered by many other artists, including Donna Summer, who brought a powerful dance spin to it. However, I'm guessing that you probably didn't care for Donna's version.)

[*Frank smiles.*] The original song was sung by Andrea Bocelli and had been out in Europe for a few years. A very good friend of mine asked me if I knew about this blind tenor and encouraged me to listen to the song, saying it was quite good. It was Sarah who woke me early one morning saying that she had listened to the song and that she thought it was a hit. She thought we should record it, if possible. It had to be given a full "Puccini treatment," and it needed an English title because "Con Te Partirò," on a global scale, just doesn't flow that nicely. Even if we created a great version, we knew we'd have to work hard to get it heard.

We felt it had to be a duet that would be sexy and funky. We first tried to do it with Bryan Adams, but due to scheduling it wasn't possible. We tried recording it with Paul Young, but it didn't work out (his Italian wasn't good enough). So we eventually decided to see if it would work with Bocelli. It was recorded in three or four takes—bang, it was in the pocket. It was also the very first song I produced with an orchestra. (On "A Question of Honour," the whole orchestra was synthesizers. The only real instrument on that record was a guitar.) Well, in the end, the song became the biggest selling single of all time in Germany. We got the track licensed to a small label in America called Angel. (It was the same label that capitalized on Enigma and released the worst Gregorian record ever recorded and had a huge hit with it— The Benedictine Monks of Santo Domingo de Silos' *Chant* album from 1994, which was one of the Gregorian chant records we threw away when making "Sadeness.")

But back to Donna Summer—it's very funny that you brought her up. Just today I finished mixing a Gregorian version of the song using the lyrics of Donna Summer's version. [*Frank plays the track.*] I loved Donna Summer; she was amazing. [*He pauses, as if reluctant to make his next statement.*] But you're right—I didn't like her version of the song.

You mentioned your work with Prince Ital Joe and Marky Mark earlier. Mark Wahlberg (Marky Mark and the Funky Bunch) had a monster dance-pop-hip-hop hit stateside in 1991 called "Good Vibrations." Of course, we all know he went on to an incredible career as a film actor. What are your memories of working with him?

Mark Wahlberg was a bit of a rookie when we worked together, and I am completely in awe of the career he has now. One of the first things that comes to mind [*Frank laughs*] – upon our initial meeting, I tried to break the ice and teased him about his very loose, baggy jeans by asking him, "Hey, didn't those pants come in *your* size?" I was always wearing skinny fit jeans and from the beginning he always called me "g-string" because he was dead set on the fact that that's the only thing that could be worn underneath my jeans.

He had been doing those Calvin Klein underwear ads. At the same time he was modeling for Calvin, he was signed to a very cool, urban rap division of Interscope Records (part of Warner Bros. back then) in the States. He was the only white kid on the label. Some of the credible black rappers of the time weren't too happy that he was signed to their label, and their pressure forced the label to keep the kid stone cold. Mark's people contacted the German office looking for someone to work with him in the European market. At the same time, I had just teamed up with Alex Christensen and together we spread the work that we were interested to work with an international artist, and so they called us.

Mark didn't want the full focus of a record to be on him—he preferred to have others with him. He just wanted to keep his career as a musician running, and since his label did not support him in the U.S. anymore, he came over to Germany. Since he stepped into unknown territory with two producers who never did a hip-hop album, we agreed to do the album under the moniker Prince Ital Joe featuring Marky Mark. Mark was a streetwise and clever guy. If our record was a big hit, it would be considered a Marky Mark song, and if it flopped, he would just say he was only helping a friend out with the recording. Mark was a great rapper and the flavor Prince Ital Joe added was very unique. We created some mixes incorporating techno, Euro-dance, reggae, dancehall and gospel. Also, both came up with great lyrics on the fly.

The funny thing with Mark was that he found it difficult to keep up with the techno-speed of the music. We ended up using special recording equipment that was able to pace his rapping with the beat of the music. Remember, this was in the early '90s, and luckily my studio was one of only a few that had this technology at the time, and the results were excellent. "United" went to number one, and while "Prince Ital Joe featuring Marky Mark" became the biggest selling act of the year, I guess it *was* considered a Marky Mark hit.

You also created the 1997 self-titled album of crossover Israeli singer Ofra Haza, which was an eclectic mix of middle eastern themes and Euro-dance sounds. You even managed to incorporate some Enigma flavor into the set. What are your recollections of working on the album (her last major release before her tragic AIDS-related death)?

It was an album I really didn't want to do because it happened at a time when I was very occupied with Sarah. I had an old friend who was working at BMG in Munich, Germany, and he told me they just didn't know what to with her. They didn't want to an ethnic album, and she didn't want to do a pure pop album. They thought someone like me would be perfect—not too poppy and not too sophisticated. I kept declining, but then Sarah began a big promotional tour. BMG came to me with a great offer, and when I saw Ofra, she was so unbelievably beautiful I just couldn't say no. She was so striking, I was like [*he laughs*], "Don't ever go away!" I guess I was really driven by my penis.

It was an interesting record, though. Her Arabic ad libs, the wailing she was able to do, were in many ways like Gregorian chant music. I suggested she just sing whatever comes to mind, let it out, and we'll record everything. I started composing songs based on what we recorded. I'd look for matching keys and ask to her change or add a note here and there. That's how we did it.

We got along really well. There were some challenges with the project. The gentleman guiding her was bit of a micro-manager at the time. However, I think that came from the fact that he had discovered her when she was very young (I believe), and he had been looking out for her ever since. Ofra was a practicing Jew, which created some restrictions in the way we could work. Still, it was all manageable, and working with her was a very nice experience. However, we had too many people involved, and with all of their opinions, things stop flowing organically. I think that's why the record didn't do as well as it could have. It did super well in Israel, but in the rest of the world it went unnoticed.

She died shortly after its release. She wasn't sick at all during the recording. She was looking for a partner, as I recall. I think her father was dying, and it was very hard for him to have a daughter who was not married. So, she was in her early 40s at that time and had been completely career driven, and I'm sure her biological clock was ticking. After the record, she didn't do much promotion because there were a lot of problems at the time with Palestine and the Gaza Strip and so on (and she was a hard-liner defending Israel's policies). Being so outspoken about her viewpoints wasn't really a door-opener in Europe at the time, and it would have been challenging bringing her to talk shows with all that was going on.

In any event, she picked the wrong guy. She contracted AIDS, and she was too ashamed to get treatment. Well, very sadly, she died. It happened very fast.

I found your work with Ms. Haza to be a wonderful reflection of her vocal talent. It was also but one of many brilliant productions that fill your musical résumé. I'm curious what you see yourself doing in the years to come?

I am so happy about the success I had in the past and when I had it. I am in the house I live now in because of that. I'm not sure what my future holds. Fortunately, because of Sarah and my Gregorian project, I was able to move into live entertainment. If I had relied on record sales, pop songs and dance tracks, I wouldn't have been able to continue.

I will tell you I am in the process of getting out of the business. Let's say I find a new talent that is potentially the next Bon Jovi. I will not get a deal from a record company because there is no money to be made in new talent for the label. It's so expensive to develop a new artist; they just won't do it. It's a fact. So I don't really see myself being able to continue to create new music, as I have in the past.

How seriously do you view the ongoing changes and challenges of monetizing music in the industry today?

I just read an article discussing the end of the jazz label Verve Records. By the time this book comes out, Decca and Deutsche Grammophon will probably be extinct. Sony Masterworks is basically closing. The current number one album on the *Billboard* classical charts has sold 220 copies. How can you produce new music with this kind of sales? They say that within 10 years, if you want to hear classical music, you either will have to find a live concert or rely on the collection you already have because there will be no more classical recordings.

I have a young artist [I have been working with]—a crossover tenor—who I believe could be the next Bocelli. He is 19 years old from Italy, and he looks like Justin Bieber. He sings higher than any soprano you have ever listened to. He's outstanding. We did a record, and I truly enjoyed doing a masterpiece recording with such an amazing talent, but I wonder how I will ever get this project sold. And if I get a deal, it will be so horrendous, that I won't be able to look myself in the mirror asking the kid to accept the conditions.

I don't need the money—that's not the point, really. However, if you aim for global success, you can't achieve it without the machine of a major label behind you. You can't replace that machine. Nobody can work a record on a global level by themselves. And even if you had this force behind you, even the most powerful people in the industry can't break a new artist anymore. What happened with Napster, YouTube, streaming, etc.—they have brought us to the end of an era. The music business is at an end.

Someone said to me they think people will get tired of streaming and want to hold the CD once again. Where will they buy it? All the stores are gone. There will only be Amazon.

You know what happens on Amazon? They tell labels what *they* want to sell. If they want more books like *Fifty Shades of Grey*, they tell publishers to give them more books like that. So, increasingly, the dealers dictate what gets sold. I just don't see that as a great way of moving forward.

I understand your viewpoint. It was a very different time in the '90s, wasn't it? Looking back at the music industry of that period, what was the key element one needed to possess in order to have a shot at success?

You often hear that the key, if you want to call it that, was having a commitment to very hard work. That was part of it. Some might say it was a person's talent [that made the music work]. People like to say these things, but it wasn't always as easy as just that. If it was just talent [that created success], then I might not be here speaking with you today. Or you wouldn't be interested in speaking with me. So, in the whole scheme of things, talent may have ended up being about 25 percent of the whole picture. No, in my opinion, the secret was having a lot of luck and pulling the strings in the right way and using your connections at the right time.

"I am so happy about the success I had in the past and when I had it," says musician, producer and composer Frank Peterson (courtesy Frank Peterson).

Alfredo "Larry" Pignagnoli, Producer, Label Owner
"Saturday Night" (Whigfield, 1994)

"During the '80s, we lived in a renaissance period, but if you wanted to survive in the '90s, you had to adapt to the changing environment."—Larry Pignagnoli

Alfredo "Larry" Pignagnoli is an Italian musician, producer, songwriter and record label owner well known for a series of huge international hits during the '80s. It was the era of Italo-disco, a genre that combined elements of classic disco with the electronic musicianship that defined the decade, and Pignagnoli was at the forefront of this sound. His trend-setting productions topped the charts of Europe, the UK and virtually any territory that supported dance floors, and many of his productions have come to be regarded as classics of the period—Spagna's "Call Me," Fun Fun's "Colour My Love," and "Challenger" by Baby's Gang among them.

As the popularity of Italo-disco faded with the arrival of the '90s, a new brand of electronics-based music, which included genres such as techno, Euro-dance, progressive house and hard-trance, among many others, took over the clubs and radio. While many of Italo-disco's artists and producers stepped out of the spotlight, Larry was among the few who remained influential and enjoyed prosperity on the new dance-pop music front. Still based out of Italy, his Off Limits Srl label launched a series of artists whose radio and club releases met with tremendous success, rivaling his achievements in the previous decade. Whigfield's extraordinarily popular "Saturday Night" and tracks by artists such as the Gambafreaks, Benny Benassi and In-Grid brought new energy and originality to an ever-evolving beat-fused landscape. Off Limits recently released Spagna's latest singles, "Baby Don't Go" and "Straight to Hell.

Though Pignagnoli rarely grants interviews, he makes an exception for this project and offers his succinct yet telling observations about his experience in the world of '80s and '90s dance-pop and beyond.

Larry, please tell me a little about your youth, growing up in Italy and what inspired your interest in music.

I was born in the Italian countryside, in Emilia. I was a kid in the '60s, and I listened to rock, blues and pop. Then I went to work in the country, helping my parents—they were farmers. What influenced my creativity was the match between two opposite worlds—the energy of the '60s on one side and the slow, poetic, but hard work of the country on the other. Playing music was the only way to escape. The guitar was the only instrument I could afford, and I fell in love with it.

How did you begin to get involved with '80s Italo-disco music in the genre's early days? You rather quickly became one of its most important innovators working with the popular X Energy label in Italy, and you enjoyed great commercial success.

I played in the clubs with a music band and we had to make people dance. Some months after, together with two of the members of the band (Ivana and Theo Spagna), we started producing our own songs. The first ever was "Take Me to the Top" by Advance in 1982, followed by "Happy Station" and "Colour My Love" by Fun Fun. With such great feedback and results, we decided to continue on the production side, and we put an end to our band era.

You've had a very close relationship with Ivana Spagna, and you were tremendously successfully building Spagna's solo career with massive international hits, such as "Easy Lady," "Call Me" and "Every Boy and Girl."

Ivana Spagna was the singer of our original band, and she's been my life partner for over 15 years. It was a relationship with no borders between job and private life, and so it was an all-encompassing experience. We were closed in our world. But it has been a successful partnership.

Was there a method or formula that you followed when creating that great music of the '80s?

There wasn't a specific method. Sometimes songs were born at the piano and then later rearranged. Sometimes we created a musical backing, and after we added a top line. In both cases, we tried to add specific sounds and melodic elements that could make the track recognizable.

The '80s was such a dynamic, creative, prosperous era for Italian dance music. Few could have predicted how hugely popular it would become throughout Europe. Why do you think Italians had such a strong talent for creating this style of music at that particular time?

I think that the success of Italo-disco has to be attributed to the simplicity of its arrangements and melodies—they were easy to remember and sing. It was a lucky mix between disco and dance coming from the U.S., and the melodies of the Italian opera tradition. I believe that combination determined the success of Italians in that field.

As the '90s began, how did the music climate in Italy change?

Trends change; it's a natural process. As a new era began, Italo-disco, which had gone global, lost some of the characteristics that made it successful. With the '90s came new technologies and the desire of artists to escape the Italian borders. During the '80s, we lived in a renaissance period, but if you wanted to survive in the '90s, you had to adapt to the changing environment.

You've managed your publishing company, Off Limits, since the '80s. What inspired you to create the Off Limits recording label in the '90s, which became very successful as a dance music production house?

I wanted to experiment with more musical freedom and follow my own road. But in doing so, I had to take on more risk. We simply tried to create dance-pop tracks that could be equally suitable both for the radio and the worldwide clubs, and in many cases they were well-received.

You were able to create a whole new roster of artists on Off Limits that became synonymous with Italian '90s dance-pop, among them In-Grid, Whigfield, Ann Lee and Benny Benassi.

With these artists, I had, and still have, good relationships, both professional and non-professional. These are very special people, and I can say success didn't go to their heads.

In 1994, "Saturday Night" by Whigfield vaulted to the number one spot in the UK and reportedly sold over a million copies in that country. That was a rather remarkable feat for an Italian production.

"Saturday Night" was the first and luckiest single on the Off Limits label. There was a mix of factors that made it go straight to number one in UK. The most important, in my opinion, was the originality and simplicity of the track—not to mention the artist's obvious vocal abilities.

Was the United States a market you were interested in or concerned with penetrating?

I never produced a track thinking of success in a specific market. However, with Benny Benassi we had good success in the U.S., even eventually winning a Grammy [2008 Best Remixed Recording, "Bring the Noise," recorded at Off Limits studios].

The '90s were the last days of substantial physical product sales. Napster and digital downloading began to change everything. How did you feel about these massive changes and the effect they might have on Off Limits?

Technology changed the way of music history once again. We had to accept this and try to ride the wave of changes and new opportunities offered by digital music. We had no other choice.

Labels are often accused of being the "bad guys" of the music industry. Many artists say their labels cheated them, didn't understand them and didn't support them. What is your view of the integrity and fairness of music industry labels during the '80s and '90s and as it stands today?

Roles in the music industry are different but pursue the same aim: the label wants the track and the artist to succeed in order to earn money; the artist wants to become famous and earn money.

Years ago (and often even today), artists look forward to receiving support from the label that invested in and promoted their track. If the track worked, everybody was happy. If the track didn't work, you tried again—and again.

Today, investments from labels are at a historic minimum, and artists are exploring the do-it-yourself world, self-promoting with social media and distributing autonomously.

Artists are normally young people and can't quantify the value of a label's work. They tend to attribute the success only to themselves and blame the labels when success doesn't come.

As an active label today, how do you manage your business with music consumers who often expect to get their music for free or at a very low cost?

Well, nowadays, labels have few options but to look for alternative sources of income, such as a financial return on artists' shows—one of the few ways left that are still remunerative.

What are your thoughts about the current shift away from vocalists and the emphasis on DJs and producers?

I believe the system of producing music is more or less the same as it was before. The difference today is that the main artist is no longer the singer (the vocalist is confined to the role of "featuring"), with the DJ/producer supervising the production and taking the lead role.

Sony/BMG in Germany recently acquired the works of Off Limits publishing from the '90s. Where do you see the Off Limits label going in the future?

We only sold the publishing side of the catalogue, so Off Limits continues to work part of the past and recent repertoire and, obviously, future songs. We keep on producing, and we continue to provide specialized services to artists in areas such as neighboring rights collection, artist management and digital distribution.

What are your thoughts or feelings about your own personal career in dance-pop music and the remarkable success you have enjoyed?

I'm aware that I've been blessed and have received a lot in my career, and I know that my success cannot to be attributed only to me. But it also comes from part of my character—never being satisfied with my results. So my journey, my search for new artists and success, goes on.

Has there been a highlight or certain moment from your career that stands out for you?

The greatest satisfaction I've received is the fact that I've been able to deliver on most of my promises, making completely unknown artists famous and contributing very positive changes to their lives.

Dance music is sometimes thought of as being less important or less valuable than, say, rock, R&B, etc. What do you think has been the value of dance music to society and pop-culture?

Yes, that's true. Dance music is snubbed, but, interestingly enough, it's still always present on the worldwide charts. I think that this genre is at the forefront, as dance music is and always has been a true innovator in the pop music field. It's dance music that creates trends, being so tightly intertwined with technology and the world of youth.

Italian composer, musician, producer and label executive Larry Pignagnoli created many iconic European dance-pop hits throughout the '80s and '90s, including Spagna's "Call Me" and Whigfield's "Saturday Night" (courtesy Off Limits Srl).

Paul Spencer, also known as Dario G
"Sunchyme" (1997)

"Though we had a huge hit with ["Sunchyme"], don't confuse me with someone who actually knew what he was doing."—Paul Spencer

In September of 1997, amidst a plethora of relentlessly driving tracks that intoxicated a sea of gyrating dancers in clubs across the planet, there arrived a gentle, uplifting, almost magically melodic song with a surprisingly big beat. It was called "Sunchyme," a track that combined irresistible world rhythms, steel drum effects and the powerful exhilaration of the melodic, African-style chant it borrowed from the Dream Academy's 1985 hit, "Life in a Northern Town." The song was performed by an entity known as Dario G, led by mastermind musician Paul Spencer, and its hypnotic effect induced an energizing feeling of overwhelming peace and positivity. It was so effective at capturing popster attention on the radio and in the clubs that the track reached the Top Three of the British pop chart and was a major hit across Europe. It also went all the way to number one on Billboard's U.S. dance survey and was reinvented countless times by various remixers in the years that followed. As recently as 2010, a new mix of the song was used to support the BBC Wildlife Fund.

Dario G, a trio that also once included Scott Rosser and Stephen Spencer, was named after Dario Gradi, the manager of Crewe Alexandra, an English football team. Paul, Scott and Stephen quickly became synonymous with dreamy, yet beat-conscious and exhilarating dance-trance music, scoring a sizable hit with their 1998 debut album, the buoyant Sunmachine (released in the U.S. on Kinetic/Reprise Records). Paul and his mates quickly returned to the top of the international singles charts with the track "Carnaval de Paris," an instrumental journey awash in bagpipes, steel drums, brass and euphoric atmosphere (ideal as an anthem for France's '98 World Cup). A third single was lifted from the set, "Sunmachine," which featured samples from David Bowie's "Memory of a Free Festival." In 2001, Paul silenced those who may have doubted his ability to continue the hot streak. His then latest single, "Dream to Me," lifted from the Dario G album In Full Colour (and borrowing from the Cranberries' "Dreams") became a top hit in Germany, the UK and throughout Europe. More sensational, upbeat tracks such as "Say What's on Your Mind" followed.

The well-educated Spencer can best be described as a very cerebral musician and composer with a sharp sense of humor and a natural, disarming demeanor. His personality is humble, direct and engaging, that of a "working class" musician who just happens to have a celebrated history in dance-pop music. He resides in Northern England with his wife (to whom he proposed at the top of New York's Empire State Building) and children, living a grounded but comfortable lifestyle. Paul is still actively creating surprising musical compositions, such as "Ring of Fire," "Game On" (featuring Pitbull and TKZee) and his 2014 teaming with Dame Shirley Bassey, "We Got Music."

There isn't a lot of information out there about your youngest days and how you got started in music, Paul. Would you describe your early history?

It's funny. I had a very odd career path, and I wouldn't follow the same path if I could do it over again. I was a classically trained pianist from a working class background. My mum and dad had normal jobs. My grandma was actually in show business—she used to be a booking agent for local comedians and acts on the circuit. She used to book talent for the TV show *Opportunity Knocks* from the 1960s and '70s.

In my home town, most people took jobs in the big industries in the area, like the railway and, at the time, factories like Rolls Royce and Bentley. So, it was like, "Which one are you gonna do?" It happens in most towns. I wanted to do something different. I started playing the piano and was weirdly obsessed with watching the keys disappear in a piano as you pressed them. I was fascinated by the operation of the instrument. I took lessons, and I got quite good at it.

As a boy, the competition thing was interesting for me. I was good, but if I wasn't as good as someone else, I'd want to increase my grade level and be better than them. I found that within a few years I was ranking higher with the grades than people who were two years older than me. I enjoyed playing, but I think what motivated me was the competition. I was pushed on by wanting to be better than other people. I went to a music college, where the competition was mostly regional, like Manchester. But it included people from all over the world. My confidence was initially low, but within a year I won an award (The PRS–John Lennon Songwriting Award, issued by the famous collection agency for songwriters),

This 1998 publicity photograph issued by Kinetic/Reprise Records in the U.S. (for the release of Dario G's *Sunmachine* CD) shows Paul Spencer aboard a tuk-tuk in Thailand. The artist says he was on the roof of the vehicle at one point and was nearly arrested by Thai police (photograph by Andy Earl, author's collection).

and I received £2000. I bought a sampler, a sequencer, speakers, a desk—all the equipment I needed to launch.

How does the group Dario G get started?

The group as a trio—myself, Scott Rosser and Stephen Spencer (no relation)—was very short-lived, lasting only about a year and a half. But the duo of Scott and I lasted longer. I met Scott at college in Manchester. He was from South Wales, and we lived together in college. We met in 1989 and decided to carry on working together. At that time, I was a keyboard player, and being in a band made you rely on others. But once I had my own equipment, I realized I didn't need to be in a band. The band was in the machine, so-to-speak, and you could make your own music. I had that idea in common with Scott, who had been into bands like Erasure and artists like that. The whole Manchester rave culture and house music thing started taking off (it had begun in the late '80s). Now you basically made a record in a bedroom on your own or with your mates and brought a singer down. Scott and I moved to my home town after college, and we just kept at it.

We met another guy named Stephen Spencer—he wasn't a musician as such. He was an industry person, a distributor. He knew Scott and I had this vibe going, this energy, and in a short time we created "Sunchyme."

I wondered if you ever worked as a DJ during your evolution as a musician.

Just a little bit. That whole DJ culture, after my classical training, was something I looked down on. That's a bit of a regret, really—that being a part of the DJ culture was not something that was advised to me. It might have been valuable if someone had suggested that I spin records to understand better the demand for those records and sounds. It would have been very valuable to better understand what the room wanted, what the club wanted, rather than just how everything works musically. On the other hand, it might be to my advantage because I can do other things besides club music.

I did have the odd DJ gig now and again, but it was also quite an expensive thing to do back then—vinyl costing £7 or £8 per record—unless you were sent records by the labels or worked in a record shop. You can't regret things. Those turns you think you maybe should have taken could have led to a different or worse outcome.

In 1997, "Sunchyme" was launched as the first single from Dario G. In addition to topping the U.S. Billboard *dance chart, the song was a Top Five sensation throughout Europe. It peaked at number two in the UK, edged out only by Elton John's "Candle in the Wind." It has been described as one of the most beautiful dance-pop songs of the era, combining trance and classical qualities with new age and house music. It was truly a breathtaking sonic journey. Please tell me about the origins and evolution of this song and the debut album,* Sunmachine.

[*Paul unveils some of the equipment that may have been used to compose the track "Sunchyme" and reenacts a sort of condensed version of his original experimentation with chords, steel drum effects and melodies that became the signature elements of the song.*]

It took about a week to create the song. When we added the steel drum effects and the sample from the Dream Academy ("Life in a Northern Town"), I began to recognize what we had. As a musician and songwriter, you want to create something that plays as you but that people will want. You need to create music that people will like. It's the same with any product. At that time, I was going clubbing a lot and loving club music. When I was working on this track, I was actually picturing a club in Birmingham, a very dark, simple, blacked-out type of club. In those days, the end of the night was 2 a.m., and I was imagining the point where the lights are going to come up. I imagined the tune the DJ might play at that point, a song that gets a little bit more time than the rest. I pictured that slow intro when everyone has that end-of-the-night euphoria, when you're a little bit tired.

When I first heard the track actually played in the club environment, it didn't quite match what I had envisioned. I still was listening to the technical things about the song, and I was worried about what I didn't think was right about it. Interestingly, when the song broke out, it wasn't really being played in the clubs. It went straight to radio because of the connections that the other Mr. Spencer had gotten. He had gotten it to break on regional radio stations like KISS-FM at the time. Some songs don't edit well to radio, but "Sunchyme" did. It blew up so quickly. It literally went from the DAT tape to the radio station.

It's difficult to say why the song resonated with so many people. It's probably easier for you to tell me. Maybe it was the combination of European sounding pianos, African choirs and the Jamaican steel drum sound. So, it had a sort of triangle of different parts of the world to it. It was the most successful record I've ever had in terms of sales. After two or three months of swamping radio, it didn't feel like my record anymore. It felt like a record on the radio—such a surreal place in my mind, next to all the current records at the time. I guess it's a good piece of music, but I've made other pieces of music, put more effort into them, and have had far less success.

I couldn't listen to the album within days of finishing it because it's never up to what you want it to be. "Sunchyme" was great—I can listen to that over and over again. "Sunmachine" featuring David Bowie, which became a Top 20 UK single, not so much because it disappointed me—what we did with it. It was written in a rush; the right ideas and synergy didn't fall into place as good as I wanted. "Carnaval de Paris"—great, our second huge hit. "Voices"—well, that turned out really great because it was featured on *The Beach* soundtrack, and it found a home. Danny Boyle, the director of the film, chose the song personally for the soundtrack. But "Voices" was one of the reasons Warner Records dropped us. It wasn't another *dance* hit—it was something different. The other tracks on the album? I just remember the stress, and it wasn't necessarily a happy time. It's really, really weird.

Do you recall your reaction to the success of the project?

Quite often, when you have the kind of success like I had with "Sunchyme," you're off thinking about the next thing. It's why so many artists and musicians are often in quite dark places. I'm not, but I have been intimidated by success. The dream of most musicians at that time was to have a Top 40 hit. Then you realize your track is growing, and you're hearing more and more good news. It becomes addictive—a little thrill here, a little thrill there.

[Shortly after] "Sunchyme" was made, I was actually touring America as a keyboard player with a rock band—Monaco, which was Peter Hook's (of New Order) group. I was using the same keyboard on which I had created "Sunchyme." I was on a phone call outside Boston's [Fenway Park] stadium with Scott and asked him what was the latest with our song. "It's gone A-list on Radio One," he said. That was very good news. Monaco was doing well, too, and I wasn't sure which was going to be more successful. As it happened, though it was a great thing to do, Monaco didn't have a great deal of further success. But if I hadn't been in the band, I wouldn't have had that pre-set sound in my keyboard that I used to create the hook of "Sunchyme." I loved my time playing with Monaco, and will always be grateful for it.

I'm curious about the unusual video created for "Sunchyme," which featured what appeared to be an African tribe donning colorful body paint. Many found the video visually striking—in sort of a "Lion King" kind of way.

I hated it! I had envisioned people on a beach having a good time, like in Ibiza. I didn't picture people being painted and jumping into rivers and dressed as lions. It wasn't really my idea of what would best represent the music. I suspect if that video had been used on a different piece of music that wasn't as popular, I don't think it would have taken hold. It was kind of silly and experimental. But because the music had caught on so well, the video got airplay and took on its own life.

When we were assigned to Warner, we were given some reels to look at by different directors. We didn't like a lot of them, which were dark and more rock oriented. We had in our heads the idea of sunshine, beaches and happy people. Then we saw one by this extremely accomplished director who had done an advertisement for British Airways, which was very colorful. Color was so important to us. The director's original idea was to have people dressed up as mice, and they would fight each other with sticks that had bits of cheese on them. We were like, "No!" The second idea was what you see in the official video.

It had a sort of racial harmony feel to it, which is cool. Each animal was the same under the paint. It didn't matter what was on top. It was a fun way to do things I suppose. I believe it was used by the Red Cross as part of a racial equality campaign back in '97–'98. But for us, it had too many political overtones at the time, and we honestly just wanted it to be about having fun. People didn't want to go to a club or watch MTV to be challenged; they want to relax.

The 1998 single "Carnaval de Paris," recorded for the FIFA World Cup that year, was another tremendous hit, reaching number five in the UK and number two in Germany, topping the pan–European chart as well. It became an immediate stadium anthem and remains enormously popular to this day. How did this infectious track get its start?

Again, Stephen had this marketing idea—more what people wanted, not necessarily what we wanted to make. We were thinking of Robert Miles and the second single he had after his smash "Children." [His follow-up] was just the same notes reordered, and it went nowhere. So, we didn't really want to make that mistake and make "Sunchyme Version 2." We played around with a few ideas, and the World Cup was coming around. We were all big football fans. The song began as a real free-for-all to represent different nations of the world with a melody. I used to play trumpet in school, and so that came in handy in our creation of the track.

Though we had a huge hit with it, don't confuse me with someone who actually knew what he was doing. [*Paul laughs.*] It was a bit chaotic. We were under a bit of pressure to follow up the "Sunchyme" record. But now we had as much studio time as we wanted, we had musicians, and we just had to come up with an idea. You're also under the pressure of time. When you have a hit, they want another one within six months.

Why did the Warner label in the U.S. drop you after so much breakout success?

[*He laughs in a knowing kind of way.*] It's hard for me to say. But I *do* know why. We struck gold with "Sunchyme," single two wasn't quite as successful, and we didn't really have a single three. Because of the way our contract was formed, the advance on the next album would have been massive. I think they thought we couldn't hit the mark again. They were also looking for the next thing. I remember Eiffel 65 started hitting it big at that time. I think labels would rather gamble on something that's starting to take off in the clubs than work something further that's already out there.

What a brutal business!

Oh—it's incredibly brutal. It can really squash your creativity. You need shark teeth because your teeth get kicked in many times. I'm not talking about managers or people in A&R. But as a musician, a creator, a conceiver of ideas, you put your heart out there and spend weeks and months on something. Then the decision-makers come along and say, "Eh, it's okay. What else have you got?" It's that kind of a world.

Just last year I did a Latin dance song with Shirley Bassey called "We Got Music." It was a fantastic record—it's Shirley Bassey! Got turned back by radio. Teeth kicked in. You just have to come up with your next row of teeth and keep smiling.

I think every musician hits several points in their life where they say, "I'm not doing this anymore." That's where strength of character and your background come in. You need to be very level-headed, especially when you enjoy success, as those levels are very high. That's why people come off stage and hit the booze and drugs. Whatever gives them a continued high. You can see how this business can make people crash.

I'll just add this—I hate to see people in entertainment who have committed suicide sort of put up there as heroes—Kurt [Cobain]—that sort of thing. I hate that they are sometimes idolized that they took their lives. What about the guy in the band that made his music and now is back home with his three kids? There are so many great musicians who did their thing, went home, do the washing, take care of their kids, go camping—nothing that will ever make tabloid news. I'd rather be in that situation than have the crazy rollercoaster lives some people have. But that's what makes stars, and I find that a real shame.

By the summer of 2001, you were ready to release your next album, In Full Colour. The evocative and powerful electro-dance single "Dream to Me" reached the Top 10 in the UK and Germany and the dance-pop track "Say What's on Your Mind" had some success as well. How did you approach these projects?

This project involved more watching what was around us—things like noticing where the money was to be made. We did more writing and less relying on samples. We got one songwriter on board, but we should have had more. We should have had a whole army of songwriters pitching to us, but we didn't. Again, it's having regrets about how you should have done things differently. If I was managing Dario G back then, I would have done it the way artists like Avicii and David Guetta do it today, with a machine that's well set up and organized so they can do their thing. I'm not sure what that thing is, but obviously there's an end product there that really works.

The label mentality seemed that they needed to know how good your album would be before they started spending money on you. They didn't want singles back then; they wanted albums so they knew how to budget. But albums take time, sometimes as long as 18 months to make. With time, fashion changes. So we needed to create songs that were more broad and pop-based and then do remixes that reflected the current trends. In *Full Colour* was definitely more pop sounding.

The *In Full Colour* album didn't even get a full release in the UK. I can't complain because we did get a Top 10 hit out of it ("Dream to Me"). To get a second bite of the cherry was really a fist pumping moment. There were people (whether in my mind or in the real world or, indeed, both)—they knew I was dropped from Warner, and I was on the waste pile. You couldn't go back. That was the thing about having a hugely successful record. They thought, okay, you had two big hits, but you can't do it again. Then we came back with "Dream to Me," and it's Top 10. But then, right on schedule, you get dropped again anyway.

Your period of commercial success came just prior to the arrival of Napster and some dramatic changes in how people get their music. How does the state of the industry today affect your ability to create new music?

Back then, I remember, like most musicians, standing open-mouthed thinking, "Why aren't they stopping [Napster]?" I recall in the '90s you could buy this dodgy viewing card that would get you all the cable channels descrambled. It was basically stealing subscription TV, though somewhat hard to do. Well, it was stamped out by the broadcasters fast. But the music industry did nothing. I still don't understand why they didn't come together and shut down Napster. Maybe I'm over-simplifying things, but if they could stop subscription TV theft, why couldn't they handle this? It's something like 18 years now since mp3s first became popular. I have people tell me they have my records, but they haven't paid for them. And then they giggle. It's not funny. Should I have a chef come over and cook my lunch? Oh, and can you cook it for free? You've heard this story a million times.

Now, in the modern day, I think of crafting a music career as the occupation of the more privileged. Otherwise, it's at the point where you'll have to do a day job to support your music. I'm seeing it now with musicians and artists I know. They can't support their lifestyles and families with the money they earn from music. There's no way. Some are working proper jobs and trying to do the rest of the music work when they can.

There are other challenges today. In order to be successful or to connect with a major label, you've got to have a huge social media following, which you can buy or fake. But there's success in there somewhere, and only the wealthy will be able to do it. How do you finance a tour? In the past, you needed the record label behind you. Do they do tour support anymore? Now you have to figure out how to finance a tour yourself. Again, it's an advantage to have wealthy support. So, I see music becoming something maybe only the privileged can afford to create.

On the other side of the coin, anyone can make music now on a notebook. But these other factors will affect how far you can go with it.

Social media is another story. I got into Facebook and those things a little late, and now you have to pay to even reach your fans. When you go to a label with a project, it's not only about the music. You have to be able to show [you have] a large amount of followers and things like that. There are fake ways of building up your Twitter and Soundcloud presence. It's so complicated, and I'm still learning it. I'd much rather concentrate on just making good tunes.

I'm blessed in one way—I have friends and connections in the business and, more than likely, I can still go and meet them face to face. That's an advantage of the success I've had. Whether that means they are interested in a deal is another story. Are they gonna start from scratch with me or give my song to someone like Paloma Faith, who has a ton of fans? Nobody really knows what they're doing—it's really just this kind of evolution, isn't it?

What do you want to still accomplish?

Outside of staying healthy and sane, which I've done a pretty good job of so far, within music I want to just stay in it and have some more success.

Do you think you can have more success?

Yes, but in a different way from the past. I still have the fire. The fire might not grow as erratically as in the past because I'm more professional now than I've ever been before. It will be all about getting the balance right and getting a good team around me or joining a team that has the momentum going already. It's quite a challenge to get your head around it, really, but I have confidence. It isn't easy.

I don't feel that pressure so much to have that number one hit again today. Yes, we all want another global smash. We all dream of that. I still work on new projects, and I keep them very secret from each other. It's not the end of the world if they tell me a big radio station won't play my song unless it's really big. I don't care if they say, "Oh, you're over 25, and that doesn't quite fit in with our mix." If you look at what's played today, if they are young lads and girls in their late teens or early 20s, they always have pictures circulating proving that they are young. If there isn't a picture, there's sort of this demand to prove that you are in this young people's circle. There's certainly a fashion demand for having younger producers, especially here in the UK. I don't understand that, but I know it's closing the doors to lots of strong music (from older people) and creating openings for music (for younger creatives) just because the face fits. It's funny though; I was just 26 when I made "Sunchyme," and even then I wouldn't have fit into the culture as it is today.

In addition to rattling '90s' dance floors worldwide, Dario G's "Sunchyme" has served as a theme to numerous sporting and charity events over the past 17 years (courtesy Paul Spencer).

I think of social media again. You read Facebook, and you read about people's success all the time, particularly in entertainment. You find yourself comparing yourself to this worldwide level of success. It's difficult to *not* feel down when your own activity doesn't seem to compare to it. But, in reality, you're seeing the two or three big nights these other people have, which is made to look like a constant stream of success. On the other hand, you also don't want to be like the other people who are constantly moaning. It's these extremes, isn't it?

I post normal things on Facebook, not that celebrity type of stuff, not motivational pictures with an Enya soundtrack. I guess I'm better at, well, fun type of stuff. Some people don't get my humor, like when I said, "Everyone should re-post what they were doing three years ago! I'd really like to see those pictures again!" People responded, "Are you sure?" Come on! I didn't want to see that photo of your toes on the pillow three years ago. Please don't share it again now! [*Paul laughs.*]

Throughout your career, is there a highlight from the past you enjoy reliving or that made you feel particularly satisfied or happy?

Obviously there was the success of "Sunchyme." Having that hit was just massive. Then having "Dream to Me" hit—that felt so good. It was like having one for the doubters. The Dame Shirley recording—a song I wrote on my own. And, of course, there is my family. They are always my priority.

Then there were things like this. [*Paul reaches to the back portion of the room he's seated in and pulls out a framed uniform shirt from a 2001 celebrity soccer game in which he played.*] This is possibly more treasured than a [gold record], because it's signed by [German soccer star and manager] Lothar Matthäus and [German racing driver] Michael Schumacher. To be invited to play in those games was just like—oh my God. That was almost like a reward for me being out there and for what I had done. Yes, and for just trying to be a nice person—that's the way it felt to me. To have mementos like this is just out of this world.

Dance music tends to receive a good deal less attention than other forms of popular music, like rock, country, R&B and rap. It's been a bit neglected in pop culture history. From your perspective, what is the good that dance music has brought to the world?

The beauty of this music is more than skin deep. The dance beat is the wrapping of the melody, really. You can take the beat away, and there's still a lot of heart and soul there. Dance music is a rhythm and a good feeling, just like all music, whether it's supplied by a percussion instrument, a guitar, strings or woodwind instruments. If you are going to say dance music is at the bottom of the ladder, I'd say turn that ladder sideways, because all music genres are the same, equal in their potential to create good feelings. Enjoy the spectrum!

LIGHTNING ROUND WITH PAUL

Giorgio Moroder or Nile Rodgers?

I just have to veer on the side of Chic and that sound. Nile Rodgers, pre–2012. I just feel he has been over-marketed the last few years; not his fault.

Applause or record sales?

I choose track or record sales because you know they are applauding you with their purchase. Even illegal downloads—they all show the listener wants to enjoy your work again and again.

Meet your ancestors or meet your descendants?

Wow! [*He pauses for a minute or two to think.*] This isn't a Lightning Round; it's like a slow-moving fog round. I'll go for ancestors. Having kids myself, you don't stop worrying about the future, but looking back, it would be nice to see what those who came before me did in a totally different environment.

Extended versions or radio edits?

Straight away with this one—radio edits. I tend to lean on the pop side of things. I will say some extended versions tend to work rather well, though, like New Order's "Blue Monday."

Fabulous nightlife or the great outdoors?

Nightlife. Being outdoors kind of bores me. Fresh air is a different buzz.

Rafael "Dose" Vargas, formerly of 2 in a Room
"Wiggle It" (1990)

"Well, when you're as young as I was, you feel invincible and whatever you dream can happen. Nobody can stop you."—Rafael Dose Vargas

In the original 1990 video of "Wiggle It" by 2 in a Room, a plethora of sexy and very genuine looking young women madly bump and grind on a beach, as Dominican rapper Rafael "Dose" Vargas delivers catchy rhymes about the joys of acid grooves. Well, as one YouTube commentator spells it out, "This right here is my shit." Vargas and production partner Roger Pauletta, along with co-producer and Cutting Records owner Aldo Marin, kicked off the decade with a fever-inducing jam that became the *party anthem, inspiring listeners to keep shakin' it up for the past quarter of a century.*

Though one might expect the man behind such a fiery beat to be an extrovert, Dose is a very soft-spoken man. With a splash of playfulness, Vargas' Twitter page describes him as the "illest writer, producer and recording artist since '88." But he is actually quite modest when speaking of "Wiggle It," his singular Top 15 pop and number one dance chart achievement. Truth be told, if he were to brag, there are many other milestones in his varied music career over which he could gloat. Though these accomplishments are often eclipsed by his frequent categorization as a "Wiggle It" one-hit wonder, he seems unbothered by popular culture's tendency to have a bit of tunnel vision.

From his home in Miami, Vargas talks about his journey to fame, which began in the heart of the Bronx.

Dose, please tell me a little about your youth and how you came into music.

I was born in New York City to Dominican parents from Santo Domingo who migrated to the U.S. in the late '60s. I was born in 1969 and grew up in Washington Heights. I enjoyed all types of music around the house, including everything from R&B to merengue. As a teen in the '80s, I listened to a lot of Latin music because of my parents, but I quickly embraced rap music and the hip-hop culture. I was the ultimate b-boy, being both a breakdancer and MC, and I became a fan of Run-DMC, LL Cool J, Mantronix, Eric B. & Rakim and KRS-One. I wanted to emulate them when it came time to make my own music.

My original plan as a teen was to go on and become an architect like my cousin Avildio. I attended the High School of Art & Design in New York City to follow in his footsteps, but

I quickly started to lose interest in architecture and gravitated towards music production and MCing, after aligning with fellow students with the same interests.

Did you get into the club scene?

Oh, wow, the clubs were my inspiration when I first started going to them, like Heartthrob [formerly the Fun House] and Red Zone over on West 54th. I snuck in when I was 17 and remember seeing the reaction of the people to the music. Hearing that music playing so loud with the bass just made me want to rush home and make music. I wanted to make people enjoy themselves—I wanted my music to bring them the kind of happiness I saw in the clubs.

How did you get your first break in the recording industry?

I guess it's who you know, right? It was something like that for me. My childhood friend (Edwin Morel) introduced me to DJ Benji Candelario, who happened to be the best friend of Cutting Records label owner Aldo Marin. Benji arranged a meeting between Aldo and me at the Music House, a popular neighborhood record store, which Aldo also owned at the time. So I was able to introduce myself to Aldo and present my music demo. To make a long story short, I walked away with my first record deal and two weeks later recorded, pressed and released my first single titled "Outlaw" under the artist name Dose Material.

Later that year, I got together with another popular neighborhood DJ named Roger Pauletta and recorded (as 2 in a Room) the hip-hop and house-infused "Do What You Want" for the Cutting Records 1989 release *The Album, Vol. 1*, which included productions by DJs Todd Terry, Little Louie Vega, Carlos Berrios and Benji Candelario. Being that I had the only vocal track in the project, Roger Pauletta and I became the faces of 2 in a Room.

I was working the 12-hour graveyard shift at a printing company every weekend when "Do What You Want" was released as a single. After a few weeks, it started going up the dance charts around the world, and I started to receive requests from promoters for live performances. Since I worked nights on weekends, it was very difficult to juggle my new-found success with my day job/night job. [*Dose laughs.*] Fortunately, I had a cool boss at the printing shop who let me leave and return during work hours. I was able to take my limousine rides to and from my performances in the city for a few weeks. I eventually started getting a lot of gigs outside of New York, and I had to resign from printing company.

At this point, where did you feel your career would go?

Well, when you're as young as I was, you feel invincible and whatever you dream can happen. Nobody can stop you. With that initial taste of success and popularity, I was determined to become a better performer and recording artist. So I spent a lot time in recording studios and educated myself in music industry matters, figuring this could be my new career.

*"Wiggle It"—what a great party song. Everybody knows the track. It's one of those '90s hits that stays fun and never seems to get old. It reached number one on **Billboard**'s dance chart, number three in the UK and was a Top 15 hit on the U.S. pop chart. Tell me about the evolution of this song.*

Roger had a large record collection, and we put our MPC60 synthesizer to work. We went into the studio every day and combined disco samples, electronic drums and hip-hop so we could make people dance and enjoy themselves.

Around 1989–90, the hip-house movement was really taking off. We released "Wiggle It" in 1990, when mainstream MCs were rapping over house tracks. It was the perfect set-up for me because I really wanted to rap, and I loved house music. I was 20 years old, we had just come off a hit with "Do What You Want," and house was taking off worldwide—so it was just like perfect timing. I think the song just had a really catchy hook—it was irresistible, and it took us to the mainstream.

I remember when Hot 103 FM in New York City tested "Wiggle It" for the first time on their weekly "Hot or Not" survey, and we received a 97 percent favorable rating from the listeners. The song became an instant hit right after that.

We made it to number 15 on *Billboard*. It would have gone higher, but we did something that the powers that be weren't happy with. The label wanted us to do a radio show here in the States (I don't remember what state it was in), but we went on a three-month European tour. We were told there would be consequences if we didn't do the U.S. show, but we couldn't contractually change our tour dates. So the plug was pulled on record promotion in the U.S. Despite all that, "Wiggle It" went on to sell a million-plus copies. So it all worked out. [*He smiles.*]

You were part of another successful dance act around the same time—the 740 Boyz, a Dominican-American group.

Yes. We toured a lot throughout Europe, right through 1995, in part because I was part of these two groups—2 in a Room and the 740 Boyz. Double duty. I was running around like crazy.

2 in a Room had other successful songs on the U.S. dance chart, including "El Trago (The Drink)" in 1994 and "Carnival" early in '96. How difficult was it to find the right material to follow-up "Wiggle It" and to ride the fence between hip-hop and dance music?

Yeah, that was a tough thing since "Wiggle It" was such a massive hit. It was a challenge in some ways. There is a lot of pressure on artists and labels to recapture that success with every single released. I went through this situation three times in my career. It also happened when I was part of 740 Boyz. One of our early singles ["Shimmy Shake"] went gold and platinum in Europe in '95, and the pressure was on to duplicate that. Then in '97, I created the group Fulanito and had another huge first hit single with "Guallando" (from the Cutting Records release *El Hombre Mas Famoso De La Tierra*). It then became the standard by which all the other singles I released were measured. It's like I've been a one-hit wonder three times. Seriously. [*He smiles again.*]

For a while, I was trying to figure out if I was going to be a hip-hop artist or a house artist. Mixing the two was more like a trend rather than a genre. After the success of "Wiggle It," which included several gold and platinum plaques and worldwide touring, it was difficult to even land a moderate hit and 2 in a Room became part of the past. It was sort of like the curse of the one-hit wonders. After collaborating with Victor and Danny Vargas of Wepaman fame in 1994 and attaining success with 2 in a Room's "El Trago," I refocused and decided to continue recording music for the dance market. That's when I created the 740 Boyz.

You experienced so much during this decade. It must have been a very exciting time in your life. What stands out for you the most?

There were many special events, but my very first performance ever at the *Helter Skelter* concert in London (where I shared the stage with many popular artists and DJs I looked up to) was my favorite moment. It was my first time leaving the States as an artist and getting on a plane (outside of going to the Dominican Republic as kid). I was scared to death, but I'll never forget the feeling I got when I performed "Do What You Want" and heard everybody in the audience singing along.

Did the influence of drugs in the business or at the venues affect you at all?

In the club scene, alcohol fuels the business, so it's always around you. When you're a successful recording artist, you get offered all the free alcohol you want. I always felt concerned about my audience in dance clubs because the majority of the patrons walk out of the club under the influence and may get behind the wheel. To this day, I still plead with my audience at the end of every show by saying, "please don't drink and drive."

At the same time, you were also a young, great looking, hot new music star. You must have been chased by fans constantly.

[*Dose laughs.*] Having a hit record does wonders for your sex life. But truthfully, I was kind of an awkward kid. I was kind of an art nerd. But once I had the hit records, I became really cool. Every girl wanted to become my girlfriend. I was the man. But before that I was a total zero.

Was the end of 2 in a Room around 1995 the result of an amicable parting with your partners?

I was partnered with Roger Pauletta from 1989 to 1992, and we still work on music projects from time to time and still have a strong friendship to this day. From 1993 to 1995 I was partnered with Elvin Ovalles, who later joined my Latin group Fulanito (from 1997 to 2002). He later went on to become a music executive.

If you could do this whole '90s journey over again, would you do anything differently?

[*He laughs.*] Can I give you a list? On the whole though, I was very blessed. I've had a charmed life as a result of all the people who gave me opportunities. Yeah, there were certain things that could have gone better—woulda, coulda, shoulda. But I have no regrets.

Though his mega-hit "Wiggle It," performed under the moniker 2 in a Room, may be a legendary '90s party track, Rafael Dose Vargas spends more time today performing the hits of his band Fulanito (courtesy Rafael Dose Vargas).

I know 2 in a Room is looked at as a one-hit wonder, but I've done a lot more in my career besides that song. I hit it big in three different types of music. I'm definitely *not* a one-hit wonder when it comes to Latin music. I must have at least 10 bona fide hits in that world. You can't have that many successes and really be given that one-hit wonder title.

You know, in 2001 or '02 VH1 came to my house in Miami to interview me for their one-hit wonder show. It was weird to be on such a show after having five number one hits at that point. In all fairness, they did mention what I was doing at the time in the Latin market.

You look quite youthful, but I suppose it is accurate to say you are on the fringe of so-called middle age. How do you feel about entering this stage of your life?

There are days where aging seems a little scary, but I don't have a lot of time to dwell on it. Pretty much every week I am performing somewhere. About 15 percent of my gigs are connected to 2 in a Room, but the other 85 is all about Fulanito. So I don't stop. I admit, I don't party as hard as I used to.

I look forward to doing some new things, too. I would really like to get into acting. I've been testing the waters, taking a lot of classes and getting myself ready to give it a try. I always wanted to try it, and I think this point in my life is a good time to see what I can do with it. I think being able to work in both English and Spanish will also be an asset. Having done a lot of videos gives me experience in front of the camera, and I think I'll be able to incorporate all this into the next phase of my life.

You've spent a big part of your life making people dance and lifting their spirits through your music. What comes to your mind when you think about the evolution of dance music over the years?

I've always enjoyed making feel-good music, and dance music (in any style or genre) will usually make people feel very happy. I really appreciate today's dance sound, both musically and lyrically, but, in my opinion, I think it's hard to beat that '80s and '90s dance music I listened to when I was young.

Lightning Round with Dose

Diana Ross or Beyoncé?

Beyoncé. Diana is the boss, but I love the mix of R&B and hip-hop in Beyoncé's music. I think it's awesome.

Extended versions or radio edits?

I love radio edits. They get to the point.

SUV or sports car?

I'm an SUV guy. I like to feel like I'm in a living room driving around. I'm not the 45-year-old guy who needs the sports car. I'm not there yet.

Music or lyrics?

Lyrics—I've been a lyrics guy from day one. I like singing more than humming.

Cardio or weights?

Cardio—I need it to be able to jump around on stage.

Instagram or Twitter?
I think Twitter is more popular, right? But I'm more into Instagram—I like visuals.

Saver or spender?
I save when I need to, but I'm a spender.

Giorgio Moroder or Nile Rodgers?
Giorgio. I find him more fascinating.

'70s or '80s?
I'm really an '80s baby, but I'll pick the '70s. I wish I had been able to enjoy the party years of the '70s—it looks like they were a lot of fun.

Martha Wash, former guest vocalist with C + C Music Factory, Black Box
"Gonna Make You Sweat (Everybody Dance Now)" (1990)

"Despite all the changes in music styles, the music business, changes in how the world is running, I've never noticed any significant difference in how audiences respond to me or the music. In an inconsistent world, that's been a very consistent thing."—Martha Wash

The 1990s had barely begun when the releases of two unexpectedly powerhouse music acts took the new decade by storm. Black Box ("Everybody Everybody"/"I Don't Know Anybody Else"/"Strike It Up") and C + C Music Factory ("Gonna Make You Sweat [Everybody Dance Now]") were suddenly the re-energized future of dance-pop and house music, and they shared one thing in common—the magnificent voice of soprano Martha Wash.

Ms. Wash's dramatic, commanding vocal prowess first found favor with the masses in the late '70s, when she teamed with Izora Armstead to sing back-up vocals for gender-bending disco icon Sylvester. Known as Two Tons of Fun, the ladies helped turn Sylvester's "You Make Me Feel (Mighty Real)" and "Dance (Disco Heat)" into venerated, gospel-fused classics of the era. In the '80s, under the moniker the Weather Girls, the ladies were responsible for the monster camp party hit "It's Raining Men."

When Martha lent her vocal expertise to "Gonna Make You Sweat (Everybody Dance Now)," a project conceived by producers and songwriters Robert Clivilles and David Cole (operating as C + C Music Factory), few could have anticipated the track's phenomenal impact. A number one house music smash that climbed to the summit of the pop and dance charts in the U.S., the song was also a mammoth success across Europe. The anthem instantly hooked the masses with Wash's soul-penetrating command to hit the dance floor. Likewise, the high energy hits of Black Box, thanks in part to Martha's take-charge style, caused booty shaking stampedes in clubs worldwide, not to mention eyebrow-raising record sales.

There was a fly or two in the glittery ointment, however. Martha was initially uncredited for her work on the projects, and promotional videos featured slim, sexy, lip-synching females appearing to be the vocalists of these songs. After much publicized legal wrangling, Wash was eventually credited for spurring legislation that made it mandatory to provide proper vocal acknowledgements on music videos and CDs.

Martha went on to release her first self-titled solo album in 1992, which featured multiple number one dance tracks (notably the stirring single "Carry On"), and she remains one of the most revered member of clubland's elite royalty to this day. She unveiled a new album in 2013, Something Good, and reached the top of Billboard's dance chart in 2015 with "Free People," a collaboration with veteran DJ Tony Moran. She scored an additional major hit the same year with "I'm Not Coming Down." Wash is also currently a member of the trio First Ladies of Disco (inspired by the book of the same name), an act that also features disco heritage artists Evelyn "Champagne" King and Linda Clifford. The group achieved a Top 10 dance hit in 2015 with "Show Some Love," released on Martha's own label, Purple Rose Records.

Martha, who was quoted in the 2013 book First Ladies of Disco *as saying she never trips on her disco era fame, is equally level-headed about her experience in the '90s. An artist who cut a new path for herself and others during this era of change, Martha talks about her experiences one hot, late summer afternoon from her home in New York.*

Martha, you enjoyed an extremely successful music career throughout the '70s and '80s. Do you recall what was going through your mind as the new decade was about to begin?

Oh, I wasn't really thinking ahead about what I wanted to do in the '90s. Nothing like that. I was basically a "take it one day at a time" type of person. I really was like that my whole life. I was still working as the Weather Girls in the late '80s, and I didn't think much about having to follow up the success we had with "It's Raining Men." I never worried about that saying, "You're only as good as your last hit." By the late '80s, [The Weather Girls] had done our second album and hadn't had any big hits off that set. Our music was more popular in the UK and Europe than here in the U.S., and I guess the time was right for a change. But I still wasn't thinking of myself in terms of going out solo. I was content with doing primarily demo work.

Let's take a look at Black Box. How did you become the vocalist for their 1990 album project, Dreamland?

My manager at the time, Doug Kibble, got the call with an offer for me to go over and record some tracks for a company called Groove Groove Melody in Italy. They were studio musicians and producers [Daniele Davoli, Mirko Limoni and Valerio Semplici]—I don't know if you would call them a group exactly. We met them and recorded the songs. I remember I was okay with the songs they wanted me to sing ("Everybody Everybody," "Strike It Up," etc.), but I had a problem with the quality of English used in the lyrics. When I heard the songs they played for me at the time—and I was privately questioning them a bit in my mind—I just thought, okay, this is what they want. I knew I had to try and make it happen. They were nice to me and very professional. I finished and went home and didn't hear anything after that.

When did you first discover that they had used the French model Katrin Quinol to lip-synch your voice in the marketing of their Black Box project?

I don't remember the city I was in or the hotel I was staying at, but I turned on the TV and saw the video they had created for "Everybody Everybody." I was just floored because there was this young woman lip-synching to my voice. I told my manager something like, "You won't believe what I just saw!" I think—before we really had a chance to think about it and the implications—we were just completely confused about what was going on. I quickly realized that many people knew my voice and were going to realize this woman in the video was *not* me. It simply wasn't true.

In the videos for Black Box (and in C + C's "Gonna Make You Sweat," in which Zelma Davis appeared, lip-synching to your voice), marketers chose to feature slim, youthful women whose looks were generally considered more appealing than a woman with a plus-size figure. It was widely publicized that you were extremely displeased with this approach. When the controversy flared up, did you have the opportunity to observe the public's reaction to the issue? Do you think they cared?

I think it was a 50/50 reaction. My hardcore fans were absolutely upset. They knew these women were not the artist they admired, regardless of their appearance. And they were offended, as I was, that marketing of these videos further implied there was something to hide about the true vocalist. Then you had the other more casual fans who really didn't care. They liked the music. Period. They didn't care so much. But I was right that my diehard fans would be upset about Katrin Quinol, and they were.

The two projects, C + C and Black Box, in a way, almost overlapped each other, perhaps by a few months. So there was this double-whammy effect.

Do you recall the C + C Music Factory recording session for the "Gonna Make You Sweat" track?

With C + C, I was told I'd be singing a demo song for another artist. A demo is just supposed to give guide vocals for the artist that's going to actually record the project. If you listen to the song, I basically delivered the hook. I had already worked with David Cole doing other demos in the past, but interestingly enough, he wasn't in the studio when I laid down my vocals for this one, only Robert. I remember I had wanted to talk to him about the song because I usually got instructions from him about what he wanted me to do. So I talked to him over the phone while in the studio and then went in and started singing. I remember thinking as I was singing the hook of the song that it was set so high, it was like I was reaching for the ceiling trying to hit the notes. "Damn, this is high," I was thinking, basically screaming at the top of my lungs.

Martha Wash is the picture of sophistication in this publicity shot issued by Logic Records in the U.S. to promote her 1998 greatest hits collection (photograph by Len Prince, author's collection).

I don't know what happened to the vocalist who they had originally in mind to actually sing the song or why they didn't use her version. David had come to me previously and asked me if I wanted to be a part of his production company. I thanked him but declined, and we were cool about it. It just wasn't something I was interested in doing at that point—being a part of a production entity like that. I didn't want to be necessarily tied down, as I'd been with a production company in the past (with Two Tons of Fun). I didn't want to do that again. He was okay with that; we just moved on, and I treated this session as my usual demo work for him.

How did the producers justify the use of your demo recording in the final mix and what happened next?

Well, that's just it; they didn't justify it. When my manager tried to get in touch with their manager, there was no real response. After a while, we started to get really annoyed that nobody wanted to respond to the very big issue that we were reaching out about. That forced us to initiate a lawsuit.

Even if these records hadn't been such big hits, I feel sure I would have pursued these matters anyway. This was not the first time this sort of thing happened in the history of the music business. My biggest issue was that people who knew me and knew my voice from working with Sylvester, Two Tons of Fun and the Weather Girls—letting something like this go would have eroded my integrity. I knew I had to stand up for myself. In a broader sense, I also knew if they got away with deceptions like that, other artists down the road were also going to suffer.

"Sweat" was the first track C + C released from the project, and the album hadn't come out yet. When the song became so successful, I don't think they were finished with the album. This is all just my theory. But I've always maintained that "Gonna Make You Sweat" blew up so quickly that they probably had to scramble around trying to get the album finished. But they still had to take advantage of this huge song that was breaking right now, and I think they probably just had Zelma Davis, the other key female vocalist that was part of the project, just go out there and lip-sync to my voice. I think the record company probably pushed them to get everything done and just to take advantage of all the publicity. They had a hit song, and people were waiting on the album, and they had all this controversy with me. That's a whole lot of publicity you can't buy. Well, nowadays maybe you can. But back then, no. I think the record company had an attitude of "Never mind what's going on with Martha Wash; we'll deal with her later."

Were you nervous about the lawsuit failing or, in essence, taking on the record industry and the risk of a possible backlash from the corporate side?

Look, this business can be, at times, very cut-throat. I knew that. I can't say I worried about things like that at the time. I really tried not to listen to warnings like that or what some people had to say. I got so much advice that I should do this and that—blah, blah, blah. I was concerned about how the public would receive the controversy. That was my focus. I considered myself a working artist who loves music. The controversy was very new to me, and I just had to have the confidence and energy to go through the process and the interviews.

My attorney, Steven Ames Brown, argued the cases so successfully that it became mandatory that artists singing on a recording have to be credited and properly featured. [*Martha was given vocal credit on Black Box's "Strike It up" single, though the video remained unchanged visually.*] That was the best thing that came out of the whole debacle. The new legislation affected not just dance music, but all music.

Today, do you think much about this rather historic episode from the '90s?
It's funny, it's been something like almost two and a half decades since this all happened, and I *don't* think about it much at all anymore. When I do, it just seems so old to me.

Following this tumultuous period, you were awarded a contract for a self-titled solo album with RCA in 1992, which yielded two number one dance chart hits, "Carry On" and "Give It to You." What were your thoughts going into this project?
I was ready for it. I was a little tired of all the controversy by that point, and I felt it was worth a try. I knew sometimes these things work, and sometimes they don't. There are many artists that put out an album, and you never hear from them again, or they go back to back-up work, session singing or whatever. I thought about that, but I thought it was an opportunity worth trying. I was anxious to see what would happen.

The only thing I regretted about it—and it had nothing to do with the album itself—was that I didn't get the opportunity to go out and promote it. I had gotten on the road and was out for four or five days to start a campaign for it. I was in Chicago and was scheduled to perform at a big launch party for the album that evening. Earlier in the day, I fell and dislocated my knee. I was laid up for three months. Think about that—your album has just come out, and you've got all this work to do for it. If you take a three month break at that point, people are going to start forgetting about it very quickly. They move on to something else.

There were great songs on that set. I just didn't get to push it the way I wanted to. Although I was very happy that "Carry On" and "Give It to You" went to number one on the dance chart, I was sure I could have done even more with those tracks on the pop side had I been able to tour.

Although we released *The Collection* album in 1998, which had a number one dance hit with "Catch the Light," it wasn't in the cards for me to do a follow-up album, at least as far as the record company was concerned. RCA had moved me to a boutique label called Logic, and rather than do an album of all new material, they simply put together a collection of my previous stuff. It had only four new songs on it.

You continued to have hits in the '90s, however, notably with producer and DJ Todd Terry. The reinvention of the Musique classic "Keep on Jumpin'" and "Something Goin' On," both featuring club diva Jocelyn Brown, topped the dance charts.
Yes, Todd Terry was very popular at the time. The funny thing about recording "Keep on Jumpin'" was Jocelyn was in London at the time, and I was in New York. We recorded in two different studios and countries, but I guess there was still good chemistry. That's really not that unusual when it comes to recording duets, especially today.

While the music may have evolved, did you observe any differences in your audiences during each era of dance music—the '70s, '80s, '90s and beyond?
That's an interesting question. Despite all the changes in music styles, the music business, changes in how the world is running, I've never noticed any significant difference in how

audiences respond to me or the music. In an inconsistent world, that's been a very consistent thing. I've watched changes in some of the demographics of my audience. For instance, today I notice more and more young people following my music and learning about who I am. They may even have heard my older work because of their parents. That's been a very cool thing. But other than that, my audience and their reception to my music has been very steady and very enthusiastic.

I think of "It's Raining Men" sometimes, and I notice how that song had such a broad appeal to so many people. You'll hear that song at a wedding, a bar mitzvah, you name it—and every age group wants to dance to it. It made a lot of very different people very happy. That's another thing I enjoyed about my audience in every decade—the diversity.

You've also had a chance to witness first hand the radical changes in the music industry, including what some people refer to as the progressive demotion of the vocalist as the producer/DJ increasingly shines in the spotlight. What are your thoughts about that?

I actually disagree with those who think this is a modern-day trend. I understand the dilemma, but it's been going on since the '90s, and I'm a singer who knows what it is like to *not* feel a proper sense of credit. I can't say I necessarily agree with the rise of the DJ as the *entire* focal point of contemporary dance music, but it's clearly a development in the culture.

As you know, Evelyn "Champagne" King, Linda Clifford and I recently joined forces under the direction of James Washington as a group called First Ladies of Disco. We released the single "Show Some Love," which has been very successful. The focus on this track is very much on the three of us, our voices and our message. Yes, we had some great DJs remixing the track, but the focus has stayed on our art and what we want to deliver to our audience. The success of the track tells me there's still room out there for both DJs and vocalists, such as the other ladies and myself.

You've taken some very progressive steps in your own career by launching your own label, Purple Rose Records, which released the First Ladies of Disco project. How does it feel for you to be the vocalist and the executive now?

It's about trying new things for me. If you want to keep living and advancing, then you have to make an attempt to move things forward yourself, not relying entirely on others to do it for you. Again, sometimes it

"We are hardworking people; we can be relevant given a chance, and—just like everybody else—we can reinvent ourselves," believes Martha Wash. In 2015, Wash collaborated with heritage stars Linda Clifford and Evelyn "Champagne" King (under the moniker First Ladies of Disco) for the hit "Show Some Love" (photograph by Gor Megaera, courtesy James Washington).

works, and sometimes it doesn't. But that's okay—that's part of life. You have to find what works for you—find your niche in a business that's very different from the way it was 20 or 30 years ago. I guess Purple Rose is evidence of me moving forward.

I really started the record company just for me at the beginning—a more proactive way of keeping my name out there and my music going. When James approached me about trying First Ladies of Disco, we talked it through and ended up feeling this might be something good for my label. We are very encouraged by the results and are looking at starting a brand within the label focused on heritage artists. We're not dead. We are hard working people; we can be relevant given a chance, and—just like everybody else—we can reinvent ourselves. The fact that we made it to the Top 10 of the *Billboard* dance chart in 2015 is amazing, and it shows me it *can* be done. Nothing is easy in life—you gotta work for it.

Many people in this book will address the question I'm about to pose to you, but few have the decades of accomplishments behind them that you possess. From the classic age of disco through today, what has been the benefit of dance music to pop culture?

I think that question probably comes from an awareness that dance music has sort of been the stepchild of the industry. Disco and dance music have been around a long time, which is a testament to its durability. Yet, I believe there is only one category at the Grammys today that addresses dance music specifically—I think it's best remix or something like that. For some reason, the artists and producers and songwriters who created these tremendously popular songs don't merit a category, like rock, or R&B and hip-hop. I find that very sad.

I've seen people react to dance music; I know the power it has. It has always made people feel good. Though dance music styles have changed, it has remained about partying and feeling alive. I'm an old school girl, and I won't hesitate to tell you I love the music of the '70s and '80s best. But no matter what era you favor, dance music has had the power to make you forget your problems—at least for a little while. Maybe that's been the biggest benefit it has provided.

Lightning Round with Martha

Diana Ross or Donna Summer?

Oh, Lord! Oh, hell! [*There is a long pause.*] Well, I can tell this is not going to be a lightning round for me. I go back to the Supremes, but I came up in the same era as Donna and loved her, too. I'll go with Donna.

Live in concert or in the studio?

Live in concert.

Extended version or radio mix?

Extended version.

Perfect hair or perfect teeth?

Perfect teeth.

Facebook or Twitter?

Oh, wow. I'll say Twitter because I'm still trying to figure out everything about Facebook.

Fiction or non-fiction?
   Fiction.

Five good friends or one best friend?
   Damn! I'll say one best friend.

Change the past or guarantee the future?
   A lot of people try to change the past. Whatever happened, happened. I'd rather guarantee the future.

Kristine Weitz, also known as Kristine W
"One More Try" (1996)

"So much of what gets introduced to us in this world isn't very heartfelt. I think you can feel that I love writing music and performing."—Kristine Weitz

In 2004, *The Advocate* acknowledged the career of Kristine Weitz, better known as Kristine W, describing her as a singer/songwriter who helped shape nightlife of the [late] '90s. Such an impressive assertion is readily supported by a series of hugely popular, back-to-back number one *Billboard* dance chart singles released by the singer beginning midway through the decade. Perhaps one of the best examples of Kristine's power to dominate the dance floor can be found in her signature anthem "Land of the Living" (from the 1996 RCA album of the same name). The track, a rousing tribute to the art of survival, was a monster hit that did much to cement the artist's reputation as a compelling, yet equally off-the-elbow vocalist with a flair for irresistibly hope-fused lyrics and powerful beats. (It also ironically and eerily foreshadowed the entertainer's personal battle with leukemia some years later.) She has become eternally bonded to the track, as well as a lengthy string of inspiringly passionate chart-toppers, including "Feel What You Want" and "One More Try."

Her breakthrough hits launched a succession of dance floor fire-starters that have kept Ms. W a highly relevant figure in the 21st century. Modern era successes like "Lovin' You," "Be Alright," "Everything That I Got," "Love Come Home" and the 2016 smash "Out There" (many of which were created under her own production banner, Fly Again Music) show the artist to be an ever-evolving hitmaker. Kristine's palpable appreciation for real life experience consistently provides the foundation for songs that forge a connection between the brain, the gut and the feet. It's a highly sought after skill by performers in the dance genre who crave longevity in the business. As a result, it's no surprise that she remains one of dance music's most durable, recognizable and venerated performers today.

Tall and strikingly attractive, this career entertainer, business entrepreneur and mother of two speaks about her life in music one weekday afternoon from her home in Las Vegas, Nevada. As she examines her masterful journey in an industry that regularly tosses all but the most steadfast aside, Kristine is a thoughtful interviewee who often pauses for several moments before answering the questions posed to her.

I know you've experienced many challenges in life, Kristine, almost from the very beginning. Tell me about your early days and growing up.

My mother was a single parent after my dad passed away when I was just three years old. He died at 32 years of age—so it was a shock. My dad was a country singer and a rancher. He had also been an air force pilot and captain who had flown defoliant chemicals used in the Vietnam war.

It was very strange what happened. He went into the hospital with flu-like symptoms on a Friday, and he was dead on Sunday. He had internal bleeding. The pilots slept by the chemicals as they guarded it back in the war—as a result he could have had leukemia or something like it. Almost everyone that was stationed with him also died very young—within 10 years of being in Asia. Ironically, I would get leukemia in 2001.

My mom is a very educated person with a degree from Whitman College, and she majored in three subjects: psychology, philosophy

Kristine W, seen here in an RCA Records publicity picture, scored a remarkable string of number one hits on *Billboard*'s dance chart, beginning with "Feel What You Want" in 1994 (photograph by Tony Duran, author's collection).

and sociology. But she couldn't get a job. It was a limited area, a small farming community, and there weren't a lot of opportunities. She couldn't bring herself to move to Seattle or Portland, and take us away from our grandparents who had just lost their son, so she started singing in a restaurant. She was a strolling waitress, singing from table to table with her guitar. That's how her career took off—the necessity to stay alive. There were four of us kids in the family between the ages of one and five. It was really tough. But my mom was a really good singer, and my parents' love of music was a gift that really helped us survive.

When I was a little kid, I'd sit under a table and listen to my mom rehearse. My grandmother moved in after my dad died, and she was a classically trained violinist and pianist. She taught me to play the piano. She was a really great musician, and she helped my mom to learn music as well. I was immersed in music, and if I wasn't singing, I was writing poems. Music became an escape for me—a way to let my feelings out. Music saved my family, and I always looked at it as, well, *hope* I guess.

I would sing in church and play my guitar on Sunday—it was my gig. I was a fast study, and I became really good at it. I could project my voice through the whole church, and I didn't need a microphone. People started to come to church to see what I was going to sing that week. I'd sing a different song every week, and I really enjoyed that so much. I would also go two or three times a week to the old folks' home and sing for the seniors while they'd eat. They were sort of a captive audience [*she laughs*], and it helped me get rid of all my stage fright. My grandmother told me I had to sing all the time—it was the only way I was going to get good and relax enough to become an effective live stage performer.

I was obsessed with Donna Summer from the time I was a kid. What she was doing was what I was feeling—up tempo music and that whole disco/dance thing. "Hot Stuff" and "Last Dance." The minute I saw her movie *Thank God It's Friday*, I couldn't stop playing "Last Dance." I remember my sister saying, "You play that song one more time, and I'm gonna kill you!" I bought all her music, and had her poster on my wall.

You eventually made your way to Las Vegas?

Yes. As a matter of fact, I won a state talent show singing "Last Dance." I ended up winning a big talent show in Reno, Nevada, at the age of 16. By then, I was six feet tall, so I'm sure they thought I was 21. I never got asked for ID. I wore a lot of make-up and a red dress—I was living it! That led to me enter pageants, which I won, and ended up on stage at the *Miss America Pageant*. I took the scholarship money from winning swimsuit and talent and headed directly to the University of Nevada, Las Vegas. It was scary heading off on my own, but I started auditioning, singing radio jingles and performing in college bands. I shared a one-bedroom apartment with two other girls and a Great Dane, had a mattress on the floor and started sluggin' it out. I went to Vegas knowing I could work my way through college, and I knew I could sing a lot of styles of music there.

How did you begin your recording career in dance music?

While pursuing my degree, my mentor (and like a dad to me), John R. Lewis, who I dedicated my *Land of the Living* album to, helped me put a band together called Kristine and the Sting, and I started performing at the casinos and the lounges, night after night. I tried out a lot of my own original material on the crowds. I made an indie record called "Show and Tell" and sent it to all the radio stations. It ended up being a pretty big hit in the area. I started traveling to California to record some stuff with an R&B production house that had done some work with Janet Jackson and others. I'd write songs and record them, and that eventually became [the material that encompassed] my first album, *Perfect Beat* (1994).

I started getting a few breaks. My best friend, Julie Michaels, an actress in the movie *Road House,* was playing my music on the set. That's how my song "Do You Really Want Me" got in that movie. Around the same time, I was performing in Vegas at the Hilton, and movie director Adrian Lyne came in during my show. He fell in love with a song I was singing, and that's how I got to sing my song "EZ Come EZ Go" live in the movie *Indecent Proposal,* with Robert Redford and Demi Moore. So my recording career was taking off.

One of the most powerful, beautifully sung and uniquely structured dance songs of the era is "Land of the Living" from 1996. It encompassed exceptionally well-crafted storytelling and achieved truly remarkable lyrical and musical depth. Can you tell me how the song and the album came to be?

I was performing on stage at the Hilton, six nights a week, two shows a night. A producer came in from London, and he had heard about me from an A&R guy in New York. He was president of a British label called Champion Records. He and his friends were listening to me, and they thought I was lip-synching. They couldn't believe that was my voice coming out of a white girl. [*She laughs.*] I just remember them going to all sides of the room checking out the equipment (and me) while the show was going on. Later, they said to me, "If that's really you singing, would you prove it by singing for us right now?" So I sang something a cappella. They said, "You need to sign with us and come to London!" That's how the whole project got started.

There was no money involved. They just wanted me to come to London to see what they could make happen. I didn't get paid for anything. I would have to keep my band on retainer while I went over there, and it was going to cost me a lot of money. But I took the leap of faith and went over there and recorded "Feel What You Want"—in one day, literally. I had to get back to Vegas and return home. A few months later, they got in touch with me and said the song was blowing up. Well, it was taking off in Europe, and then it hit New York, where DJ Junior Vasquez was playing it all the time. So we kept working on the album, and I created songs like "Land of the Living" and "One More Try." Again, I wasn't paid anything. My expenses got paid, like my hotel rooms when I traveled, but it was a gamble—like rolling the dice. Next thing you know, the album was done. "One More Try" ended up being a pop radio crossover hit, and that was insane. My live shows in Vegas were giving me the ability to fund these projects. But it was very hard work.

"Land of the Living," the song, can be said to reflect people's determination to survive. It had a distinct connection to those living with AIDS at the time and later turned out to be a reflection of your own health challenges.

Yes, exactly. In 1997, "Land of the Living" was chosen as the third single. It became an anthem for people with AIDS because that was during the time people began to feel that maybe they *could* live with AIDS. It was right at the time when AIDS had stopped becoming a death sentence. So the gay community really connected with the song. To be truthful, however, I wrote the song about surviving the brutal entertainment business.

Let me clarify what I mean by that. To be a working musician is just so hard. In Vegas, at that time, you worked six nights a week, two 90-minute shows a night. Or you had the option of doing three one-hour shows a night. You had to work incredibly hard to keep everyone's attention all of the time because you're competing with thousands of slot machines right outside the door. Vegas has a really tough crowd. Half the time you'd wonder if they'd even remember your name. It's a grind. It could be fun, too, but it takes a lot of practice and focus. I had to be the producer and the star; I had to hire and fire people. It's a tremendous amount of pressure—you perform all night, get up in the morning, and head to rehearsal to learn music. The more popular you become, the more people come back to see your show. They want to see something different. Adding new songs equals more rehearsals, more costumes, and more expenses. Not so glamorous.

Thinking about "Land of the Living," I can tell you watching my mom work so hard in the clubs also influenced me in writing the song. I kind of wrote it for both of us—soldiers in music.

"Land" was not written about surviving getting sick, as some may think. However, it was like a prediction of things to come for me. I *really* had to live those lyrics in 2001 when

I was diagnosed with AML leukemia. I remember when I was in the hospital at UCLA being treated, I told myself, "Okay, when you wrote that song, you meant it. And now you've got to live it. This is for real. This isn't about words or music—this is about you not being on the planet anymore." It was surreal thinking about the lyrics to that song, about the lights coming down and no flowers at my door—wow. That was my reality. I was holed up in the hospital for a year. I didn't want to tell too many people because I didn't want to believe it myself. I had two babies, one and a half and two and a half years old at the time. I had to keep a lid on my emotions so that I could focus on survival.

Your leukemia diagnosis must have been extremely sobering.

My odds of surviving were so low—like a 30 percent chance of survival, even with all the treatments. Leukemia is cancer of the blood, so it's not like something they can cut off you. The treatment is so horrific, and most people do not survive it. It's so many rounds of chemo for so long, followed up by a stem cell transplant of the good cells that they've been able to extract from you over the months. I've had so many blood transfusions. It's insane.

I think I was able to survive it because of my determination and my children. As a mother, you have so much fight in you. You want to survive to be there for your kids. In my own life, I don't know what I would have done without my mother and grandmother and that maternal power. I just could not leave my kids here without their mother. Losing my dad was devastating; that's for sure. But I think when you lose your mother—it's a whole different type of grief that happens. People like Madonna, Rosie O'Donnell, and others who have lost their mothers—I admire them surviving that loss.

You're a survivor, and in the process you've racked up some amazing accomplishments. Virtually every song you've released as a major single has gone to number one on **Billboard's** *dance chart. Your recent album,* **New & Number Ones,** *nicely showcased your repertoire. What is it about your songwriting (and performances) that resonate so strongly with dance music fans?*

Maybe it's because I just love it so much. I think my audience can feel it because it's real. So much of what gets introduced to us in this world isn't very heartfelt. I think you can feel that I love writing music and performing. It's like food—the love is in the recipe and the preparation, on the plate. I think that's the ingredient I bring to the table. When you come see me perform, when you hear me sing on a record, I think you can feel there's something genuine in the message.

I love dance music. It's a fun, but challenging genre for me. You can tell sad stories, but at 128 beats-per-minute, you can't be that bummed out. I've talked about how ungrateful a person is, for example, how they hurt me—a tragic song—but the beat and production are so much fun that it makes the message palatable. I love that about dance music. You can deliver happy messages, sad messages. To me, it's a great template.

Let's talk about the record industry itself. Do you have any observations about the long-standing absence of women in key executive roles within the music business?

Yes, it's mainly a man's business with mostly men running the industry, both live and on the recording end. That's beginning to change, fortunately. I never worked with a female entertainment director, a female A&R person, or any female executives at the labels I was signed to. The only females were in public relations or working as assistants. It's not that I don't work well with men, because I do. I just believe that I would have benefited from there being more females in executive positions. They could have brought their energy to the promotion of my music.

How much pressure is there on women in the business, just in terms of looks and image? As a woman gets older in the music industry, how do you feel she can best meet that challenge?

Well, of course anybody who says there isn't pressure or that it isn't a challenge to age in this business is lying. I don't care if you're going to a grocery store or trying to sell a record, you're constantly judged based on your looks. It's really tough on women in terms of aging—not on men—just women. Paul McCartney can get up there, and nobody cares how many wrinkles he's got or how saggy he is. We have a crazy society where youth and beauty are put on such a high pedestal that very few people can live up to the expectations of the media and the society we are creating. We still value looks way over intelligence. It's very sad. It's a game, and I guess you have to decide if you're going to play or not. And if you stay in the game, what you're willing to do if you decide to play.

I just do the best I can. I take care of myself, eat well, and do my best to stay hip and cool and hang out with people who share those ideas. I work with people from all over the world—not just a certain little circle. I try to keep it global to maintain a broader perspective.

You've come through the transition that's taken place in the way we listen to music, going from vinyl and CDs to downloads. How do you feel about these changes? How difficult is it to make a living as a dance music artist today?

Before you make any money today with an album download, it's often stolen. I don't know what the statistics are, but I think it's stolen and shared sometimes hundreds or thousands of times before you make an actual sale. My project manager has a full time job reporting sites (and trying to shut down those sites) where my music is illegally available. Artists have lost the ability to monetize recorded music for the most part. I started my own label, so perhaps I can do a little better that way. But, still, you have so many expenses right off the top—recording costs, shooting the cover photos, producing videos, hiring remixers, paying promoters of all kinds, etc. Then you make the music available on digital platforms that take a good percentage right off the top.

So what's the future of singers and songwriters in an age where people largely expect to get their music for free?

That's the great unknown. The garden is not being watered, so how do you sustain it? I think we're all at the crossroads now. The cost to create music is high; it takes a lot of time to create it. Even if you do all the work before you go into the studio, pre-production, it costs a fortune. For example, to use an average studio, engineer and decent microphone, it can cost $150 or more per hour. The price continues to escalate with more and more studios shutting down. Meanwhile, the artist is making less and less. So how long can anyone keep doing this? I think that's why you see big labels getting smaller or going out of business, and we're seeing artists selling anything from underwear to cookware and whatever they can think of to brand and sell. The trend now is if you recognize my face and name, I've got something to sell you! [*She laughs.*]

Many artists have given up making new music and rely on their back catalog. Look at radio. It's pretty much pay-for-play to get in rotation on the major pop stations. You have to pay a promoter or promotion company a ton of money to make it happen, but even then there's no guarantee. Thankfully, places like SiriusXM satellite radio will play songs based on the merits of the music. Sirius channels like BPM and Utopia are straight up about it. They'll tell you if they like the track or not, but at least it's real, and they'll add your music based on how well they think it will go over with their audience. There are some fabulous dance outlets on radio and the internet like Fusion (now known as Nexus) out of Chicago, C89.5 in Seattle, Pride Radio and others. They're making big noise, and that makes me happy. I find myself listening to a lot of Internet stations because they play a greater variety and take more chances. I love that. You can actually hear songs with vocals there—*yeah*!

I think it's key for artists now to work on licensing our music and performing live as much as possible. I've recently licensed my songs for workout compilations and TV, and that's going well. I have to say, it's a blast being a part of someone's workout.

Another trend that took hold in the early 2000s was the shift in focus from the vocalist to the producers, DJs and remixers. What do you think inspired that change?

Yep! And it's still going on. I think it happened because the Internet gave the power over to the remixers, some of whom didn't want to share the billing with artists. They didn't want to have to deal with the vocal talent anymore. And, let's face it, some of the divas were probably very difficult to work with. I think we're in a new period where we all are re-learning how to work together.

We're also talking here, in some ways, about the importance of loyalty on the part of your audience and their support of your work. The gay community has certainly been among your most loyal fans. Would you agree with that?

For sure, and I love and appreciate their support. That's where my loyalty is as well. I remember (at the time my career was really starting to blow up) I worked with labels where the execs that were running corporate were always advising me not to perform at so many gay events or to deal so much with the gay press. "We're not going to be able to cross you over," they'd say. "You need to cut the line with all this gay stuff." I refused to follow that advice. I made the conscious decision to follow my heart and whatever came of my decisions, I would live with it.

How is reaching number one on the Billboard dance chart today a different experience from reaching the top spot in the '90s?

I think the main difference is that there were more clubs back then, and getting to number one meant you'd work so much more. There are not as many clubs in the U.S. and abroad anymore.

I will say, however, reaching number one today is still a huge accomplishment because the field is so competitive. You're competing with everybody—*everybody*. Country singers, rock singers, R&B—everyone puts out dance mixes on everything they release. Michael Bublé even had a remix. Even rappers are fighting for a position on the dance chart. To get into the dance Top Five today is a real fight. To date, I have 20 Top Five *Billboard* dance hits. I think that's what I'm most proud of. It's more difficult to reach those positions now than it was back in the late '90s.

Disco and dance music artists have rarely received the accolades that are bestowed on those popular in other genres of music, but the sounds continue to endure. Why do you suppose that's the case?

If you just go back and recall a classic disco song, like a Donna Summer–Giorgio Moroder production, you'll hear all those lush strings—the work of live musicians, horn sections, guitar work, kick-ass drummers. It was so incredibly musical—it's insane. When you think about what they created and knowing they didn't have all the technology they have now, I mean, the musicianship is just ridiculous. Just a wall of magnificent sound! Fast forward through the '80s and '90s to now. The history and evolution is phenomenal.

Maybe one reason dance music hasn't gotten the respect other genres receive is because people haven't taken the time to really listen to it. The quirky dance songs sometimes get all the attention. People can be drawn to that music, especially if it's played non-stop on the radio. You can almost get programmed to like it. However, there's cheesy rock out there, too. You have to take the time to listen and explore dance music, just as you would any other genre.

"I don't care if you're going to a grocery store or trying to sell a record, you're constantly judged based on your looks. It's really tough on women in terms of aging—not on men—just women," observes Kristine Weitz (photograph by Ruskin Studios, courtesy Kristine Weitz).

That's the key to the genre gaining more respect in the future, and it's starting to happen now.

Lightning Round with Kristine

Wallet or smart phone?

Wallet for sure! That's easy because I can always get another cell phone, but the wallet has all my tangible ID and cards. That's a disaster if you lose it.

Money or fame?

Fame, if you get it for the right reason—a platform that would be helpful to others. All you have is your legacy, and I would value fame if it helped other people somehow.

Five good friends or one best friend?
Five good friends—I think you need all the help you can get.

Facebook or Twitter?
Facebook because there's more information and you can get to know the person better. Twitter is pretty fast food.

Speaking of fast food, McDonald's or Taco Bell?
Neither. You will never see me at either.

Meet your ancestors or your descendants?
Ancestors. There are so many that I've heard so much about, and I would love to be able to spend time with them.

Afterword
by DJ Susan Morabito

Anyone who followed nightlife in New York City during the '90s will testify to the magnetism and influence of DJ Susan Morabito. As a legendary record spinner for the Big Apple's most famous dance halls (Sound Factory, Tunnel, Twilo, Roxy, Limelight, Palladium, Roseland, etc.), Morabito (the simplified moniker she goes by today) was a glass ceiling breaker. In an industry virtually ruled by males, she became the premier female DJ (and one of the most popular ever, especially among the city's dance-ravenous gay community). Her sessions at the GMHC Morning Party on the Beach at Fire Island Pines and the Dance on the Pier (aka the NYC Gay Pride Pier Dance) were rousing celebrations from the era that are still talked about today.

Susan's career flourished throughout the decade, and she shared her talent for bringing people together on the dance floor with many major venues throughout the country, including Avalon in Boston, Probe in L.A. and Amnesia and Salvation in Miami. She continues to be a DJ in high demand by today's international club scene.

Returning from performing a stellar set at the 2015 Black & Blue: District Red Light Montréal event in Canada, Morabito takes a few moments to look back at her experience as one of clubland's most revered orchestrators of dance floor euphoria.

I was born and raised in Cleveland, Ohio. I've always had a deep passion for music for as long as I can remember. I was always listening to the radio as a kid, and I'd save my lunch money to buy records. I enjoyed telling my friends about songs I found that maybe weren't that well known. When I was 14 or 15 years old, I had aspirations of becoming a radio DJ because, at the time, that's all I knew. However, I soon learned that radio DJs have the gift of gab, and they are guided by a program director. So, basically, it was somebody else telling the DJ what to play, and those choices were controlled by the record labels. I quickly kind of nixed that idea.

A few years later, I went to my first gay club. I wasn't out yet, but I walked in with a group of friends, and I was amazed, excited and enthralled by what I saw—which was several hundred people on the dance floor with their arms up in the air, all feeling great. The music was disco (it was about 1980–81), but I had never heard these tracks before. I walked around the bar by myself, letting my friends do their thing. I wanted to explore this place. It was the first time in my life that I felt like I belonged somewhere—a gay bar. Here I was, knowing I was gay, but not really even knowing what that meant. Being gay wasn't acceptable in the mainstream in those days, and yet here I was in this environment with drag queens, lesbians and gay men. I realized I wasn't a freak after all. I think my generation and those prior to mine were people who came out with a lot of shame, and being here was liberating.

I started looking around for the source of all this great dance I was hearing—I wasn't quite sure how it was being pumped into in this place. Way at the top of some steps, I found a guy in a booth playing records. I stood there and watched him closely. I was so impressed and amazed with his process and how he was choosing what he wanted to play. I saw the impact he was having on this room full of people, and it made a huge impression on me. Just amazing! What this man was doing was probably far more powerful than what most radio DJs could ever hope to achieve. There was a spontaneous, combustible energy just happening right in front of my eyes.

After that revelation, I started seeking out more gay clubs and befriended a DJ named Greg Whitbeck. I asked him if he would teach me to play. He told me to hang out in the booth with him, shut up and listen. And so I did. I learned how the music was structured. I went out and bought some 12-inch singles, practiced at home, and, little by little, I started getting jobs. I began working at lesbian bars and eventually some gay men's bars. I visited New York and started going to the big circuit parties there, such as those held at the Saint. That's when I realized how far a DJ can take a musical journey. Seeing this happen—well, I knew it was on a level that Cleveland would never see. I understood if I wanted to be involved in *that* kind of creativity, I'd have to move to New York. By the late '80s, I did.

I had a few gigs here and there and did my best to network. I worked at Vinylmania Records, a shop on Carmine Street in the village, which was where many top DJs bought their records. Connections were there for me. DJ Manny Lehman also worked at the store and helped me get my first job at the Ice Palace on Fire Island. Around 1993, it really started coming together for me. There was one particular gig on Fire Island Pines that changed the game. After playing my set, I suddenly was no longer that cute boy in the booth (everyone thought I was a boy). I had ripped the roof off! Then I became *Susan Morabito*. I now had a name, and it all took off from there.

Susan Morabito (courtesy Susan Morabito).

I think my success was based on a couple of factors. One was my taste in music. What music would you play during this period of the '90s that would draw people in? I found the right mix. I also believe I was what you would call a journey DJ, meaning there was a flow to the music that I played. When you're really on, one song flows right into the next one, seamlessly. I took people on this three-part journey (the beginning, middle and end), almost like a three-act play in the theater. Here's a better way to describe it—it was almost like sex, with a build-up or tease, a climax and the come down (or what is also known as the cuddle). People can identify with that description. But it never happened the same way twice. I never know what I am going to play next in my set to create a journey. The beauty of DJing is that it is a spontaneous art form. It's a give and take with the crowd, and I happen to be a very emotional DJ. I think my audiences responded to that in the '90s, and they continue to in the present.

I was one of the first female DJs to become well known. Sharon White was a successful DJ before me, and the first woman to play the Saint. Her career changed, and she dropped out of the scene in the '90s (though she's now back). I was really the only female spinning at the time, and that was a novelty. I stood out from the pack of big DJs of the day because I wasn't male. But being female was sometimes a challenge in the business. My sexuality was never a barrier to acceptance, but my sex was. I heard some gay men saying, "You're a woman. How would you know what *we* want?" *I heard that a lot.* Two promoters admitted that they wouldn't initially hire me because I was a woman. Later on, they did. But eventually being a woman started working in my favor because when the guys started realizing "she *does* know what we want," it created a buzz. There's sexism out there whether you're gay or straight. It's a man's world. It's a white man's world. It is what it is. You work with it, you work around it and you get past it. You don't waste time bitching about it.

There was a great energy in the clubs during this era. By the time my career started taking off in the '90s, people were surviving with AIDS. There was a celebratory vibe in the air, especially in the gay clubs. People were throwing their hands up, and they were happy. When the Saint closed, the circuit parties really heated up, and they began to spread throughout the country—Washington, D.C., Detroit, Houston, Miami, San Francisco, L.A., Montreal. And I must be honest if we are going to speak about circuit parties—the '90s was the decade of feel-good drugs. Whatever one's stance is on recreational drug use, I can't deny I felt that people in the clubs were far more engaged with the music and each other as a direct result of it. (They also didn't have cell phones and weren't distracted on the dance floor by their devices or going on Grindr.) Let's face it, people loosened up when they had a drink or took whatever substance they were on. I saw so many guys in clusters doing X, swaying back and forth and embracing in what was then called an "ecstasy hug." As a DJ, you contribute to energy in the club. The drugs played a big role in these warm feelings on the dance floor, but the music of the '90s was also integral, and the two elements worked hand-in-hand.

One of the best songs from the '90s that comes to my mind was Alison Limerick's "Where Love Lives." It is an excellent example of a house track from the period that was sophisticated, lush and incredibly well-produced. It has a divine piano, lovely vocals and is structurally put together so well. To this day, people go crazy for that song, and it has stood the test of time. There are many other tracks from this era that have been able to do that. We had some great, song-oriented hits back in those days, but we also had some wonderful instrumentals and dubs. There was nothing like a great track *without* any vocals. Both styles had their charm. And though the '90s launched a more electronic sound, it was still a music-oriented period in dance music. You had great sax and piano highlights in much of this music (and the combination with the electronics was beautiful). Of course, whether that sax and piano were real instruments or electronic plug-ins is debatable.

I'm a better DJ today thanks to the experiences I had back in the '90s. Ego became less important to me as time went by, but the music has remained my passion. I'm a big fan of today's dance music. It's very different from the '90s, but I absolutely love it. Dance music, whether from the '70s, '80s, '90s or beyond, evolved with different styles—whether it was disco, house, techno, electronic, chill, tribal, or a dozen other variations. In the long history of dance music, going as far back as the age of disco, it's always been that way. Just as in the past, today's sound is a mix of pop and commercial material and more experimental underground sounds. There's good stuff and bad in all categories. But it's important to remember that good and bad, when speaking of music, will always be a subjective thing. I can say most genuinely that I love the journey dance music has taken, and today's sounds are incredibly exciting.

Most people tend to feel the music they grew up with was the best, and they tend to stop following dance closely once he or she reaches a certain point in their life. They aren't going music shopping 20 hours a week, as I still do today, and perhaps they aren't going out quite as much as they did in their youth.

Like the music, I believe the club scene today is also evolving. New York's nightlife, admittedly, is not what it was in the '90s, and there are a lot of reasons for that. Real estate is insanely expensive, and club space is even scarcer. People don't want smoking outside their co-ops or the noise from the clubs and the sounds of people leaving in the wee hours. That after-hours vibe is harder to find now. And more people spend their nights online. A big reason why some people went out in the past was to hook up with somebody. You can do that in the comfort of your home now, using just a cell phone. But the club scene *is* bouncing back, and I see the future giving rise to smaller clubs like in the days of early disco. The day of the '90s mega-club, however, is over.

In spite of all the changes that have taken place over the years, I love being a DJ today, just as much as I did in the '90s. I love what I do. My job stays exciting because dance music keeps evolving and moving forward, and, in turn, it continues to give me a youthful vibe. Like the music, I continue to reinvent myself, rebrand and update my sound. I believe that's important, whether we are talking about a career such as mine or those of the artists that have been discussed in this book. Through reinvention we are all able to break away from preconceived notions of the past and enjoy the embrace of a younger generation. And I can assure you of one thing. They can hear the difference between someone with experience and someone who doesn't have it.

I am very proud of my connection to dance music, from the '90s right through to the present day. Dance music has brought us together and created community—it always has. It is all-encompassing; everyone is a part of it.

There is just as much magic on the dance floor as any other place on earth.

The CD Rack
Recommended Listening

The following is a sampling of some noteworthy dance-pop tracks by artists who found success in the '90s and are not profiled elsewhere in this book. Some are well-known classics, and others are a bit more obscure. A few may have been completely missed by aficionados when these recordings first hit music store shelves decades ago. However, all are significant products of the era by important artists who contributed great energy, excitement, and—most importantly—a lot of fun to the period.

Ace of Base: "Happy Nation"/"Wheel of Fortune"/"All That She Wants"/"The Sign"/"Living in Danger"/"Beautiful Life"/"Lucky Love"/"Don't Turn Around"/"Cruel Summer"
Adamski: "N-R-G"/"Killer"
Adeva: "It Should Have Been Me"/"Independent Woman"
The Adventures of Stevie V: "Dirty Cash (Money Talks)"
Alex Party: "Saturday Night Party"
Alexia: "Uh La La La"
Alice Deejay: "Better Off Alone"
Alison Limerick: "Where Love Lives"/"Make It on My Own"/"Gettin' It Right"
Amanda Lear: "Fantasy"/"Blood & Honey" ('98)
Amber: "Sexual (Li Da Di)"/"This Is Your Night"
Amii Stewart: "Friends" ('91)/"Knock on Wood" ('98 and '99)/"Extralarge"/"Don't Stop (Pushin')"/"Don't Be So Shy"
Amy Grant: "Baby Baby"/"Every Heartbeat"/"Good for Me"
Ann Lee: "2 Times"/"Voices"
Annie Lennox: "Little Bird"/"Walking on Broken Glass"/"No More 'I Love You's'"
Aqua: "Barbie Girl"
Aretha Franklin: "A Deeper Love"
Armand Van Helden: "Witch Doktor"/"You Don't Know Me" (featuring Duane Harden)
Army of Lovers: "Crucified"

American contemporary Christian music singer Amy Grant, seen here in an A&M Records publicity shot, dipped her toe in the dance-pop lake with her Top 10 1991 album *Heart in Motion*. The set yielded several upbeat hits, including the number one "Baby Baby" and the fiercely catchy "Every Heartbeat" (photograph by Albert Sanchez, author's collection).

Arthur Baker (and the Backbeat Disciples): "Let There Be Love"
ATB: "Don't Stop"/"9 PM (Till I Come)"
A*Teens: "Mamma Mia"/"Super Trouper"

Audrey Landers: "Sun of Jamaica"/"Shadows of Love"
The B-52's: "Roam"/"Love Shack"
Bananarama: "Preacher Man"/"Last Thing on My Mind"/"More, More, More"
Barbara Tucker: "Beautiful People"/"I Get Lifted"/"Stop Playing with My Mind"/"Hot Shot"/"Everybody Dance"
Barry Manilow: "Could It Be Magic"/"I'd Really Love to See You Tonight" (Dance Mixes)
Bass Bumpers: "Can't Stop Dancing"/"The Music's Got Me"/"Move to the Rhythm"
Betty Boo: "Doin' the Do"/"Catch Me"
Billie Ray Martin: "Your Loving Arms"/"Imitation of Life"/"Space Oasis"
Blondie: "Atomic"/"Maria"
Blue System: "Love Is Such a Lonely Sword"/"Déjà Vu"/"Magic Symphony"/"Lucifer"/"History"/"Body to Body"/"Dr. Mabuse"/"Laila"/"Love Will Drive Me Crazy"/"Only with You"
Blur: "Girls & Boys"
Bob Marley Vs. Funk Star De Luxe: "Sun Is Shining"
Bobby D'Ambrosio featuring Michelle Weeks: "Moment of My Life"/"The Day"
Bombalurina: "Itsy Bitsy Teeny Weeny Yellow Polka Dot Bikini"
Bombfunk MCs: "Freestyler"
Boy Krazy: "That's What Love Can Do"/"Good Times with Bad Boys"/"On a Wing and a Prayer"
The Brand New Heavies featuring N'Dea Davenport: "Stay This Way"/"Never Stop"/"Dream Come True"/"Midnight at the Oasis"/"Spend Some Time"/"Dream on Dreamer"/"Back to Love"/"Close to You"
Brooklyn Bounce: "Get Ready to Bounce"
Brothers in Rhythm Present Charvoni: "Forever and a Day"
Brownstone: "If You Love Me"/"I Can't Tell You Why"
The Bucketheads: "The Bomb! (These Sounds Fall into My Mind)"
Cappella: "Move on Baby"/"U Got 2 Let the Music"
Captain Jack: "Captain Jack"
Carleen Anderson: "Mama Said"/"True Spirit"
Cathy Dennis: "Touch Me (All Night Long)"/"You Lied to Me"
Ceybil Jefferies: "Love So Special"/"Open Your Heart"
Cher: "Love and Understanding"/"Believe"/"Strong Enough"/"All or Nothing"/"Dov'è L'Amore"
Chyp-Notic: "Nothing Compares 2 U"/"I Can't Get Enough"/"I Do It All for You Baby"

CJ Lewis: "Sweets for My Sweet"
Claudja Barry: "Love Is an Island"/"I Will Always Love You"
Clivilles & Cole: "A Deeper Love"
Club 69: "Let Me Be Your Underwear"/"Drama" (featuring Kim Cooper)/"Much Better" (featuring Suzanne Palmer)
Club X featuring Gladys Bankston: "Shower Me with Love"
Corina: "Temptation"
Corona: "The Rhythm of the Night"
Crush: "Jellyhead"
The Crystal Method: "Comin' Back"
Crystal Waters: "Gypsy Woman (She's Homeless)"/"100% Pure Love"
Cut 'n' Move: "Take No Crap"/"I'm Alive"/"Give It Up"
Dana Dawson: "3 Is Family"/"Show Me"/"Got to Give Me Love"/"Romantic World"
Dance 2 Trance: "Power of American Natives"
Danni'elle Gaha: "Secret Love"/"Do It for Love"/"Stuck in the Middle"
Danny Tenaglia: "Elements"
Darude: "Sandstorm"
David Hasselhoff: "Crazy for You"/"Do the Limbo Dance"/"Everybody Sunshine"
David Morales: "Gimme Luv (Eenie Meenie Miny Mo)"/"The Program"/"In De Ghetto" (and the Bad Yard Club, Crystal Waters)/"Needin' You" (David Morales presents the Face)
D'Bora: "E.S.P."/"Dream About You"/"Love Desire"
Deborah Cox: "It Could've Been You"/"Nobody's Supposed to Be Here"/"It's Over Now"/"Things Just Ain't the Same"
Deborah Harry: "I Can See Clearly"/"Sweet & Low"
Deee-Lite: "Groove Is in the Heart"/"E.S.P."/"Runaway"/"Power of Love"
Denise Lopez: "Don't You Wanna Be Mine"
De La Soul: "A Roller Skating Jam Named 'Saturdays'"
Des'ree: "You Gotta Be"
Diana Ross: "Take Me Higher"
Digital Underground: "The Humpty Dance"
Dina Carroll: "Ain't No Man"/"Special Kind of Love"/"Here"/"Livin' for the Weekend"/"Mind Body & Soul"/"Without Love"
DJ BoBo: "Love Is All Around"/"Somebody Dance with Me"/"Pray"/"There Is a Party"/"Freedom"/"Everybody"
DJ Miko: "What's Up"
D.N.A. featuring Suzanne Vega: "Tom's Diner"
Dolce & Gabbana (D&G): "More More More"

Donna Gardier: "I'll Be There"/"Reach Out"/ "Good Thing"
Donna Giles: "And I Am Telling You I'm Not Going"
Donna Summer: "Carry On"/"Melody of Love"/"I Will Go with You (Con te Partiró)"/"Love Is the Healer"
Doop: "Doop"
D:Ream: "Things Can Only Get Better"
Drizabone: "Real Love"/"Pressure"/"Catch the Fire"
Dune: "Can't Stop Raving"/"Hardcore Vibes"
Dusty Springfield: "Reputation"
Edelweiss: "Starship Edelweiss"/"Beam Me Up"
Eiffel 65: "Blue (Da Ba Dee)"
808 State: "Cubik"/"Bombadin"/"Cubik: 98"
Elaine Hudson: "No More the Fool"/"On a Long and Winding Road"/"Feeling Free"/"Good God"
Electronic: "Getting Away with It"
Elvis Crespo: "Suavemente"
EMF: "Unbelievable"/"Lies"
Enrique Iglesias: "Rhythm Divine"
En Vogue: "My Lovin' (You're Never Gonna Get It)"/"Hold On"/"Lies"/"You Don't Have to Worry"
Erin Hamilton: "Dream Weaver"/"Satisfied"/"The Flame"/"The Temple"
E-Rotic: "Max Don't Have Sex with Your Ex"
Eternal featuring BeBe Winans: "I Wanna Be the Only One"
Eve Gallagher: "Love Is a Master of Disguise"/"Change Your Mind"/"You Can Have It All"/"Love Come Down"/"Heaven Has to Wait"
Faithless: "God Is a DJ"/"Salva Mea"/"Insomnia"
Falco: "Titanic"/"Data De Groove"
The Family Stand: "Ghetto Heaven"
Fancy: "When Guardian Angels Cry"/"No Way Out"/"Love Has Called Me Home"/"How Do You Feel Right Now?"/"Gimme a Sign"/"Mega-Mix '98"/"Na Na Na Na Hey Hey Hey Kiss Him Goodbye"
The Farm: "All Together Now"
Felix: "Don't You Want Me"/"It Will Make Me Crazy"

The elegant ladies of En Vogue (comprised of Maxine Jones, Terry Ellis, Cindy Herron and Dawn Robinson, seen here in a EastWest publicity photograph) were queens of the *Billboard* dance and pop charts in the spring of 1990. Their R&B-dance smash "Hold On" was lifted off the album *Born to Sing* (author's collection).

Fire Island featuring Loretta Holloway: "Shout to the Top"
501 featuring Ondrea Duverney: "Inside"
Fizz featuring Crystal Gayle: "When I Dream"
49ers: "Touch Me"/"Don't You Love Me"
Frankie Knuckles: "The Whistle Song"/"It's Hard Sometime"/"Workout"/"Too Many Fish" (featuring Adeva)/"Whadda U Want" (featuring Adeva)
French Affair: "My Heart Goes Boom (La Di Da Da)"
Fun Factory: "Close to You"/"I Wanna B with U"/"Celebration"
Fun Fun: "Give Me Love"
Funky Green Dogs: "Fired Up!"/"The Way"/"Body"
Gabrielle: "Dreams"/"Because of You"/"Going Nowhere"/"Sunshine"/"When a Woman"
Gala: "Freed From Desire"
Gerardo: "Rico Suave"
G.G. Anderson: "Immer Nur Du"
Gigi D'Agostino: "Gin Lemon"/"Elisir"/"The Riddle"/"Bla Bla Bla"/"La Passion"/"Another Way"
Gina G: "Ooh Aah.... Just a Little Bit"/"Higher Than Love"/"Fresh!"/"I Belong to You"/"Gimme Some Love"/"Ti Amo"
Gisele Jackson: "Love Commandments"/"Happy Feelings"/"Foolin' with My Love"/"Me, Myself & I"
Gloria Estefan: "Turn the Beat Around"/"Everlasting Love"
Gloria Gaynor: "I Will Survive"/"(If You Want It) Do It Yourself" New Music Versions ('90)/"Can't Take My Eyes Off You"/"How High the Moon" ('93)/"First Be a Woman"/"Love Affair" ('93)/"Rippin' It Up"/"Oh What a Life"/"Mighty High" (featuring The Trammps)
Grand Fiesta: "Ritmo De La Noche"
Guru Josh: "Infinity"
Hannah Jones: "No One Can Love You More Than Me"/"You Only Have to Say You Love Me"/"More to This"
Harajuku: "Phantom of the Opera"/"On My Own"/"Can You Feel the Love Tonight"/"Colors of the Wind"/"Someday" (featuring Stephanie O'Hara)
Ini Kamoze: "Here Comes the Hotstepper"
Incognito: "Don't You Worry 'Bout a Thing"/"Always There"/"Everyday"/"Pieces of a Dream"/"I Hear Your Name"/"Givin' It Up"
Ireen Sheer: "Tennessee Waltz"/"Lüg, wenn du kannst"/"Ireen Sheer-Hit Mix"
Irene Cara: "All My Heart"
Jaki Graham: "Ain't Nobody"/"Absolute E-Sensual"
Jam & Spoon: "Right in the Night"/"Find Me (Odyssey to Anyoona)" (featuring Plavka)/"Kaleidoscope Skies"
Jam Tronic: "End of the Road"/"I'd Do Anything for Love"/"An Angel"
Jamaica: "Tell Me Where It Hurts"
Jamiroquai: "Space Cowboy"/"Canned Heat"/"Cosmic Girl"
Janet Jackson: "Escapade"/"Alright"/"That's the Way Love Goes"/"Runaway"/"Scream" (with Michael Jackson)/"Love Will Never Do (Without You)"/"The Pleasure Principle"/"Together Again"
Jennifer Lopez: "Waiting for Tonight"/"Let's Get Loud"
Jennifer Paige: "Crush"
Jennifer Rush: "I Can't Say No"/"Out of My Hands"
Jinny: "Keep Warm"
Joy Salinas: "Rockin' Romance (I Go Slow)"
Judy Cheeks: "Respect"/"Reach"
Juliane Werding: "Singles"/"Männer Kommen Und Gehn"
Juliet Roberts: "I Want You"/"Caught in the Middle"
Junior Vasquez: "If Madonna Calls"
Kai Tracid: "Dance for Eternity"/"Your Own Reality"
Kathy Sledge: "Take Me Back to Love"
k.d. lang: "Lifted by Love"/" If I Were You"
Kelly Marie: "Runaway"
Kim Appleby: "Don't Worry"/"G.L.A.D."
Kim English: "Nite Life"/"Supernatural"/"Learn 2 Luv"/"Missing You"/"Jumpin' and Bumpin'"/"Tomorrow"/"Unspeakable Joy"
The KLF: "Justified & Ancient" (featuring Tammy Wynette)/"3 A.M. Eternal (Live at the S.S.L.)"/"America: What Time Is Love?"
Kym Mazelle: "Don't Scandalize My Name"
Kym Sims: "Too Blind to See It"/"Take My Advice"/"A Little Bit More"
Kris Kross: "Jump"
Kristina Bach: "Hey Ich Such Hier Nicht Den Groben Lover"
Kuva: "Isn't It Time"
Kylie Minogue: "Shocked"/"Better the Devil You Know"/"Step Back in Time"/"What Do I Have to Do"/"Confide in Me"/"Did It Again"/"Breathe"
LaBelle: "Turn It Out"
L.A. Style: "James Brown Is Dead"/"I'm Raving"
Lara Fabian: "I Will Love Again"
LaTour: "People Are Still Having Sex"
Laura Branigan: "Bad Attitude"/"Moonlight on Water"/"Dim All the Lights"

Len: "Steal My Sunshine"
Lighthouse Family: "High"
Linda Eder: "Never Dance"/"Something to Believe In"
Lisa Lisa & Cult Jam: "Let the Beat Hit 'Em"
Lisa Stansfield: "All Around the World"/"This Is the Right Time"/"Change"/"What Did I Do to You?"/"Never, Never Gonna Give You Up"/"I'm Leavin'"/"Set Your Loving Free"/"Someday (I'm Coming Back)"
Little Louie Vega with Marc Anthony: "Ride on the Rhythm"
Livin' Joy: "Dreamer"/"Don't Stop Movin'"
Loft: "Love Is Magic"/"Don't Stop Me Now"/"Mallorca"
Londonbeat: "I've Been Thinking About You"/"You Bring on the Sun"
Loni Clark: "Rushing"/"U"/"Love's Got Me (On a Trip So High)"
Lonnie Gordon: "Bad Mood"/"Happenin' All Over Again"/"Gonna Catch You"/"Dirty Love"
Loona: "Bailando"
Los Del Rio: "Macarena"
Lou Bega: "Mambo No. 5"/"I Got a Girl"
Loveland featuring Rachel McFarlane: "The Wonder of Love"
Lucilectric: "Mädchen"/"Liebe Macht Dumm"/"Süss Und Gemein"
Lulu: "Independence"/"Goodbye Baby and Amen"/"Every Woman Knows"
Luther Vandross: "The Best Things in Life Are Free" (with Janet Jackson)
M People: "Moving on Up"/"One Night in Heaven"/"Excited"/"Open Your Heart"
Madison Avenue: "Don't Call Me Baby"
Madonna: "I'm Breathless"/"Vogue"/"Keep It Together"/"Justify My Love"/"Erotica"/"Deeper and Deeper"/"Fever"/"Bedtime Story"/"Don't Cry for Me Argentina"/"Frozen"/"Ray of Light"/"Nothing Really Matters"/"Beautiful Stranger"
Magic Affair: "Omen III"
Mariah Carey: "Someday"/"Emotions"/"Dreamlover"/"Fantasy"/"Heartbreaker"
Marianne Rosenberg: "Frage Niemals"
Mark 'Oh: "Love Song"/"Tears Don't Lie"
Marky Mark and the Funky Bunch: "Good Vibrations" (featuring Loleatta Holloway)
Marusha: "Somewhere Over the Rainbow"/"It Takes Me Away"
Masterboy: "Generation of Love"
Mauro Picotto: "Komodo"
MC Hammer: "U Can't Touch This"/"Dancin' Machine"/"Addams Groove"

Collaborating with English producer William Orbit (Blur, All Saints) on her critically acclaimed 1998 album *Ray of Light*, Madonna (seen here in a Maverick/Warner label press photograph) once again reinvented herself with a sound that merged rave, electro-dance and Brit-rock. The album won four Grammy Awards and was listed as one of the 500 Greatest Albums of All Time by *Rolling Stone* (photograph by Mario Testino, author's collection).

MC Sar and the Real McCoy/**Real McCoy:** "It's on You"/"Another Night"/"Run Away"/"Automatic Lover (Call for Love)"/"Come and Get Your Love"/"One More Time"/"(If You're Not in It for Love) I'm Outta Here"
Meja: "How Crazy Are You?"/"All 'Bout the Money"
Michael Jackson: "Black or White"/"Remember the Time"/"Who Is It"/"Blood on the Dancefloor"
Michelle Gayle: "Happy Just to Be with You"/"Sensational"/"Looking Up"
Mr. President: "Coco Jamboo"
Moby: "Move"/"Feeling So Real"/"James Bond Theme"
Modern Talking: "You're My Heart, You're My Soul" ('98)/"Brother Louie" ('98)/"Space Mix"/"You Are Not Alone"/"Sexy Sexy Lover"
Mo-Do: "Eins, Zwei, Polizei"
Montell Jordan: "This Is How We Do It"
Mousse T.: "Horny"/"Sex Bomb" (featuring Tom Jones)
Mylène Farmer: "Désenchantée"/"Je T'Aime Mélancolie"/"Que Mon Coeur Lâche"/"Beyond My Control"/"Souviens-Toi Du Jour"/"Regrets" (with Jean-Louis Murat)

Nicole: "Abrakadabra"
Nicole McCloud: "Long Train Runnin' (Without Love)"
Nightcrawlers: "Push the Feeling On"
Nomad: "(I Wanna Give You) Devotion"/"Just a Groove"/"24 Hours a Day"
Norma Jean Bell: "I'm the Baddest Bitch (in the Room)"
N-Trance featuring Rod Stewart: "Da Ya Think I'm Sexy?"
Olive: "You're Not Alone"/"Miracle"/"Outlaw"
Opus III: "It's a Fine Day"
The Orb: "Little Fluffy Clouds"
The Original: "I Luv U Baby"
The Outhere Brothers: "Boom Boom Boom"
Passion Fruit: "The Rigga-Ding-Dong-Song"
Patricia Kaas: "Reste Sur Moi"/"Les Lignes De Nos Mains"/"Quand J'Ai Peur De Tout"
Patti LaBelle: "The Right Kinda Lover"/"All Right Now"
Paula Abdul: "Crazy Cool"/"My Love Is for Real"/"Vibeology"/"The Promise of a New Day"
Pet Shop Boys: "Being Boring"/"Where the Streets Have No Name (I Can't Take My Eyes Off You)"/"I Wouldn't Normally Do This Kind of Thing"/"Absolutely Fabulous"/"Go West"/"Can You Forgive Her"/"I Don't Know What You Want but I Can't Give It Any More"
Phyllis Nelson: "Don't Stop the Train" ('99 Almighty Remix)
Praxis featuring Kathy Brown: "Turn Me Out"
Q featuring Tracy Ackerman: "Get Here"
Qkumba Zoo: "The Child (Inside)"
Quad City DJ's: "C'mon N' Ride It (The Train)"
Ralphi Rosario: "You Used to Hold Me '94" (featuring Xaviera Gold)/"Take Me Up (Gotta Get Up)" (featuring Donna Blakely)/"Wanna Give It Up" (featuring Linda Clifford)
Randy Crawford: "Forget Me Nots"/"Wishing on a Star"/"Give Me the Night"
Rapination: "Love Me the Right Way" (featuring Kym Mazelle)
Reel 2 Real featuring The Mad Stuntman: "I Like to Move It"
Revenge: "Pineapple Face"
Ricky Martin: "Livin' La Vida Loca"
Rob Base & DJ EZ Rock: "It Takes Two"
Roberta Bai: "We Are Family"
Robert Miles: "Children"
Robert Owens: "I'll Be Your Friend"
Rollergirl: "Dear Jessie"
Rosie Gaines: "Be Strong"/"Closer Than Close"
RuPaul: "Supermodel (You Better Work)"/"Don't Go Breaking My Heart" (with Elton John)/"Back to My Roots"
Sabrina: "Cover Model"/"Rockawillie"/"Siamo Donne"/"Yeah Yeah" (Remix)/"Shadows of the Night"/"Angel Boy"
Sabrina Johnston: "Peace (in the Valley)"/"Friendship"
Saint Etienne: "Only Love Can Break Your Heart"/"Nothing Can Stop Us"
Salt 'N' Pepa: "Let's Talk About Sex"/"Whatta Man" (with En Vogue)/"Shoop"
Samuli Edelmann: "(Sinä Olet) Aurinko"
Sandra: "Hiroshima"/"(Life May Be) A Big Insanity"/"Johnny Wanna Live"/"Don't Be Aggressive"/"I Need Love"/"One More Night"/"Won't Run Away"/"You Are So Beautiful"
Sandy B: "Make the World Go Round"/"Feel Like Singin'"
Sash! Encore Une Fois"/"Ecuador"/"Stay"

RuPaul Andre Charles, recording and performing as simply RuPaul, hit the big time in 1993 with the album *Supermodel of the World*. The single off the set, "Supermodel (You Better Work)" was a left field hit, reaching the Top 50 in the U.S. and UK (photograph by Albert Sanchez/Rhino Records, author's collection).

Scatman John: "Scatman (Ski-Ba-Bop-Ba-Dop-Bop)"/"Scatman's World"
Scooter: "Move Your Ass"/"The Age of Love"/"Fuck the Millennium"
Secchi: "I Say Yeah" (featuring Orlando Johnson)/"Keep on Jammin'"/"A Brighter Day" (featuring Taleesa)/"One Love in My Lifetime"/"Flash"
Shades of Love featuring Meli'sa Morgan: "Body to Body (Keep in Touch)"
The Shamen: "Move Any Mountain"/"Phorever People"/"Boss Drum"
Shanice: "I Love Your Smile"
Sharada House Gang: "Gypsy Boy, Gypsy Girl"
Shawn Christopher: "Another Sleepless Night"/"Don't Lose the Magic"/"Make My Love"/"Thinking About the Way"/"Sweet Freedom"
Sherree Ford-Payne: "Shoulda Coulda Woulda"
Shirley Murdock: "Let There Be Love!"
Sin with Sebastian: "Golden Boy"/"Shut Up (And Sleep with Me)"
Sinitta: "Shame Shame Shame"/"Aquarius"/"Love and Affection"/"The Supreme EP"
Sir Mix-A-Lot: "Baby Got Back"
Sister Sledge: "We Are Family" ('93 Sure Is Pure Remix)/"Thinking of You" ('93 Remix)
Sonia Davis: "Bette Davis Eyes"
Sophie: "Dedicated to You"
The S.O.U.L. S.y.s.t.e.m. featuring Michelle Visage: "It's Gonna Be a Lovely Day"
Soul II Soul: "People"
Sound Factory: "Good Time"
Sounds of Blackness: "The Pressure Pt. 1"

Minneapolis/St. Paul, Minnesota–based vocal and instrumental collective Sounds of Blackness merged R&B, jazz, gospel and dance genres, achieving a rousing club smash with "The Pressure, Pt. 1" in 1991. Among the vocalists in the ensemble were Cynthia Johnson (formerly of Lipps, Inc.) and Ann Nesby (photograph by Kwaku Alston/A&M Records, author's collection).

SOX featuring Samantha Fox: "Go for the Heart"
Sparks: "The No.1 Song in Heaven"
The Spice Girls: "Wannabe"/"Spice Up Your Life"/"Stop"
Steps: "One for Sorrow"/"Tragedy"
Suzanne Vega: "Tom's Diner" (DNA Remix)
Suzette Charles: "Free to Love Again"
Tag Team: "Whoomp! (There It Is)"
Technotronic: "Get Up! (Before the Night Is Over)"/"This Beat Is Technotronic"/"Move This"
Thelma Houston: "What He Has"/"Throw You Down"/"Out of My Hands"/"High"
Thomas Anders: "The Sweet Hello, the Sad Goodbye"
Tina Moore: "Never Gonna Let You Go"
Todd Terry: "Something Goin' On" (featuring Martha Wash and Jocelyn Brown)/"It's Over Love" (featuring Shannon)
Toni Braxton: "Un-Break My Heart"/"You're Makin' Me High"/"I Don't Want To"
20 Fingers & Gillette: "Short Dick Man"
The Twins: "Not the Loving Kind" (Remixed)/"Love Is Blind"
2 Brothers on the 4th Floor: "Can't Help Myself"/"Never Alone"/"Dreams (Will Come Alive)"
2 Colors: "You Look Like the Sun"
2 Cowboys: "Everybody Gonfi Gon"
2 Eivissa: "Move Your Body"/"Oh La La La"/"Open Your Eyes"
2 Unlimited: "Get Ready for This"/"Twilight Zone"/"No Limit"/"Workaholic"/"Tribal Dance"/"Let the Beat Control Your Body"
U2: "Mysterious Ways"/"Lemon"/"Discothèque"
U96: "Club Bizarre"/"Das Boot"
Urban Cookie Collective: "Feels Like Heaven"/"High on a Happy Vibe"/"The Key, the Secret"/"Sail Away"
U.S.U.R.A. "Open Your Mind"/"Tear It Up!"/"Sweat"
Utah Saints: "What Can You Do for Me"
Vanessa-Mae: "Toccata & Fugue in D Minor"
Vanilla Ice: "Ice Ice Baby"
Vengaboys: "Boom, Boom, Boom, Boom"/"We Like to Party"/"Up & Down"/"We're Going to Ibiza!"
Wamdue Project: "King of My Castle"
WestBam: "The Roof Is on Fire"/"The Wall"/"The Mayday Anthem"/"Celebration Generation"/"Crash Course"/"BeatBoxRocker"
Whitney Houston: "I'm Every Woman"/"It's Not Right but It's Okay"/"My Love Is Your Love"/"Queen of the Night"/"Heartbreak Hotel"
Will Smith: "Gettin' Jiggy Wit It"
Wreckx-N-Effect: "Rump Shaker"
Yothu Yindi: "Treaty"
Zombie Nation: "Kernkraft 400"

Vanilla Ice was the stage name of Robert Van Winkle, a white rapper who conquered the top of the *Billboard* pop chart with the hip-hop dance single "Ice Ice Baby" (which incorporated the bassline from Queen & David Bowie's 1981 hit "Under Pressure.") The song was originally the B-side of Vanilla Ice's single version of the rock-disco classic "Play That Funky Music" by Wild Cherry (photograph by Michael Lavine/SBK Records, author's collection).

Index

The Adventures of Priscilla, Queen of the Desert (film) 171, 173, 174
Aitken, Matt 68, 69, 73
Amber 3, 5–7, 153, 158, 159, 231
Amos, Tori 90
Anzilotti, Luca 13–15, 79
Archer, Tasmin 25
Armstead, Izora 210
Austin, Thea 13–20
Avicii 87, 92, 200

Backstreet Boys 9, 43, 44, 83, 88, 165
Baha Men 5
Baker, Arthur 146, 231
Band of Gypsies 135
Basement Boys 154–156
Bassey Shirley 196, 200
Baxxter, H.P. 103
The Beach (film) 198
Belolo, Henri 126
Benassi, Benny 30, 191, 193
The Benedictine Monks of Santo Domingo de Silos 187
Benitez, Jellybean 140
The Berman Brothers (Frank and Christian Berman) 5–8, 159
Bizarre Inc. 21, 23–27, 111
Black Box 210–212, 214
Bocelli, Andrea 187, 189
The Bodyguard (film) 83
Bowie, David 22, 55, 56, 87, 195, 198, 238
Boy George 3, 27
Branson, Richard 180, 183
Brenner, Ulli 125
Brightman, Sarah 187, 189
Brown, Angie 21–29, 111
Brown, Jocelyn 24, 27, 60, 88, 214, 238
Brown, Steven Ames 214
Butler, Maurice (Turbo B) 13

C + C Music Factory 10, 210, 212, 213
Cabrera, Albert 145
Captain Hollywood (project) 47–50, 101, 102

Carey, Mariah 7, 9, 144, 182, 235
Carlson, Sannie 30–38
Cherry, Cynthia 154, 155
Cherry, Neneh 28, 89
Christensen, Alex 188
Cintron, Marty 39–46
Clifford, Linda 211, 215, 236
Clivilles, Robert 210, 232
Cole, David 210, 212, 232
Coleman, Bill 2, 156, 157
Coolen, Nance 47–54
The Cover Girls 46, 144, 146, 149
Cox, Tim 135
Cretu, Michael 178, 180, 182
Cruiz, Taio 86, 92
Culture Beat 97, 99–101, 105, 127, 128

Daniels, Lee 19
Dario G 195–203
Davis, Clive 6, 41, 42, 80, 81
Davoli, Daniele 211
Dawson-Harrison, Tony 49, 102
Deee-Lite 1, 2, 10, 65, 232
Denton, Sandy "Pepa" 110
Dion, Céline 148
Dr. Alban 77, 88, 164–170
Dream Academy 195, 197

Eiffel 65 200
Eisele, Michael 101
El Mar, Jam 102
Enigma 10, 178, 182–185, 187, 188
Enriquez, Jocelyn 7, 153, 158
En Vogue 9, 233, 235, 236
Esser & Strauss 49, 41
Estefan, Gloria 2, 144, 146, 147, 149, 150, 234
Everything But the Girl 39

Fairbrass, Fred 55–67
Fairbrass, Richard 55–67
Fairstein, David 182
Farian, Frank 39, 41, 42, 51, 106, 125, 126, 130
Fenslau, Torsten 97, 98, 100, 103
Ferguson, Stacy Ann (Fergie) 44 54 (film) 5, 7, 153, 158
First Ladies of Disco 11, 211, 215

Flick, Larry 1–4
Ford, Penny 13–15, 17, 18
French, Nicki 68–76
Fulanito 206–208

Garrett, Siedah 137
George, Allen 117, 188
Gibson, Debbie 3
Gordon, Eddie 109, 110
Gordy, Berry 117
Grant, Amy 144, 231
Gregorian 178, 179, 189
Guetta, David 3, 28, 90, 149, 200

Haddaway, Nestor (Haddaway) 10, 77–85
Hallström, Sten (StoneBridge) 86–96, 118
Hanks & Jacks 48–50
Harris, Niki 17
Hartmann, Karin 77, 79
Haza, Ofra 188
Hector, Hex 7, 11
Hed Kandi 28, 91
Hendrik, Tony 77, 79
Hernández, Ariel 39–41
Hernández, Gabriel 39–41
Hirschburger, Klaus 181
Hook, Peter 198
Hooper, Nellee 156, 157
Houston, Whitney 6, 13, 16, 25, 81, 83, 116, 119, 125, 182, 238
Hubert Kah 181
Humphries, Tony 155

Iglesias, Enrique 42, 233
Indecent Proposal (film) 220

Jackson, Michael 3, 14, 17, 47, 69, 116, 117, 125, 127, 133, 136–139, 144, 147, 152, 156, 182, 220, 234, 235
Jam & Spoon 97 102, 234
James, Cheryl "Salt" 110
Jamieson, Bob 131
Joling, Gerard 53

Katzmann, Nosie 97–106
Kemmler, Hubert 181

239

Index

King, Evelyn "Champagne" 177, 211, 215
Knuckles, Frankie 3, 11, 234
Kravitz, Lenny 83, 90

La Bouche 7, 10, 50, 123–132
The Latin Rascals 144–147
Le Click 125
Lennox, Annie 6, 81, 83, 144, 231
Limerick, Alison 229, 231
Limoni, Mirko 211
Lynch, Sybil (Sybil) 107–115

Madonna 2, 3, 10, 13, 17–19, 35, 36, 40, 47, 52, 55, 89, 93, 127, 149, 150, 161, 168, 222, 234, 235
Manzoli, Rob 55, 58
Marin, Aldo 204, 205
Marky Mark and the Funky Bunch 44, 179, 186–188, 235
Masters at Work 3
Maynard, Robin Jackson (Robin S) 3, 10, 86, 88, 89, 116–122, 176
McCray, Lane 10, 123–132
McFarlane, Fred 117, 118
Meecham, Andrew 24
Meredith, Dean 24
Miller, Rozalla (Rozalla) 3, 133–143
Milli Vanilli 39, 41–43, 125, 126
Monaco 198, 199
Morabito, Susan 11, 227–230
Morales, David 3, 11, 86, 89, 232
Moran, Tony 3, 11, 86, 120, 144–152, 211
Morrison, Mark 28
Münzing, Michael 13, 14, 79

Napster 11, 43, 93, 131, 141, 160, 167, 182, 189, 193, 201
Naté, Ultra 3, 7, 153–163
Nawapa, Alban (Dr. Alban) 77, 88, 164–170
Negro, Joey (DJ) 89
A Night at the Roxbury (film) 39, 77, 82
No Mercy 5, 39–46, 126
Novak, Dave 131
NSYNC 9, 43, 44, 83, 88
Nwapa, Alban 77, 88, 164–170

Oceanic 61
Oldfield, Mike 181
O'Loughlin, Eddie 108–110
Orbit, William 235
Overweight Pooch 172

Pacino, Al 139, 140
Passion Fruit 129, 236
Pauletta, Roger (Rog Nice) 204, 205, 207
Peniston, CeCe 3, 10, 171–177
Peterson, Frank 178–190
Pignagnoli, Alfredo "Larry" 30, 32, 35, 191–194
Pirates of Pop 98
Pizarro, Gladys 157
Pop, Denniz (Dag Krister Volle) 88, 164–167
Prick, Charly 51
Prince Ital Joe 186–188

Quinol, Katrin 211, 212

Rayne, Dana 130
Real McCoy 3, 5, 6, 10, 235
Right Said Fred 10, 55–67
Riva, Davide 32
Rodgers, Nile 87
Rodway, Steve (Motiv8) 27
Rogers, Ce Ce 107
Ross, Diana 68, 133, 139, 146, 232
Rosser, Scott 195, 197
Rozalla 3, 133–143
RuPaul 236

S, Robin 3, 10, 86, 88, 89, 116–122, 176
Salt 'N' Pepa 58, 110, 113, 236
Sanders, Kim (Culture Beat) 127
Sandra 178, 180–183, 236
Santana, Carlos 169, 179
Saraf, Amir 125, 129
Scooter 102, 103, 237
Seedorf, Stacey (Stay-C) 50
Semplici, Valerio 211
740 Boyz 206
Shekoni, Kayo 130
Sia 89, 90
Silverman, Tom 6
Sinatra, Frank 64
Snap! 3, 10, 13–18, 49, 50, 79, 100, 128, 176
Soft Cell 66
Soulsearcher 13, 18
Sounds of Blackness 237
Space Jam (soundtrack) 120
Spagna, Ivana 30, 32, 191, 192, 194
Spencer, Paul 195–203
Spencer, Stephen 195, 197, 199
Springate, John 69
Stansfield, Lisa 28, 235
Stars on 54 5, 7, 153, 158
Stock, Mike 68–70, 75, 109, 110

Stone, Robin 3, 10, 86, 88, 89, 116–122, 176
StoneBridge 86–96, 118
Strasser, Alex 77, 79
Summer (vocalist w/Snap!) 17
Summer, Donna 3, 17, 55, 68, 79, 118, 144, 149, 152, 187, 220, 225, 233
Swanston, Nigel 135
Sybil 107–115

Taylor, Elizabeth (Liz) 138
Terry, Todd 3, 11, 24, 41, 91, 120, 205, 214, 238
Thornton, Melanie 10, 123–125, 129
Timberlake, Justin 17, 44, 71, 83
Top of the Pops 17, 18, 25, 37, 71, 89, 110, 118, 135, 155, 195
Turner, Carl 24
Twenty 4 Seven 47–54
2 in a Room 204–209
Two Tons of Fun 210, 213
2 Unlimited 10, 52, 100, 128, 238
Tyler, Bonnie 68–70, 83

Urban Cookie Collective 140, 238

Vanilla Ice (Robert Van Winkle) 16, 238
Van Nelsen, Jo 99
van Rijen, Ruud 47–50
Van Winkle, Robert (Vanilla Ice) 16, 238
Vargas, Rafael "Dose" (2 in a Room) 204–209
Vasquez, Junior 3, 11, 86, 221, 234
Vega, (Little) Louie 3, 158, 205, 235

W, Kristine 3, 150, 218–226
Wahlberg, Mark (Marky Mark) 44, 83, 179, 186–188, 235
Wash, Martha 3, 24, 144, 151, 210–217, 238
Waterman, Pete 71, 109, 110
Waters, Crystal 129, 232
The Weather Girls 210, 211, 213
Weitz, Kristine (Kristine W) 3, 150, 218–226
Wes (Madiko) 148
Whigfield 30–38, 191, 193, 194
White, Sharon 229

Young, Paul 187

Zedd 152
Zimmermann, Jens 98, 100

www.ingramcontent.com/pod-product-compliance
Lightning Source LLC
Chambersburg PA
CBHW060259240426
43661CB00060B/2838